The
Power
Motive

The
Power
Motive

DAVID G. WINTER

Wesleyan University

THE FREE PRESS
A Division of Macmillan Publishing Co., Inc.
NEW YORK

Collier Macmillan Publishers
LONDON

The Free Press
A Division of Macmillan Publishing Co., Inc.
866 Third Avenue, New York, New York 10022

Collier-Macmillan Canada Ltd.
Toronto, Ontario

Library of Congress Catalog Card Number:
72-92869

printing number
1 2 3 4 5 6 7 8 9 10

To
My Father
and
The Memory of My Mother

Contents

List of Illustrations

List of Tables

Preface

This book is an attempt to apply the systematic and objective techniques of psychological investigation to the study of power, which is a topic about which everyone (including myself) has strong, confused, and of course uniquely correct ideas. I have started with the broadest possible topic—the striving for power, or the Will to Power. My definitions, measurement techniques, findings, and speculations are of course not unassailable. Rather, my intention is to construct a framework that will help organize and make sense of the whole domain of power (a domain that one researcher has called a "quagmire"). At least this book has helped me to do so.

No one can hope to be unassailable when he writes or talks about power; it is a subject too close to us all, and our views are saturated with strong emotions and moral scruples. In the book, I try to be objective; here, therefore, I shall set down my own opinions and feelings about power.

Power fascinates me and frightens me. Perhaps for these reasons, in moments of irony I feel that power is vastly overrated. When it looms before us, it looks so big—power is the "Pillar of Society," in Ibsen's ironic sense—but from the perspective of distance or time, it

seems so small and petty. After several hundred years, who remembers
—or cares about—the names of England's ministers of state at the
time of Shakespeare's death? Or the dukes, electors, archbishops, and
other minor potentates who commissioned the music of Bach and
Mozart? They sought power; and now they have their just reward. Yet
power cannot be dismissed so lightly. Like most people, I feel awe
when I see the physical traces of the empires of Ashoka, Caesar,
Phillip II, or Disraeli; and I feel terror when I look at old films of
Nazi Germany.

I think that Americans have made a special kind of error in thinking about power, because of our national habit of dividing all things
into "good" and "bad," and then setting the good free to destroy the
bad. Applied to power, this habit usually leads us in the end to tragedy
—such as Woodrow Wilson at Versailles, or Vietnam. I think that the
good and bad of power are so closely woven together that they cannot
be separated—and so I propose a new metaphor. Power is neither the
essence of "nourishment" (Nietzsche) nor "poison" (Henry Adams).
To me, power is like *fire:* it can do useful things; it can be fun to play
with and to watch; but it must be constantly guarded and trimmed
back, lest it burn and destroy. To use Bachelard's words about fire,
power both "shines in heaven" *and* "burns in Hell."* Therefore, it
seems to me that the proper attitude toward power is respect tinged
with some suspicion.

*   *   *   *   *

It will be obvious that this book drew on the ideas and work of
many people besides myself, and I am grateful for these contributions.
I am particularly indebted to David McClelland, whose ideas and approach to research are obviously reflected in these pages; and to
Abigail Stewart, who suggested, argued, criticized, and encouraged at
many points, especially during the writing and revising of Chapters
6 and 7. As chairman of the Wesleyan psychology department, the
late Jules Holzberg always encouraged my research.

Many others helped by gathering, analyzing, or making available
data, giving ideas and suggestions, or reading part of the manuscript.
In alphabetical order, they are: John Atkinson, David Bonnano, Rufus
Browning, Howard Conley, Arthur Couch, Elliot Daum, Richard Don-
ley, Hubert Duijker, Carole Efron, Rudolph Fisch, Tammis Forshay,
Dwight Greene, Alan Hartley, Heinz Heckhausen, Daniel Jones,
Nancy King, Stanley King, Susan Knight, W. Nicholas Knight, David

* G. Bachelard, *The psychoanalysis of fire.* London: Routledge & Kegan Paul,
1964, p. 7.

Kolb, Loretta Konstan, George Litwin, Robert May, H. Andrew Mich-
ener, Theodore Payne, Alfred Petrocelli, Karl Scheibe, Connie Sutherland, James Uleman, Jan van Dijk, Joseph Veroff, Gerald Wade,
Robert Watson, Hans Wendt, and Frederick Wiecking.

Financial support for this research came from many sources:
NIMH Research Grant #MH-16,687 and Wesleyan University Faculty
Research Grants and Summer Grants to me; NIMH Undergraduate
Research Fellowships #MH-08,027 to Daniel Jones, Robert Watson,
and Abigail Stewart; and PHS Grant #FR-07,107 to Wesleyan University. Finally, a fellowship from the John Simon Guggenheim Memorial
Foundation enabled me to complete the final manuscript. This support
was essential to the research, and I am grateful to the agencies and
people involved.

D.G.W.

The
Power
Motive

CHAPTER 1

The
Study
of Power

This book is an account of research designed to identify and measure the striving for power as one important motive or disposition in individuals. Since power has been defined and studied from so many different points of view, I want to emphasize that the "power motive," as I shall use the term in this book, has a special and restricted meaning. It will not be identical to other social science concepts related to power. I do not believe that the power motive is the only important human motive, or that all of a person's behavior can be understood by studying only his strivings for power. I do not believe that research on the power motives of individuals is the only way to study power in society. Nor do I believe that the study of power always has to be kept separate from values and judgments about power, even if that were possible. My own beliefs and values about power are set forth in the Preface. I do believe that our judgments and values concerning power ought to be as informed as they can be by research and scholarship. I believe, moreover, that the study of the power motive in individuals is one important and useful way to approach the broad and complex topic of power itself. Hence this book.

Men have written about the role of power in human affairs at least since Plato described the decline of the ideal state and the rise of the despot:

> When nature or habit or both have combined the traits of drunkenness, lust, and lunacy, then you have the perfect specimen of the despotic man. . . . When a master passion is enthroned in absolute dominion over every part of the soul, feasting and revelling with courtesans and all such delights will become the order of the day. . . . Goaded on to frenzy, . . . he will look out for any man of property whom he can rob by fraud or violence. . . . When the numbers of such criminals and their hangers-on increase and they become aware of their strength, then it is they who, helped by the folly of the common people, create the despot out of that one among their number whose soul is itself under the most tyrannical despotism.[1]

In later ages, thinkers such as Machiavelli, Hobbes, Nietzsche, and Adler concluded that man's nature and the origins of human society could be explained by the striving for power. Power and related words are important concepts in modern social science. In the present day, "power" is a popular explanation for many different social events: wars and threats of wars, national independence movements, the mobilization of new groups both inside and outside the established political process, racial turmoil, and the unrest of young people. In each case the quick and easy explanation is often "power." The word has acquired many different and conflicting meanings, so that using "power" as a superficial explanation of everything may in the end explain nothing.

Many thinkers in the Western tradition were not comfortable with the idea of power or with explanation of action and society based largely on power. One tradition, reflected in the words of Plato quoted above, argues that man's potentially unbounded lust for power is a demonic flaw that corrupts and destroys him (Acton, 1887; Ritter, 1952; Sorokin and Lunden, 1959; Rubinoff, 1968). Thus power-seeking must be tempered, whether by humility arising from classical moderation and restraint (Babbitt, 1924; Winter, Alpert, and McClelland, 1963), by both avoiding the desire to rule and at the same time looking after the needs of the ruled (see Bainton, 1968, on Erasmus), by law and custom (Craig, 1958), or by a sense of responsible cynicism about class interests and a search for transcendent symbols (Niebuhr, 1932).

Another tradition, often dismissed by "realists" as pious sentimentalism, suggests that power can be overcome by some kind of other

[1] *The Republic*, Chapter 32 (IX. 572–574). Translated by F. M. Cornford. New York & London: Oxford University Press, 1941.

ideal, such as sacrifice, altruism, or social interest (Adler, 1928). At the extreme is the anarchist tradition, in which (according to many interpretations) power is rejected completely and supposedly replaced by love, self-expression, or some other principle (Kropotkin, 1902; Goodman, 1962; Sampson, 1965 and 1971; Van Duyn, 1969).

Individuals, especially if they are prominent in public life, almost never say that their actions are motivated by a desire for power; instead they talk of idealistic abstractions such as "service," "duty," "responsibility," or perhaps "legitimate power." This has led some psychologists to conclude that, just as sexuality was repressed and denied during the nineteenth century, so today power strivings are repressed and achieve only disguised expression through defense mechanisms such as distortion, displacement, projection, and rationalization (Schmuck, 1965).

In the first chapter of this book, I will discuss four specific aspects of power. First, what does "power" mean? Second, what are the differences between power and such closely related concepts as dominance, authority, force, and leadership? Are these different kinds of power, or different bases of power? Is the power motive related to some of these bases, or to all of them? Third, is power a property or capacity of persons (something that people have), or does it reside in relationships or situations? If a person's power depends mainly on the situation that he is in, then what is the use of talking about his power motive? Finally, how is the conceptualization of power as a motive different from other psychological variables involving power, such as authoritarianism, internal control of fate, and Machiavellianism? These four topics cover much of the psychological theory and research on power, so that this chapter is a prologue to the discussion of power as a motive.

In Chapters 2 and 3, I turn to an analysis of the concept of motive, and then present the precise point of view and research strategy that were used to define and measure the power motive in this book. This excursion may seem either pedantic or superficial; yet I feel that in dealing with concepts such as "power" and "motive," where so many different theories and research traditions come together and overlap, it is important to be clear and precise about what is meant and what was done. Chapters 4 and 5 contain the principal research results on the actions, values, and background characteristics that are related to the power motive. These results are heterogeneous and wide-ranging, because in many cases some of the most interesting research was initiated by the unusual and creative ideas and projects of students. Chapter 6 presents a portrait of the power-motivated man, through a study of the legend of Don Juan. In turn, the legend itself suggested hypotheses about the action correlates and the social and historical context of the power motive. These are presented in Chapter 6, and are an introduction to what is probably the most interesting, controversial, and provocative part of the book in Chapter 7. Does the power motive, as defined and studied in the earlier chapters, help to understand and unravel the complicated role of power in human society? How are wars, social movements, and political leaders who strive for power related to the power motive? This final chapter is based on a few studies of some groups and leaders, so that there is nothing definitive and final about my conclusions. As the justification for what has gone before, its real purpose is to stimulate others to do further research to support—or challenge—these conclusions.

WHAT IS POWER?

Our English word "power" derives from the Old Latin root *potēre*, which means "to be able"; thus Locke and the British associationist philosophers argued that we form our idea of power from observation of our abilities—from "observing in ourselves, that we can at pleasure move several parts of our body which were at rest" (1690, II, 7, VIII). In a like manner, Freud described the differentiation of the ego and the world in terms of the awareness of power or ability: the child "must be very strongly impressed by the fact that some sources of excitation . . . can provide him with sensations at any moment, whereas other sources evade him from time to time" (1930, pp. 13–14). In a similar fashion, Heider relates power to the factor of "can," or ability, contrasted with the factor of environmental force as a determinant of action (1958, pp. 82–100).

　　Three qualifications need to be made in order to give a useful definition of power. First, I am concerned here with social power—when one or more persons have an effect on the behavior or emotions of another *person* or persons. Emotional effects can be inferred from observation of behavior. Power over things is of interest in this context only insofar as it leads to social power. Second, I exclude cases where the effect of one person on another is merely accidental instead of intentional. To say that someone has an ability or can produce an effect strongly suggests that he can do something when, how, and in the way that he wants to do it—according to his intention. I recognize that intentions may be denied or unconscious, so that the definition may often be elusive and arguable. To distinguish between intended and unintended effects, we shall need a way of measuring unconscious or denied intentions. Finally, social power can be thought of as a capacity as well as an action: one person (for convenience called O) could affect the behavior or emotions of another person (called P) when and if O wanted to. There is nothing mysterious about calling social power a capacity, for it can always be defined operationally in terms of some set of directly or indirectly observable events.

Is it important to consider the intentions of the person who is affected (P)? Dahl (1957, p. 202) argues that O has power only when he gets P to do something that P would not otherwise do. I think that this is too limited, because getting someone else to believe that he really *wants* to do what you want him to do is surely a very sophisticated technique for getting power. Thus I agree with Duijker (1961), who argues that although the resistance of P may be strong evidence for O's power, it is not a necessary condition of it.

Thus social power is *the ability or capacity of O to produce (consciously or unconsciously) intended effects on the behavior or emotions of another person* P. In this form, the definition is very close to that used by psychologists, sociologists, and political scientists (see Lasswell and Kaplan, 1950, pp. 74–80; Cartwright, 1959, pp. 185–193; Duijker, 1961; Van Doorn, 1963, pp. 6–8; and Champlin, 1970). The task of this book is to determine whether there are differences in the extent to which people want power, or strive to affect the behavior of others according to their own intentions; to measure these differences; and to determine their further consequences and associated characteristics.

POWER AND RELATED CONCEPTS

The literature on power is full of discussion about the differences between power and other related concepts such as "influence," "leadership," "authority," "dominance," "force," and "control." From one writer to the next, different words are often used for the same concept, and the same word is used for different concepts, as Schopler (1965) points out. Russell (1938) differentiated priestly power, kingly power, naked power, revolutionary power, and economic power. Weber (1947) analyzed power (*Herrschaft*) according to the way in which it was legitimized among followers: by appeal to rationality, by tradition, or by the transcendent claims of charisma. French and Raven (1959) distinguished five different kinds of power according

TABLE 1.1. CLASSIFICATION OF THE FORMS OF INFLUENCE AND POWER
(*Adapted from Lasswell and Kaplan, 1950, p. 87*)

The Means of Influence

The Goal of Influence

	Power	Respect	Rectitude	Affection	Well-Being	Wealth	Skill	Enlightenment
Power	Political Power	Homage	Inculcation	Fealty	Compulsion	Polinomic Power	Directorship	Indoctrination
Respect	Councilorship	Sponsorship	Suasion	Esteem	Charisma	Credit	Guidance	Authoritativeness
Rectitude	Mentorship	Approbation	Moral Authority	Devotion	Chastisement	Ethonomic Influence	Injunction	Censorship
Affection	Personal Influence	Regard	Moral Influence	Love	Guardianship	Benefaction	Zeal	Edification
Well-Being	Violence	Terror	Discipline	Rape	Brute Force	Brigandage	Forced Labor	Inquisition
Wealth	Ecopolitical Power	Standing Power	Simony	Venality	Subsistence Power	Economic Influence	Employment	Advertising
Skill	Expertness	Admiration	Casuistry	Ingratiation	Prowess	Productivity	Management	Intelligence
Enlightenment	Advisory Influence	Fame	Wisdom	Sympathy	Regimen	Economic Foresight	Instruction	Education

Note: Reprinted from H. D. Lasswell and A. Kaplan, *Power and Society*, by permission of the Yale University Press.

to their bases: reward, coercive, legitimate, referent, and expert power. In his catalogue of individual needs or dispositions, Murray (1938) included dominance, aggression, and autonomy as presumed distinct concepts. In a *tour de force* of classification, Lasswell and Kaplan considered both the base and the goal of influence in order to generate 64 different forms of the influence process (or power), as shown in Table 1.1. Yet even this table does not exhaust the possibilities. Duijker (1961) discusses those cases where person P anticipates the intention of person O and acts accordingly. Such Ps often say that they acted of their own free will, out of love, friendship, respect, cooperation, or service—but not because of the power of O. Yet the whole behavior sequence fits the definition of power. When and how are we justified in overruling P's claim and categorizing the behavior as power?

It is clear that theorists are adept at elaborating conceptual distinctions within the broad domain of power; but are all these distinctions important? Presumably each different "kind" of power has some special antecedents and consequences, but we do not know how important these special features are. Does each "kind" of power lead to the same goal and the same satisfaction for O? To the same effects on P? To the same overall social effect? In other words, what is the purpose of distinguishing different "kinds" of power; and when we have done so, how many different kinds are there?

An element of moral evaluation runs through many of the typologies of power. What a particular writer thinks of as "good" power is usually described as "leadership," "guidance," or perhaps "authority"; while "bad" power is called "authoritarian dominance" or "coercion." Thus the particular concept used will depend very much upon the observer's point of view, his interests and habits of classifying, and perhaps the consequences to him and others of using any particular concept.

More formally, I prefer to think of the broad definition of social power that I gave above as a semantic space, in which are located all of the power concepts and many others that are not so obviously power-related, such as respect, cooperation, and loyalty. In most cases, I think that we can get agreement on whether a particular sequence of actions by O and P fit within this broad definition. Sometimes it may be difficult to pinpoint the precise location of any particular word, because that word may have a variety of different meanings and connotations.

How many dimensions are needed to describe and organize such a semantic space? I think that three dimensions are enough for most purposes. For the first dimension (A), I suggest the *relative inequality of status or strength* of O and P. If O is stronger or of higher status than P ($A+$), we tend to use words such as "force" or "authority" to describe the interaction. If the two actors are of equal status, we are more likely to call it "influence" or perhaps "peer leadership." At the opposite pole is the curious case where O is actually of lower strength or status than P. Examples here would include the moral persuasion of Gandhi, the "surrender tactic" of the powerless (see Haley, 1969), and the so-called dictatorial power of a small and helpless baby. In all these latter cases, for a lower-strength or lower-status O to have any effect on P, he must have high *legitimacy or moral force*, which I propose as the second dimension (B).[2]

This second dimension (B) refers to the location of the action sequence in a moral nexus. Often, but not always, this moral nexus is also reflected in a society's legal system. If power is viewed as legitimate or moral ($B+$), then we call it "rule," "authority," "command," or "legitimate claim." If it is thought to be illegitimate or immoral ($B-$), then we usually think of it as "authoritarianism," "dominance," "naked power," or even "terror." Here the orientation of the observer is especially important. Many people would describe Hitler's power as illegitimate or immoral; but to those Germans who accepted his legitimacy, Hitler was an inspiring charismatic ruler (see Speer, 1970).

Finally, I think that the resistance of P should be taken as the third dimension (C). If P resists strongly ($C+$), we are likely to emphasize force in our label; but if P willingly goes along with O's intention (C-0), we would use such categories as "leadership" or "arousing enthusiasm," or we might even avoid calling the action sequence power at all. For some purposes, it might be useful to distinguish nonresistance (C-0) from active and willing compliance ($C-$). Figure 1.1 shows how many different words that relate to power can be located in this three-dimensional semantic space. The

[2] Gandhi's nonviolent resistance worked in part because many British people recognized the legitimate moral force of his actions. A demanding baby is taken care of because most parents feel that they ought to do so. Thus the space $A-B-$ in Figure 1.1 (illegitimate power of a weaker actor) is effectively empty. In those cases that might seem to fit here—where the action of an actor who is weaker and perceived by P to be illegitimate still has an effect—I think that the "weaker" O actually has the potential for gathering greater strength than P. Even those British officials who did not concede the legitimacy of Gandhi's demands often gave in because they knew that the alternative was violence, chaos, and the enormous potential strength of the Indian population. Thus such cases really can be placed in the space $A+B-$.

Figure 1.1 The Semantic Space of Power-Related Concepts

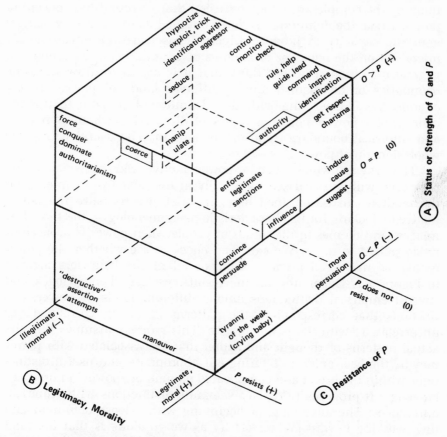

Dimensions: (A) Relative inequality of *O* and *P* in status, strength, etc.

(B) Legitimacy or morality of the action

(C) Resistance of *P* to *O*'s action

three dimensions seem to be very similar to the more general dimensions of meaning proposed by Osgood, Suci, and Tannenbaum (1957): legitimacy suggests evaluation, status inequality suggests potency, and resistance fits with activity.

This diagram is intended to bring some order into the complicated domain of power-related words, and to show that after a word or action fits into the general definition of power, most further categorization and labelling depend upon the point of view, knowledge, and values of the observer. For this reason, I propose a special strategy for untangling the complexities and confusion that surround the concept of power. I take the definition of power outlined above as a very general one: the capacity to produce effects (consciously or unconsciously intended) on the behavior or feelings of another person. Beyond this general definition, I do not think that it is useful to draw semantic boundaries or distinguish among different kinds of power on any *a priori* basis. Operating with this definition, I propose to use the concept of a power motive as a way of discovering whatever natural and empirical boundaries and distinctions may be useful within the whole domain of power.

The way in which such a power motive can be isolated and measured will be discussed more fully in the next two chapters; but the method can be outlined here. In brief, we measure the power motive by looking for its characteristic phenomenology—the thoughts, images, and themes in the minds of people when power is aroused or made salient to them. We can then check to see whether the power motive as measured predicts some or all of the behaviors arrayed in Figure 1.1. Depending on the results, we can then go back and suggest empirical distinctions among different kinds of power, distinctions that correspond to the patterns of action correlated (or uncorrelated) with the power motive. This strategy assumes that the actual patterns of thought and action that are associated with power may be the best guide to figuring out appropriate and useful distinctions within the broad and complicated domain of "power" in ordinary language. It proposes to replace semantic distinctions with empirical differences. The advantage of beginning with a loose definition and then working toward greater clarity as we go along is that the final arrangement is likely to be more useful in understanding behavior.[3] In the beginning, then, I take "power" to mean all of the different

[3] The research on achievement motivation provides an instructive example of this advantage. Before the work of McClelland *et al.* (1953), the word "achievement" had a very broad series of overlapping meanings. McClelland *et al.* started with a general definition (ego-involvement), concentrated on identifying the patterns of thinking or imagery associated with achievement, and then looked at which behaviors were associated with this pattern and which were not. As a result, they distinguished at least two quite different kinds of achievement: "entrepreneurial," or self-defined achievement, which was predicted by their measure of the achievement motive; and "academic," or other-defined achievement, which in the form of school grades has been consistently unrelated to their measure. If we look back, such a distinction may seem obvious; but apparently it was not, judging by the number of authors who have questioned the validity of the *n* Achievement measure on the grounds that it doesn't predict grades (cf. McArthur, 1953; Arnold, 1962, pp. 101–114; and Klinger, 1966).

sequences of action that fit within the definition of power that I have given.

IS POWER A PROPERTY OF PERSONS
OR OF SITUATIONS?

In everyday language, power is something that a person or persons have. "Napoleon was powerful." "The President forced Congress to pass his program." "English public schools trained young men to rule the British Empire." It is easy and natural to attribute power to people in this way, for we usually perceive power through the effects of specific persons on other specific persons. Thus we might conclude that leaders have power because they have some special uncommon characteristic; that successful men of influence have a special kind of power "skill," just as scholars have a special mental ability or athletes have physical prowess; and that history is the record of actions of "Great Men" who influenced and led the people of their tribes, their faith, or their nation. This way of thinking about power has great appeal, both because it is close to our phenomenal experiences of power, and because it allows us to reduce the complexities of human interaction and social structure down to a contest of persons —weak and strong, heroes and villains. This is the personal or "psychological" interpretation of power.

Opposed to such an analysis is the situational interpretation of power. Leaders have power because they are in the right position, or because they happen to have abilities that are required by the situation at that moment; men of influence are drawn from the upper social classes and other small elite groups; the "Great Men" of history are merely symbols of the emergence, growth, and decline of such broad social groups, or of inevitable historical trends. Those who accept the situational perspective on power often disparage the personal perspective, because to them it merely reflects the naïve ideology of bourgeois individualism and neglects the great impersonal forces of history. In the extreme version of the situational analysis, the powerful man is just the man who happens—scarcely of his own choice or effort—to be riding the crest of the right wave at the time when the searchlight of public attention (and of history) flickers past in brief illumination.[4]

---

[4] In political science, these two perspectives are reflected in the dispute about the existence of a "power elite" or "ruling class" as proposed by Hunter (1953) and Mills (1956), refuted by Dahl (1958) and Polsby (1960), and again rebutted by Bachrach and Baratz (1962) and Domhoff (1967).

A rigorous and extreme situational analysis of power would leave little scope for the operation of a power motive or individual disposition to strive for power. If such a motive existed at all, it might at most be thought of as a kind of mental epiphenomenon without any inherent effects on behavior—as simply the thoughts in the minds of the ruling class as they held (or sought) power. Alternatively, personal factors might predict attempts to get power, but situational variables would determine success in power-seeking. Before discussing the power motive, I want to work out some resolution between these two perspectives. Are they really irreconcilable, or is there evidence supporting each point of view? I will focus on social psychological theory and research on leadership; because the two perspectives meet sharply here, and because leadership (or attempted leadership) is certainly one action that should be associated with a power motive.

Shortly after World War I psychologists began to study leadership in a systematic way. They usually accepted the personal interpretation of power, and so for several decades they tried to discover that set of physical and personality characteristics that would predict leadership—leadership of almost any sort of group, at almost any sort of task. The results were rather meager (see Mann, 1959; Gibb, 1969). There were small positive correlations of leadership (or leadership status) with height, weight, intelligence, and a variety of rather vaguely defined personality traits such as "self-confidence," "personality integration," "dominance," and so forth. Results varied considerably from study to study and on the whole were not very impressive. Many problems made comparison among different investigations difficult: populations varied widely; personality measures were often inadequate; and "leadership" was variously defined by status, by peer nomination, or by the display of certain behaviors that were arbitrarily counted as "leading." Nevertheless, by about 1950 most psychologists agreed that much more of the variation in leadership was to be explained by the situation rather than by the traits of individual persons. Hollander expressed this conclusion as follows (1964, pp. 4–5, 15):

What was overlooked . . . in the view that leaders are uniquely endowed . . . was the actual fact of daily life, that is, that persons function as leaders in a particular time and place, and that these are both varying and delimiting conditions; that there are several pathways to leadership, sometimes from higher authority, other times from group consent. . . . Indeed, if any point stands forth in the modern day view of leadership it is that leaders are made by circumstances even though some come to those circumstances better equipped than others. . . . The leader's emergence or waning of status is thus inextricably linked to the prevailing situation.

Many studies designed within this perspective demonstrated the enormous importance of situational factors in determining the allocation of power: (1) Certain *positions* (the more central ones) are associated with being a leader in the study of Leavitt (1951) that has been replicated numerous times (see Collins and Raven, 1969, pp. 141–145). Sommer (1967) and Howells and Becker (1962) discuss other effects of position. (2) the *socioeconomic status* of individual members and of the group as a whole affects the choice of leader and the distribution of influence (Strodtbeck, James, and Hawkins, 1958), as does the implicit or *informal status hierarchy* (Zander, Cohen, and Stotland, 1959). The *sexes* apparently have unequal access to power and leadership in small groups (Strodtbeck and Mann, 1956), as well as in society at large. The effects of other ascribed status variables, such as *race* and *ethnicity,* are obvious and well documented. (3) The *personality characteristics of group members* (such as authoritarianism); (4) the *size and degree of organization of the group;* and (5) the *nature of the task,* or the purpose of the group, all have great effects on who emerges as the leader or most powerful person (see Gibb, 1969). All of these variables can be expressed as different bases of power which are allocated according to particular norms and values and perhaps also structural "laws" of human interaction.

Stated in general terms, the principal conclusion of this research is that if a group is permitted to choose its leader, the choice will be influenced by the task and the goals of the group and the corresponding resources of different group members. Those people who are perceived to facilitate the attainment of the group's goals will be chosen as leaders. Actually, this statement needs to be refined and qualified; and when this is done, I think that there is considerable scope for the influence of personal factors in determining power. For example, the members of a group may change their ideas of the group's task and goals. These changes may be due to fluctuations in the group's morale, changes in the kind of members recruited into the group, the development of relationships among the members, or persuasion by one or more members of the group itself. The fundamental question is, therefore, not whether the leader actually does facilitate goal-attainment, but whether the members think that he does. While the situation affects the allocation of power and leadership, it is the situation as perceived and judged by the group members. These perceptions and opinions can be influenced and manipulated just like any other perception or judgment. Thus if a person who seeks power is constrained or blocked by the perceptions and judgments of his followers, he may be able to change these perceptions and thereby to create power. Skill in defining situations, in convincing others of these definitions, and in portraying one's own role as important or indispensable to the achievement of these redefined group goals would thus permit a person to have power within the constraints of a situation. Many social psychological studies of leadership, involving atomistic studies of previously unacquainted group members who work together at tasks of dubious interest for a single brief period of time, would obviously be unable to detect the subtle effect of one member gaining leadership through changing the perceptions of the rest of the group over time.

What is the evidence that such an effect can occur? Talland (1954) carefully identified those members of psychotherapy groups who emerged as leaders after some time. He found that these leaders had not been more accurate in sensing group opinion before discussion, nor were their own opinions closer to the group mode. However, during the life of the group they were able to bring members' opinions into accord with their own views. In other words, leadership rested more on being able to redefine the group's opinions and goals in terms of one's own, than on having the modal opinions, by chance, at the beginning.

Working with children of ages four through eleven, Merei (1949) found that when a child who had showed power in previous groups was introduced into a group that had already formed fixed traditions and patterns of leadership, that child was at first displaced, and his leadership was no longer followed. Nevertheless, over time the introduced ex-leaders managed by a variety of strategies to play the role of leader and to regain part of their power. One strategy was *order-giving:* "Though keeping within the frame of activities he had just learned . . . and according to their rules, he told the children what to do—that is, he ordered them to do exactly what they would have done anyway (p. 28)." Another strategy grew out of order-giving: he introduced *small changes* and *innovations* in the group's procedures and traditions—some added ritual, a faster pace of activity, a wider terrain, or perhaps more concerted action. A final strategy for the restoration of power was the arbitrary *assumption of ownership and possession* of all important objects in the room. Often these objects were then "given" back to their original possessors. The possession and assignment had no functional importance, since all the children continued to play with the things that they were playing with before. Yet in some subtle way, "ownership" and the formal power of measuring and allocating (which is the original meaning of the verb "to rule") came to rest with the restored leader. These ploys of would-be child leaders remind me of the techniques that Renaissance European kings used to wrest land and power back from the feudal nobility.

Although Leavitt and others found that position in a communication network was related to power and leadership, there is nothing to prevent the would-be power-holder from knowing this principle, sizing up the situation, and then choosing his position so as to maximize his power. Indeed, some evidence in Chapter 4 suggests that people high in the power motive do just that. Every organization has its Machiavelli, who compiles a manual of cold-blooded advice on how to manipulate positions, wants, and opinions in order to increase his power. Skill in interpreting situations to others and altering their desires and perceptions is one of the principal skills of a politician (see Lasswell, 1936, chap. 6). Calling these behaviors "skills" emphasizes the extent to which they can be taught, and the extent to which their development is a matter of choice, intention, and practice. If we like the person, we call these skills "charisma," and we talk about how the charismatic leader is able to articulate the yearnings of his people and present himself as the embodiment and fulfillment of these yearnings (Erikson, 1964, 1969). If we don't like the person, we talk about the cunning ways in which he has unscrupulously played upon the hopes, fears, and expectancies of people so as to secure his own power.

Finally, certain kinds of situations inherently give individuals great scope to gain and exercise power, as Van Doorn (1963) points out: (1) Dramatic revolutionary conditions in which there is a crisis of confidence in institutionalized authority. Here individuals who have skills and a few resources can readily attain some power. The growth of feudal domains and other small-scale bands of followers around a bandit leader, after the collapse of larger institutionalized empires, is a classic historical example (Hobsbawm, 1965; Shils, 1965). (2) Differentiation within a large society creates new bases of power within the newly differentiated groups; as in the growth of social classes and other forms of stratification, empires, armies, ecclesiastical bureaucracies, and trade unions. Increasing complexity gives increasing scope for power to those officials who were originally carefully controlled from above; they become "viceroys." (3) Related to the second trend, increasing size and complexity of voluntary associations brings about a transformation of representative power into autonomous oligarchic power. Those who hold power originally "on behalf of" members become insulated from the effective control of the members (see Lipset, Trow, and Coleman, 1956, especially chaps. 1 and 18). (4) Technological change, for example, the growth of mass media of communication, may create new opportunities for power. Greenstein (1969, pp. 33–62) discusses the general characteristics of such situations in more abstract terms. In each case, the scope for the operation of personal factors in getting power is increased. Not everyone takes advantage of these opportunities. Not everyone who could become a bandit leader, a viceroy, a spokesman-representative for an organization, or a "media personality" does in fact become one, or even wants to become one. Although they have the chance of getting power, many people prefer to seek truth or beauty instead.

This same effect of personal factors and preferences can be observed in stable organizations and situations, where the scope for having power may be determined by situational factors such as position, status, or class. Not every person uses all of his potential power. Cartwright (1959, p. 203) and Gamson (1968, pp. 94–98) cite examples of people who are "under-users" of their power. These people may not be aware of the power that they have; they may not have the skills to use their potential power effectively; or they may simply be interested in other things (affiliation, leisure), or be fearful of the use of power. Dahl (1963, chaps. 5–6) discusses the same phenomenon in political analysis: some people do not use the power resources that they have, while others go to great lengths to increase and use their power resources. Even such a powerful position as the American presidency has been filled by different men in different ways. Some sought to increase the power of the office, while some allowed power to diffuse toward other positions and offices (see Hargrove, 1966; Donley and Winter, 1970; and Chapter 7 of this book). For these reasons, I think that we have to distinguish between the scope of potential power, which is often, though not always, set by the situation, and the inclination to expand and use that power, which may be more closely related to individual motives.

When we look at the personal and the situational perspectives on power in this way, I think that they can be reconciled. While there is abundant evidence for the importance of the situation, there is also evidence that individual factors and motives affect a person's power —not instead of the situation or in opposition to it, but in combination with situational factors. Many of the more recent reviews of research on leadership have come to just this conclusion (see Hollander and Julian, 1969). That is the perspective that I shall use in this book; I shall discuss it more formally in Chapter 2 and at the beginning of Chapter 7.

PSYCHOLOGICAL VARIABLES INVOLVING POWER

The rest of this book is devoted to the identification, measurement, and characteristic action correlates of the power motive. I believe that the power motive is one key personal variable that is important for understanding power behavior. Since psychologists have already suggested a number of other personality variables that relate to power, I think that it is important to try to distinguish them from the idea of a power motive. For example, there are: perceived locus of the control of reinforcement (Rotter, 1966; Minton, 1968); personal causation (de Charms, 1968); sentiments about power, such as authoritarianism (Adorno, Frenkel-Brunswick, Levinson, and Sanford, 1950), or Machiavellianism (Christie and Geis, 1970); power as attributed by others (Lippitt, Polansky, Redl, and Rosen, 1952); and the tendency to categorize interpersonal relationships in terms of power (Duijker, 1961). In part, these concepts are semantic distinctions, but they are also empirically measured, distinct variables. How do they fit together? Do they overlap with the power motive?

To a strict empiricist, such questions can be answered only by looking at the intercorrelations of the actual variables. I will present some of these in Chapter 3; but here I want to discuss how all of these concepts can be distinguished from the power motive at the level of psychological theory.[5] Such a distinction is important, because research traditions and personal viewpoints have led many people to assume that certain variables, such as authoritarianism or internal control of reinforcement, exhaust the scope of the psychological analysis of power; thus that any other variable relating to power must be related to their own favorite if it is to be valid.

By the power motive, I mean a disposition to strive for certain kinds of goals, or to be affected by certain kinds of incentives. People who have the power motive, or who strive for power, are trying to

[5] In a similar way, Weiner *et al.* (1971) analyze the components of attributed achievement behavior into effort (motivation), ability, task demands, and luck. Such an analysis is similar to the present discussion and could readily be adapted to power behaviors.

bring about a certain state of affairs—they want to feel "power" or "more powerful than. . . ." Power is their goal. We would expect that they tend to construe the world in terms of power and to use the concept of "power" in categorizing human interaction, but they do more than that. Not only do they categorize the world in terms of power, but they also want to feel themselves as the most powerful (cf. Duijker, 1961, for this distinction).

The sense of internal control of reinforcement, or personal causation, can also be distinguished from the power motive. A person who feels that he controls his own fate may *feel* power (although internal control of reinforcement strongly suggests autonomy, while power seems more akin to "control of the fate of others"). Thus the sense of fate-control refers to a present state of affairs, a feeling, or an expectancy about attaining a goal. The power motive suggests a striving toward a goal or incentive; such striving could occur in the presence as well as the absence of the goal itself.[6]

Both Machiavellianism and authoritarianism appear to be sentiments about the nature of power, or power as an aspect of man's nature, rather than dispositions to strive for power. The Machiavellian has certain beliefs about people—"Barnum was probably right when he said that there's at least one sucker born every minute"— and certain beliefs about operating tactics which follow from his beliefs about people—"It is wise to flatter important people." In his behavior he is likely to be an "operator," a manipulator, and successful in detached aggressive bargaining (Christie and Geis, 1970). All of this suggests a particular style of exercising power, a style that may be successful in certain contexts such as American society in the 1960s. However, this style is not the same thing as the power motive. I can surely imagine a person who strives for power but who does not consciously endorse Machiavellian sentiments; and I do not think that everyone who is cynical about the exploitability of people necessarily strives for power himself.

In like manner, authoritarianism denotes an interlocking set of

---

[6] One might argue that motive and satisfaction cannot co-occur; for example, we do not normally feel thirsty when we have just drunk. Social motives appear to be different, and in principle insatiable. This is certainly true of power, about which Thomas Hobbes said "The nature of power . . . is like the motion of heavy bodies, which the further they go, make still the more haste" (1651, p. 69). Minton (1967), in his review of studies using the Rotter I/E measure, hypothesizes that E (a sense of external control of reinforcement) would produce a need for control, or power motive. Plausible as this may seem, there is little empirical evidence for such a relationship, and data reported in Table 3.13 suggest that I/E and the power motive are unrelated.

sentiments and ideology about power relationships—who should have power over whom, why, and how. The authoritarian believes that power is good and that inferior people should be deferent toward superiors, presumably as a resolution of his own intense ambivalence about authority. He is anti-intraceptive, superstitious, projective, and so forth (Adorno *et al.*, 1950). These are beliefs, but they may not necessarily lead to power strivings. Again, I can think of the typical minor bureaucrat in a totalitarian society as a person who scores high on the F-scale but who nevertheless lacks the power motive himself.

Finally, I want to distinguish the power motive from the empirical fact of whether a person occupies a position of power. Such positions may be initially allocated on the basis of characteristics such as membership in elite groups. However, over time there is usually some dropping out (nonusing of power) at the top, and some recruitment to the ranks of the powerful from below (in common with other analysts, Domhoff calls this "co-optation," 1967, pp. 4–5). The *status* of having power is the *goal* of the motive. Over time, I would expect that (other things being equal) those high in the power motive will tend to move into positions of power, and that those low in the motive may move out of the positions of power that they have inherited or that they occupy by accident. In other words, I think that a person's power status at any one time and his power motive are very different concepts.

This completes a brief review of some important problems and issues in the psychological study of power. I intend this discussion to set the stage for the identification and study of the power motive.

CHAPTER 2

The Concept of Motive

This chapter is devoted to an examination of the concept of motive, a review of the ways in which psychologists have tried to measure motives, and an outline of the strategy that I have used to identify and measure the power motive. Since some recent theorists have charged that motive concepts, along with other generalized personality dispositions and constructs, are ambiguous, of little explanatory power, and therefore unnecessary, I feel that it is worthwhile to start from the beginning and explain why "motive" is an important and even indispensable concept. While the research strategy used here has been employed to measure many motives (see Atkinson, 1958), it has often not been fully understood, partly because it is complicated, and partly because its technique and assumptions have not been fully spelled out in the past. Therefore I propose to give a rather full account of that strategy in this chapter. Finally, since the relationship between motive and behavior is by no means a simple one, I want to discuss some models that Atkinson has proposed to specify this relationship.

"MOTIVE" AND THE EXPLANATION OF BEHAVIOR[1]

We use the concept of motive, or the everyday word "reason," to explain someone's behavior in a special way. Take a homely example: "Why did John cross the road?" A typical explanation of this behavior in terms of motive might be "to buy a newspaper" or "because he wanted to buy a newspaper." This kind of explanation implies several things: (1) First, we are talking about a change of behavior, a change that was apparently voluntary or uncompelled. John was walking along the road, or standing, or sitting; then he crossed the road. Moreover, this change of behavior cannot be explained in terms of any obvious external force, such as an obstacle on the sidewalk or a request from someone else to cross the street. In these latter cases, we would explain the action of crossing the street in terms of reasons or causes external to John. Thus "motive" is a way of explaining those changes in behavior that cannot readily be explained by external forces alone. (2) A motive explanation refers John's immediate behavior to some more *general disposition* or *tendency*. John tends to (wants to, likes to, or often does) buy newspapers, probably because he likes to read them. (3) Implied in the motive explanation is that the particular act (crossing the road) is an efficient means of reaching a *goal* (buying the newspaper). John believes that newspapers exist, that they can be purchased at newsstands, and that the building on the other side of the road is a newsstand. If John knows the culture well, his beliefs are likely to be right. (4) The motive explanation involves some predictions about John's future actions: First, that after crossing the road, he will walk to the newsstand, enter it, pay for the paper, and take it. Second, that John is likely to repeat either this same sequence of actions or else some other series of actions that will reach the same goal. Tomorrow, perhaps at about the same time, he may buy another newspaper. If at that time he finds himself already on the other side of the road, then he probably *won't* cross the road, because that action is no longer an efficient means to his goal. Given the goal, John will vary the particular actions as appropriate. (5) Under unusual circumstances, we can also predict other actions. If the store is not a newsstand, or if the newspapers are sold out, John is likely to look for another way to get a newspaper. He might walk on; he might borrow someone

---

[1] The following discussion draws heavily on the philosophical analysis and critique of Peters (1960).

else's newspaper; or if his real purpose was to find out the news, he might turn on a radio or television set. In other words, John will vary his behavior according to the circumstances and events that he encounters, and he will persist in order to achieve his goal.

(6) However, the motive explanation will not tell us certain other things about his behavior. We do not know whether John will walk, run, jump, or perhaps even use a pogo-stick to get across the road. We do not know whether he will cross the road at a right angle or take a diagonal course directly to the front of the newsstand. To answer those questions, we would ask about his *habits* of crossing streets or moving about, whenever he moves toward any goal.

So long as John reaches his goal, his habits do not matter. There is an indefinitely large number of precise ways in which he could get to the store, and an even larger number of ways whereby he could get a newspaper. Whether we use a motive explanation or a habit explanation depends on what we want to know and predict. If we want to predict the broad course or trend of John's behavior under certain circumstances, then we make hypotheses about his motives or dispositions to reach goals—the content of his behavior. If we are interested merely in how John moves about, wherever he is going or wants to go, then we make hypotheses about his habits of moving or the way in which the nervous system, muscles, and skeleton of his body function in movement—the process of his behavior.

I think that this simple example illustrates the use of the concept of motive and also suggests many of the features of a motive explanation that will be formally dealt with later. Nevertheless, many psychologists reject motive explanations in favor of some other kinds of explanation which they feel are simpler or more scientific. Let me illustrate these other explanations with the case of John. We might say that John crossed the road because he was "conditioned" to cross it or because he learned to cross roads. Perhaps he has been trained since early childhood to cross a road whenever he sees one. This explanation focuses on the stimulus, or the situation external to John. It might be an appropriate explanation of some unusual tendency, phobia, or compulsion; but it will hardly cover the present case, because John doesn't always cross roads whenever he sees them—only on certain occasions, such as when he wants a newspaper. The learning explanation can be extended a little bit to fit this kind of contingent behavior: "In certain situations [stimulus-pattern of 11:00 A.M. on Sunday morning, lack of newspaper, perception of newsstand across the road], John has learned to cross roads." Does John have a learned response of road-crossing at 11:00 A.M. on Sundays to buy newspapers? No, because he might have got the newspaper in many other ways. What can be called his "learned response" is simply a general tendency to get newspapers, which tendency can be carried out in an indefinitely large number of different ways under different circumstances. But here we are again with what amounts to a motive explanation. The more complete and accurate we try to make the habit explanation, the more we give, in effect, a motive explanation.

I think that there are fundamentally two different kinds of be-havior—motives and habits. Although these two have been confused in the past, I think that they call for two different kinds of explana-tions, and that these explanations ought to be distinguished by two different concepts. Behavior that is intelligent, variable, and oriented toward some *future* goal (or stimulus) cannot be expressed as a habit or learned response, because many alternate responses could reach the goal and no one response is necessary to reach it. If we try to describe fully the behavior as a learned response to a stimulus pattern, we always end up by speaking directly or indirectly of stimuli which occur "within" the person rather than in the situation; which stimuli involve the future and the results of his action. "Future-oriented internal stimuli" is simply another way of talking about a motive or goal. We need this kind of construct to enable us to know and predict the kinds of things that it will predict, as I suggested above. In contrast, behavior that is a stereotyped response to a par-ticular external present (or past) stimulus configuration is a habit or learned response: crossing roads at traffic lights (or ignoring traffic lights), picking up the left foot after putting down the right foot when walking, and so forth. When a person (inappropriately) shows such a habit response in circumstances where we would expect the more variable operation of a motive, we often call it a *phobia*.

I think that psychologists tried to use the construct of habit or learned response as an explanation of all behavior because they began by studying learning under experimental conditions where the environment of the organism was restricted to a few stimuli which became part of well-learned S-R habits, with all important contin-gencies under the complete control of the experimenter. Most of the behavior that they observed looked as though it were simply chains of stimulus-initiated habits. As learning theory developed and became more sophisticated, most psychologists have distinguished motive from habit in one way or another: "molar behavior" (Tolman), "operant behavior" (Skinner), "incentive" and "fractional anticipatory goal response" (Hull and Spence), and "behavior which is intrinsi-cally regulated" (Koch). I prefer the simpler term "motive," but I think that it could be translated into these other expressions without much difficulty.

Another explanation of John's behavior that would be favored by some psychologists is that some internal "drive" or need operated to cause him to cross the road. Perhaps he acted to relieve some basic tissue need such as hunger or thirst. (In a roundabout way, a psychologist may claim that something called "anxiety," associated with these needs, is "reduced" by newspapers.) Perhaps he was driven by the need to restore some kind of internal homeostasis, or perhaps getting a newspaper touches off some kind of event in the "pleasure centers" of his brain (Olds, 1955). These explanations have a mechanical quality that is attractive to some, but they are incomplete if we follow them through. A good deal of research on motivation and learning has shown that there is no obvious connection between many often-performed actions and any conceivable state of tissue deprivation. Insisting on such an explanation, as, for example, by invoking the "reduction of conditioned anxiety" or neural connections with pleasure centers, only amounts to circular reasoning. John does the act, and our theory is that all behavior is related to anxiety-reduction or neural pleasure: therefore the behavior is caused by anxiety-reduction or pleasure.

We want to know John's motives so that we can understand and predict John's behavior, and any general statement that "all behavior is motivated to avoid anxiety" or "pleasure is the master motive" simply avoids the question. If such a general statement is correct— that is, if it avoids circularity by specifying independently defined mechanisms—then it may tell us something about the nature of motives in general; but this is not what we want to know. Like all other organisms, John avoids anxiety or gets pleasure; but he does it in particular ways with particular behaviors. A general explanation of the physiological mechanisms of all motivated behavior or of the processes by which motives are learned would be valuable if it were complete and accurate; but from such an explanation alone we still cannot answer important questions: What are the ways in which John gets pleasure? What are his motives? How can we discover these motives? How did John develop these motives? Thus physiological explanations of motives do not fully substitute for motive explanations, although they can be a valuable supplement to them.

What about a psychoanalytic explanation of John's behavior? How would it be different from the motive explanation given above? Freud argued that there are only a few fundamental motives:[2] ego motives related to the processes of self-preservation, libidinal motives,

---

[2] Freud's term *Trieben* has often been translated "instincts," but I think that "impulse," "propensity," or "motive power" might be better renderings.

and perhaps a wish for death. Actually, "libido" is not itself a motive, but the name and explanation of a broad class of more specific and differentiated libidinal motives of individuals. While the concept of libido is an explanation of one mechanism of motivated behavior (the reduction or abolition of sexual tension), in practice it also leads an observer to look for specifically sexual aspects of particular motives. Thus it can increase the variety and sophistication of motive explanations.

Freud's other contribution to the study of motivation was his insight that most motives are either in conflict with other motives, or else blocked by real or imagined fears of punishment. Thus motives are partly unconscious and often achieve only a disguised expression in behavior, so that any particular action is likely to be a compromise or fusion among several different motives and mechanisms of defense (or defensive motives). Many defenses are quite primitive, in that they involve "primary" mental processes such as hallucination or judgment of equivalence on the basis of emotional similarity in the mind of the perceiver (displacement, transference, symbolic representation). Because of conflicts and defenses, then, any particular motive is likely to relate to a much wider and stranger array of actions than would be the case if it were strictly rational and without conflict. For this reason, neither a person's own explanations of his behavior (his "reasons" or self-report of motives) nor momentary observation of that behavior by an external judge is likely to be a very good way of measuring motives, and therefore of understanding and predicting what we want to understand and predict with a motive explanation. A careful reconstruction of the structures and defenses of several major motives may be necessary to understand and predict the behavior of a particular person.

I do not want to discuss the evidence for or against the whole of psychoanalysis here. To the extent that careful research and experience shows that Freud's concepts of libido and unconscious motivation are useful, they permit an enormous refinement and extension of motive explanations to cover behaviors that previously had defied explanation, or that had been thought to be "accidents"—that is, resulting from factors external to the person.

To return to John crossing the street: He *says* that he does it in order to get a newspaper, and taking this as his motive is probably good enough for most purposes, even for psychoanalysis. But what if there were no newspapers there? Or if he crossed the street again and again? Or if he looked anxiously and furtively around as he walked? Or if, once having bought the newspaper, he tore it up into little pieces and scattered them around while madly singing and dancing? For the ordinary behaviors of life, psychoanalysis is content with the ordinary kind of explanation of action that has been given above; but when the behavior or verbal fantasy begins to show "surprising and unusual connections," as Freud put it, then the search for hypothesized unconscious goals can lead to the fuller explanation of this behavior.

MOTIVES, DISPOSITIONS, AND SOCIAL LEARNING THEORY

In recent years, social learning theorists have made a different kind of criticism of motive explanations (see Vernon, 1964; Mischel, 1969). The basic claim of social learning theory is that all behavior can be explained and predicted by a full specification of the reinforcement history of the person and the forces present in the situation. At first, this seems similar to the attempt to explain motive as habit; but social learning theorists would accept the notion of "internal future-oriented stimuli," which is the principal postulate of motive explanations. Social learning theory accepts the idea of goals, but rejects the notion that for a person there are broad classes of equivalent goals, such that he can be said to be "generally motivated for power" or "assertive." Social learning theory argues that behavior is highly specific to the particular cues of each individual situation; thus that there is no use in postulating broad generalized categories of motives or personality, for people simply are not that consistent across situations or over time. Mischel (1969) reviews some evidence and argues that behavior shows little generality across situations or over time; thus he claims to reject any kind of generalized personality disposition, trait, or state as a useful explanation of behavior. Since motives are included in this general condemnation, I think that it is important to look at the claims of this position.

No one argues that behavior can be predicted from a knowledge of only the present stimuli, for individuals simply differ in their responses to what are objectively the same conditions. This is the starting point for personality theory and motive explanations; and to deal with this fact, social learning theory necessarily introduces variables that, taken together, function as motive or dispositional constructs. First, individuals differ in their inherent capacities to learn or to be reinforced, and in their differential capacities to learn by classical conditioning, positive instrumental learning, and avoidance learning (Eysenck, 1957; Berlyne, 1968). Second, the term "reinforcement history" stands for a variety of different concepts that account for individual differences in learning in particular situations. There are differences in the rewardingness of particular stimuli or incentives; differences in the coding or categorizing of stimuli; differences in attending to and selecting particular stimuli as "relevant"; differences in the acquired emotional meaning of stimuli (Mischel, 1969, pp. 157–159); and differences in the capacity for self-reinforcement, or the ability to generate one's own internal rewarding stimuli (Katz, 1967; Mischel, 1969, p. 166). All of these individual difference variables, taken together, in effect constitute motive or personality variables. The term "motive" can be specified in Mischel's terms as a combination of directed attention, acquired emotional meaning for a significant category of stimuli, and a capacity for certain kinds of self-reinforcement.

Nevertheless, Mischel makes important criticisms of the empirical usefulness of dispositional constructs. Research purporting to demontrate the validity of personality characteristics typically yields correlations with behavior that are in the range of ±.30; although such coefficients may be statistically significant, they are not impressive and they do not account for a very large percentage of the variance of behavior. Mischel argues that the definition and measurement processes are partly at fault. Questionnaires and judges' ratings reflect response sets, stereotypes, and halo effects as much as they pick up actual differences in behavior. Often there are no clear empirical definitions of the variables to be rated. Measures of criterion behaviors are sometimes the same as measures of dispositions (questionnaires, judges' ratings), so that the research only predicts from one kind of rating scale to another. Unsophisticated research designs do not take account of possible interactions between personality and situational variables.

These criticisms[3] are serious and suggest several important re-

---

[3] Another point in the criticism of personality theory is that viewing behavior as the result of relatively stable dispositions located within the person is both therapeutically and ideologically conservative; for it suggests that the causes of behavior and problems of behavior are to be found mainly in the person, rather than in his situation or society; and it underestimates the effects on behavior of a changed situation. I don't want to get into a full discussion of the politics of personality theory, but I do think that two points can be made: (1) While social conditions are the ultimate "cause" of most dispositions and actions, their effects may be different at one stage of the person's life than at another; and the effects at the first stage may be partially irreversible, or at least important in determining effects at later stages. This complicated way of saying that earlier learn-

quirements for improved research on motivation and personality. First, the motive must be defined in clear, reliable, and empirical terms. Second, the criterion behaviors should include "real" behaviors as well as "paper-and-pencil" behaviors, and these should be measured insofar as is possible by nonreactive techniques (see Webb, Campbell, Schwartz, and Sechrest, 1966). Finally, the overall research design should anticipate and make allowance for the interaction of personality and situational variables, by means of a formal model if possible. When this latter step has been carried out in the past (for example, Couch, 1962; Atkinson and Feather, 1966; Fishman, 1966; McGuire, 1968; Greene and Winter, 1971), the level of correlation coefficient obtained has increased substantially. The research reported in this book uses the idea of personality-situation interaction, although without a more precise mathematical formulation. Overall, I feel that the critique of Mischel and other social learning theorists suggests some important cautions for motive research, but I do not think that it should keep us from doing it. Alker (1972) outlines a paradigm for such new kinds of personality research.

SCIENTIFIC CLARIFICATION OF "MOTIVE"

If the concept of motive or goal is essential to the explanation of behavior, why then have psychologists so often resisted such concepts, and so often tried to reject motive explanations or to reduce them to something else? Is there a problem with the word "goal"? Because a goal is a future event that influences present behavior, it must necessarily be represented in the mind of the organism or person while he is moving toward it. This creates no problem for ordinary people, who are accustomed to "look forward" to Santa Claus or to a summer vacation; but it used to create problems for those psychologists who did not like the implied "mentalism" of such a construct. Yet in the end other similar constructs ("expectancy," "fractional anticipatory

---

ing has some kind of primacy effect is, I think, the necessary axiom of personality theory. A modified way of putting it is that the effects of some personality disposition (or variable) may be different from its causes. (2) To talk of dispositions is not necessarily to talk of fixed and unchanging dispositions. Whether any particular aspect of personality changes, and if so under what circumstances, are empirical questions; though as I shall argue in the next chapter, the great concern for high test-retest "reliability" has often prevented psychologists from asking them.

goal response") had to be introduced to represent the future in the present "mind" of the person. With the great advances of cognitive psychology, I do not think that we have to fear "mentalism" in the notion that a future goal in the mind of a person can somehow direct his present behavior.

A second objection to the concept of goal or motive is that it is too vague—anathema to those who want to model psychology after what they perceive to be the highly successful enterprise of positivistic, "tough-minded" physics. But I don't think that the term "goal" has to be vague. By using some of the characteristics of motivated behavior, "goal" can be specified in ways that will enable observers to identify with accuracy and agreement both when behavior is directed toward a goal, and what that goal is.

What are the characteristics of goal-directed or motivated behavior? First, it is likely to be more and more predictable up to the point when the goal is reached; thereafter it is quite unpredictable *with respect to that particular goal*.[4] If the goal is soon reactivated, or if the person has other goals, then his subsequent behavior is predictable with respect to these other goals. Second, as a person approaches a goal, he becomes less distractable, which can be tested by introducing obstacles and barriers. Sometimes (though not always), the speed of response will increase, or the latency decrease, toward the goal. Overall, motivated behavior shows intelligent variation with conditions insofar as the person is intelligent and experienced with the conditions. He is likely to have a cognitive "map" of the goal and the actions and regions associated with it, and he can verbalize and describe this map. He will have positive and negative anticipations. He will make choices in characteristic ways. Finally, at the goal itself, his behavior will become so predictable that it can be called a stereotyped "consummatory response." Each of these characteristics of motivated behavior could be operationally specified and refined into a way of identifying and measuring motives; but there are certain advantages and problems associated with using each, as I shall discuss below.

What then can psychology, as a science of behavior, do with motives? How do we know a person's motives? Psychology can define

[4] Strictly speaking, this is true only of approach motives: in the case of avoidance motives, behavior is less predictable as the person continues to move away from the (negatively-valued) goal. Thus in both cases there is a gradient of predictability with respect to distance from the goal. The distinction between approach and avoidance motives will be considered later in this chapter and also in Chapter 3.

and measure motives, and can then study particular motives intensively. How does the motive influence behavior? What are the alternative courses of action that a person high in that motive might take? How do different situations affect the motive? How did it develop in the person originally? These are the questions that guided the research on the power motive reported in this book.

MEASURING MOTIVES

How can a motive be measured? The obvious way is to look at one or more of the features of motivated, goal-directed behavior mentioned above. These include the following (see Murray, 1938, p. 124; McClelland, 1951, pp. 478–521; Klinger, 1966):

1. Increasing predictability of behavior as the goal is approached.

2. Intelligent variation of instrumental behavior according to conditions, especially in the presence of obstacles or barriers.

3. Increasing persistence, possibly associated with faster, more efficient, improved performance (so long as the motive level is not excessive and, therefore, debilitating).

4. Reports from the motivated person as to what he believes his motives and motive strength to be.

5. Emotional (autonomic) responses in anticipation and realization of the goal.

6. Characteristic choices and interests.

7. Cognitive clusters that include "maps" of the goal and associated instrumental actions, positive and negative anticipations, and sensitized perception of goal-related objects.

Which feature offers the best way of measuring a motive? Each has been used by one or more investigators, and each has some advantages and disadvantages (see McClelland, 1958, which is the basis of much of the following discussion).

First, we might measure motives by looking at the trend of a person's action (characteristics 1 and 2). What does he appear to be striving for when not under the pressure of some immediate task? This procedure fits our commonsense notion of what a motive is— a trend or course of behavior. Surely if a motive is important to the person, then it ought to show up often in his behavior. Murray and his associates used this technique. Trained judges carefully studied a person's behavior trends by both direct observation and scrutiny of important personal documents such as autobiographical accounts. Sometimes one or more experimental procedures (tasks involving performance, frustration, or persistence) were added to the dossier of information from which judgments were made (Murray, 1938; and O.S.S. Assessment Staff, 1949). After conference and discussion, the judges decided on motive ratings for the person. Although this procedure has several advantages, it also involves some very serious difficulties and pitfalls of the type noted by Mischel. It is very difficult to be sure that all judges are defining each motive in the same way; or if they are given standard instructions, that they are using them in the same way. Such a difficulty is greatly increased when the judges are untrained peers of the person being assessed. Even if the definitions are clear, the assessments are easily contaminated by the judge's own motives, biases, projections, implicit theories of human behavior, and relationship to the person assessed. Even if these problems could be overcome, any judge can observe only a few very limited samples of behavior. The particular actions that he observes could well be related to any one of several different motives taken by themselves, in fusion, or in conflict. In order to decide which motive is involved, observations beyond the available sample may be required.

Moreover, judges' observations are likely to be made under conditions that are quite restricted, as well as simply limited in time. For example: judges will not observe much eating behavior by a very hungry person if they observe him only when he has no access to food. A person with a strong power motive might show little power behavior in a situation where he felt that there were no worthwhile power goals. Of course, attempts can be made to overcome this problem by observing in a variety of situations, and inquiring about the unobserved parts of the person's life. But what is a fair or appropriate sample of situations? Inquiries are either second-hand accounts from other people, which simply puts the problem at one remove, or second-hand accounts from the person himself, which I shall discuss below under the topic of self-reports. Even under ideal observation conditions, the motive might be blocked by fear, social desirability, or another motive.

Since motives energize behavior and thus usually lead to stronger or faster responses, learning theorists and others such as Cattell (1958) detect and measure motives by looking for those actions which are performed with special vigor, speed, energy, or persistence (characteristic 3). Yet "energy" is difficult to define in a way that will apply to all motives. For example, not every motive will always cause faster or stronger instrumental activity. (The power motive might sometimes lead to instrumental behavior that is superficially not vigorous, and even devious.) If we try to create an experimental situation to assess vigor or persistence, how do we know that we have designed the right one? Feather (1961) found that under certain conditions of low expectancy, men high in the achievement motive actually showed *less* persistence than men low in the achievement motive and high in Test Anxiety. For these reasons, I don't think that measuring the energy of response is likely to be useful as a way of assessing complex human motives.

Often when we want to find out someone's else's motives, we simply ask him (characteristics 4 and 6). After all, who is in a better position to understand a person's motives than that person himself? Psychologists have refined this procedure into questionnaires or other instruments. In some such self-report measures, the questions are straightforward and clear, so that it is obvious to the person who responds that his motives are being studied (for example, the Stern Activities Index or the Edwards Personal Preference Schedule). Other instruments conceal their purpose by asking questions which are seemingly unrelated to motives, but which are thought on empirical grounds to be diagnostic of them (for example, the Strong Vocational Interest Blank or the MMPI). Despite the intuitive appeal of self-report procedures, they too have several serious difficulties. Although a person possesses a special and intimate kind of knowledge about himself and his goals, he is unlikely to spend time in systematic recollection of them. What he does remember is likely to be fragments of his life organized around certain selected goals or themes—goals influenced by things such as the desire to make consistent sense of his life and purposes, and social pressures about the goals that people ought to have (or ought to admit to having). At best, a person's self-report of goals is a rationalized interpretation of selected memories, rather than an unbiased and systematic sampling of particular day-to-day goals. Those goals which are contrary to individual moral standards or social customs are likely to be repressed altogether, or at least denied in a psychological assessment setting. In Chapter 1, I suggested that power is often just this kind of goal.

So far, we have assumed an optimal assessment situation, such as an intensive series of interviews with a sensitive clinician. In actual practice, "self-report" usually means having subjects fill out questionnaires in a setting that is closer to a psychological experiment. Because the typical questionnaire has standard questions with a very limited choice of standard answers, there is the serious danger that the goals and motives most relevant to a particular person will not be included, or that the alternative answers given will not fit the person's own conception of himself. Moreover, the meaning and interpretation of the item wording may differ greatly from experimenter to subject, just as in the case of judges' ratings. Questionnaire administration, as an experimental situation, is subject to the operation of experimenter-bias, unintentional influence, and demand characteristics in the same way as any ordinary psychological experiment (see Rosenthal, 1966; Orne, 1962, 1970): social desirability, trying to figure out the purpose or use of the questionnaire, trying to please (or displease) the experimenter, and so forth. Finally, response sets and other tendencies to reply to items apart from the content of those items will affect self-report assessment procedures (see Couch and Keniston, 1960; Berg, 1967).

Because motivated behavior is accompanied by a variety of cognitive representations, anticipations, and images (characteristic 7), some psychologists have attempted to measure motives through recording and analyzing these networks of cognitive associations. Freud's use of free association is a classic example of the technique. The subject (or patient) is encouraged to report whatever is "in" or "comes to" his mind, without censoring and without regard for coherence or logical connection. After some practice and further encouragement against "blocking" or editing, the subject can produce an extended chain of free association; from these associations the analyst or investigator can infer his goals and motives. When it worked, free association was thought to approach being an accurate report of *fantasy*, or the autonomous flow of fanciful images directed toward the fulfillment (or representation) of a wish or need (Murray, 1937, pp. 115–116). Thus fantasy was thought to be a full and reliable source of information about motives, if it were properly interpreted. Since dreams were also an important source of fantasy, their analysis and interpretation became a standard clinical method for discovering motives.

Since it is time-consuming, difficult, and costly to obtain and record extensive samples of free association or dream-reports from large numbers of people in order to study their motives, it is not surprising that many researchers have tried to devise quicker and more direct ways of obtaining and recording fantasy or fantasy-like material. These are based on the presumed relationship between fantasy and perception. When input from the external environment (stimuli, suggestions, events) occurs together with fantasy, these external cues are incorporated into the fantasy production. In extreme cases, all perception of external phenomena is seriously distorted by internally generated wishes; in such cases the internal needs are said to be "projected," or perceived as existing in the environment. In more ordinary circumstances, our interpretation of the environment is influenced by or organized along the lines of our motives, although our comprehension of the environment itself is not seriously distorted. This intermediate process, combining stimuli from the environment and from fantasy processes, or "assigning meaning to the physical stimulus," was called "apperception" by Murray (1933, p. 319). Since our apperceptions contain elements of our motives, or are affected by them, they could be a source of information about motives if they were properly interpreted.

To standardize the situation and the stimuli which were involved in apperception, Morgan and Murray (1935) devised the Thematic Apperception Test (TAT), in which they presented a person with a series of twenty cards. Each card was a picture that was vague in that it could suggest a variety of different motifs, themes, or stories. The subject was asked to make up a story about each picture, following certain standard questions that covered the elements of a plot, but otherwise was completely on his own with no suggestion that there was any one "correct story."

There were probably many reasons why Morgan and Murray settled on this particular test to measure apperception. Previous psychoanalytic experience with the bizarre distortions and misinterpretations that projection produced was an obvious influence. Murray's interest in art and literature led him to the problem of the interpretation of literary and artistic creations. Finally, at about this time, he devised an experiment that proved to anticipate many of the features of the TAT and even of the strategy for using it in research that is employed in this book (Murray, 1933). Several girlfriends of his eleven-year-old daughter were weekend guests, and the game of "Murder" was scheduled for exciting entertainment on Saturday evening. Murray used the occasion for some informal research. He arranged sets of pictures clipped from a magazine, and on three separate occasions showed them to the girls. Each time, they were asked to rate "how good or bad is the character of the person" on a scale of 1 to 9, and to "write down what you think the person in the photograph is thinking or saying." Ratings were made at noon Saturday, after a ride in the country and well before the game of Murder; immediately after the game Saturday evening; and at noon Sunday after a sleigh ride. As expected, judgments of badness increased after the excitement and fear of the game of Murder; but Murray also reported that the made-up sentences changed in ways that seemed closely related to the changed emotional and motive state of the girls. For example, one picture elicited the innocuous "What shall I do next?" before the game; afterward the same girl attributed to it the sentence "So all your children are sick. Well, I hope they die." One girl reported a vivid dream of burglars during Saturday night. This demonstration that verbal reports of apperception were so sensitive to changes in motives and moods suggested that the technique could be adapted to measure enduring motives.

Morgan and Murray thought that they had devised a systematic method for investigating fantasy, because they had felt that the plots of the stories obtained were a fairly direct transcription of the conscious and unconscious motives of the story-teller.[5] While the pictures themselves affect the stories, their use was actually a partial advantage over free association, since it brought some of the previously random elements of the external world under greater control of the investigator. The essential elements of the TAT were that (1) the subject was shown an ambiguous stimulus and (2) he was asked to make up a dynamic story about the stimulus.[6] Since it was first introduced, the TAT has been modified in numerous ways by other researchers. Stories have been written rather than told orally; pictures have been changed, and also shown on large screens to groups; and sentence stems have been substituted for pictures (French, 1958). These changes do not seem to affect the essential elements of the test. Thus,

[5] Of course "fantasy" in the strict sense is not the same as the content of TAT stories, as Holt (1961) carefully argues. Rather (as Murray also said), the TAT story is some combination of fantasy and secondary process.

I also want to avoid the term "projective test" in discussing the TAT, because to me it brings in unnecessary and confusing assumptions and arguments about the nature of projection or the different kinds of projection. Murray originally argued that the apperceptive processes involve strict projection only in unusual and pathological cases. Normally they are made up of associative traces, conscious images, and imaginal meanings (1933, pp. 312–314, 323). The later use of the term "projective test" blurred this very clear distinction. The questions of how motives are expressed in apperception, and under what circumstances apperception is projective in the strict sense, are surely empirical ones. Murray himself recognized this point several years after he devised the original rationale for TAT interpretation (1958, p. 190).

[6] This contrasts with the Rorschach Test, which asks for a description rather than a story with a plot; and also with the Iowa Picture Interpretation Test, in which the subject does not make up a story, but instead selects one of several alternatives provided by the experimenter as the "most likely story." The latter procedure in effect converts the TAT into a questionnaire, rather than a measure of spontaneous apperception.

following the tradition of McClelland, Atkinson, Clark, and Lowell (1953), I shall use the term TAT to describe stories written by people, in groups, to pictures shown with a slide projector on a screen. The pictures that I have used are different from those of the original Murray set. Following the same tradition, I shall use Murray's symbol "n" to indicate the power motive as operationally defined and measured by the TAT—n Power. (This does not imply that the power motive is ultimately based on any physiological need, as Murray sometimes implied.)

After several decades of use, the TAT remains a popular clinical instrument, because it is thought to measure "deeper" levels of personality—things which are not so much under the conscious control and censorship of the subject (see Combs, 1947). Nevertheless, the TAT is not without problems insofar as its scientific use in research is concerned (see Murstein, 1963). These problems are basically four: (1) Do movies appear directly or inversely in the TAT? That is, do the stories that a person tells reflect (a) all of his motives, (b) only those motives that are not presently satisfied, or (c) some combination of motives and defensive transformations of these motives (see Lazarus, 1961, 1966)? It seems impossible to give any *a priori* answer to this question, although each alternative has its staunch advocates. Yet some sort of answer is required if the TAT is to be useful in research. (2) Assuming that the TAT does in some way reflect motives, how is a particular motive to be measured? For example, what should be the scoring definition of the power motive in TAT stories? Given the number of different conceptions and definitions of power, and making allowance for the effects of reaction-formation and sublimation, different researchers could probably justify scoring almost anything as "power" in a TAT story. Again, there seems to be no easy way of deciding the matter in advance of doing research; yet a scoring definition is needed in order to do the research itself. (3) Regardless of the scoring system used, the TAT appears to have rather low reliability; that is, the stories that a person tells at one time seem to be different from the stories that he tells at some later time. If this is a criticism, it is based on the assumption that personality or motives do not change, since if they did change, low reliability would be expected (although mere low reliability is hardly a virtue). (4) In any case, the TAT does seem extraordinarily sensitive to the effects of the immediate situation and mood in which it is taken (Murstein, 1963, pp. 236–257).

THE McCLELLAND-ATKINSON RESEARCH STRATEGY

The McClelland-Atkinson strategy for defining and measuring motives, which is used in this book, proceeds by answering problems 1, 2, and 4 all at once. First, the scoring system for a motive is defined through observing the effects on fantasy when that motive is experimentally aroused. In other words, the sensitivity of the TAT to the immediate situation is used in order to provide a more objective way to answer the first two problems. First, a group is exposed to an experience that arouses a motive such as hunger, achievement, or power; while a matched control (or "neutral") group has no such arousal experience. Birney (1968, pp. 858–860) reviews the different experiences that have been used to arouse the achievement motive.

Both the aroused and the neutral groups then take TATs. The differences between the stories written by the aroused group and those written by the neutral group can then be thought of as due to the effect of the aroused motive; in other words, they can be taken as a measure of the motive itself.[7] That is, a person who has a strong motive can be thought of as being in a more or less continuous state of arousal, or as being more likely to be in this state of arousal at any one time. In other words, he customarily reacts to (or assigns meaning to) the stimulus picture-cues in the way that most people do only under special, strong, externally induced conditions. Thus his TAT stories should be similar to those of the group in which arousal of the motive was induced, as compared with the stories of the neutral group.

The principal assumption of the McClelland-Atkinson technique is, therefore, that the manifestations of the motive in the person with the strong motive (whom I shall call "aroused" in explicit analogy to the "aroused" group) are substantially the same as the manifestations of the motive under the process of experimental arousal. More formally, the assumptions are that what is called a motive: (1) can be experimentally manipulated and aroused, (2) is also present in different strengths among different people, and (3) that these two manifestations are the same or equivalent. Thus the problem of defining the scoring system for a motive is handled by exploiting the known sensitivity of the TAT to situations. If the arousal conditions are

[7] Of course, one group could be tested under both neutral and aroused conditions. Unless the order of conditions is counterbalanced, this will lead to the problems that arise when the TAT is given to the same person(s) twice (see Reitman and Atkinson, 1958, p. 679).

appropriate, then the resulting shifts in fantasy are diagnostic of the motive. Such a strategy avoids *a priori* speculation about whether motives are expressed in fantasy directly or in substitute form by the simple statement that motives are expressed in the way that they are expressed (see Murray, 1958, p. 190).

The scoring system is based on the differences between aroused and neutral groups, although in constructing such a system there is ample scope for testing every conceivable *a priori* idea about how the motive might be expressed in fantasy. Some of these *a priori* ideas tend to work out; some do not; and others work only in modified form. Construction of such a scoring system usually takes a great deal of work by many different investigators, as will become apparent in Chapter 3 when I describe the development of the *n* Power scoring system. The essential task is to detect differences and to try out hypotheses about differences, and then to refine these into clear written definitions of each category of the scoring system. The result should be a system that can be readily communicated to others and that can, on the basis only of written instructions and practice materials, be learned to a very high standard of reliability.

The main feature of the McClelland-Atkinson strategy that I have left unspecified, which is one of the main problems of the strategy, is the arousal experiment(s) itself. How can the effects of the arousal experience be used to define the motive, when some definition of the motive is necessary in order to design an arousal experiment? If I say the scoring system for *n* Power is defined by the observed shifts in fantasy after experience *x*, then am I not really defining power as *x*? And isn't this as arbitrary and, therefore, disputable as any other way of defining power?

The validity of any one motive arousal experiment is always open to question, for there is no guarantee that that experiment is an ideal, appropriate, or complete way to capture the essential features of the particular motive. But one must start somewhere. Therefore it is necessary to begin with a very broad general conception of power, and to design an experience that is likely to arouse the power motive according to this broad definition. After doing this, it is important to design and execute a whole series of different arousal experiments, each sampling the broad domain of power in a slightly different way or from a different perspective. Those shifts in fantasy that occur in all, or most, of the experiments can be isolated as a more valid and meaningful measure. Thus the strategy does not rest on any one arousal experiment. Any one arousal experiment may be open to question; but results common to all of a series of different arousal experiments are more defensible. The greater the variety of such experiments, the greater is the representative design or "ecological validity" of the final motive measure (Brunswik, 1956).[8] The final test of the measure is whether it predicts important actions related to the motive in question—its "construct validity" or "relational fertility" (McClelland, 1958). I think that relational fertility and the ecological validity of the system go together. Thus the empirical usefulness of the n Achievement measure is due in part to the number of separate arousal experiments that were carried out before the final scoring system was fixed.

Instead of using experimental arousal or manipulation of the motive, why not compare one group which we believe is already high in the power motive with another group which we believe is low? Veroff (1957) used student candidates for offices in university organizations as a criterion group for defining the power motive, assuming that they "must be" high in n Power. Such a procedure sacrifices some scientific confidence, because it studies "response-response" covariation instead of manipulating the motive experimentally (Spence, 1948). As a result, the differences in the stories of the two groups may be caused by factors other than the motive in question. Indeed, the two groups may not even differ on that motive! While the experimental arousal technique also makes assumptions about the definition of the motive, at least "you know what you're getting"—if subjects are assigned randomly to the aroused and control groups, and if the arousal procedure is carefully and fully described. In other words, the method of experimental arousal permits more complete specification of the independent variable (i.e., the differences between the two groups), and easier separation of "motive" from other confusing variables. There would seem to be no logical flaw in the criterion groups method *if the group is really an appropriate criterion for the*

[8] Some of the arousal experiments may not "work"—they may not produce the same shifts in fantasy as the others, which purport to measure the same motive, do. In such a case, one may begin to learn empirically about the boundaries of the motive in question. Birney (1968, pp. 855–860) discusses examples of this in the case of n Achievement. One might work toward distinguishing different "kinds" of, say, power motives according to the results of arousal experiments. "Power-A" would be that pattern of fantasy shifts produced by experiments a_1, a_2, and a_3; while "Power-B" would be the pattern produced by experiments b_1, b_2, and b_3; and where neither type of power motive is aroused by experiments of the other type. This sounds cumbersome; but because it is based on the experimental manipulations of motive-related situations, it seems an alternative that is preferable to *a priori* theorizing about the number of different kinds of power or power motive.

motive in question, and only for that motive. And this is precisely the problem with using criterion groups, for any given outcome (status, past action) can be the result of many different motives, as well as a variety of social variables. It might seem obvious that politicians should be an appropriate group for defining the power motive; yet any number of different motives and nonmotivational factors can lead men into politics (Browning, 1968; also Chapter 4 of this book). Thus the criterion groups method is likely to lead to confusion.

I followed the McClelland-Atkinson research strategy in the present research on power motivation. The final measure of the power motive was based on several different arousal experiments, tentative conceptualizations of the motive, and further revisions (see Chapter 3). I have not yet explicitly discussed the issue of TAT reliability, which I mentioned above as a continual problem with thematic apperception techniques. This omission is intended; I shall treat the problem at length in Chapter 3 in the context of the reliability of *n* Power scores.

MOTIVE AND BEHAVIOR

I argued above that the relationship between motive and behavior is complex: for example, motive interacts with variables in the situation to produce action; and an action can be the result of many different motives, either singly, in combination, or in conflict. At this point I want to discuss the models proposed by Atkinson (Atkinson, 1957; Atkinson and Feather, 1966; Atkinson and Birch, 1970) as a more formal conception of the relationships between motive and action. In a general way, these models guided the research reported in this book, although the results and interpretations are not formulated with mathematical precision. However, I believe that models such as these —which organize motives, as measured by TAT procedures, and other psychological and social variables that determine behavior—will be important in understanding both motives and power, and in interpreting the results of research.

In a series of early experiments on achievement motivation, Atkinson (1953) found that *n* Achievement related to performance on a particular task only under certain conditions. A formally dressed, brisk experimenter who described the task as a test of intelligence, in which scores would be taken as the full measure of ability, produced a positive correlation between *n* Achievement and performance. When an informally dressed experimenter appealed for cooperation in doing the task because it would help him in his research, *n* Achievement was unrelated to performance (Atkinson, 1953); but such conditions did produce a correlation between n Affiliation and performance (French, 1955; Atkinson and Raphelson, 1956). These results led Atkinson and his associates to think of task performance (or Action tendency A in the model to be described) as some function of the joint product of motive a (M_a) and the expectancy that action A will lead to the goal a of the motive (E_a). In symbolic terms:

$$\text{Action tendency } A = f\ (M_a \times E_a)$$

The relationship between motive and expectancy is deliberately multiplicative, so that if either one is zero, then the contribution of that motive to Action tendency A will also be zero. This formulation indicates that *any* motive ($a, b, c, \ldots z$) may contribute to the tendency to perform *any* action ($A, B, C, \ldots Z$), so long as there is some expectancy that the action will lead to the goal of that motive. Expectancies are the result of previous learning (contiguity and repetition) and perception; although, within the limits of plausibility, they can be modified by experimental instructions and similar techniques. They are more or less independent of motives. Thus the total Action tendency A is the summation of motive × expectancy terms for all motives, although of course these products will be nearly zero for all but a few motives in any particular case:

$$\text{Action tendency } A = \sum_{i=a}^{z} f\ (M_a \times E_a)$$

where z = the total number of motives

Further refinement of the model and results from new experiments led Atkinson to propose that the *amount of incentive,* or incentive value of the particular goal, should be included in the calculation of Action tendency, and so he proposed the following extended formula (1957):

$$\text{Action tendency } A = \sum_{i=a}^{z} f\ (M_a \times E_a \times I_a)$$

where I = the amount of the incentive of the particular goal

This allows explanation of the case where a strong motive and a high expectancy of success do not lead to action, because the perceived value of the goal is very low. An everyday example would be the hungry man who is nevertheless reluctant to eat unappetizing food. At least the revised formula predicts that he should more eagerly eat good food!

So far I have considered only appetites or approach motives—the desire *for* something, to *get* something, to *reach* a goal. Yet many purposes or motives can best be defined as something that we are trying to *get away from* or avoid. These fears or avoidance motives (Miller, 1944) have the same characteristics as other motives, except that the goal is negative: behavior (i.e., avoidance behavior) is increasingly predictable the nearer the person is to the negative goal; and the person makes negative choices, and has negatively-toned cognitive elements. Presumably avoidance motives are the result of punishment experiences rather than reward experiences. In any case, avoidance motives should follow the Atkinson formula, always with the caution that we are speaking about avoidance behavior (i.e., *not* carrying out an action), and negative incentives of reaching a goal. Since the effect of avoidance motives is negative, it should be subtracted from action tendencies, and, therefore, should be included in the formula as a subtractive term (although avoidance motives may energize a variety of particular behaviors such as withdrawal or conformity, as well as producing apathy or freezing).

What things are we likely to avoid? This depends upon the culture. For middle-class white American males, failure at an achievement task is usually something to be avoided and success is usually something to be approached. Thus there are said to be two achievement-related motives—Hope of Success (approach) and Fear of Failure (avoidance). Depending upon their previous experience, especially the general salience of achievement behavior and the balance of reward and punishment techniques used by their parents, most middle-class white American males will have certain levels of Hope of Success and Fear of Failure.

For American women the situation is different. Cultural stereotypes about appropriate sex-roles dictate that women are not "supposed to" succeed at many kinds of achievement tasks, and that they should be covertly punished if they do succeed. Thus they develop a *motive to avoid success*, or a Fear of Success (Horner, 1968, 1969), which can of course exist along with a Hope of Success or Fear of Failure. In order to handle these culture-related and status-related differences in motive and incentive socialization, the formulation has to be expanded. Within any content area (power, achievement, affiliation), there are "successful" outcomes (getting power, success, or friends) and "unsuccessful" outcomes (losing power, failure, or having no friends). For any particular person, approach and avoidance motives might be attached to either outcome *or to both.* Either outcome might be approached by some and avoided by others. The overall Action Tendency will be some combination of all approach and avoidance motives. How can such an avoidance motive be represented symbolically? It should be a subtractive term, multiplied by the same expectancy and by its own incentive term (Aversive I_a), which indicates the amount of the negative incentive. Thus the overall Action Tendency is the summation of all approach tendencies (motive $\times$ expectancy $\times$ incentive) minus all avoidance tendencies (avoidance motive $\times$ expectancy $\times$ aversive incentive)[9]:

$$\text{Action tendency } A = \sum_{i=a}^{z} \begin{aligned} &f\,(M_a \times E_a \times I_a) - \\ &f\,(M_{\text{avoid } a} \times E_a \times \text{Aversive } I_a) \end{aligned}$$

Since the expectancy term (E_a) is the same in each case, this is equivalent to:

$$\text{Action tendency } A = \sum_{i=a}^{z} f\,\{[(M_a \times I_a) - (M_{\text{avoid } a} \times \text{Aversive } I_a)] \times E_a\}$$

Thus the complete calculation of the action tendency would involve the consideration of separate approach and avoidance tendencies for each motive relevant to the action and its results—i.e., where E was significantly greater than zero. This means four separate tendencies: approach and avoidance for reaching the goal (i.e., Action *A*), and approach and avoidance for not reaching or failing at the goal. Fortunately, in actual practice this simplifies quite a bit, the more so if we know the culture. Thus, for well-designed experiments with white middle-class American college males, it is usually enough to calculate Hope of Success and Fear of Failure for the achievement motive, ignoring Fear of Success and Hope of Failure as well as other motives. But I think that it is important to keep the whole complexity of the model in mind in order to be prepared for different results, and to understand these results, when other groups are studied.

[9] This is an extended generalization of the Atkinson models, but it seems consistent both with Atkinson's overall theory and with the results and theory of Horner.

The formulation thus far suggests an organism at rest. In actual practice, people are almost always doing something. Behavior is a continuous stream, rather than a series of disjunctive events. Thus the tendency to perform any action is actually equal to the summated tendencies for that action, minus the summated tendencies to continue to perform what is presently being performed (see Atkinson and Cartwright, 1964). The former term is more or less constant in the short run; but the latter term will be entirely different for each different action that might be already in progress. Thus the same levels of motive, expectancy, and incentive for some new action, A, will produce different results when combined with the values for different actions, B, already in progress. The formulation can be represented as:

$$
\begin{aligned}
\text{Tendency} \\
\text{to change} \\
\text{from } B \\
\text{to } A
\end{aligned}
=
\begin{bmatrix}
\begin{aligned}
\text{Action} \\
\text{tendency} \\
A
\end{aligned}
= \sum_{i=a}^{z} \begin{aligned} & f\,(M_a \times E_a \times I_a) - \\ & f\,(M_{\text{avoid }a} \times E_a \times \text{Aversive } I_a) \end{aligned}
\end{bmatrix}
-
\begin{bmatrix}
\begin{aligned}
\text{Action} \\
\text{tendency} \\
\text{to persist} \\
\text{at } B
\end{aligned}
= \sum_{i=a}^{z} \begin{aligned} & f\,(M_a \times E_a \times I_a) - \\ & f\,(M_{\text{avoid }a} \times E_a \times \text{Aversive } I_a) \end{aligned}
\end{bmatrix}
$$

Notice that I use the goal subscript a in all summations. This is because the summation for each action tendency has to take account of all relevant motives for that tendency (i.e., motives for which E is greater than zero). It often happens that some of the same motives are involved even when actions change; when this happens, the motives would be included in both terms. For example, I stop eating soup and start eating meat, then I go on to dessert, with the food motive continuously involved. This phenomenon of the same motive leading to a series of different goal-related actions, can be called "boredom" (or "curiosity"), and can be formally expressed as the rapid decay (or increase) of certain incentive values. Despite appearances, the formulation is not getting out of hand. It simply indicates that a change of our action is determined by the relative probabilities of gratifying whatever motives are important at the time, and the amount of gratification that might be obtained.

Atkinson and Birch (1970) have recently added other terms to the model to take account of things such as the following: does expression of a tendency affect the motive level (or the incentives) for that tendency? This is called "consummatory force." What effect will substitution among closely related tendencies have? How do time lags and resistance enter in? The model begins to take on a formidable appearance, although it does suggest some interesting possibilities for computer simulation. I think that we should remember, however, that when comparing two groups or two different laboratory conditions, most of the variables can be considered to be constant and hence dropped out of the formulation. The increasing complexity and mathematical sophistication of these models should not obscure their original purpose, which is to assist in understanding and predicting behavior by specifying the ways in which motives and other variables fit together. Actually, the models are largely hypothetical in the sense that only a few deductions from them have been tested, and these tests have usually involved studies of the achievement motive among college men. Alternate models have been suggested by Heckhausen (1968), Weiner *et al.* (1971) and Heckhausen and Weiner 1972), and so it is premature to decide on a final version. As I shall argue in Chapter 7, more work needs to be done in order to measure the expectancy and incentive terms in the case of the power motive. I have discussed these theoretical models in order to show the complexities of the relationship between motive and action, and yet the fundamental importance of the concept of motive. At the very least, let those take caution who still think that a motive such as the power motive can simply and obviously be inferred from power-related actions!

A CONCLUDING NOTE

All of the ways of measuring motives are based on the presumed characteristics of motivated or goal-directed behavior. Since each method makes certain assumptions about motives and thus is vulnerable to certain hazards and confusions, different methods of measuring what seems to be the "same" motive probably would not intercorrelate very highly. This is true of *n* Achievement (de Charms *et al.*, 1955; McClelland, 1958, pp. 37–40; 1961, pp. 331–335; Birney, 1968); Chapter 3 will report that *n* Power does not correlate with self-report measures of power interest. One could claim that the motive measures possess low "concurrent validity," in that they do not correlate with other methods of measuring the presumed "same" thing. However, I do not think that we can presume that the other measures are in fact measuring the "same" motive. Therefore I believe that, for purposes of motives, concurrent validity is not very important; for it only assesses the degree to which one measure correlates with other measures, rather than the degree to which it correlates with significant behavior. I think that this latter kind of corrrelation ("construct validity" or "relational fertility") is a much more important test of the usefulness of a measure of a motive.

CHAPTER 3

Developing
a Measure of
the Power Motive

Following the McClelland-Atkinson strategy outlined in the last chapter, several researchers have carried out experiments designed to arouse the power motive. In this chapter, I shall review these experiments, the conceptions of power implicit in them, the scoring systems for n Power that resulted from them, and their action correlates. (Lacking any easy alternative, I shall refer to each of these early scoring systems by the name of its author.) Then I shall describe how these earlier scoring systems were combined and integrated into one revised system that successfully differentiates the stories of aroused and neutral subjects in each of the arousal experiments. By "n Power," I mean only this revised scoring system. I shall describe ways in which this measure of n Power can be separated into approach and avoidance components. Finally, I shall report the psychometric properties of the revised n Power measure and discuss the issue of reliability.

THE VEROFF SCORING SYSTEM

Veroff (1957) first attempted to measure the power motive by using 34 male candidates for student office at the University of Michigan as an aroused group of subjects. After a month of campaigning and two days of student voting, these candidates had gathered at the polls to await the results. They had to wait for about two hours while the votes were counted. To heighten the salience of the election (and presumably the power cues of the situation), Veroff asked the candidates to estimate their chances of winning on a 6-point scale. Then all candidates took a modified TAT. Thirty-four male students in an undergraduate psychology course at the same university served as the neutral control group. They were told that the TAT administration was part of a procedure about which some graduate students were interested in obtaining normative data. The Veroff design actually involved a combination of two strategies: (1) the use of criterion groups to define power, since candidacy for a student office was assumed to indicate high power motivation and being in an undergraduate psychology course was assumed to indicate lower power motivation. Veroff recognized that candidacy might also be related to other motives and characteristics. (2) Additionally, the candidates were thought to be in a special state of power-arousal because they were waiting to learn about the election results, and had just been asked to estimate their own chances of winning. As with other arousal experiments, the rough definition of "power arousal" embodied in this experiment is always open to question. Because all votes had been cast and the election actually "decided" at the time of the experiment, the power-aroused candidates were helpless in the sense that there was nothing that they could do to affect their chances of gaining power. Conceivably this could create an anxious, vulnerable state of mind that would express itself in negative and defensive fantasies. Any measure of the power motive that was based on such a situation might therefore reflect anxieties and defenses as well as the power motive.

In a general way, Veroff developed his n Power scoring system from an examination of the differences between stories written by the two groups of subjects, but the system had several *a priori* features in addition to these empirical differences. First, he used two principles from the n Achievement and n Affiliation scoring systems (McClelland *et al.*, 1953, chap. 4; Atkinson, 1958, chaps. 4–5): (1) The system was divided into two parts: *Power Imagery* and *Sub-*

categories. Imagery was to be scored if there was any reference to a power goal, according to certain criteria. Only if the story were scored for Imagery could it be further scored for the subcategories, which were conceived of as a measure of the intensity or elaboration of the power theme or goal. (2) The names and approximate scoring definitions of the subcategories themselves were directly taken from the previous scoring systems, which in turn were based on a particular model of the sequence of adjustive or problem-solving behavior (Dashiell, 1949) that is illustrated in Figure 3.1. Morgan

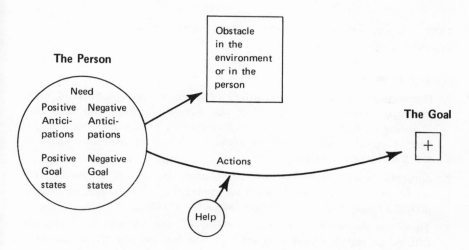

Figure 3.1. The Dashiell Model for Conceptualizing Motive Subcategories (adapted from McClelland et al., 1953, p. 109, and Dashiell, 1949)

and Murray (1935) suggested an informal model of analysis that is similar. In other words, Veroff used existing models in designing the formal characteristics of the Veroff *n* Power scoring system. He assumed that the power motive would be organized around the same subcategories that worked for other motives.[1]

[1] Veroff realized that many of the subcategories did not significantly differentiate the aroused and neutral groups; but as the differences were always in the predicted direction, he left them in the final scoring system. Apparently he did not consider using the "Nurturant Press" subcategory. It should be noted that Veroff's test of differentiation was based on an overall median split on score, rather than the more sensitive parametric analysis used by McClelland *et al.* (1953, pp. 140–146). In any case many of the subcategories occurred very infrequently in both groups. Veroff does not mention looking for any *new* subcategories.

Finally, Veroff began his search for precise scoring definitions with a fairly explicit definition of power, viz., "control of the means of influencing another person(s)."[2] The two groups of stories were examined more for the purpose of delineating the kinds of evidence for power goals of this type than for constructing an empirical definition of Power Imagery. These assumptions, as well as the nature of the arousal experiment, need to be taken into account when we examine the action correlates of n Power as scored by the Veroff system. A brief outline of the system is given in Table 3.1.

TABLE 3.1 A BRIEF SUMMARY OF THE VEROFF SCORING
SYSTEM (*Adapted from Veroff, 1957*)

Power Imagery:

1. Someone in the story shows affect or is *emotionally concerned about getting or maintaining control of the means of influencing a person.* Wanting to win a point, to show dominance, to convince someone, to gain a position of control, to avoid weakness or humiliation, or to teach or inspire another person.

2. Someone is actually *doing something about getting or keeping control of the means of influence,* such as by arguing, demanding or forcing, giving a command, trying to convince, or punishing.

3. There is a statement of an interpersonal *relationship which is culturally defined as one in which a superior person has control of the means of influencing a subordinate person.* This relationship must involve activity, and the subordinate (or the effect on the subordinate) must be mentioned.

Subcategories:

Need: An explicit statement that someone needs, wants, hopes for, or is determined to attain or maintain control of the means of influence.

Act: An explicit action toward control of the means of influence.

Goal Anticipation: Someone anticipates attaining the goal of control of the means of influence ($Ga+$), or is concerned or doubtful about getting such control ($Ga-$).

Blocks: Disruptions or obstacles to gaining control of the means of influence, in the person himself (Bp) or in the outer world (Bw).

Goal States: Someone attains the power goal and feels happy ($G+$), or is unsuccessful and feels unhappy, angry, frustrated, etc. ($G-$).

[2] Veroff (1957, pp. 1–2, and personal communication).

Thema: The power concern is the principal plot of the story, and there is no other theme or plot.

Fifteen years of research on the action correlates of the Veroff measure has produced results that are not completely clear or consistent. Sometimes the measure predicts power-seeking behavior; other times it seems to predict avoiding power (Veroff and Veroff, 1972). I shall review this research under three general headings: interpersonal behavior, career and life outcomes, and national characteristics.[3]

Interpersonal behavior. In his original validation study conducted with the 34 men in the neutral arousal group, Veroff (1957) found that Veroff *n* Power was related to two aspects of classroom behavior, as rated by instructors on a 3-point scale: (1) being argumentative or liking to argue and contradict; and (2) being eager to get points across in order to convince the instructor or other students of a point of view. McKeachie (1961) found that men high in Veroff *n* Power tended to get high grades in college mathematics and psychology courses if the class emphasized student participation in discussion. Skolnick (1966) examined data collected in the longitudinal Oakland Growth Study, and found significant relationships between Veroff *n* Power and adult judges' ratings on: *drives* for social ties and control, the *manifest trait* of aggression, and free-play and situational *behaviors* which suggested popularity, sociability, and assertion that created an effect on the group. The motive scores and all ratings were obtained in late adolescence.

Although the picture seems clear so far, it should be noted that these findings all involve the perception and evaluation of adolescents by adults. When she looked at sociometric ratings by peers, Skolnick found that Veroff *n* Power correlated with ratings of "assured," but not "bossy," "fights," or "a leader."

[3] Here, as elsewhere in this book, only research on males is reported. The reason is that research on the achievement motive in women (French and Lesser, 1964) had shown that role-orientation was an important moderator variable in predicting both the experiences that would arouse the motive and the behaviors correlated with the motive. The work of Horner (1968, 1969) further suggests that the structure of the scoring system itself may differ in some cases. Research on the power motive in women, as it is moderated by variables involving role, or Self Definition, is now under way (Winter and Stewart, 1972). Meanwhile, Veroff and Feld (1970) and Veroff and Veroff (1972) discuss the correlates for women of the Veroff scoring system.

Moreover, some laboratory experiments on interpersonal behavior in pairs and small groups present conflicting results. Terhune (1968a) found that men high in Veroff n Power were exploitative both initially and over the long term when playing a two-man mixed-motive "Prisoner's Dilemma" game. In an international relations simulation, three-man teams that were high in Veroff n Power tended toward conflicting rather than cooperative acts, great military effort, and deception (Terhune, 1968b). Yet Berlew (1959) found that in *ad hoc* small discussion groups, men high in Veroff n Power tended less often to ask and give suggestions and give opinions, tended less often to describe other members of the group with power-related adjectives, and were less accurate in making judgment of other members of the group with respect to power. The Berlew results could be explained by arguing that high Veroff n Power was somehow inhibited or defensive because of the temporary nature of the groups, or that excessive power motivation debilitates power performance (following the Yerkes-Dodson law); but it is hard to see how the Terhune experiments were any different in these respects. The most we can conclude is that the Veroff scoring system seems to predict either one extreme (power assertion) or the other (power avoidance) in small group experiments.

Career and life outcomes. The same pattern of opposite extremes appears when we look at the results of administering a four-picture TAT in an interview setting to a representative sample of the adult American population in 1957 (hereafter called the National Sample study; see Veroff, Atkinson, Feld, and Gurin, 1960; Veroff and Feld, 1970). The following demographic subgroups were high in Veroff n Power (in the sense that 55% or more of the group was above the overall male median score): those with an annual family income of $10,000 or more, those over age 35,[4] and those from metropolitan areas or suburbs. These results are all consistent with the power-assertion interpretation. But other demographic subgroups that scored high were: those with a yearly family income of $2,000 or less, those with only a grade-school education, blacks, those from broken homes (who had lost one or both parents, or whose parents had been divorced before they were sixteen), and those men over age fifty who were widowed. These latter results suggest either that n Power is related to power-avoidance, or else that it is a de-

[4] Some 52% of the men over 35 scored above the median in n Power, as compared with only 47% of the men under 35.

fensive fantasy substitute for power behavior (cf. Lazarus, 1961, 1966).

Both trends also emerge in the analysis of career choices and satisfactions. Lindman (1958, quoted in Veroff and Feld, 1970, p. 23) found that high Veroff n Power adolescent boys chose careers that were either very high or very low in power potential. Browning and Jacob (1964) found that politicians and candidates for offices of relatively high influence potential scored higher in Veroff n Power than politicians and candidates for offices of lower influence potential, both in an Eastern American city and in a Louisiana parish. In an analysis of the National Sample data, Veroff and Feld (1970) found that Veroff n Power was low among salesmen and foremen—two occupations that would seem to involve power; more generally, it was low in those occupations that were prestigious (using the 1953 NORC ratings), that involved extensive social interaction, or that had great potential for supervising other people. And, among those men who were salesmen, foremen, or who were in prestigious, social, or supervisory jobs, Veroff n Power was correlated with feeling dissatisfied about work! Men in jobs that involved being supervised by others tended to be higher in Veroff n Power. Again, it appears that the Veroff scoring system involves avoiding power. Yet in a study of career advancement and motivation among Mexican businessmen, Andrews (1967) found that Veroff n Power was associated with more rapid advancement in a patriarchal firm that emphasized conformity and dependence, but not in a more "modern" firm. Litwin and Stringer (1968, pp. 72, 84) found that among MBA students and actual managers, Veroff n Power was related to preferences for a work climate that was high in structure (rules, regulations, and channels), in responsibility (being one's own boss), and in expressing conflict; but that was low in risk-taking.

How can we interpret all of these results? Since the National Sample data involve simultaneous measurement of motivation and career, it is not clear whether the motive scores determined the careers or were reactions to them (see Veroff and Veroff, 1972). Such a problem can be resolved only with longitudinal data of the type that I shall present in the next chapter. Veroff and Feld assumed that the career choices and satisfaction data were at least somewhat the result of motive levels, and they concluded that while Veroff n Power may sometimes involve the assertion of power, usually it leads to avoiding weakness—particularly avoiding weakness in those situations where failure to influence or to exercise power would be clearly visible. More precisely, "the more public a person's power or lack of it in a role, the more likely it is that the negative features (power-avoidant behavior) of the motive will be engaged in role behavior" (p. 330). In other words, visibility or "expectation of vulnerability" appears to act as a moderator variable that determines which aspect of the motive is expressed in action. Veroff and Veroff (1971, p. 64) further specify visibility or expectation of vulnerability as the extent to which there is "pre-emption by another, of freedom to choose in a social choice situation." This suggests the influence of the expectancy term in the Atkinson model (see Chapter 2) or perhaps Rotter's Internal/External control of the means of reinforcement. Thus we could say that success/failure was not public or visible in the Prisoner's Dilemma experiments because subjects did not know or meet each other, did not expect to meet each other, and could communicate (when permitted) only by written messages. Thus their power motivation was not vulnerable, and so it was expressed in exploitative behavior. In the Berlew studies, there was a half-hour sustained interaction in the small group, and participants knew that they would be encountering each other afterward. Hence power motivation was "vulnerable" and led to low assertive behavior and inaccurate judgments.

This interpretation is further supported by the data on marriage and parenthood in the National Sample study (Veroff and Feld, 1970, *passim*). Veroff *n* Power was associated with generally positive reactions to parenthood among men whose eldest child was of pre-school age (0–4 years). J. P. B. Veroff (1959) found, moreover, that high Veroff *n* Power fathers tend to be relatively *more* affectionate with nursery school age sons. However, when the eldest child was an adolescent or adult (over age 13), men high in Veroff *n* Power felt that parenthood was restricting and generally negative. These trends were especially marked for high Veroff *n* Power college-educated men, who in addition said that they felt inadequate as parents. In other words, small children, who are an easy and legitimate object of paternal influence, elicit power assertive reactions and consequently satisfaction; but as children grow up and become a highly visible threat to the father's power, the negative aspect of the motive becomes primary. Veroff *n* Power was positively associated with reported happiness of the marriage relationship among men having only a grade-school education, but the relationship reversed for men with college education. Veroff and Feld suggest that the former group probably have traditional marriages in which the husband is (at least overtly) more powerful; while the college men are more likely to have "companionate" marriages in which power is more equally shared (p. 84). Such an assumption makes the results congruent with the emerging conception of Veroff n Power.

National characteristics. McClelland (1961) gathered children's readers from some 44 nations and selected, translated, and coded for motive imagery 21 stories per country. By making the assumption that these scores reflected the concerns or motives of significant elite groups in each country, he then used the scores as estimates of national motive levels, or as an indirect measure of "national character" (see Inkeles and Levinson, 1969). McClelland reports that the pattern of high Veroff n Power/low n Affiliation was associated with having a totalitarian form of government. In further analysis of these scores, Southwood (1969, quoted in McClelland, 1971b) found that 1946–50 Veroff n Power scores were correlated $+.27$ ($p<.10$) with an index of "internal war" for the time period 1955–60. However, Firestone (1969, p. 48) found that 1925 scores correlated $-.35$ ($p<.10$) with "number killed in domestic violence" during 1955. The inconsistency of these latter two results may be due to the different time-lags involved, or else to the possibility that there is no consistent relationship between Veroff n Power and domestic violence.[5] In any case, the power motive is associated with totalitarian government. Whether one considers this to be evidence for assertive power or for action out of a fear of weakness presumably depends upon one's view of totalitarianism.

Overall assessment of the Veroff scoring system. The most comprehensive conclusion about the Veroff system for scoring n Power is that it measures some combination of both positive and negative aspects (approach and avoidance) of the power motive. The demographic correlates suggest that Veroff n Power is in part a defensive manipulative concern with getting one's way in a threatening world. Which aspect will appear in behavior seems to depend upon the public visibility of the exercise of power, or the likelihood of public failure in the situation. Most of the evidence suggests that the negative, defensive, avoidant aspects of the power motive will predominate, unless the target of power is a very easy one.

Such an analysis suggests several possible conclusions. Perhaps TAT measures are related to action in an inverse or substitute way

[5] A further possibility is that the relationship is negative for rich nations (most of those in Firestone's 1925 sample were such), but positive for poor nations (more of which were included in Southward's 1946–50 sample).

rather than in a direct way—those who don't have power show power concerns in TAT stories (Lazarus, 1961). In other words, fantasy is not a good direct way to measure motives.

Many people would take these results as confirmation of the popular theory that all power drives are really exaggerated attempts to overcompensate for feelings of inferiority (Adler, 1927, 1928), or that the striving for power is somehow neurotic (Horney, 1937). An additional conclusion might be that power, as the result of a crippling or stunting of man's highest and best goals, is bad and should, therefore, be avoided.

However, these results may be due to the nature of the Veroff n Power scoring system. Does this system exhaust the possibilities for measuring the power motive? Might there be other more positive and approach-oriented aspects of n Power which aren't being picked up fully? The actual arousal situation that Veroff used did stress the anxiety-laden and threatening aspects of power, since, it heightened the salience of power in a situation where any instrumental action (such as campaigning) was no longer of any avail, and where failure was publicly visible. Thus it seems plausible that these defenses and anxieties about power may have been picked up in the scoring system itself. This possibility is supported by the finding of Wolowitz and Shorkey (1966) that paranoid schizophrenic males tend to have high n Power, using a modification of the Veroff scoring system.

More support for this interpretation comes from a study by Slavin (1967, quoted in Veroff and Veroff, 1971, p. 64), who studied Boy Scouts who were seeking leadership positions. Some were made to feel that they had been selected, while others were made to think that they had not been successful. The latter group subsequently showed higher Veroff n Power than the former group. Litwin and Stringer (1968) studied eight-day simulations of business organizations under three different conditions of "climate." They found that after exposure to a warm and friendly climate (in which people paid attention to other people's feelings, there was democratic decision-making, and norms of equality prevailed), Veroff n Power increased significantly on subsequent testing. The argument is that because of a lack of structure and direction (i.e., anomie) and the requirements of lengthy group decision-making processes, the warm and friendly climate in a competitive business situation actually led to anxiety and threat specifically about power, and this caused increased Veroff n Power scores.

Finally, subsequent researchers expressed some dissatisfaction with the actual definition of Power Imagery in the Veroff scoring system (Uleman, 1966, 1972; Winter, 1967). Power, particularly power in a bureaucratic organization, may be "control of the means of influence"; but this definition seems rather remote from the primitive phenomenological sense of power (see Chapter 1). In practice, the definition is difficult to apply directly to many kinds of stories, where power in the sense of having impact is involved and yet "the means of influence" seem quite remote and abstract. For this reason, as well as because of the conflicting pattern of empirical results. Uleman and Winter each made separate attempts to revise the Veroff scoring system. Each began with a new arousal experiment and developed a new scoring system. I shall discuss each in turn.

THE ULEMAN SCORING SYSTEM

Uleman (1966, 1972) began with a general conception of power as the actual face-to-face influence of other persons for its own sake.[6] He studied members of two college fraternities in the Boston area. To arouse power, he asked the 22 members of one fraternity (chosen at random) to serve as experimenters in a psychological study of "the effects of frustration on imagination." In this capacity, each person in the aroused group would frustrate one person from the other fraternity during a two-person interaction sequence that normally involved gambling for small stakes. Members of the aroused group were taught specific techniques to insure that they could control the results, always win, and thus presumably frustrate the other person (tactics such as the hidden strategy of a matchsticks game, the use of marked cards, and so forth). The persons to be frustrated were simply told that they were participating in a gambling game. The aroused subjects were cautioned not to reveal their special status. Thus the power arousal consisted of being assigned the role of psychological experimenter, which permitted them to exercise legitimate influence or control; the actual and certain expectation of being in control and thus able to "frustrate" another person; and finally the

[6] Uleman later called his measure n Influence. Originally, he called it a new measure of n Power (1966); subsequently he decided to distinguish this motive from Veroff's n Power and adopted the term n Influence (1972). In any case his conceptualization and arousal experiments fit into the definition of power given in Chapter 1, and so I present his results here. Whether one views the Uleman arousal experiment as measuring a different *kind* of power or as expanding the ecological validity of the revised measure of n Power is a matter of preference and judgment.

presumed prestige and power connotations of science, psychology, and the role of experimenter (cf. Orne, 1962). A four-picture TAT was administered to each pair just before the games began (TAT_2), at which point the "experimenters" were presumably in a state of power arousal and the "subjects" were simply waiting for the gambling games to begin. Both groups had previously taken a four-picture TAT under neutral conditions (TAT_1).

Uleman developed a scoring system by looking at the differences between aroused and neutral subjects on TAT_2, and also looking at the differences between TAT_1 and TAT_2 for the aroused group. He did not have the kind of *a priori* definition of power that Veroff did, nor did he restrict himself to the list and arrangement of subcategories previously used for *n* Achievement. Consequently the scoring system that he developed, as outlined in Table 3.2 and illustrated in Figure 3.2, is quite different from Veroff's *n* Power measure. While

TABLE 3.2 A BRIEF SUMMARY OF THE ULEMAN SCORING SYSTEM (*Adapted from Uleman, 1972*)

Criterion for scoring Imagery (Imagery must occur in order for the subcategories to be scored, but Imagery receives no weight itself in the total score.):
One party (P_1) takes over and intentional action toward some other party (P_2), so that P_2 reacts. The reaction may include any response, whether overt or not. A party is a person, or a group which acts as a unit.

Emphasis modifiers (subcategories):

Prestige: A party has high status, prestige, fame, wealth, etc.

Organization: A party is an oganization (i.e., with a formal hierarchy), or it acts as a member of an organization.

No Self-deprecation: Absence of deprecation, humiliation, embarrassment, or the like, of one party. Deprecation can be statements and feelings of the party, as well as stylistic treatment by the writer of the story.

No Reminiscence: Absence of idle thoughts about the past (thoughts without implications for the present or future) by a party.

No Dread: Absence of dread, fear, or apprehension about the future by a party.

Consultation: A party plans a future activity with another party, or seeks and/or gives advice regarding the future.

Threat: The action-reaction sequence involves an intentional threat to another person's vital interests, and an attempt to neutralize the threat.

Counter-Reaction: The action-reaction sequence involves a clear and overt action by P_2, which explicitly relates back to P_1 in some way.

Separation: A party actively separates from or leaves another party; or is actively kept apart from another party.

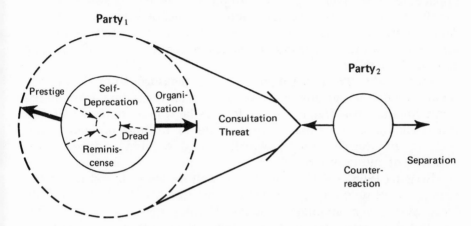

Figure 3.2. Conceptualization of the Uleman n *Influence Subcategories (from Uleman, 1972)*

"Influence Imagery" is a criterion for scoring the subcategories, it itself is not scored. Comparing the Uleman and Veroff systems, we see that Uleman included many elements that suggest reciprocal, interactive influence rather than controlling the means of influence— for example, the subcategories Counter-Reaction, Consultation, and Threat. Some categories reflect positive features of power-exercise (Prestige, Organization); and the system explicitly subtracts points for negative and defensive features as Self-Deprecation, Reminiscence, or Dread. Overall it seems to reflect a more positive orientation toward power than does the Veroff system. This difference is probably due to the fact that Uleman's arousal involved the certainty of legitimate power, as opposed to the very uncertain anticipations among Veroff's aroused subjects. After some reflection, Uleman named this measure *n* Influence rather than *n* Power.

Data about the action correlates of the Uleman *n* Influence measure are drawn largely from Uleman's original study (1972). Using TAT_1 scores on all subjects, he found significant relationships to "dominance," as assessed by self-ratings ($r = +.28$, $p<.10$), peer sociometric ratings ($r = +.35$, $p<.01$), and the CPI Dominance scale ($r = +.31$, $p<.05$). There were no relationships to Machiavellianism, the EPPS Dominance scale, the F-scale, and the Marlowe-Crowne Social Desirability scale. N Influence was also unrelated to the number of offices in organizations that a person had held ($r = .10$, $p = $ n.s.), as was the Veroff n Power measure when applied to these TAT protocols.[7] Applied to neutral TATs from the Veroff arousal experiment, the Uleman measure was related to the Allport-Vernon "Social" scale ($r = +.30$, $p\sim.12$), but unrelated to the instructors' ratings of argumentativeness or of frequency of trying to convince others.

Among the 22 "experimenters," the measure from TAT_1 was related to the actual amount won during the gambling (which the "experimenter" was free to vary so long as he won more than half and thus took the entire final amount), and to feelings of being comfortable, natural, in control, satisfied, and not tense on the post-experiment questionnaire.

Berger (1968, 1969) used the Uleman measure in a study of the effects on attitude change of writing counterattitudinal essays. Subjects were given simulated "feedback" that they had been either successful or unsuccessful. Among those given "successful" feedback, n Influence was related to subjects' own ratings of how persuasive they had been. Among all subjects, n Influence was related to the amount of change of own attitude after writing the essays, independent of the kind of feedback given. The latter result might seem hard to reconcile with a notion of power, but it could suggest that the Uleman measure reflects involvement in a nexus of mutual influence, and a sensitivity to feedback about influence attempts.

In a study where pairs of subjects were to resolve differences of opinion about which "ESP symbol" had been telepathically received from a "sender" (Uleman, 1971b), the member of the pair higher in n Influence tended more often to prevail. Uleman notes that this situation is devoid of monetary, achievement, or status rewards, and suggests that influence for the sake of influence is the only incentive present. Because Veroff n Power was essentially unrelated to prevailing influence, Uleman suggests that it reflects, in contrast, a concern with the external status aspects of power and influence. Yet this distinction between the two scoring sysems is hard to reconcile with a verbal conditioning experiment (Uleman, 1971a), in which the

[7] Winter (1967) later confirmed both of these negative findings for the Veroff and Uleman systems with data from the Harvard Student Study.

reinforcement was feedback that the subject's position in a hypothetical 25-person hierarchy was rising. Uleman found that among those subjects with a high Behavior Intention (see Dulany, 1968), there was a further substantial correlation between n Influence and increases in the appropriate response (i.e., learning) over five blocks of trials. Veroff n Power showed no such relationship. Uleman interprets the results by assuming that information about increasing position or status is more rewarding to subjects high in n Influence, so that they learn faster; yet presumably the information was not attractive to subjects high in Veroff n Power, because they did not learn faster. These results seem to contradict the earlier distinction between the two motives.

Overall assessment of the Uleman scoring system. In his latest monograph (1972), Uleman explicitly differentiates n Influence from Veroff's measure of n Power along the lines that I have already suggested. The subcategories of n Influence do seem to be more positive or approach-oriented than those of Veroff n Power; and the action correlates do suggest a confident, nonhierarchical style of interpersonal influence, although not enough research has been done with the measure to tell exactly what it measures. A fundamental question is thus posed: Are influence and power (or confident vs. defensive power) two aspects of the same thing or two wholly separate dispositions? Is a clear-cut decision between these two really required by the pattern of results so far? The two systems do not correlate very highly, nor does either successfully differentiate the aroused and neutral stories of the other (discussed more fully below); but that is not to say that some further system which incorporates elements of both might not do so. Do both arousal experiments fit the definition of "power"? If the answer is yes, then another scoring system that works for both experiments is needed; if it is no, then two quite separate measures remain. Uleman decided that influence and power were different things. I don't think that there is fully persuasive evidence for making such a distinction, at least before another attempt is made to bring them together.

Moreover, some of the subcategories in the n Influence scoring system seem narrow and particularistic in definition, and perhaps specific to certain pictures (e.g., Threat and Separation). How useful would these categories be with very different subjects and pictures? It is also a little disconcerting that neither the Uleman nor the Veroff system appears to be related to holding office in organizations, among the subjects of the Uleman experiment (see footnote 7). Nevertheless, many of the ideas in the n Influence system were important in working out a third scoring system (Winter, 1967), and were of considerable value in the development of the revised scoring system that was used in the research reported in this book.

Uleman "hypnosis" arousal experiment. At an early stage in his research, Uleman conducted an experiment designed to arouse power by a demonstration of hypnosis to a class of college students (Uleman, 1966). One-half of the class, selected randomly, saw the demonstration and then took a TAT; the other half took the TAT before the demonstration and without knowing about it. In the end, Uleman decided to substitute the "experimenter-gambling" arousal, but the TAT protocols from this prior experiment were available for subsequent analysis and will be discussed again later in this chapter.

THE WINTER SCORING SYSTEM

The previous studies illustrate the great difficulty of trying to study power under controlled experimental conditions. The best that we can create in the laboratory seems only a pale reflection of power in the real world; yet it seems impossible to study "real power" with sufficient control and precision. Therefore the researcher either ventures a little way into the field and encounters confusing and complex arousal conditions, as did Veroff; or like Uleman he designs laboratory manipulations in the hope that they will capture those things that are important about power. I decided that using films might be an ideal way of capturing the full range of vivid experiences associated with power, yet under reasonably controlled laboratory conditions (Winter, 1967). Therefore, to arouse the power motive, I showed a film of the 1961 inauguration oath and speech of President John F. Kennedy. The film was made from the National Broadcasting Company videotape. It seemed an ideal arousal, since the occasion had overtones of each of Weber's types of power: rational-legal (the transfer of elected executive power in a routinized way), traditional (the historical line of presidents since George Washington), and charismatic (the appeal of Kennedy himself). In order to control for the effects of seeing any film at all, the neutral group was shown a film in which a businessman discussed science demonstration equipment. Subjects were 91 male MBA students at the Harvard Business School, who had volunteered for a "study of human response to mass media content." As they appeared for the experiment, they were assigned to either of two adjacent rooms in a manner that was as random as possible. The aroused and neutral groups were thus run simultaneously in virtually identical settings. In each case, the film was shown after a brief introduction. Immediately after the film, each group took a six-picture modified TAT and then filled out a brief questionnaire asking for background data, mood during the film, and reactions to President Kennedy.[8]

Some independent evidence of the arousal properties of the Kennedy film came from subjects' comments on the questionnaire: those who saw this film mentioned pride, leadership, identification with a cause, respect, fascination, and similar feelings. Subjects in the neutral group reported essentially neutral feelings, ranging from slight boredom to mild interest. In the questionnaire, all subjects were given a list of 31 adjectives and asked to check those that described their mood during the film (the adjectives were from Green and Nowlis, 1957). The aroused group checked the following adjectives significantly more often than did the neutral group: strong, vigorous, pleased, contemplative, energetic, lonely. The neutral group more often checked: skeptical, uncertain, startled.

[8] Originally, I thought of this experiment as a study of the response to a charismatic leader (see Winter, 1967). However, it soon became clear that the results could more clearly and usefully be thought of as an arousal of the power motive, and so they are discussed in this way. What a charismatic leader does may be something else; or, as I now believe, it may simply be the arousal and vicarious gratification of the power motive.

This experiment was conducted in May, 1965. Undoubtedly the assassination of Kennedy less than two years earlier had an effect on the subjects, arousing thoughts of death, fate, violence, grief, and the like. Are these distractions from the power theme? It can be argued that the assassination and its lingering residue of grief actually intensified the feelings about Kennedy as a heroic, powerful figure. During 1965, as the United States involvement in the Indochina war increased, and as the intervention in the Dominican Republic occurred, many young Americans believed that things would somehow be better if only Kennedy were alive and president, since the role of the Kennedy administration in the Indochina involvement had not been fully disclosed at that time (*New York Times*, 1971). Thus nostalgia and the mythic elevation of Kennedy were very high at the time of the arousal experiment, and it can be argued that it was a more successful arousal of positive power than it would have been if conducted in the summer of 1963 or in the summer of 1971.

Originally, I distinguished pro-Kennedy and anti-Kennedy subjects on the basis of questionnaire responses, because one could not know in advance whether ideological agreement or disagreement would interact with the power arousal. Subsequent analysis showed that the shifts in TAT content occurred among both subgroups.

Development of the scoring system through empirical differentiation. While I followed the traditional model of motive imagery and subcategories that elaborate or indicate the intensity of that imagery, I decided in advance not to use only the Dashiell model for naming and organizing these subcategories. The scoring system was developed through a combination of simple empirical searching for differences, application of *a priori* ideas of what was "power," and then modification of these *a priori* ideas in the light of the actual differences that emerged. As a precaution, I divided the TAT protocols of both the aroused and neutral subjects into three batches. A preliminary scoring system, developed on the first batch of each group, was cross-validated by blind scoring of the second batches of each group mixed together. Then the scoring system was further revised, and again cross-validated by blind scoring of the third batches of each group mixed together. This blind cross-validation gives some assurance that the differences reflected in the scoring system have some objective existence outside the mind of the analyst. Full knowledge of which protocols come from which group can thus be used to develop a scoring system that maximizes actual differences; yet this system must then successfully differentiate aroused and neutral subjects when applied to additional protocols, where the scorer does not know the group to which each story belongs. Such a procedure seems to be an important precaution in content analysis research (see Brown, 1965, pp. 515–516).

The search for empirical differences, conceptualization, checking, repeated search, and repeated checking is a complex and difficult process. Although it has been used often before, the actual step-by-step method has not been described in detail. Therefore I shall present some account of this technique as it was actually carried out in practice (see Winter, 1967). It will be helpful to describe briefly each of the six pictures that was used:

Description	*Source*
1. A group of soldiers in field dress; one is pointing to a map or chart.	Uleman (1972) study
2. A boy lying on a bed reading a newspaper.	Harvard Student Study and Winter, Alpert, and McClelland (1963)
3. "Ship's Captain" talking to a man wearing a suit.	Harvard Student Study

4. A couple in a restaurant drinking beer; a guitarist is in the foreground.

Uleman (1972) study

5. "Homeland": man and youth chatting outdoors.

#24 in Atkinson (1958, appendix 3)

6. A couple sitting with heads bowed, on a marble bench.

May (1966) study

These pictures were selected in order to cover certain general themes that were thought relevant to power, such as authority, aggression, love and sex, and help. The hypotheses used to select pictures need only to be rather general, since most pictures elicit a wide variety of stories, so that there is scope for unexpected effects to appear. Nevertheless, the specific pictures used are a determinant of story content, and so there is always uncertainty that the "right" pictures have been selected. Veroff (1957) used pictures which were more tied to power in the sense of influence or argument, and he did not use any pictures with women or figures in uniform. This may have affected the nature of his scoring system.

The first stage of analysis is to look for simple empirical differences between the two groups of stories, picture by picture. Often the most unusual or bizarre stories give the most useful clues to differences. It is very helpful to list brief summaries of a few stories from each group in adjacent columns, preserving some of the striking words and phrases, as in the stories written to picture 3 below:

Aroused Group

001. Smuggler captain confidently bluffs revengeful customs inspector and escapes. Tells him to go to hell.

002. Captain angry at a reporter; he vents emotion on crew and has a record run.

003. Captain of high-efficiency ship assures company man that this tough attitude is for the company's own good.

Neutral group

101. Captain worried and trying to vindicate himself for late arrival.

102. Businessman pays premium price so captain will agree to take his cargo.

103. Captain is frustrated but has to be polite as he answers the questions of a newsman.

A brief look at these parallel story fragments suggests certain story elements that are present more often in the aroused group than in the neutral group. These themes are then put down, picture by picture, as below:

Picture 1   Crucial situation, fear of death
            Command in the context of a challenge
            Men are enthusiastic, cooperative

Picture 2   Someone worrying about his future—good job?
            Effort-relaxation cycle, but effort prominently mentioned
            Dissatisfaction at low status

Picture 3   Illegal activity, violence—collision, revolution, bawled out
            Someone vents emotions, tough attitude
            Counteraction when control is threatened (vs. failure to try to vindicate self)
            Leader chastises so as to get good performance

Picture 4   A reacts to B's pleasure, which he usually caused
            Someone is fooling someone else on the sly
            Elite people, impressive settings

Picture 5   A is helping B, though it doesn't always work
            Gratitude for advice
            Prominence—crowds approving, star shortstop, etc.
            Make a name for self

Picture 6   Poverty, help for a better life
            B despairs at something A has done

The next step is to try out the themes from one picture on stories written to another picture, so that certain common themes emerge. Notice the number of themes relating to leadership and one person's effect on another. There is the explicit sense of a formally-designated leader commanding a group (1),[9] and the less formal situation where one person causes pleasure or fear in another (4) or helps him (5). The leadership theme is further elaborated by the other's positive responses (1) or gratitude for help given (5). A second general theme seems to be prominence or status. Sometimes individuals are very concerned about getting it (2), sometimes they react violently when it is challenged (3), and sometimes they use it to make an impression on others and thus increase their status (4). Often status is simply emphasized through a title (1) or mention of a lavish or

[9] The numbers refer to picture number (or story number).

expensive setting (4). Another element is that the aroused stories seem to evolve great significance, rather than ordinary and routine events. There may be decisive battles (1), or widespread poverty and economic depression (6).

The results of this initial comparison seemed promising, and certainly seemed to involve power, both as outlined in the definition given in Chapter 1, and as discussed by many theorists. These general themes were next organized according to the model of Power Imagery and Subcategories:

Power Imagery. A person with the status of a leader acts in the story. Status can be indicated by a title, such as "colonel," or "commanding officer." The story must give some specific actions of the leader; it cannot just describe his presence. Actions include transmitting information, making requests, explaining things. The story cannot be scored if it is concerned primarily with the men's complaints, or their argument.

Subcategories:

An expressed concern by the leader for his men. This can include concern as a spur to performance.
Mention that this is an elite or exceptional group—highly skilled, great experience, etc.
Trust and enthusiasm for the leader by the men.
Fear, such as fear of death or anxiety, so long as it does not mean loss of power or capacity to command and act.

A preliminary scoring system developed along these lines was not very successful at differentiating the stories of the second batch of experimental and control subjects mixed together and scored blindly. What was the reason for these disappointing results? There might really have been no differences between the two groups; that is, the scorer might have been ignoring counter-examples from each group when he knew the source of the story. For just this reason, blind cross-validation is essential to establishing the validity of any scoring system derived in this way. Alternatively, the first scoring system may have been too ambiguous and loose, so that important scoring decisions were later made in an arbitrary way. Moreover, many of the definitions seem closely tied to the specific pictures used.

To find out the real reason for the results, the researcher has to go over the cross-validation stories. In effect, this meant starting again from the beginning with a picture-by-picture search for empirical differences, though now with some general sense of the likely trends. For example, after looking again at the aroused stories written to picture 4 (the couple drinking), it suddenly seemed clear that they often emphasized the man's desire to have sex in a way that reflects his impact, rather than in a way that involved love. He was *creating an effect* in order to *get what he wanted*. Viewed in this way, the theme seems closely related to the differences in stories written to picture 1. Below I quote at length from the account of rethinking the differences to that picture (Winter, 1967):

> Originally, the differences in the stories seemed to focus around the *presence* of some kind of leader, who was involved in an action. We had looked primarily at the elaboration of the status of the leader and at the enthusiastic response of the men. The basic criterion for Imagery was simply "a person of status acting."
>
> In fact, this definition did not work out well in the cross-validation stories. Many neutral stories also had someone identified as a "general" or "commanding officer" who was giving instructions. It seemed apparent that the original definition would not capture the essential differences between the two groups. We looked again at the stories. Before, we had noticed that the aroused group more often used a dramatic setting. The picture itself was of a military officer pointing to a map or chart, surrounded by other men dressed in fatigue uniform. The aroused stories seemed to describe this scene more often as preparation for a crucial battle, while in the control stories it was often some kind of routine situation.
>
> Therefore we began to consider more carefully *the nature of the action itself*. This included not only the specified action of the leader, but also the action of the group—e.g., preparing an attack, briefing before a bombing mission, or simply receiving routine instructions. Both groups referred to combat situations. When we looked at the neutral stories which had a combat situation, however, we discovered that usually the leader and group were defending, relieving, etc. One story explicitly mentioned that "they haven't taken the offensive." In contrast, virtually all of the aroused combat stories involved an attack or preparation for an attack, raid, etc. Even where the other side had attacked first and they were planning defense, this defense involved something such as a "full scale counterattack."
>
> Gradually, then, we began to focus more on the *kind of action*, regardless of the formal setting or the explicit mention of the status of the leader. This suggested that the aroused group wrote more stories about vigorous, aggressive, assertive, penetrating actions; while the neutral group treat the same idea (combat) in ways that were routine and not vigorous and assertive. After this shift of emphasis concerning imagery, we felt that some of the original criteria for imagery, *viz.* the status of the leader, could best be viewed as a *subcategory* which modified or added emphasis to a basic concern with vigorous action to create an impact on other people.

The above process was repeated for each picture. Power Imagery now was principally defined as "strong vigorous action." The aroused group wrote more stories involving giving help and advice; and while these are certainly weaker forms of action, they do create some kind of impact either on some specific person(s) or else on the world at large—just like exploitative sex and military attacks. The aroused stories to pictures 2 and 5 often had no explicit statement of other people as being affected, but they did describe some character who was trying to increase his fame or position in the world. This is close to the scoring definition of n Achievement, but it does contain an element of power also. Table 3.3 presents a brief outline of the final Winter scoring system, which was then successfully cross-validated on the third batch of stories from the two groups. Figure 3.3 presents

TABLE 3.3 A BRIEF SUMMARY OF THE WINTER SCORING SYSTEM (*From Winter, 1967*)

Power Imagery:

Scored if someone ("the actor") is *concerned about his impact; that is, about establishing, maintaining, or restoring his prestige or power* in the eyes of the world. This can be inferred from:

1. The actor demonstrates or increases his impact on people through taking direct, vigorous, expansive action: attacks, sexual exploitation, force, and even helping or counseling.

2. The actor takes some action which is sufficient to arouse and focus or draw in the positive or negative feelings of another person. Here any act can count, so long as it arouses some emotional response.

3. The actor is explicitly concerned about his reputation.

Subcategories:

Prestige of the Actor (PA+ and PA−): High or low status, titles, reputation, fame, etc.

Feelings of the Respondent (FR+ and FR−): A respondent shows strong positive or negative feelings and emotional reaction.

Self-perception of the Actor (SPA+ and SPA−): The actor has feelings about himself as a result of his increased or decreased impact.

Act: Overt activity to establish, maintain, or restore impact.

Set: The story takes place in an important, extraordinary, or particularly dangerous setting.

Thema: The power or impact theme is the principal plot of the story.

the conceptualization of the subcategories. I shall omit any detailed discussion of the Winter scoring system and its action correlates (see

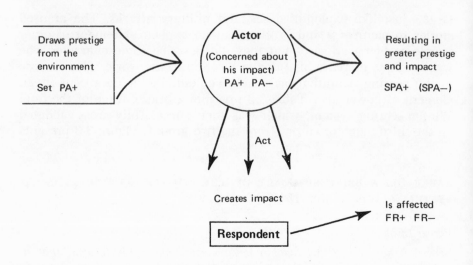

Figure 3.3. Conceptualization of the Winter Scoring System

Winter, 1968 and 1972), because this system was ultimately revised and combined with elements of the other scoring systems as discussed below.

THE REVISED *n* POWER SCORING SYSTEM

At this point there were three different scoring systems, each purporting to measure the power motive. Each system had its own conceptualization, set of scoring definitions, and associated action characteristics. How do they fit together? How can we decide which is the most appropriate? Perhaps the three systems reflected (at least) three different aspects of the power motive, or even three different motives, as Uleman decided. On the other hand, the three different systems could represent three partial approaches toward some common or general measure of the power motive; partial and limited both because of the limitations and particularities of the separate arousal experiments (including the pictures used) and also because of the particular point of view of each researcher as he developed his scoring system. No single experiment can make a preemptive claim to being the ideal one, yet each experiment captures an aspect of the power motive. Nevertheless, when each scoring system is applied to the stories of the other experiments, as shown in Table 3.4, they are not very successful at differentiating aroused and neutral stories from the other experiments. Moreover, the systems do not intercorrelate very highly, as shown in Table 3.5. Lacking a firm basis, then, for choosing one system or for simply considering that each system measures a different motive, I thought it reasonable to try to combine all three systems. If an integrated system would work for each of the four arousal experiments, it might also show a more understandable and stable pattern of action correlates.

For these reasons, then, a revised system for scoring n Power was developed out of all three scoring systems, taking the Winter system as a point of departure. First, the Winter system itself was reexamined. Some aspects of the system (particularly the third criterion for scoring Power Imagery) seemed to overlap with n Achievement, and this had created some confusion and error when other scorers tried to learn and apply the system. There are good

TABLE 3.4 PERFORMANCE OF THE VARIOUS SCORING SYSTEMS ON DATA FROM THE DIFFERENT POWER AROUSAL EXPERIMENTS

| Scoring System | Does the scoring system significantly differentiate aroused and neutral subjects in the experiment conducted by: | | | |
	Veroff	Uleman-Gambling	Uleman-Hypnosis	Winter
Veroff (1957)	yes	no	no[a]	—
Uleman (1966, 1972)	no	yes	no	—
Winter (1967)	no	trend[b]	yes	yes
Revised n Power scoring system used in this book[c]	yes	yes	yes	yes

Note: Chi-Square or Fisher Exact Test for above/below the median on total score, for aroused/neutral subjects, was used in all comparisons reported in this table.

[a] According to Uleman (1966).

[b] For subjects in the Form A-B sequence, $p \sim .10$; for subjects in the Form B-A sequence, $p = $ n.s. (See Uleman, 1972, for details about the forms and sequences.)

[c] This scoring system is discussed in the following section and in Table 3.7.

grounds for keeping power and achievement separate, even though both were aroused by the Kennedy film. (See the later section in this chapter on power versus achievement.) Hence Power Imagery was redefined so as to exclude achievement strivings more explicitly. Second, the stories from the Kennedy film experiment were reread to determine whether aspects of the Veroff scoring system that had not been included in the Winter system nevertheless could be applied to differentiate aroused and neutral stories. In other words, there was an explicit attempt to merge the two definitions of Power Imagery, but with the simpler and less ambiguous definition of "having impact on another person." Veroff's "controlling the means of influence of another person" seemed to be a special case of this more general criterion. Third, the various subcategories of each system were re-arranged and combined where possible. The result was that the basic Dashiell framework was retained, but with the addition of sub-categories of "Prestige" and "Effect" from the Uleman and Winter

TABLE 3.5 INTERCORRELATIONS OF VARIOUS n POWER SCORING SYSTEMS

	Veroff System	Uleman System	Winter System
Uleman System	.03–.37[a]		
Winter System	.32[b]	.39[b]	
Revised n Power System used in this book	.39–.47[c]	.44[b]	.51–.77[d]
Hope of Power[e]	.39[b]	.46[b]	.39[b]
Fear of Power[e]	.06[b]	.03[b]	.29[b]

[a] Range of coefficients reported by Uleman (1971a, 1972) and from TAT protocols from the Harvard Student Study (N = 83).

[b] TAT protocols from the Harvard Student Study.

[c] Range of coefficients from TAT protocols from the Harvard Student Study and TAT protocols from businessmen and politicians (Browning, 1960; N = 93).

[d] Range of coefficients from TAT protocols from the Harvard Student Study and TAT protocols from Wesleyan University undergraduates (N = 59).

[e] Subscores which are discussed later in this chapter.

systems. Throughout the work, the definitions and arousal experiment stories from the Veroff and Uleman experiments were consulted. Table 3.6 gives a brief outline of the revised scoring system that resulted, and indicates the source of the various definitions and subcategories in this revised scoring system. Appendix I gives the complete

TABLE 3.6 BRIEF OUTLINE AND SOURCE OF POWER IMAGERY AND SUBCATEGORY DEFINITIONS OF THE REVISED n POWER SCORING SYSTEM

Category	Source(s) of the Category
Power Imagery	
1. Strong vigorous actions which express power.	From Winter, modified to include important features from Veroff and Uleman.
2. Actions that arouse strong affect in others.	From Uleman and Winter.
3. Explicit concern about reputation or position.	From Winter.
Subcategories	
Prestige ($Pa+$, $Pa-$)	From Winter and also Uleman, together with Uleman's "Consultation" and "Organization."
Stated Need for Power (N)	From Veroff.
Instrumental Activity (I)	From Veroff and Winter, also Uleman's "Threat."
Block in the world (Bw)	From Veroff.
Goal Anticipation ($Ga+$, $Ga-$)	From Veroff; also with modifications from Winter's "Self-Perceptions."
Goal States ($G+$, $G-$)	From Veroff; also with modifications from Winter's "Self-Perceptions."
Effect (Eff)	From Winter's "Feelings of the Other" and Uleman's "Counter-reaction" and "Separation."

revised scoring system, together with instructions and practice materials for learning to use it. Unless otherwise stated, this is the scoring system which has been used in all of the research reported in the rest of this book; the terms "*n* Power" and "the power motive" will refer to scores obtained by the application of this revised system.

Finally, all stories from all arousal experiments were rescored according to the revised system to make sure that every aspect of the system worked for a broad data base. To be included in the final scoring system, any subcategory or criterion for Power Imagery had to (1) differentiate aroused and neutral subjects in at least one arousal experiment with a significance level of .05 or less, and (2) when applied to all arousal experiments, differentiate aroused from neutral subjects with a combined probability of .05 or less.[10] Table 3.7 shows the results of this analysis. Because many of the stories had been used or read in the course of designing the revised scoring system, they obviously could not be scored blind, although the scoring was as objective as possible; hence the results in Table 3.7 may be more favorable than they would be with wholly blind scoring. The purpose of the scoring was to show that in principle the revised system worked for the whole range of experiments. Table 3.5 above presents the intercorrelation of all the various systems on various samples of data.

Subsequent research by Watson (1969) gives additional evidence of the ability of this revised scoring system to reflect the arousal of the power motive. Watson tested 42 black college undergraduates in small groups of between 4 and 7. After subjects in each group had written four stories to TAT-type pictures, the group was asked to improvise a dramatic episode lasting five to ten minutes. After the improvisation, subjects wrote four more stories to a different set of pictures. In the improvisation task, subjects were asked to imagine that they were members of a black action group whose leader had just been arrested and beaten by the police, and who were meeting to decide what action to take. The improvisation was introduced by

---

[10] Combined probabilities were estimated with a method described by Mosteller and Bush (1954, p. 329), in which the Fisher Exact probability for the differentiation between aroused and neutral by median split in each single experiment is converted to its Chi Square equivalent. These equivalents are then summed for the number of experiments (in this case three), and the probability of this summated Chi Square taken with $d.f. = 3$. Subjects rather than stories were taken as the unit of analysis, which is a conservative procedure. In cases where the subcategories are organized as pairs (*Pa*+ and *Pa*−; *Ga*+ and *Ga*−; *G*+ and *G*−), a subcategory is retained in the revised system if the other member of the pair *and* the combination meet the two criteria described above.

TABLE 3.7 PERFORMANCE OF THE REVISED n POWER SCORING SYSTEM IN DIFFERENTIATING AROUSED AND NEUTRAL STORIES FROM ALL AROUSAL EXPERIMENTS

Probability of Aroused/Neutral Differences in:

Category	Veroff Experiment	Uleman[a] Experiments	Winter Experiment	Combined Experiments[b]
Power Imagery				
Criterion 1	.02	.07	.0001	.001
Criterion 2	.34	.12	.02	.05
Criterion 3	.10	n.s.	.03	.05
Total Imagery	.001	.15	.0001	.001
Subcategories				
Pa+	.05	.04	.003	.001
Pa−	.22	.24	.18	.20
Pa+ or Pa−	.11	.06	.001	.001
N	.11	.19	.09	.05
I	.02	.01	.03	.001
Bw	.002	.18	.02	.001
Ga+	.22	.28	.14	.20
Ga−	.07	.30	.04	.05
Ga+ or Ga−	.01	.38	.02	.01
G+	.22	.03	.04	.01
G−	.02	.38	n.s.	.10
G+ or G−	.02	.26	.13	.02
Eff	n.s.	.01	.001	.001
Total Score	.004	.01	.0001	.001

Note: All probability figures in the three left-hand columns table are based on the Fisher Exact Test for aroused/neutral subjects by above/below the combined median on total score, including all stories.

[a] The "Hypnosis" and "Gambling" experiments are combined because of the small number of subjects.

[b] Combined probabilities are estimated by converting the Fisher Exact Probabilities for the different experiments to their Chi Square equivalents, summing, and taking the probability for the resulting Chi Square with $d.f. = 3$ (see Mosteller and Bush, 1954, p. 329).

a black experimenter, and all TAT pictures were of black persons. Watson used two counterbalanced sets of pictures, and after correcting for slight differences in the initial n Power levels obtained with each set, found that power motive scores increased considerably from before to after the role-improvisation (mean change $= +1.60$; $p<.01$, 1-tailed, for difference from 0). Improvising a role in such a situation certainly should arouse the power motive among black undergraduates in the United States in the late 1960s; so that these results add to the evidence for the validity of the revised n Power scoring system and increase our confidence in it.

DISTINGUISHING APPROACH AND AVOIDANCE ASPECTS OF THE POWER MOTIVE

In Chapter 2, I suggested that there are two different kinds of motives: getting to a positively-valued goal (approach), and getting away from a negatively-valued goal (avoidance). This distinction, originally based on Miller's analysis of conflict (1944), was introduced in the context of Atkinson's model of the relationship between motive and behavior. Depending on socialization experience and cultural norms, presumably any goal can take on either positive or negative valence; thus there will be two different kinds of motives associated with any goal. Atkinson calls these two aspects "Hope" and "Fear." It seems likely that both aspects of the power motive exist and are widely distributed in our society, since power has been both valued and sought, and also condemned and feared. Thus each person should have some level of interest in power, concern about power, or power salience. This in turn should involve some combination of approach or Hope of Power, and avoidance, or Fear of Power. (As I suggested in Chapter 2, it is also possible that there are approach and avoidance motives attached to losing power or failure at power, respectively; but I want to defer this complexity until Chapter 5.) For the moment, let us consider the three motive scores: overall salience, approach, and avoidance. Each may have different effects on behavior, and thus different action correlates, although all three should be related to power in some systematic ways. The practical problem is, therefore, to distinguish the approach and avoidance aspects of the power motive. I already suggested above that the Veroff scoring system somehow includes many defensive, avoidant aspects, but now it is necessary to make the distinction more clearly and systematically.

How have avoidance aspects of motives other than power been measured? Researchers on n Achievement and n Affiliation used a variety of different techniques. McClelland, Atkinson, Clark, and Lowell (1953) first called attention to the approach/avoidance distinction after observing that many people with moderate n Achievement scores appeared fearful and defensively oriented, whereas persons with high n Achievement scores were hopeful or approach-oriented. Thus they simply assumed that low or moderate n Achievement scores indicate high Fear of Failure. Hardy (1957) and Byrne (1962) distinguished approach and avoidance aspects of n Affiliation in the same way. However, there was little independent evidence for the assumption that moderate scores indicate avoidance, and later researchers have assumed that the Hope and Fear components of a motive are completely independent.

Several researchers have tried to distinguish Fear of Failure by means of an external criterion, rather than by means of arousal experiments as with n Achievement. Atkinson's model (1957) suggested that subjects motivated primarily by Fear of Failure would reverse the Zeigarnik effect and show counterrational shifts of aspiration level (down after success; up after failure). Persons showing these shifts could, therefore, constitute a criterion group for Fear of Failure. Clark, Teevan, and Ricciuti (1956) examined the TATs of such persons, and suggested that the subcategories of the n Achievement scoring system be divided into positive ("goal imagery") and negative ("deprivation imagery") subscores, with the latter being a Fear of Failure score. However, it was never clear that this "negative categories subscore" actually measured Fear of Failure according to the predictions of the model (Atkinson, 1958, pp. 594–595, footnote).

Moulton (1958) used a similar criterion procedure, and began to work toward a separate scoring system for Fear of Failure Imagery, with separate subcategories modifying this Imagery. He also retained only the positive subcategories in the measure of the Hope of Success. Heckhausen (1963) incorporated several changes in this procedure. He dropped the scoring of Imagery as such, took out several subcategories, and completely redefined the others. The result was two separate and comprehensive scoring systems for the Hope of Success and the Fear of Failure, using goal-setting as a criterion of validity. Heckhausen's scoring systems have been extensively used in further research in Germany (summarized in Heckhausen, 1963, 1967, and 1968).

Birney, Burdick, and Teevan (1969) argued that Fear of Failure should be defined by using experimental arousal and noting shifts of TAT content, in the same way that the *n* Achievement scoring system was devised. Their reasoning was that using any single behavior or even group of behaviors as a criterion inevitably commits the investigator to one or another model about the avoidance motive and its effects. If the model is no longer viable, then the generality of the scoring system is jeopardized. Moreover, using criterion groups often unconsciously narrows research with the measure to areas closely related to the criterion variables. Experimental arousal of the Fear of Failure had not been done before Birney *et al.* began their investigation (although Heckhausen's criterion-based measures did show sensitivity to subsequent experimental arousal; see G. Reiss, cited in Heckhausen, 1968, pp. 140–143). Nevertheless, Birney *et al.* found it difficult to find any differences between aroused and neutral subjects' protocols, so finally they turned to the criterion groups method and developed a system that ultimately was able to discriminate in their original arousal experiment.[11]

Meanwhile Atkinson and his colleagues at the University of Michigan decided to measure Fear of Failure through direct questionnaires. Using either the Mandler-Sarason Test Anxiety Questionnaire (Mandler and Sarason, 1952) or a more specific Achievement Anxiety Questionnaire (Alpert and Haber, 1960), this group produced many important studies of the two aspects of achievement motivation (Atkinson and Feather, 1966). Such measures worked well in most of these studies; yet there was no very extensive theoretical rationale for using them or theoretical explanation for why they worked.[12]

[11] Although the measures of Birney *et al.* and of Heckhausen are conceptually distinct and empirically uncorrelated, they appear to predict the same domain of behavior in American and German subjects, respectively. This may suggest cross-national differences in the structure of Fear of Failure, as noted by Heckhausen (1968).

[12] Although there is consistent evidence that *n* Achievement, or at least the approach aspect of it, cannot be measured by direct questionnaires, Atkinson and Feather nevertheless used questionnaires to measure the Fear of Failure. In part this was simply because the questionnaires were there, and seemed to work. Nevertheless, these questionnaires may actually be measuring some component of generalized anxiety or arousal (Heckhausen, 1968, p. 120) rather than any specific avoidance aspect of the achievement motive. On the other hand, it may well be that the avoidance aspects of all motives tend to be highly related, and are, therefore, measurable by generalized anxiety or arousal. This possibility is supported by some findings on the relationship between Fear of Power and arousal which are presented later in Chapter 5. McClelland (1971a) also suggests that direct questionnaires often measure responses to strong, persistent, fixed demands imposed by others (originally by parents). If these demands are supported by aversive punishment, then an avoidance motive would be a likely result.

Finally, other researchers decided to leave the original scoring system more or less intact, and to code a story as Hope or Fear on the basis of its overall content regardless of the particular subcategories scored. De Charms and Davé (1965) scored Hope of Success and Fear of Failure on the basis of the story's outcome (+ or −) with respect to the achievement goal (not simply overall optimism, anxiety, or hostile press). De Charms (1957) and Fishman (1966) also used this procedure for differentiating approach and avoidance aspects of n Affiliation, while Byrne, McDonald, and Mikawa (1963) used a measure of the quality of interpersonal affect of the story in a similar way.

How is one to choose from among so many different ways for separating approach and avoidance, and measuring each? From this brief review, it should be clear that there is no one generally accepted method with impeccable credentials. The best results so far come from the systematic and creative use of a method that seemed useful to a particular investigator at a particular time.

Ideally, the method used should make conceptual and intuitive sense, and should give meaningful results that are related to approach and avoidance actions for the motive in question. My theory is that the overall motive score, as developed and refined through the arousal experiments, reflects the overall salience of the motive *in both its positive and negative aspects*. That is, the total n Power score represents the sum of approach and avoidance motives in the area of power.[13] Power approached and power avoided still register as power thought about; hence both contribute to the score. Therefore, I think this score should be partitioned in some way to distinguish between the approach and avoidance motives. Simply dividing up the subcategories, however, will not always work; apparently because these subcategories deal with the intensity of the motive, rather than its valence. Is there some additional way of classifying stories as Hope or Fear, after they have been coded for the overall level of the power motive (or power saliency)?

To explain how such a classification was finally developed, it is first necessary to review some research with preliminary versions of the Winter scoring system (Winter, 1967, 1972). Early findings had suggested that the action correlates of Winter n Power were

[13] Actually, this is true only if there has been a broad "sampling" of approach and avoidance situations in the experiments designed to arouse the motive. Thus by accident of limited design, it appears that the first measure of n Affiliation tapped primarily avoidance motives in the area of affiliation (see Shipley and Veroff, 1952; Atkinson, Heyns, and Veroff, 1954).

arranged in a bipolar factor, with office-holding slightly toward one pole and drinking, reading vicarious magazines and watching vicarious television programs, and sexual aggressiveness at the other pole. The overall Winter n Power score correlated with the absolute score on this bipolar factor, i.e., with the magnitude of approach toward either pole. (Later research has modified this conclusion somewhat, as shown in the findings reported in Chapters 4 through 6).

At this same time, McClelland, Davis, Kalin, and Wanner (1972, chap. 8) were investigating the relationship between n Power and drinking. They found that Activity Inhibition, as measured by the frequency of use of the word "not" in TAT stories or other verbal material, loaded strongly on the bipolar factor in the "office-holding" direction. They further discovered that drinking could be predicted by a combination of high n Power and low inhibition (rarely using "not"). Therefore, McClelland *et al.* developed a series of additional scoring categories that distinguished the high n Power stories of men who were also high in inhibition (used "not" often) and who were low drinkers, from the high n Power stories of men who were low in inhibition (rarely used "not") and who were heavy drinkers. In other words, the additional categories were designed to capture more precisely the distinction that was made by the bipolar factor and the Activity Inhibition measure. These additional categories are outlined in Table 3.8 (see McClelland *et al.*, appendix IV, for a complete version). They are applied after Power Imagery has been scored, and are intended as an alternative to the usual subcategories in Table 3.6. McClelland *et al.* labelled the high power/low inhibition categories "Personalized Power," or p Power, and the high power/high inhibition categories "Socialized Power," or s Power.

Although p Power and s Power scores were derived from studies of drinking, there is some evidence that they predict differently to other activities as well (McClelland *et al.*, 1972, chap. 8 and appendix IX; McClelland, 1970), and so they came to be thought of as two aspects of the power motive—though not completely independent aspects (see Table 3.10).

This distinction between personalized and socialized power suggested a promising way to isolate the approach and avoidance aspects of power, because the categories involve the valuation or valence of the power goal. Nevertheless, I thought it useful to retain the familiar subcategories of Table 3.6 as a measure of the overall *intensity* of the power motive, whatever its valence. To work with both sets of subcategories at once would create considerable confusion and overlap among different subscores. Therefore, I reworked the categories as defined by McClelland *et al.* into one binary scoring decision. If a story has been scored for Power Imagery and the subcategories in the usual way, it is then further classified as either Hope of Power or Fear of Power according to these new criteria. All of the points already scored for the story are then added to the Hope of Power score or to the Fear of Power score, as the case may be. The p Power definitions became the basis for classifying a story as Hope of Power, and the s Power categories the basis for classifying it as Fear of Power. (Stories that are not clearly Hope or Fear are classified as Hope, on the basis of an additional validation study which is described below. Thus the Hope of Power and Fear of Power subscores sum to the total *n* Power score.) Table 3.8 gives an outline of both the McClelland *et al.* p and s Power categories and the Hope/Fear code that was derived from them. Appendix I gives the full scoring definitions for the Hope/Fear code.

Why are the combined s Power categories labelled Fear of Power and the combined p Power categories called Hope of Power? Shouldn't it be the other way around? My own decision about which should be called which was based on the different action correlates of the two measures, as discussed in Chapter 4 and especially Chapter 5. To anticipate that discussion, Fear of Power scores were associated with a variety of things (such as paranoia) that seemed to involve both interest in power and a negative valence of power, or an avoidance of power. Thus the score is called Fear of Power. In contrast, Hope of Power scores seemed to predict actions that suggested an approach to power; hence the score is called Hope of Power. While the Hope/Fear distinction was derived from the p/s distinction of McClelland *et al.*, it is important to recognize that my interpretation of the meaning of the two scores diverges considerably from theirs, and even contradicts it in some respects. I shall discuss these differences at the end of Chapter 5, after discussing the Fear of Power measure.

Does the Hope/Fear recasting of the p/s distinction still differentiate persons scoring low and high, respectively, in Activity Inhibition as measured by the usage of "not" in the TAT stories? Protocols from 100 subjects were scored for Hope of Power, Fear of Power, and Activity Inhibition. The results, presented in Table 3.9, suggest that, as predicted, Fear of Power is related to Activity Inhibition in the same way as the s Power categories of McClelland *et al.* Since stories that were not clearly Hope or Fear (in terms of the original p and s Power categories) showed the same relationship to Activity Inhibition as those that were clearly Hope and Power, they were considered as

Hope. In other words, all stories are classified as Hope of Power unless they show one or more signs of Fear of Power.

Table 3.10 further shows that there is rather substantial overlap between the two different systems, in that Hope of Power scores are

TABLE 3.8 BRIEF OUTLINE OF p POWER, s POWER, HOPE OF POWER, AND FEAR OF POWER SCORING DEFINITIONS

Personalized Power (p Power) and Socialized Power (s Power) Categories[a]:

P[b] *Personal Goal:* The power goal is not for the good of others, and is explicitly for the good of the actor.

S *Social Goal:* The power goal is for the good of some specific other person(s), and is unsolicited by them.

S *Instrumental Activity:* The actor is doing something about reaching the power goal.

S *Self Block:* The actor struggles with himself about his ability or potential for power, or experiences interpersonal conflict that casts doubt on his competence.

P *Opponent Block:* Explicit mention of the opponent in a power struggle.

S *Power Contrast:* The power or reputation and prestige of the actor are deceptive because he has a flaw. Mixed affect at the outcome of a power attempt. Exaggeration or irony by the writer of the story.

Hope of Power and Fear of Power[c]:

All stories are classified as Hope of Power *unless* one of the following characteristics is present, in which case the story is classified as Fear of Power:

1. The power goal is for the direct or indirect benefit of some specific other or generalized cause.

2. The actor has doubts about his ability to have power, or experiences confusion and emotional conflict about power during the story.

3. Contrast, irony, or explicit statement by the writer of the story that power is deceptive or has a flaw. Reversed affect-outcome relationship (happy after failure, sad after success).

---

[a] Adapted from McClelland, Davis, Kalin, and Wanner (1972, appendix IV).

[b] P = counted toward p Power score for the story.

  S = counted toward s Power score for the story.

[c] A complete version is included in Appendix I of this book.

correlated with p Power and Fear of Power scores are correlated with s Power. Again I emphasize, however, that the reader should keep in mind the conceptual and philosophical differences between the two systems. They may be two different ways of looking at the same thing, or they may be two rather different things. Only more research with both systems can give definitive evidence.

How do the Hope of Power and Fear of Power scores relate to each other and to the total n Power score? Table 3.11 presents correlations among these scores, drawn from several different samples. The trends are quite consistent. There is a good deal of overlap between overall n Power and Hope of Power, although this may vary according to the pictures used to elicit TAT stories and the subjects tested. Anticipating the findings in Chapter 4, Hope of Power generally predicts the same kinds of actions as does overall n Power, although often the total score gives more significant results. In contrast, Fear of Power is uncorrelated with Hope of Power, less highly correlated with overall n Power, and very often predicts completely different actions from either Hope of Power or total n Power. Every one of these charac-

TABLE 3.9 RELATIONSHIP OF HOPE OF POWER AND FEAR OF POWER TO ACTIVITY INHIBITION IN THREE SAMPLES

| Motive Subscore | Mean Motive Subscore for Those with Activity Inhibition[a] Scores that are: | | |
	Below median[b] (N = 46)	Above median[b] (N = 54)	Difference
Hope of Power	50.54	51.46	.92; p = n.s.
Fear of Power	47.89	52.54	4.65; t = 2.35 p = .01 1-tailed

Note: The samples are: 57 Wesleyan undergraduate males in an introductory psychology course; 21 Wesleyan undergraduate males in an advanced psychology course; and 22 executives in a large United States corporation.

All motive scores are standardized within each sample (mean = 50 and standard deviation = 10), because different pictures, administration conditions, and times for writing stories were used in each sample.

[a] Measured by frequency of usage of "not" in TAT protocol.

[b] Medians calculated separately for each sample.

teristics seems consistent with the distinction between approach and avoidance motives suggested by Atkinson and Feather (1966) and Birney, Burdick, and Teevan (1969). Hence the Hope of Power and Fear of Power scores, as defined and measured in this way, are assumed to reflect the approach and avoidance aspects of the power motive.

Combining of the subscores. In the past, subscores for approach and avoidance have been analyzed and combined in many different ways. Heckhausen (1963, pp. 67–68; 1968, p. 119) lists the logical possibilities: (1) the combination of approach and avoidance, which is called "total motivation" and is presumed to reflect the overall salience of the particular content area; (2) approach and avoidance simply treated as two separate and independent variables; and (3) avoidance subtracted from approach, which is called "re-

TABLE 3.10 INTERCORRELATIONS AMONG VARIOUS POWER MOTIVE SCORES IN TWO STUDENT SAMPLES

	Overall n Power	Fear of Power	p Power	s Power
Hope of Power	.90**	−.13	.74**	.57**
	.66**	−.25*	.46**	−.02
Fear of Power	.28*		−.03	.43**
	.57**		.21	.49**
p Power	.72**			.50**
	.55**			.26**
s Power	.72**			
	.37**			

* p<.05.
** p<.01.

Note: The upper correlation within each pair is based on a sample of 63 male high school students, and the lower correlation in each pair is based on a sample of 72 male and female college summer school students. The TAT was administered on three different occasions to the high school sample; the correlations shown here are for the first administration only. The patterns for the second and third administrations are similar, except that Fear of Power and s Power are unrelated in the second administration.

I am grateful to Ellsworth Fersch and David C. McClelland for making these results available to me.

sultant motivation" and which comes directly from Miller's original analysis of conflict behavior (1944). Using this last procedure, a zero score can occur in two different ways (approach and avoidance both high or both low), and so the procedure entails the assumption that approach and avoidance act in directly opposite ways and, therefore, cancel each other out.

I have used mainly the first two procedures in this book. The total n Power score (Hope and Fear combined) is the basis for many of the findings reported in Chapters 4 through 7. One would expect many actions to be correlated with the overall salience of power, and so it is reasonable to use the total score. However, total n Power is

TABLE 3.11 INTERCORRELATIONS OF n POWER AND SUBSCORES IN VARIOUS SAMPLES

Sample	Correlation of total n Power score with:		Correlation of Hope of Power with Fear of Power
	Hope of Power	*Fear of Power*	
Total Sample of Wesleyan Students (N = 325)	.80**	.52**	−.09
Upper-middle-class American Executives (N = 22)	.71**	.28	−.22
Harvard Class of 1964 Students (N = 255)	.91**	.37**	−.05
Oxford University Students (N = 58)	.86**	.54**	.04
German Engineering Students[a] (N = 96)	.80**	.48**	−.15

** p<.01.

[a] Data from Erdmann (1971).

highly correlated with Hope of Power, so that many of these actions correlates may in fact be related to the approach motive. I have used the second procedure, which assumes that approach and avoidance are independent, each with its own correlates, mainly in Chapter 5 to study the Fear of Power. Apart from the work of Heckhausen and Birney, Burdick, and Teevan (1969) on the Fear of Failure, there has been relatively little previous emphasis on the separate characteristics of avoidance motives as such. I have not used the third procedure in this book, since the primary purpose was the investigation and conceptualization of the total score and the two subscores. McClelland, Davis, Kalin, and Wanner (1972, chap. 8 and appendix IX) have used this procedure with p Power and s Power. Measuring resultant motivation would be important for future research designed according to the Atkinson model; and researchers who wish to do so can simply standardize each subscore and then subtract Fear of Power from Hope of Power.

RELIABILITY

In Chapter 2, I noted that one of the important problems with TAT measures in general, including motives as measured by the McClelland-Atkinson research strategy, was their apparent low reliability (Murstein, 1963, chap. 6). Low test-retest correlation coefficients are often taken to mean that the TAT lacks temporal reliability or stability; that it measures something that is so emphemeral and unsturdy that it is useless for research purposes. I have deferred the discussion of reliability to this point so that I could present data on test-retest reliability for the revised measure of n Power, and refer to previous findings with n Achievement. I think that the concept of reliability is more complex than it seems at first; reliability means more than just test-retest correlation coefficients. Therefore I want to discuss the issue at some length.

The concept of reliability. In the strict sense of the word, a measure is "reliable" if it gives the same reading for a person or a group under the same or nearly the same conditions (McClelland, 1958, p. 18). Thus a thermometer is "reliable" if it gives consistent readings against some absolute standard of temperature. A thermometer that is not consistent in this way would be a bad instrument for measuring temperature; a measure of personality that is not consistent is likely to be a useless instrument. Since n Achievement typically shows test-retest correlations ranging from +.20 to +.40, many writers argue that the measure is, therefore, unreliable, and that there are grounds for rejecting the TAT as a way of measuring enduring motives. Of course TAT measures have some inherent instability, as does any other procedure; if this were large, it might be grounds for questioning their usefulness. In practice, however, the extent of inherent instability is confused and obscured by many other factors. These factors make the direct analogy with the thermometer inappropriate.

(1) Using any measure once may render it unsuitable for subsequent use—the measure may have a kind of "self-destruct" quality. Thermometers naturally adjust (or can be shaken down) to the proper temperature after use; but psychological instruments may react with the person tested so that the instrument cannot be used again in the same way. If the measure has this quality, it will show low apparent reliability; yet the initial measure may be quite valid in the sense of correlating with other behaviors (McClelland, Atkinson, Clark, and Lowell, 1953, pp. 191–194). What about the TAT? Persons are asked to compose imaginative stories; if they later take another TAT, they may consciously try to make their stories different the second time, or they may treat the test as a measure of memory and try to make them the same. In other words, there may be a "refractory phase" for associative processes (see Telford, 1931). There is some evidence that this refractory effect even occurs within a single sequence of TAT stories. N Achievement scores appear to vary by picture in a cyclical fashion, independent of the picture (McClelland et al., 1953, pp. 187–189; Reitman and Atkinson, 1958, p. 679). I shall present evidence below that a similar "sawtooth" effect (cyclical variation of reliability coefficients) occurs during successive TAT administrations. One hypothesis to account for these refractory or sawtooth effects is that motives are organized into a hierarchy according to salience, intensity, or "regnancy" (Murray, 1938, pp. 45–54). On a first administration, the TAT elicits expression of the most salient or regnant motives; but because of the typical instructions to be creative and imaginative, the second administration bypasses these regnant motives and instead elicits expression of other, less salient motives (see also Sechrest, 1968, p. 564). On a third administration, regnant motives are more likely to "reappear." Thus there is picture-by-picture and administration-by-administration fluctuation in motive score. Klinger (1971, chap. 13) presents a more formal theory of regnancy and drift in the fantasy process.

An experiment by Haber and Alpert (1958) gives some support to this hypothesis. They administered the TAT twice, and found reliability higher for pictures that were less ambiguous in the sense of having stronger cues for the particular motive in question. Morgan (1953) found that reliability was improved if the time that subjects had to write stories was sharply reduced. In other words, on a second administration the regnant motive may still be elicited if the picture cues for the motive remain sufficiently strong, or if the person has less time to run down his hierarchy of motives in the effort to make up an interesting and creative story.

(2) Reliability can be meaningfully assessed only when testing conditions are the same or nearly the same. TAT responses are affected by a great many relevant and seemingly irrelevant situational and contextual cues, some under the control of the experimenter and some not (see Murstein, 1963, chaps. 7–8; Klinger, 1971, chap. 12). Thus it is very difficult to reinstate exactly the same set of stimulus and background conditions for a subsequent administration. At the very least, important variables such as individual differences in experience during the period before testing and the course of world events will be beyond the control of the researcher. Even the most heroic efforts to reinstate identical conditions and to eliminate the effect of individual differences in experience prior to testing may actually produce extraordinary response sets. Klinger administered the TAT three times to 144 male undergraduates, each time under the following controlled conditions (1968, p. 157):

. . . Sessions were identical for a given S—same room, procedure, instructions, time of day, and day of week. . . . Ss were tested alone in a 7 ft. × 7 ft. audiometric room . . . all communications with Ss employed printed matter, signs, audio tapes, slides, and films, thus eliminating sources of experimenter bias. . . . The Ss were instructed at the start of each session to sit quietly in the lit room for 25 min. in order to reduce the variable associative effect . . . then shown a brief (1 to 7 min.) silent film . . . and given a 10 min. arithmetic test.

Klinger found n Achievement and n Affiliation reliabilities among all three administrations to be at chance level; but one wonders what effect these rather extraordinary procedures had on his subjects' motive-arousal. The point is that potentially every aspect of the entire context of an experiment may affect some critical aspect of personality and behavior (Orne, 1970). A procedure that is formally "identical" still may not be appropriate if it creates its own unique effects on motive arousal.

(3) Finally, a true instrument will not reproduce the same measure if the thing to be measured has in fact changed. Any interval of

time beyond a day or two adds the effects of learning, growth, and change to an estimate of test-retest reliability in the strict psychometric sense (Kenny, quoted in Kagan and Lesser, 1961, p. 279). If people's motives change, then their motive scores ought to be different when they are tested again; and there is considerable evidence that motives, being learned, can change (McClelland and Winter, 1969, chap. 2 and *passim*). There is a circular dilemma here. Since some theorists define personality as relatively *stable* patterns of behavior, a good personality test, therefore, shows little temporal change—it gives very "reliable" answers. The existence of such tests is then taken as evidence for the "stability of personality." Change and growth are neglected or slighted; those procedures which might show such change are stigmatized, therefore, as being "unreliable."

Murstein arranged the data on *n* Achievement reliability according to the time interval between tests, and argued "that the size of the correlation is analogous to a learning curve with the maximum decrease during the first 2 months, followed by only a slight further decrease over a period of years" (1963, pp. 140–141). This suggests that part of the reliability problem may be due to learning and change, rather than only to error and fluctuation.

Reliability data on n *Power.* Table 3.12 presents data concerning *n* Power reliability from several different research projects, arranged roughly by the time interval between test administrations. The results are equivalent to the figures for *n* Achievement stability cited by Murstein and others (Klinger, 1966; Birney, 1968). The Watson study (1969) is practically an estimate of split-half reliability, but it is included here as the limiting case of test-retest reliability because there was an interpolated activity between two administrations, though the activity itself probably interacted with motive levels and hence affected them in unknown ways. The same considerations apply to the McClelland, Davis, Kalin, and Wanner (1972) figure. Taking the first part of the table as a whole, reliability is moderate for very short time intervals, but decreases over time, as would be expected if motives actually change. The pattern corresponds to that shown by Murstein for *n* Achievement.

What about the predicted "sawtooth" effect over three administrations? The Harvard Student Study data show an increase in reliability estimate from administration[1-2] to administration[1-3]. (The increase in *r* from .17 to .30 is significant at the .11 level, 1-tailed.) The same increase in reliability on a third administration of the TAT also occurs among a small sample of Wesleyan undergraduates. This tends to

TABLE 3.12 THE RELIABILITY OF n POWER SCORES

Time Interval	Investigation	Correlation
Two Administrations		
10 minutes	Watson (1969): two 4-picture TATs with 10 minutes of dramatic role improvisation between. N = 42.	.45
90 minutes	McClelland, Davis, Kalin, and Wanner (1972, chaps. 6 and 8): two 4-picture TATs with 90 minutes of drinking between. N = 50.	.50
3 months– 18 months	Various Wesleyan undergraduates who took the TAT twice (see Chapter 4). N = 56.	.29[a]
about 1 year	Harvard Student Study. N = 110.	.17
Three Administrations		(*reliability[1-3]*)
3 months– 18 months	Various Wesleyan undergraduates who took the TAT three times. N = 9.	.56[b]
about 2 years	Harvard Student Study. N = 110.	.30
Four Administrations		(*reliability[1-4]*)
about 3 years	Harvard Student Study. N = 110.	.24

Reliability Studies with Wesleyan Undergraduates

| Test variable | Average *rho* (administration[1-2]) for groups where the test variable was: | |
	The same	*Different*
Pictures	.44 (3 groups)	.15 (3 groups)
Administrator	.75 (2 groups)	.03 (4 groups)
Setting (class, small group, or experiment)	.40 (2 groups)	.20 (4 groups)

support the hypothesis of McClelland, and of Reitman and Atkinson, that there is a conscious or unconscious refractory phase in the associative processes.

Because the Wesleyan undergraduate data were collected in many different administrations, under varying conditions and with an overlap of subjects, informal tests of some of the aspects of TAT reliability discussed above can be made. Six different "pairs" of TAT administrations could be distinguished. (A "pair" is a group of from five to fourteen subjects who took TATs in the same two administrations—see note *a* of Table 3.12.) If we arrange these six pairs or groups according to whether various features of the two administrations were the same or different, as is done in the last part of Table 3.12, we find that average reliability is always higher when a particular feature of the test administration is the same than when that feature is different. In other words, the more similar the second testing situation is to the first, the higher the reliability. The administrator appears to be the single most important feature, in that when the same person gave the TAT, average reliability was quite high, but when different administrators were used, reliability drops effectively to zero. Again, this is consistent with previous findings for *n* Achievement (Haber and Alpert, 1958; reference to unpublished paper by Birney in McClelland, 1958, p. 35). Furthermore, if we distinguish four kinds of differences (pictures, sex of administrator, status of administrator [faculty or student], and setting), then the rank order correlation between the *rho* for a pair and the number of differences in the two administrations is −.50. While this figure is not significant because only six groups are involved, it does indicate that increasing dissimilarity between the two sets of testing conditions will produce sharply reduced reliability.

As I said above, the issue of TAT reliability is complex. There is evidence for the operation of each of the factors that I hypothesized could confuse and obscure true stability or instability: the "sawtooth" effect, or alternation of measured motive level between administrations and even between pictures; changes in the testing situation; and changes in the motive itself over time. The first factor should not

---

Table 3.12 (*Cont.*)

[a] All *n* Power scores were standardized within each of several administrations for the Wesleyan undergraduates. This correlation is based on the first and second administrations for each subject who took the TAT twice, regardless of the particular sessions involved.

[b] Correlation computed in the same manner as that described in note *a* for all those who took the TAT three times.

affect validity, although it will tend to produce low test-retest correlation coefficients. The second factor presents more of a problem: what is the appropriate or "correct" set of testing conditions for maximum prediction of external behaviors? I don't think that there is yet any answer to the question; until it is answered, validity research will produce relatively fewer significant findings and some confusing differences between different studies. Until we know more about the precise effects of testing situations on fantasy responses (see Klinger, 1971), two important cautions are necessary for research with TAT measures of motives. First, test conditions should be as "neutral" as possible with respect to the motive in question. Klinger (1966, pp. 298–299) argued that motive scores obtained under neutral conditions tend to give the most understandable validity results. Second, if one is going to study the behavior correlates of a motive among a particular group of subjects, then *it is highly desirable that all subjects be tested in the same situation,* especially if one is comparing motive levels of two different groups. If subjects cannot be tested all at once, and if one can assume that the mean motive scores of the different groups are the same, then standardizing scores within the different administrations is an appropriate but by no means ideal alternative. The third factor—change of motive over time—should not affect "true" validity, although it may damp down the results obtained in longitudinal studies where testing was carried out long before the behaviors of interest were measured.

When all of these factors are taken into account, I think that TAT reliability, in the strictest sense of the term, is sufficient for research purposes, although I realize that not every psychometrician will agree.

Interscorer reliability. Appendix I of this book provides materials for learning, practicing, and then checking mastery of the *n* Power scoring system. Six scorers trained by this method have, so far, demonstrated median Category Agreement figures of .91 for scoring presence of Power Imagery and a median *rho* of .84 for the last three sets of practice stories. Both figures are higher than those reported for the Veroff measure (see Feld and Smith, 1958, p. 238). The manual and accompanying materials should enable a scorer to attain scoring skill sufficient for research purposes after a reasonable amount of practice.

As a test of cross-national use of the scoring system, a German scorer learned the manual in English and then scored 14 German TAT stories.[14] These were translated into English and rescored in that

14 I am indebted to Hans W. Wendt for providing these stories.

language by an expert scorer. Category Agreement on Imagery was .80 and overall *rho* was .78. Inspection of discrepancies suggested that disagreements tended to be caused by abbreviations and colloquialisms in one language that are not understood by the scorer working in the other language, rather than by any fundamental difficulties in applying the system to other languages or translating stories in such a way as to preserve motive imagery.

CORRELATIONS WITH OTHER PSYCHOLOGICAL TESTS

At the end of Chapter 1, I tried to draw a conceptual distinction between the power motive and other psychological variables related to power. Table 3.13 presents the actual correlations of the *n* Power measures with a variety of these other tests, including other purported measures of power interests or strivings. It can be seen that *n* Power is essentially unrelated to these other variables, as well as to intelligence. Perhaps some would argue that the *n* Power measure, therefore, has low concurrent validity. However, as argued in Chapter 2, I do not think that concurrent validity (or the correlations with other psychological tests) is a particularly important virtue, *if* a measure shows substantial construct validity (or correlations with important actions). The rest of this book presents findings on the construct validity or action correlates of the power motive measures.

The relationship of *n* Power to *n* Achievement requires further comment. In a sample of 260 Wesleyan undergraduates, there is a slight positive correlation between *n* Power and *n* Achievement; which, although significant because of the large sample, does not represent a high degree of association. Although the two motives may be slightly correlated for this group of college undergraduates (in the National Sample survey, Veroff and Feld, 1970, also found a slight correlation between Veroff *n* Power and *n* Achievement among college-educated husbands, especially younger ones), I think that they are really quite distinct both conceptually and empirically. Doing a job well or reaching a goal with excellence (achievement) is not at all the same as having power or control of the process (power); indeed, they may often conflict. Together, they may constitute the ascensionist fantasy of the "American Dream" (Murray, 1958, pp. 193–194). They are nicely combined in the old saying, "Build a better mousetrap [achievement], and the world will beat a path to your door [power]."

TABLE 3.13 CORRELATIONS OF n POWER WITH VARIOUS OTHER PSYCHOLOGICAL TESTS

| Sample | Variable | Correlations with: | | |
		n Power	Hope of Power	Fear of Power
Harvard[a]	Scholastic Aptitude Test (83)	−.12	−.04	−.17
	Mathematical Aptitude Test (83)	.02	.06	−.08
Wesleyan[b]	Rotter Internal-External Control (41)	.13	.17	−.01
	Machiavellianism (Mach-V) (46)	−.22	−.13	−.15
	Social Desirability (from Mach-V)	−.02	−.04	.04
Harvard	F-Scale (80)	−.05	−.07	.03
	F-Scale, positive items	−.03	−.02	−.03
	F-Scale, negative items	−.05	−.09	.07
Wesleyan	EPPS Manifest Needs: (58)			
	Autonomy	.21	.10	.17
	Exhibition	.33*	.26*	.15
	Dominance	.06	.20	−.16
	Nurturance	−.30*	.07	.07
	Heterosexuality	.49**	.33*	.30*
	Aggression	.01	.21	−.24
	CPI Scales: (36)			
	Dominance	.07	.14	−.04
	Capacity for Status	.34*	.37*	.10
	Psychological Mindedness	.19	.31	−.07
Harvard	Stern Activities Index: (82)			
	Dominance	−.16	−.06	−.23*
	Aggression	−.17	−.09	− 19
	Narcissism	−.05	−.05	−.01
Harvard	Yeasaying (see Couch and Keniston, 1960) (82)	.14	.17	−.04
	FIRO-B Scales: (82)			
	Expressed Control	−.18	−.18	−.03
	Wanted Control	.15	.17	−.02
Wesleyan	n Achievement (260)	.17**	.11	.11
	n Affiliation (58)	−.01	.02	−.04

* $p < .05$.
** $p < .01$.

The whole point of the power game is to have the world come to your door without having to build a better mousetrap—perhaps by convincing the world that in any case they should beat a path to your door!

At the level of behavior, I would predict that the principal difference between the two motives is in the reaction to negative results and the use made of such information. People high in n Achievement may not like news of failure, but they do use it to change their plans and modify their performance (McClelland, 1961; pp. 231–233). People concerned with power may try to suppress such information; first from the public, then from themselves; because that very knowledge may itself be power (see Canetti, 1962, pp. 290–296). N Achievement is associated with seeking and using expert help (Koenig, 1963), while n Power is probably associated with avoiding it or "burying" it. I would expect that n Power leads to a shorter-range time perspective than n Achievement, simply because of the moment-by-moment quality of power—if it is not constantly demonstrated, it may be lost. However, these are merely speculative hypotheses to explain an empirical lack of relationship.

In this chapter I have reviewed several scoring systems for n Power, traced the integration of all of these earlier systems into one revised set of coding rules and definitions, discussed various approaches to partitioning the overall motive score in order to reflect different aspects (or valences) of the motive, and presented some of the psychometric characteristics of the revised n Power scoring system. Because it successfully differentiates aroused and neutral subjects in four separate arousal experiments, it already possesses a kind of validity. But far more important, what actions does it predict?

Table 3.13 (*Cont.*)

Note: The number in parentheses after the variable name is the N for the correlations with the variable.

[a] Subjects from the Harvard Student Study.

[b] Subjects from psychology courses at Wesleyan University.

CHAPTER 4

The
Power Motive
in Action

This chapter begins the presentation of research results using the revised measure of n Power. It is simultaneously an investigation of the validity of the motive scores, and a study of the whole domain of power. What actions, under what conditions, are related to n Power? Probably not all power-related actions will be; but certainly there should be some, if the scoring system is claimed to measure the power motive. The validity of the n Power measure thus comes not from any single experiment, but rather from a whole network of findings.

SUBJECTS AND PROCEDURES

Most of the research reported in this chapter was carried out with male college undergraduates at Wesleyan and Harvard universities. Recently psychologists have shown great concern about the pitfalls of trying to generalize laws of human behavior from such atypical groups. College students are readily available and are usually docile about participating in research; but they are highly selected on such important variables as intelligence, social class, and race (Schultz, 1969). They are at an unusual and uncertain period of their lives.

They are so accustomed to taking psychological tests that they have developed elaborate response sets in order to outsmart the psychologist, whom they suspect of only practicing deception experiments anyway. Finally, half of humanity—women—is often ignored or excluded as experimental subjects.

All of these criticisms of undergraduate subject populations are valid. Strictly speaking, this chapter is mainly concerned with the action correlates of n Power among male, largely middle-class undergraduates at Eastern private colleges in the United States, although some findings from other groups will also be reported. Nevertheless, I think it is worthwhile to consider some important advantages of research with college students, so long as we keep aware of the dangers. For one thing, college students are of similar age and are in a relatively homogeneous situation, so that the effects of a motive can be studied without at the same time having to worry about great variation in the environment, or more precisely, in expectancies and incentives. A great advantage of working with college students is that there often exists a wealth of nonreactive or "archival" measures on them. This does not mean "secret" records that involve issues of privacy, but simply careful and relatively complete archives of interesting behaviors, gathered in such a way that the behavior itself is not affected by the record. For example, who has been an officer or elected to a committee; who has received varsity letters in a sport; who is a dormitory counselor or has written a letter to the college newspaper, and so forth. If, as Webb, Campbell, Schwartz, and Sechrest (1966) argue, psychological research should increasingly pay attention to such nonreactive measures of behavior, then perhaps there are some hitherto unrealized advantages to working with college students.

The principal sample in the present research was several hundred male undergraduates at Wesleyan University. They took a Thematic Apperception Test (TAT) during the first week of various psychology courses or as part of an experiment for which they volunteered. These TATs, as well as all those from the other research reported in this book, were scored for n Power by scorers who had previously demonstrated very high agreement with the practice materials prescored by experts that are included in Appendix I (Category Agreement above .90 and rank-order correlation of total scores greater than .85). Because different administrators and sometimes different pictures were used in these different testing sessions, it was necessary to correct for the known sensitivity of the TAT to differences in testing conditions. This was done by converting the raw motive scores into standard scores within each testing situation. (There were between thirty and eighty students in each session.) Such a procedure assumes, of course, that the "true" means and variances are the same for all groups; however, it seemed worthwhile to make this assumption in order to correct for very likely differences in the testing conditions and pulling power of different sets of pictures. Thus the n Power scores for Wesleyan student subjects are reported in standardized form, with an overall mean of 50 and a standard deviation of 10. Since scores were not correlated with story length, further correction was not necessary. Other data were obtained from various smaller groups of the Wesleyan sample through questionnaires, inventories of activities, archives, and other records. Appendix II contains the basic questionnaire that was used with most of the students.

Other results reported in this chapter came from the Harvard Student Study, in which extensive longitudinal data were gathered on several hundred members of the Harvard College Class of 1964. All subjects took a TAT in the early autumn of their freshman year (1960), and n Power scores from that test were used in all analyses of data. Finally, results from other groups, such as small businessmen in India, executives from a large American corporation, German soldiers and students, and various groups of adult men who volunteered for psychological experiments are discussed in this chapter. Sample characteristics and testing arrangements will be discussed as these studies are mentioned.

As pointed out in Chapter 3, there are actually three different power motive scores: overall n Power, which I conceive as a measure of the salience of power concerns; Hope of Power, which is a refined measure of the approach motive; and Fear of Power, which is assumed to measure the avoidance motive. Under most conditions, n Power and Hope of Power correlate quite highly and predict the same actions. Thus in most cases, the total n Power score will be used in this chapter and in Chapter 6; in such cases it can be assumed that Hope of Power shows the same pattern of relationships. Hope of Power scores will be used mainly in those cases where they alone show statistical significance—in other words, where the action or characteristic is related *only* to the approach motive. Finally, the action characteristics that are uniquely associated with the Fear of Power are presented in Chapter 5.

FORMAL SOCIAL POWER

We would expect that persons with high n Power would more often seek and occupy positions of formal social power, although it is important to distinguish between offices that have "real" power and those that are empty, routine, or "figurehead" jobs. That is, in terms of the Atkinson and Feather (1966) model, the power motive should be associated with occupying positions of office only when the expectancy and incentive of having power in the position are both high.

All of the Wesleyan students tested were subsequently asked whether they belonged to any university organizations and whether they were or had been officers in any of them. For this analysis, only those students who were juniors or seniors at the time of taking the questionnaire are considered, since by that time they had had a reasonable chance to become officers, whereas most freshmen and sophomores had had much less opportunity. Those 57 students who were or who had been officers are significantly higher than the 47 who were not, in n Power (means = 51.95 and 46.51, t = 3.00, p<.01 2-tailed) and in Hope of Power (means = 53.05 and 45.40, t = 4.66, p<.001 2-tailed).

The power motive is also associated with occupying other positions of power within the university. For example, Wesleyan has resident advisors who live in dormitories and serve as academic and personal counselors for students (particularly freshmen), give advice, and act as the liaison between students and the administration, the Dean's Office, and the professional counseling staff. They perform an informal socializing function and overall they possess considerable influence and respect. The position is highly competitive, since resident advisors are entitled to a free room of slightly better quality than other dormitory rooms, many free meals, and free local telephone service. The selection procedure is rigorous, and involves scrutiny of one's record, overall reputation among students and other residential advisors, and performance in an interview. Those 26 students who had been resident advisors are higher in n Power than the 169 who had not (means = 52.62 and 49.78, t = 1.39, p = .08 1-tailed). Students were excluded from this calculation if they were ineligible—for reasons of academic or disciplinary probation, marriage, or absence from the university.

It might be argued that holding office in college organizations or serving as a resident advisor does not represent very much "real" power in the American university as it exists in the late 1960s and early 1970s. The course of events at Wesleyan University permitted a further nonreactive test of the relationship between power motivation and having formal social power. In February, 1970, the president of the university resigned in order to seek political office. As a result, a "Presidential Search Committee," composed of trustees, faculty, and elected students was formed to look for and select a new president. This committee did not restrict itself merely to considering names, but was supposed to examine the scope and purpose of the university itself. Hence membership on the committee undoubtedly gave a high expectancy of significant power. Fifty-two students nominated themselves for the three positions which were to be elected by the student body. Fourteen of these nominees were in the sample tested. While these 14 were not higher in n Power than the overall average, there was a significant rank-order correlation between Hope of Power and the number of votes received in the election ($rho = +.64$, p<.01). Fear of Power was significantly negatively correlated with votes received ($rho = -.43$, p<.05).

Finally, certain organizations such as the college newspaper and radio station seem to have power in a university community. They are essential to the dissemination of information and the formation of opinion. Those students from the sample who reported that they were (or had been) on the newspaper or radio station staffs were higher in Hope of Power than the overall average (N = 46, mean Hope of Power = 52.43, t = 1.95 for difference from 50.00, p~.07 2-tailed).

Athletics is another form of social power, in at least two different ways. First, competitive sports inherently give a sense of power. One person or team defeats another. The language of sports journalism is full of power words and images. Symbolically, sports competition may be a vestige of the combat in dominance hierarchies observable among some animal species (Brown, 1965, pp. 16–21). Thus competitive sports are sometimes suggested as a substitute for war and other direct forms of power competition among humans. A second way in which sports are related to power involves the relation of sports to the rest of society. Success in sports is often the most important basis of popularity, reputation, prestige, and hence power among American young males (Whyte, 1943; Lippitt, Polansky, Redl, and Rosen, 1952; Coleman, 1961, chap. 5), although this may be changing nowadays. Successful athletes are often celebrities and a focus of adulation and deference for many adults (Beisser, 1967). Athletic success is even one way of entering the political system. Hence it seems clear that there ought to be a close connection between n Power and sports, although of course such factors as physical size and skill are also important.

To test this hypothesis, I asked the Wesleyan Department of Athletics to furnish lists of all students in the sample who had been awarded varsity letters in any sport, or who had participated in those sports existing on a "club" basis (crew, rugby, ice hockey). On the basis of a small pilot study, I divided sports into two groups: (1) Those which are directly competitive, in the sense that each move

made by one person or team leads to a response by the other, so
that a "game" is actually a long chain of response and counter-re-
sponse. Examples are football, baseball, tennis, and squash. (2) Those
which are indirectly competitive, in that each player or team can
perform a whole sequence of actions by himself, and his total performance is the basis of comparison to the other player or team.
Examples include track, swimming, golf, and cross country. The first
category can be thought of as man-against-man, or team-against-team
sports. They cannot ever really be played alone, and involve strategy
in addition to skill or chance (Roberts and Sutton-Smith, 1962). The
second group can be thought of as man-against-himself, or man-
against-clock sports, and they can be played alone, although there
certainly are pacing effects. Figure 4.1 summarizes this distinction.
On the basis of the pilot study, I predicted that those students who
had won varsity letters in directly competitive sports would be higher
in n Power, but that those in nondirectly competitive sports would
not; both in comparison to those who had not won letters. Table 4.1
shows that these predictions are strongly confirmed.

Figure 4.1. Categories of Sports Used in the Analysis

	Directly Competitive	**Not Directly Competitive**
Nature of the Competition	"Man against Man" "Team against Team" Strategy Sports	"Man against the Clock" "Man against Himself"
Pattern of Play	Player A ⟶ ⟵ Player B	Player A ⟶ Player B ⟶
	Examples: Football Basketball Baseball Lacrosse Tennis Squash Soccer Wrestling Hockey Rugby	Examples: Track Cross Country Swimming Golf Crew

TABLE 4.1 *n* POWER AND PARTICIPATION IN DIRECTLY
COMPETITIVE SPORTS

Group	n *Power*	Mean Scores on: Hope of Power	Fear of Power
Varsity letter winners in directly competitive sports (N = 36)	54.64	52.36	54.50
All others (N = 266)	49.69	49.95	49.66
Differences	4.95	2.41	4.84
	t = 2.84	t = 1.43	t = 2.76
	p<.005	p<.10	p<.005
Varsity letter winners in nondirectly competitive sports[a] (N = 13)	45.77	48.62	45.08

Note: All tests of significance in this table are 1-tailed.
[a] Included in the "All Others" category above.

Further evidence for the connection between *n* Power and the
kind of vigorous, even violent, physical activity found in competitive
sports comes from a questionnaire item in which 60 Wesleyan students were asked whether they had ever broken a bone or sprained a
joint. Fifty-three students had, and they were significantly higher in
n Power than the seven who had not (means = 51.30 and 44.71,
t = 1.71, p = .09 2-tailed).

POLITICS

So far *n* Power is related to a variety of actions and activities that
involve formal social power and personal impact within a large sample
of male college undergraduates. Do these findings hold true among
adults? What are the ways in which high *n* Power adults seek and
get power? Some preliminary research, using the Winter scoring
system with a small sample of middle-class adult men, showed that
n Power was correlated with the number of organizations belonged
to and the number of offices held (Winter, 1968). However, as a

source of power, membership in clubs and organizations is certainly far overshadowed by occupation among adult American males, for whom a "job" or career is probably the most important part of the self (Parsons, 1942). Politics as a career might seem to be the way to get the most power. What is the relation of n Power to political activity and careers?

Browning (1960) collected TATs and other data from carefully matched samples of men in "Eastport," a city of about 150,000 population in the eastern United States. (Analyses of these data are reported in Browning and Jacob, 1964, and Browning, 1968.) Browning distinguished four groups: (1) politicians who were party candidates for various offices; (2) matched businessmen inactive in politics; (3) businessmen active in the urban renewal program but not in regular party politics; and (4) matched businessmen inactive in urban renewal. Browning and Jacob (1964) found that candidates for offices that could be rated as high in expectancy of power were higher in Veroff n Power than candidates for offices that were rated low in expectancy of power.

These same TAT protocols were scored according to the revised n Power scoring system with rather different results, as shown in Table 4.2. There were essentially no differences among all groups, except for the leaders in the urban renewal program, who were higher than subleaders and controls. The lack of differences among the party candidates and controls[1] is a little surprising. Isn't the political system an obvious way to get power? Why are the urban renewal leaders the only group with an elevated motive score?

The massive urban renewal program in "Eastport" was the center of focus for local politics during the past two decades (see Dahl, 1961). The downtown was completely transformed, and the social

[1] Actually, there is some evidence for a relationship between n Power and political activity in Browning's data, but only under rather complex conditions. Among the candidates for high-power-potential offices in Table 4.2, those five men who initiated their own candidacy were higher in n Power than those five men who were recruited by their party *or* who had fathers active in politics ($p = .048$, 1-tailed Mann-Whitney U test). For the latter men, situational pressures and the influence of learned role models appear to override the effects of motive.

Browning (1968) points out that none of the urban renewal leaders had fathers active in politics. In other words, a man who makes his own effort to become a renewal leader, or a candidate, does tend to have relatively high n Power. This is consistent with the view that motivational effects are most clearly seen in the absence of strong situational or role-model forces (see Atkinson and Reitman, 1956; Heckhausen, 1968).

and economic life of the city radically (and not always fortunately) altered. Perhaps the "real" opportunities for social power in Eastport during these years were to be found in urban renewal and not in the regular local political apparatus. Other writers have called attention to the fact that urban renewal is a highly political process, involving delicate relationships of power among various governmental, economic, social, and racial groups; that an urban renewal "entrepreneur" must acquire, strengthen, and use his power (Bellush and Hausknecht, 1967). The symbolic association of power with dreams of tearing down and rebuilding the world is even reflected in drama and history: Ibsen's characterizations of the Master Builder and John

TABLE 4.2 n POWER SCORES OF BUSINESSMEN ACTIVE IN URBAN RENEWAL, PARTY POLITICIANS, AND CONTROL GROUPS IN "EASTPORT"

	Mean Scores on:	
Group	Veroff n Power[a]	Revised n Power[b]
Urban Renewal Leaders (N = 7)	7.57	60.22 ⎫
Urban Renewal Subleaders (N = 22)	6.00	49.60 ⎬ $t = 2.20$ $p<.05$ ⎫ $t = 2.26$ $p<.05$
Matched Controls—Inactive in Urban Renewal (N = 21)	5.52	49.97 ⎭
Party Candidates for high-power offices[c] (N = 10)	7.90 ⎫ $t = 2.33$	47.93
Party Candidates for low-power offices[c] (N = 13)	4.69 ⎭ $p<.05$	47.53
Matched Controls—Inactive in party politics (N = 17)	5.29	50.36

Note: All significance tests in this table are 2-tailed.

[a] Corrected for story-length (see Veroff, Atkinson, Feld, and Gurin, 1960).

[b] Corrected for story-length by regression equation of raw score on length; then standard-scored with overall mean of 50 and standard deviation of 10 for the entire sample of all groups combined.

[c] Using a measure of expectancy of power for the office; see Browning and Jacob (1964) for details.

Gabriel Borkman are full of power images. Adolf Hitler dreamed of rebuilding the city of Linz, Austria, began construction of the *Auto-bahn* system, and even up to the last days of World War II commissioned plans for the rebuilding of Berlin and other German cities (Speer, 1970).

To be sure, this is a *post hoc* interpretation of some unexpected results, but it does seem reasonable to conclude that urban renewal (or city planning generally), by establishing the physical and social structures of daily life and thus limiting many of the behavior alternatives available to large numbers of people, offers great possibilities for the satisfaction of the power motive. Therefore I suggest that whether any particular position in the ordinary political system attracts people with high n Power depends on several further questions: What can that political system do? What are the pressures that cause people to go into politics? What are the demands of the office? What are the opportunities? How clearly defined and specified is the job? What scope is there for altering the job and the system itself? What important opportunities for power exist outside of the traditional political system? What constraints (economic, ethnic, religious, sex) prevent people from gaining a position in the political system?

A study by Donley and Winter (1970) illustrates how levels of the power motive affect the way in which a person performs in office. Donley and Winter coded power and achievement motive imagery in the inaugural addresses of American presidents from 1905 through 1969. There was a wide variation in Power Imagery levels among the presidents, although of course there is no way to compare these presidents with other men. Donley and Winter found that the n Power score of each president made sense, in that it was related to the ways in which the president performed in office and used opportunities to expand his power.

OCCUPATIONS AND CAREERS

Turning to job or career as a source of power, a wealth of important data can be used to determine which occupations attract men who are high in n Power. First, the Wesleyan students were asked to specify the career or careers that they intended to have after college. In most cases, the responses could be classified into about ten categories, with a few answers vague or uncodable. The precise coding definitions that were employed are given in Appendix III. Table 4.3 presents the results of the study with Wesleyan students. For each occupational category, the mean n Power score of those who selected it as their first choice is tested against the overall mean score of 50.00 for the entire sample. Students high in n Power report that they would like to be teachers, psychologists, and clergymen. There is also a tendency for them to choose business, although usually the particular business role (manager, technical, finance, etc.) could not be determined from the answers given. It is interesting to note that students high in n Power are not especially drawn to law, medicine, or government and politics.

TABLE 4.3 n POWER AND OCCUPATIONAL PLANS OF WESLEYAN STUDENTS

Occupational Category	Mean n Power	t-test for difference from overall mean of 50.00
Teaching (N = 48)	53.69	2.80, p<.01
Psychology (N = 27)	54.00	2.31, p<.05
Clergy (N = 4)	55.00	1.70, p<.20
(Psychology and Clergy)	54.13	2.73, p<.02
Business (N = 22)	53.10	1.32, p<.20
Diplomacy, international government (N = 5)	53.80	—
Government and Politics (N = 13)	44.46	2.71, p<.02
Medicine (N = 14)	46.40	—
Law (N = 27)	49.00	—
Creative Arts, Writing, etc. (N = 12)	51.00	—
Architect, Urban Affairs, etc. (N = 8)	47.00	—

Note: Two hundred thirty-nine students answered questions about their occupational and career plans. In all cases, their first choice or first-mentioned career was coded according to the categories described in Appendix III. One hundred eighty could be classified, and are included here; the others were either of low frequency or were too vague to be coded.

All t-tests in this table are 2-tailed, for rejecting the null hypothesis of a random relationship to n Power (i.e., a mean score of 50.00 for the category).

This first analysis raises several problems, however. For one thing, the students were asked about plans or preferences, with little reference to reality factors such as ability. Many students were vague or uncertain, and probably several will change their plans. Even the meaning of the choices of psychologist and teacher is not clear. Are these two professions likely to be high in n Power? Or perhaps high n Power students are simply more likely to identify with (or to please) the person who asks them to fill out questionnaires—and in this case, that person was a psychology professor. It is clear that longitudinal data on subsequent career choice together with prior motive scores are needed to resolve such questions. Longitudinal data will also help to answer the question raised in Chapter 3 in connection with the National Sample data: does power motivation "precede" power positions and power behaviors, or is it mainly developed as an appropriate role response to them? (See Klinger and McNelly, 1969; Veroff and Veroff, 1972).

Fortunately, a technique devised by McClelland (1965) could be applied to data from the Harvard Student Study in order to study longitudinal career development. In 1969, the Harvard Class of 1964 issued a "Five Year Report" with biographical and career information on the members of the class, five years after most of them had finished college. This report contained data on 236 students who had been tested by the Harvard Student Study as freshmen in the autumn of 1960. At the time of the report, most students had come to some definite career choice, although in many cases they were still finishing the appropriate preparation, such as medical school, graduate school, or other training. Table 4.4 presents the average n Power scores from the 1960 TATs for each of the major occupational categories used in Table 4.3 to describe the plans of Wesleyan students. The hypotheses derived from the Wesleyan data are all confirmed with the longitudinal Harvard data. Teachers and business managers are very significantly higher than average in n Power, and psychologists and clergymen are higher than average, although the significance level is not as great.

These findings are also confirmed with longitudinal data from a study of 58 English undergraduates at the University of Oxford. They took TATs in the spring of 1961, and in 1970 were asked to write a brief paragraph describing their career history and present job. Thirty-eight responded (66%), and it was relatively easy to code their careers with the same categories used in the Wesleyan and Harvard studies. The results, presented in Table 4.5, again confirm the earlier finding that teachers, business managers, and clergymen are higher in *n* Power than those in other careers. (There were no psychologists in the English sample.)

The relationship between *n* Power and career choice have thus been confirmed with several different kinds of data, including longitudinal and cross-national information. *N* Power leads to teaching, psychology, and business management; it does not particularly lead to law, medicine, or politics and the civil service. The reader may be surprised to find business managers high in *n* Power, since McClelland (1961) demonstrated that businessmen tended to be high in *n* Achievement; although of course they could be high in both motives.

TABLE 4.4 *n* POWER AND SUBSEQUENT OCCUPATIONS OF HARVARD STUDENTS

Occupational Category[a]	Mean *n* Power	*t*-test for difference from All Others[b]
Teaching (N = 27)	4.85	2.57, p<.005
Psychology and Clergy (N = 17)	4.18	1.38, p<.10
Business Management and Journalism (N = 15)	6.60	3.35, p<.0005
Law (N = 29)	3.59	
Medicine (N = 20)	3.35	
Miscellaneous (N = 65)	3.06	
"All Others" (the three categories above combined, N = 114)	3.25	
No career information given (N = 53)	4.12	
Did not reply (N = 10)	3.92	
Mean Score of Total Sample (N = 246)	3.93	

a See Appendix III for coding definitions.

b Since the hypotheses, derived from Table 4.3, were that teachers, clergy, psychologists, and business managers and journalists would be relatively higher in *n* Power, each of these groups is tested separately against the mean of all subjects not in these categories, excluding those who did not give career information, did not reply, or had died. All tests of significance are therefore 1-tailed.

Actually, McClelland pinpointed entrepreneurs or innovators as being high in n Achievement and was careful to distinguish such entrepreneurs from the more general categories of "businessman" or "manager." (See McClelland, 1965, for the specific coding definitions used.) Compared to entrepreneurs, managers probably concern themselves less with innovation or improvement and more with coordination and overall control. In Barnard's terms, effectiveness or the attainment of external objectives is the entrepreneurial function, while efficiency or the maintenance of the system itself through ensuring satisfaction of appropriate needs is the managerial function (Barnard, 1938; also Parsons, 1951 and other writings). Furthermore, Kock (1965) found that both n Achievement and Veroff n Power were related to managerial success in a sample of executives from knit-wear factories in Finland. Lennerlöf (1967) reported that prior Veroff n Power scores correlated highly with subsequent rated success in supervisory positions in a small sample of Swedish management trainees. Perhaps the most important reason for the association of n Power with becoming a higher manager or executive can be found in the changing nature of the American business and industrial system. Galbraith (1967) argues that advances in technology and increases in the scale of markets, planning, and therefore enterprises themselves have led to the emergence of the giant corporation. Within these corporations, decision-making and control have passed from

TABLE 4.5 n POWER AND SUBSEQUENT OCCUPATIONS OF OXFORD STUDENTS

Occupational Category[a]	Mean n Power	t-test for difference from All Others[b]
Teaching and Clergy (N = 15)	10.13	2.53, p<.01
Business Managers and Journalists (N = 7)	13.86	4.27, p<.0005
All Others (N = 16)	5.44	

[a] See Appendix III for coding definitions.

[b] Since the hypothesis was that teachers, clergy, business managers, and journalists would score relatively higher in n Power, each of these categories is tested separately against the mean for all other subjects not including the hypothesized groups. All tests of significance are 1-tailed.

those who owned capital to a new group which Galbraith calls the "technostructure." The technostructure is concerned not so much to maximize return on capital, but rather to maximize the power (of the firm and of themselves) to shape society by means of the growth and control of resources of the technostructure (chaps. 10–13). With a rather uncharacteristic euphemism, Galbraith calls this new concern or motive "adaptation," but it is clear that he means power: the society, and not the individuals of the technostructure, is to be "adapted." This general concern with power is further reflected in the day-to-day activities of the technostructure: coordinating and controlling people, controlling information, and persuading the market and the public (chap. 6). Thus when we consider the changing nature of the industrial system, the finding that n Power is associated with becoming a manager or executive seems quite reasonable.

The results for teachers seem rather straightforward. Teachers have power and influence, although the ideology of the teaching profession usually stresses that this influence should be tempered with concerns for affiliation and for the autonomy of the student, so that the result of the teaching process is an independent student who educates himself in those things that he wishes to know. Clergymen used to be in a position of great influence, although nowadays the scope of this influence depends much more upon how important religion is to their clients.

Psychologists and those in related professions (psychiatry, social work) also exercise power. Many writers have described the process of therapy as essentially a power relationship (Frank, 1961; Haley, 1963; Guggenbühl-Craig, 1971). Szasz (1970) argues that the intervention procedures of "institutional psychiatry," though labelled "help" by the profession, are in fact expressions both of personal cravings for power and of societal control of so-called deviants. Psychological research also involves power. It is supposed to lead to "understanding, prediction, and control" of behavior. Ideally—and usually—it treats the "subject" as an "object" or "stimulus-response machine," for whom all of the relevant stimuli and conditions are under experimental control (Schultz, 1969). Very often the experimenter uses deception; that is, he makes a conscious and explicit attempt to impose his own misleading definition of the situation on his subjects. The power aspects of psychological research are quite apparent in some recent popular research trends. For example, the token economy is a system in which the experimenter tries to shape the behavior of (institutionalized) "subjects" by securing and using complete control of all significant reinforcing events though the use of tokens as intermediate reinforcers (Ayllon and Azrin, 1968). Milgram's studies of obedience (1963, 1965) are explicit attempts to study power and are also vivid examples of power. Even the criticisms of Milgram emphasize the importance of power in psychological research. Orne and Holland (1968) suggest that Milgram's results can be attributed to the power inherent in the social roles and demand characteristics of the laboratory situation, rather than to any extraordinary propensities for "obedience" in people. Baumrind (1964) criticizes the research on the grounds that it may jeopardize the "proper" authority and power of psychologists.

It is not surprising therefore that psychologists tend to have high n Power scores. Nevertheless, many psychologists do not feel comfortable with the notion that they have and use power, perhaps because of the strong negative connotations that the word itself has for both them and many others. Therefore these psychologists stress the beneficial results of their work. Many try to minimize power, or to reject it completely, as in so-called nondirective therapy or "leaderless" groups. Perhaps these movements are only attempts to suppress power concerns, or perhaps the profession is changing. In any case, power still seems to be very salient among psychologists, whether they like it or whether they are trying to avoid it. May (1967) concludes that "There is a selective factor at work in that [psychology] tends to attract the type of individual who denies and represses his power needs. These repressed power needs then have room to come out in his proclivities for controlling other people in therapy or in his identification with the power of his laboratory techniques . . . to control others" (pp. 205–206).[2]

Taken together, all of the careers associated with n Power involve considerable scope for influence and power, although in most cases this power has been rationalized in theory and practice as "good" or "helpful" power (see Guggenbühl-Craig, 1971). In teaching, psychology, and business management a person has considerable scope to define his role, select his actions, and advise, help, control, and evaluate the behavior of his clients or subordinates. Such characteristics seem to explain why high n Power people are drawn to such positions. While law and politics may be more explicitly concerned with power and power structures, in many cases the actual lawyer

[2] Among the Wesleyan students, those saying that they wanted to be psychologists or psychiatrists were especially high in Fear of Power, which supports both the "repression" interpretation and the rejection of power by many psychologists. See the discussion of Fear of Power in the next chapter.

or politician functions in a very routine and circumscribed role. He applies rules and procedures to specific cases, often at the request of a superior. Thus while he is involved with power, he has little scope for the expression of his own personal power needs. If a lawyer or politician begins by having a high power motive, I would predict that over time he will either change his job, or else redefine his role and functions toward teaching, therapy, or business management. The looseness of the structure (or the extent to which the situation permits restructuring along the lines of a person's own wishes) and the chance to have direct impact on others seem to be the things about a career that makes it attractive to high n Power people. Only sometimes can these be found in politics (see Greenstein, 1969, pp. 33–62).

INTERPERSONAL STYLE AS THE BASIS OF FORMAL SOCIAL POWER

Having established the relation of n Power to positions of formal power and careers of power, we now turn to the underpinning or substructure of such positions. What are the actions and strategies that high n Power people use? What interpersonal behaviors lead to positions of formal power?

Since Machiavelli, much has been written on this topic, and almost everybody has his own set of rules for the "power game" (Felker, 1969). Successful power tactics depend on a person's position and resources. Martin and Sims (1956) studied the lives of successful executives and worked out a perceptive list of tactics for exercising power: using alliances skillfully, maintaining maneuverability (often by delaying action), controlling communication, and dramatizing one's self. Haley's imaginative and provocative essay on "The power tactics of Jesus Christ" (1969) begins with the man who was alone and who had nothing—no position, no resources, and no followers. Haley defines power simply as being able "to determine what is going to happen" (p. 36), and discusses the career of Jesus in such terms. That career was the incredible success of a "messianic revolutionist" whose organization "took over the Roman Empire [and] . . . held absolute power over the populace of the western world for many hundreds of years and was only divested of that power in a violent struggle" (p. 19). Haley analyzes two essential tactics of power that Jesus developed, and I shall review them briefly as categories for organizing the findings from American college students with high n Power:

(1) *Becoming known.* The would-be leader must bring himself to the attention of people, a task that is most readily accomplished by using existing traditions (e.g., the role of prophet, the myth of a Messiah). The leader must then speak for change, while defining his words as orthodoxy or conformity to the law. He must attack the leaders of the establishment, preferably by using their own ideological framework (pp. 22–28).

(2) *Building an organization.* The leader with no resources must start his organization among the poor, the forgotten unknowns who have little to lose. Thus his movement at all times is independent of the established power structure (pp. 28–36).

Haley's first requisite for getting power is sheer visibility—one must become known to others. Becoming visible involves at least two separate stages: first, one must share time and space with other people; second, one must create some sort of impact, which serves to define the situation and the terms of subsequent discussion. Among Wesleyan students, n Power was significantly, although modestly, correlated with the reported number of hours per week spent in informal discussions or "bull sessions" ($r = .13$, $N = 113$, $p < .05$). Participating in bull sessions is, of course, the result of many other factors; but it does seem to be a crude index of the amount of time a student spends with other students. Moreover, those 50 Wesleyan students who had written letters to the college newspaper during their college career had a mean n Power of 52.54, which was significantly higher than the mean of 49.75 for the 230 who had not written letters ($t = 1.76$, $p < .04$ 1-tailed). There seems to be a tendency for students high in n Power to be more "visible" and to participate more in the discussion and definition of significant issues.

Haley's second tactic for getting power is building an organization —making and keeping alliances with other persons and groups. This involves looking for those who will be most receptive to one's influence and ensuring that smooth relationships will be maintained within this group, the ultimate "power base." Haley suggests starting with the poor and the forgotten. Freud (1921) suggested that groups are held together by ties of affection and regard toward the leader and mutual ties of affection among the members. People who themselves lack affection and regard should more easily be led to feel affection toward a leader, and thus become his secure power base.

In an attempt to study the kinds of friendships that high n Power students develop, we asked 23 Wesleyan students in an advanced psychology course the following question:[3]

What are the names of the four people whom you consider to be your closest friends at Wesleyan? Do *not* include people in this course. (Do not feel obligated to list four; you may list more or less than four.)

From the names listed, one master list was compiled and submitted to all members of the class, with instructions to indicate how well they knew each person on the list. The alternatives were:

I don't know this student at all.   (scored 0)

I know the name but don't know this person well.   (scored 1)

I know this person (have talked with him, etc.).   (scored 2)

For every name listed by any student as a personal friend, we first computed a recognition score, which was the total number of points given for that name by the whole class, according to the above scale. We then determined how well known a person's friends were by taking the average recognition score for the friends that he had listed. There was a highly significant *negative* correlation between n Power and the average recognition score of listed friends ($r = -.57$, $p<.01$) and also between n Power and the highest recognition score of any single friend listed ($r = -.50$, $p<.05$). Thus people high in n Power tend to pick as close friends those students who are less well known and relatively unrecognized by other students. To a power-motivated person, such friends are attractive because they are presumably not a threat, since they do not compete for power and prestige. Being less well known, such friends are also more disposed to form strong ties of friendship, regard, and support for the power-motivated "leader." In this respect, they are like the poor and the disinherited in Haley's terms—they have relatively less to lose. Thus they constitute the loyal nucleus of an alliance.

Additional evidence from a study by Jones (1969) supports this conclusion. (The complete study is discussed below.) Forty-three Wesleyan freshmen volunteered to write a TAT and later participate in experimental small discussion groups. It was necessary to assign subjects so that members of each group were not previously acquainted. Therefore when everyone had gathered for the first session and had completed the TAT, all subjects were asked to write down

[3] I am indebted to Robert Feldman for designing and executing this study.

the names of all persons in the room with whom they were acquainted. N Power was uncorrelated with the number of times a person himself was chosen ($r = -.06$), but was negatively correlated with the average number of times that the person's acquaintances were chosen—i.e., their recognition by peers ($r = -.23$, $p \sim .11$). The possibility that these two consistent results are an artifact of low recognition scores for high n Power people can be ruled out by the approximate zero correlation between n Power and own recognition score in the Jones study.

Evidence from India also supports the conclusion that people high in n Power are adept at using social situations to expand their network of "contacts" or "allies." Fifty-six Indian businessmen from two towns who had participated in achievement motivation development courses at a government-sponsored institute were asked to list the names of those other participants whom they had known before the course, and then the names of those whom they had come to know after the course (McClelland and Winter, 1969). As might be expected, the number of times that a person was chosen before the course was related to his n Affiliation ($r = .29$, $p<.05$). However, the gain in number of times chosen from before to after the course was significantly related to n Power ($r = .42$, $p<.01$). In other words, Indian businessmen high in n Power apparently used the courses as an opportunity to expand their friendships and alliances within their towns, and to make contacts which were in themselves rewarding and which might be useful in subsequent business affairs and negotiations.

How do people high in n Power hold their alliances together? Responses by Wesleyan students to several questions from the College Student Questionnaire (Educational Testing Service, 1965) provide some clues. The questions and the analysis of replies are given in Table 4.6. While high n Power students say that they like to compete with other people (item 145), they tend to have friends who are more similar in taste (item 160), and they are concerned to maintain smooth relationships and avoid disruption among those around them (items 162, 164). It appears as though they are willing to conform to the norms and expectations of at least their close associates, although this may be because they themselves have shaped these norms. Such sensitivity or conformity has the obvious function of maintaining their esteem and power in the eyes of the group, and is a skill essential to having power and leadership, as situational theorists of power point out (See Chapter 1; Gibb, 1969; and Hollander, 1964).

If people with high n Power are concerned to maintain relation-

TABLE 4.6 n POWER AND RESPONSES TO THE COLLEGE STUDENT
QUESTIONNAIRE

Item # and Question	Cross-tabulation of Response		

145. Generally speaking, how
do you feel about com-
peting with other people,
especially when the
stakes are high?

		Dislike Neutral	Like
	High	36	37
n Power	Medium	52	27
	Low	43	26

$\chi^2 = 4.67$, p<.10

160. With regard to the arts,
would you say that the
preference and taste of
your acquaintances are
similar to your own
tastes?

		Different	Similar
	High	27	45
n Power	Medium	24	55
	Low	34	34

$\chi^2 = 6.00$, p<.05

162. How often do you maintain a point of view
despite other students
losing patience with you?

		Rarely, occassionally	Often
	High	59	59
n Power	Low	38	64

$\chi^2 = 3.61$, p<.08

164. Do you generally like to
do things in your own
way and without regard
for what other students
around you may think?

		No, not usually	Yes
	High	69	50
n Power	Low	43	60

$\chi^2 = 5.19$, p<.03

ships with their close associates, they also say that they like to compete with others. Probably, then, they direct their competitive drives outward from the close inner group of associates, and upward at higher-status "targets." Such externalization of hostility can further unify the alliance or power base, as Freud (1921) and Haley (1969) point out.

What is the evidence that n Power leads to power competition or hostility toward higher-status persons? One nonreactive finding involved an hour examination in an introductory psychology course. Students were given a choice of questions. The first was a rather

conventional question about ego psychology. The second presented
the now famous passage from the October, 1969, speech of the
American Vice-President, in which he attacked critics of Administration military policy as "an effete corps of impudent snobs." Students were asked to discuss psychoanalytic defense mechanisms
which might account for the content of this quotation. Answering the
second question is an opportunity to "explain" and thereby have power
over an important (and perhaps resented) political figure. As predicted, those 11 students who chose the second question were higher
in n Power than the rest of the class (mean $= 55.00$, $t = 1.88$ for
difference from overall mean of 50.00, p<.05 1-tailed).

Further evidence for the association between n Power and verbal
power or hostility toward higher-status persons comes from a pilot
study by Alan Hartley that was subsequently replicated several times.
Hartley asked the following question:

If you could say one sentence—any sentence—to *anyone*, anywhere
in the world, in person and without fear of reprisal, what would you
say, and to whom?

I would say: "_____."

To: _____

The sentence was first coded for affective tone (positive, neutral, or
mildly negative vs. strongly negative). Strongly negative affect was
quite easy to code, since it usually involved profanity or obscenity.
Then the sentence was coded for the status of the addressee (high
vs. low). High status meant any addressee who would be generally
known to the public at large, or at least to a university community. As
a dividing line, the president of the university was considered to be
high status, but individual instructors or students were not. The
overall results of the study and replications are presented in Table
4.7. They indicate that high Hope of Power is associated with wanting
to say something strongly negative or hostile to someone of high
status.

Taking all of these results together, it appears that n Power is
related to having smooth relationships with those who make up one's
inner circle or power base, but having a competitive, hostile stance
toward those of higher status or power who are outside of the immediate group. This attitude is especially manifested in a verbal style
that is distinctive and, to followers, surely impressive. Thus n Power

seems to facilitate the fulfillment of both functions of a leader: achieving solidarity within the group, and directing the group toward an external goal, through the sharp differentiation of those to whom the leader is friendly and conforming and those to whom he is competitive and challenging. In Haley's terms, high n Power people attack established leaders of high status and fulfill people of low recognition and status. In psychoanalytic terms, this combination of complementary actions is very similar to narcissism, and Freud's analysis of the concept sounds like the present formulation (1914, p. 46):

It seems very evident that one person's narcissism has a great attraction for those others who have renounced part of their own. . . . In literature, indeed, even the great criminal and the humorist compel our interest by the narcissistic self-importance with which they manage to keep at arm's length everything which would diminish the importance of their ego.

TABLE 4.7 n POWER AND VERBAL HOSTILITY

Characteristic of the "one sentence said to anyone in the world."	Mean Hope of Power Score	
I. *Affect*		
Those giving a sentence with strong negative affect (N = 25)	54.20	t = 2.05 p<.025
Those giving a sentence with mild negative, or positive affect (N = 65)	49.71	
II. *Status of Addressee*[a]		
High status (N = 44)	52.32	t = 1.35 p = n.s.
Low status (N = 45)	49.62	
III. *Combination*[a]		
Strong negative affect to a high status addressee (N = 19)	55.58	t = 2.41 p<.002
All others (N = 70)	49.64	

Note: All tests of significance in this table are 1-tailed.
[a] One response uncodable.

EXPERIMENTAL SMALL GROUPS

We have seen that n Power is associated with a distinctive interpersonal style: visibility, the capacity to form alliances, and a
competitive approach toward outside powers. Such a combination
should lead to being influential in small groups; over time, this influence should lead to positions of formal social power. The small
group is thus one arena for developing power: a person can learn
awareness of the dynamics of interaction, he can learn and practice
power strategies and techniques of influence, and he can actually
achieve power satisfactions.

Wesleyan University regularly offers a small group course entitled "Analysis of Interpersonal Behavior," a self-analytic or T-Group
modelled after those described by Mann, Gibbard, and Hartman
(1967) and Bales (1970). The course is described in the college
catalogue as follows:

The aim of this course is to improve the student's ability to observe,
analyze, and understand behavior in everyday interpersonal situations.
The course will be conducted as a self-analytic group; problems for analysis will be drawn from events in the group itself. In a series of papers,
students will discuss the group experience in terms of concepts from the
sociological and psychological sources on the reading list.

In addition, during 1968–69 and 1969–70 a series of "Personal
Growth Encounter Groups," based on tape-recorded materials and
procedures developed by Berzon and Reisel,[4] was offered to Wesleyan
students. Both kinds of groups clearly gives experience and practice
in group-interaction skills, among which one is surely power. Those
57 students from the total sample who took the T-Group course or
who signed up for the tape-recorded group series were higher in
n Power than the overall average (mean = 52.26, t = 1.79 for difference from 50.00, p<.10 2-tailed). Moreover, the T-Group course was
twice run by student leaders; as expected, these four students were
themselves higher in n Power than the Wesleyan average (mean =
57.25, t = 2.18 for differences from 50.00, p<.08 1-tailed). Thus it
seems clear that persons high in n Power are drawn to participate in
and lead small groups. They apparently perceive that these groups

[4] *Encountertapes for Personal Growth Groups.* Developed by Betty Berzon and
Jerome Reisel at the Western Behavioral Sciences Institute. Distributed by the
Human Development Institute, Inc., Atlanta, Georgia.

offer experience and training in the dynamics of influence, and also direct power satisfactions.

How do they act in a small group? Jones (1969) studied several small *ad hoc* discussion groups composed of Wesleyan University freshmen. Forty-three subjects who had volunteered for the study first took a TAT. Jones then asked them to participate in a four or five-man discussion group scheduled on one of several later evenings. He arranged the groups so that all members were previously unacquainted. Each group was given approximately thirty minutes to discuss a Stoner-type problem that involved weighing risks and coming to a group decision (Brown, 1965, chap. 13). Chairs were arranged around a table (three on one side, two on the other) to insure that there was no "head of the table" effect, and as little "end seat" or "central" position effect as was possible in a five-person group, because all of these locations have been found to relate to influence in small groups (Leavitt, 1951; Sommer, 1967). Groups were told that the discussion would be tape-recorded and observed through a one-way mirror. At the conclusion of a half-hour discussion, each subject was asked to fill out a brief sociometric questionnaire indicating which members of the group were most influential, who contributed the best ideas, who guided the discussion best, who was most liked, and so on (adapted from Bass, 1949). Subjects were then paid $2.50 for their participation. Several days later, all subjects were asked to answer a few questions about their overall reaction to the discussion. The discussion problem, instructions, post-discussion questionnaire, and the final questions are all reproduced in Appendix IV.

Actually the three-and-two seating arrangement does not completely equate each location for influence potential. Howells and Becker (1962) found that in such an arrangement, persons on the "two" side of the table tend to be more influential. Jones found that those who sat on the "two" side of the table were in fact slightly higher in *n* Power (corrected $\chi^2 = 3.04$, p~.08, considering the 5-man groups only). Whether such persons were aware of the higher influence potential of such seats, at any rate they chose them. Although power may depend on positions, location, and other situational variables (see Chapter 1), nevertheless high *n* Power people tend to seek these positions; that is, they use such situational effects in order to secure power.

Jones's principal results are presented in Table 4.8. In the far left column appear the raw correlations between *n* Power and votes received on the various sociometric questions answered immediately after the discussion. The only significant correlation is that between

n Power and votes received for being "most influential," and even this correlation is rather modest. Obviously a great many factors besides motivation act to determine influence in small groups. For example, some subjects were not very interested in the discussion; they participated only for the money or out of boredom. For them, the incentive-value of power in such a situation (or the expectancy of achieveing "real" power) was low. According to the Atkinson model, a motive will relate to action only when expectancy and incentive are high. N Power should not lead to influence in all discussions, but only in those where people expect that meaningful power can be obtained—those situations about which the person really cares. Therefore, in order to predict rated influence, one must know the meaning of the situation (or expectancies and incentives) in addition to the motive.

The right side of Table 4.8 incorporates two corrections designed to take account of these factors. First, only those subjects who said that they were very "involved" are included (+4 or +5 on the post-experiment question: "How involved did you feel in this discussion?" See Appendix IV). This question is taken to be a rough measure of expectancy and/or incentive in the sense of the Atkinson model. It is unrelated to n Power ($r = -.19$), and seems to be valid in the sense that across the nine groups, the rank-order correlation between the number of "very involved" subjects and the length of the discussion was $+.85$ ($p<.01$). Thus the right side of the table considers only those subjects for whom expectancy and/or incentive is high. As a second correction, n Power was standard-scored among the "very involved" subjects in each group. This procedure removes the effect of chance differences in n Power levels in the different groups, differences which would reduce valid correlations because the number of votes cast per group is roughly the same, whereas motive score distributions varied.

With these two corrections, the correlation between n Power and "most influential" rises somewhat, and the correlations between n Power and other power-related actions and ratings also increase. Among those who were "very involved," n Power correlates significantly with encouraging others and acts initiated. Finally, categories 1 (most influential), 2 (defined problem), and 5 (encouraged others) can be taken as a combination of the most important aspects of power. Any person who gets half or more of his group's votes on at least two of these three categories can be designated as a "clear leader." Such clear leaders turn out to be significantly higher in n Power than the rest of the "very involved" subjects, as shown at the bottom of Table 4.8.

TABLE 4.8 *n* POWER AND INTERACTION IN SMALL DISCUSSION GROUPS

Correlations with raw *n* Power score for total sample (N = 43)	Variable from the Sociometric Questionnaire[a]	Correlations with *n* Power score as corrected[b] for those "involved"[c] (N = 32)
.31, p<.05	1. Whom do you think most influenced the other participants?	.38, p<.05
.12	2. Who most clearly defined the problems?	.27
.06	3. Who offered the best solutions to the problems?	.01
−.04	4. Whom do you think worked the hardest to get the job done and come to a good conclusion?	−.02
.20	5. Who most encouraged the others to participate?	.33, p~.05
−.08	6. Whom do you like best?	.05
.17	7. Whom do you think tried to keep the group running smoothly, and encouraged cooperation?	.14
.09	8. Overall, who was the "leader" in this group?	.22
.19	Percent of own group's total acts initiated	.36, p<.05
	Total number of votes, categories 1, 2, 5	.42, p<.05

Group (among those "involved"[c])	Mean *n* Power Score[b]
Clear Leaders[d] (N = 10)	54.50
Others (N = 22)	48.09
Difference	6.41
	t = 1.69
	p = .05 1-tailed

While the Jones study found relationships between n Power and informal social influence in small groups, these relationships are not very strong, and they depend on the use of independent moderator variables, such as involvement, which presumably "engage" the power motive. Jones also studied members of one section of the self-analytic group course described above. He found some positive correlations between n Power and sociometric choices for being influential, as well as between n Power and some of the dimensions of group performance suggested by Bales (1970), but these correlations were quite different for later sections of the course. Each group appears to develop its own distinctive norms, goals, roles, and structure; and it is reasonable to suppose that such group "climates" will differ in the extent to which they engage and encourage the power motive. (See Litwin and Stringer, 1968, for an excellent discussion of motive and climate.) In many cases, the situation may be so strong as to "override" individual motive differences (Heckhausen, 1968).

Our discussion of the Jones study illustrates many of the reasons why research relating personality to performance in experimental small groups has often led to disappointing correlations (Mann, 1959; Gibb, 1969). Yet these correlations can be substantially increased when researchers take the trouble to define and measure various kinds of moderator variables, as shown by Couch (1962), Atkinson and Feather (1966), Fishman (1966), and the Jones study.

Even though the corrected correlations are modest, the Jones findings are an important link in the chain of n Power relationships, because they tend to confirm predictions about likely social influence that were made on the basis of the findings about visibility, friendships, and verbal style; and they support the further link to the findings that high n Power people tend to occupy positions of formal social power.

Table 4.8 (*Cont.*)

a Number of votes received divided by number of votes cast, both excluding own votes. This corrects for varying sizes of groups (4 or 5) and the fact that some persons voted for more than one person in some categories.

b Standard-scored, among the "involved" members (see footnote c below), separately for each discussion group.

c Score of +4 or +5 on the post-experiment question "How involved did you feel in the discussion?" (see Appendix IV).

d Those who received more than half of their group's votes for at least two of the three categories 1, 2, and 5.

SUCCESSFUL USE OF POWER

While high n Power people may act in ways so that they attain power, we do not know whether they will necessarily be effective users of power. They may not be successful in all power situations. High power motivation may distract their attention and distort their perception; it may also interfere with the behaviors appropriate to the situation. For example, many roles that involve formal social power require helping or giving assistance, rather than just control. Teaching and therapy are obvious examples, but leadership in many settings requires that the leader help others to attain both individual and group goals (Gibb, 1969).

Kolb and Boyatsis (1970) studied helping relationships in a series of T-Groups, where effective help was largely dependent on information exchange, that is, giving useful interpersonal "feedback" to other members of the group. They studied eight groups, each made up of about 15 M.A. students in Industrial Management. The task of the groups was to help members achieve various personal change goals. Kolb and Boyatsis distinguished three different kinds of group members on the basis of peer nominations: effective helpers, those seen by others as giving significant and important help; ineffective helpers, seen as giving help which was not important; and nonhelpers, who did not attempt to help. They found that the ineffective helpers scored higher in n Power and lower in n Affiliation than either the effective helpers or the nonhelpers. (Using Veroff n Power, McClelland, 1961, pp. 167–170, found that this same pattern often coincided with totalitarian forms of government in modern nation-states.) In other words, excessive power motivation, especially without concerns for affiliation, may lead people to become too highly organized, superior, outspoken, and impatient—that is, dictatorial. In the long run, persons with very high n Power may thus create the seeds of their own destruction or loss of power, because their followers see them as not effective in promoting their own goals. The leaders may then be driven to an ever-increasing cycle of intensified attempts to control, and increasing disaffection of their followers.

PRESTIGE AND REPUTATION AS
POTENTIAL POWER

Actual power may be thought of as direct force or energy; but most
often power exists as a potential force that is only rarely used. Consider the dominance hierarchies that are commonly observed in
many different animal species. Brown (1965) points out that only
rarely does each animal in a group have to fight with every other
animal in order to arrive at a stable, peaceful hierarchy. First, many
characteristics or signs that are ordinarily associated with strength
and therefore success in fighting—size, elaborate feathers, plumes,
crests, manes, ferocious displays of rage—are sufficient to settle a
contest for dominance without actual combat. Brown concludes:
"The victor is ordinarily the animal who puts on the more intimidating
show" (p. 20). Second, the mechanisms of observational learning
and memory act to make the emergence of a hierarchy more efficient.
Animal C can observe that animal A has defeated B; and, remembering
that B has previously defeated itself, is therefore likely to give deference to A without a fight. Thus cognitive processes such as symbolic
representation and memory are the basis of potential power, which is
a convenient and efficient substitute for direct force.

  If power is maintained by such cognitive processes, then perhaps
power can be created by artificially altering and manipulating symbols
and memory. If power is maintained by symbols in the minds of
organisms, then power can be "faked" by the use of symbols and the
changing of memories. Several experiments with animals have demonstrated such effects. Miller, Murphy, and Mirsky (1955) took a
monkey low in the dominance hieararchy and presented it as the
conditioned stimulus for electric shock to several other monkeys who
were originally higher in dominance. The shock could be terminated
by pressing a bar, which also ended the conditioned stimulus of the first
monkey. Subsequent dominance tests after conditioning established
that the originally low-status monkey had risen several steps in the
hierarchy. The rest of the order was essentially unchanged, suggesting the occurrence of altered perceptions of the previously low-status
monkey who was the conditioned stimulus (i.e., a specific "fear"),
rather than any absolute reductions of dominance on the part of the
monkeys who received shock (i.e., general "anxiety"). Murphy and
Miller (1956) were able to achieve dominance reversal within individual pairs of monkeys by the same procedures.

  However, Maroney, Warren, and Sinha (1959) tried to alter a

dominance hierarchy by arranging "success" experiences for low-status monkeys and "failure" experiences for high-status monkeys, using as conditioned stimuli other animals not from the hierarchy. These experiences did not alter the dominance hierarchy. Thus it appears that the experiences of a particular animal are not as important in determining dominance position or potential power as the experiences or perceptions that other animals have had vis-à-vis that animal. In this connection it is important to refer to Guhl's (1964) observation that even experimentally-tranquillized, ill, or injured birds "may maintain their status provided that factors for recognition (e.g. combs) do not change abruptly" (p. 279). In other words, evidence from animal research suggests that it is not always the condition or strength of the animal as such, but rather the condition of its symbolic equipment and its reputation (i.e., other animals' experiences with it) that make up its potential power.

Man's immense symbolic ability and memory capacity set him apart from the animals; in complex human societies the symbolic forms of potential power are so elaborated that under most conditions they have almost completely replaced direct physical force. Symbolic, potential power is usually called "prestige" or "reputation." Hobbes called attention to the power of prestige (1651, p. 70):

> Reputation of power is power; because it draweth with it the adherence of those that need protection . . . also, what quality soever maketh a man beloved, or feared of many; or the reputation of such a quality, is Power; because it is a means to have the assistance, and service of many.

In his classic analysis of the concept, Nicolson (1938) suggested that prestige was a capacity to evoke extraordinary and powerful reactions with overtones of dazzlement and magic—in short, to put on an intimidating show. Max Weber suggested that "The sentiment of prestige is able to strengthen the ardent belief in the actual existence of one's own might, for this belief is important for positive self-assurance in case of conflict" (1948, p. 161). Thus prestige functions as power.

Since man's power is more fully symbolic, we expect that man can more easily create or fake power by the manipulation of symbols and memory. Symbols and memory both involve information; he who controls the creation and transmission of information therefore controls and has power (see Martin and Sims, 1956). Secrecy and secret "expert knowledge" are essential to the power of those who work in a complex, bureaucratic structure (Weber, 1948, pp. 232–235; Gamson, 1968, p. 126). As we have seen, journalists, who develop and disseminate information, tend to be high in n Power. But if knowledge is power, knowledge does not have to be "true" to be powerful (at least in the short run), if one has sufficient monopoly on the sources of information. Over time, continuous suppression and distortion of information in order to maintain power can be disasterous, if a person actually begins to believe his distortions; but this is a problem for the history or maintenance of power, and not for the attaining of it.

How is n Power related to prestige, reputation, and the control of information? It is very difficult to conduct experiments assessing how people control and distort information about their power and reputation, for if subjects are successful, then the experimenter has no way of checking their responses accurately! However, there is some evidence that n Power may be related to the distortion of information about the self. One hundred eleven Wesleyan upperclassmen were asked to indicate the lowest final course grade that they had received in college, by circling the appropriate letter symbol. Responses were then checked against their academic transcripts. Twenty-two students distorted; that is, they indicated a grade that was either higher or lower than the actual lowest final grade that they had received up to that time. These 22 students were not significantly different from the other 89 in n Power; but among those who distorted, n Power was significantly correlated with the amount of upward distortion ($rho =$ .39, p<.05). In other words, high n Power students tend to remember or to report their academic performance as better than it really was. This does suggest that n Power is related to controlling information, but further research is needed to make a convincing proof.

Early studies with preliminary versions of the revised measure of n Power showed that it was correlated with owning "prestige possessions" (cars, wine glasses, college banners, etc.) among Harvard College students (Winter, 1972), and among middle-class adults (Winter, 1968), although n Power was not related to the amount of spending money that the students had. This finding was replicated in a more thorough way at Wesleyan. Instead of using questionnaires, an observer actually visited the rooms of 70 undergraduates.[5] All of these students were living in architecturally similar single bed-sitting rooms in university-owned and maintained dormitories. The observer noted down any and all things other than the standard items supplied by the university: pictures, posters, and *objets d'art;* the colors intro-

[5] I am indebted to Connie Sutherland for her ideas and assistance in designing and executing this study.

duced by the occupant (through rugs, curtains, bedspreads, etc.); magazines; and arrangement of furniture. Table 4.9 presents the principal findings. Students high in Hope of Power are more likely to have a variety of prestige possessions, including a television set, tape recorder, rug or carpet of their own, and wall hangings. They are more likely to have an electric typewriter, which in the college environment probably qualifies as a prestige object; and they are more

TABLE 4.9 n POWER AND OBSERVATIONAL STUDY OF PRESTIGE POSSESSIONS

		Correlations with:	
		Hope of Power	Fear of Power
Number of Prestige Possessions[a] in dormitory room, Wesleyan male undergraduates (N = 70)		+.27 p<.03	−.19 p∼.10

t of difference between correlations = 2.47 p<.02 2-tailed

		Have electric typewriter	Do not have
N Power	High	12	22
	Low	5	31

$\chi^2 = 4.36$
p<.05

	Mean Hope of Power Score
Those who have their name on the door to their room (N = 23)	53.26
Those who do not (N = 47)	49.13
Difference	4.13
	t =1.67
	p∼.05 1-tailed

[a] One point for each of the following items: television set, tape recorder, stereo phonograph system, radio, rug, carpet, picture frame(s), and more than one wall hanging.

likely to put their own name on the outer door of their room—another subtle way of suggesting their prestige or importance.

A further study of 92 Wesleyan undergraduates during 1968 showed that those 29 students who had beards or mustaches were higher in n Power than those without (means = 54.07 and 49.79, t = 1.95, p~.06 2-tailed). Of course, having a beard or mustache is very much a matter of fashion: men had them in the nineteenth century; then didn't; now they are beginning to have them again. I presume that there is no intrinsic connection between n Power and hirsute adornment as such (although one could argue that long hair and potency have always been linked in Western culture, as in the story of Samson). Rather, n Power leads to a concern with reputation or prestige, and this leads to relatively quick adoption of all those trends or fashions that count for prestige in a given culture or subculture at a given time. Thus if n Power is associated with having prestige possessions, the latter term must always be specified more fully: what counts for prestige in the particular group that is studied?

At this writing, most middle-class American businessmen do not wear beards. However, within a sample of 22 executives in a large manufacturing company,[6] n Power was correlated +.45 (p<.05) with the number of credit cards that a person carried. This finding was later replicated on a sample of 108 lower-middle and working-class men (data collected by Davis, 1969; r = .19, p<.05). Are credit cards a prestige possession for the middle class? Although they may be a convenience because they make carrying large amounts of cash unnecessary, they are very often advertised as symbols of status, influence, respect, and power. Some prestige cards are known to have minimum requirements of income and other elements of status for cardholders. Moreover, making a purchase with a credit card requires more effort on the part of the clerk than does paying with cash. Getting other people to do something—to work harder, to perform special actions and rituals—may be the ultimate sign of prestige and therefore satisfaction of the power motive. The writer Tom Wolfe (1969) has called this "the ultimate power—seeing 'em jump," and he points out the extraordinary demands for personal service that are made by the powerful person in order to demonstrate his power.

In American society, one of the most universal and salient objects of prestige is the automobile. Manufacturers and advertisers make great efforts to produce highly differentiated "images" for their vehicles, and many consumers find that the performance characteristics

[6] I am indebted to Eric Strobel for conducting this study.

and subtle merits of their automobiles are conversational topics of continuing and consuming interest. If *n* Power leads to a concern for prestige and reputation, then it should be associated with preferences for certain kinds of automobiles. The first hypothesis was that *n* Power would be related to the horsepower of the car, or perhaps to some more complex measure of the car's power such as the horsepower/weight ratio (which is highly correlated with top speed and acceleration). Among college students and middle-class executives, this was not true. On reflection, it seemed understandable that people with high *n* Power did not prefer cars that were very powerful. The power of the car might compete with the driver, or detract from his power, so that he might prove incapable of handling or controlling the "raw power" of his car.

A careful reading of automobile advertisements suggested a second theme, which stressed a different aspect of power—the power of the driver over the car itself.[7] Phrases such as "The shift is a remarkable lever at the driver's fingertips," and "incredible maneuverability," as well as an emphasis on the sophisticated technical superiority and "smooth," understated image of the car bring out this second theme. In this case, the driver is in total control of the vehicle, and the power of the car is not so important as its maneuverability. How can automobile maneuverability be measured? It is made up of several different characteristics, but one simple measure is the ratio of the track (distance between the two front wheels or the two rear wheels) to the wheelbase (distance between the front and rear wheels), as shown in Figure 4.2. The more box-like the car, the more maneuverable, other things being equal. In addition, the height of the car and such features as number of gears, independent rear suspension, disc brakes, and the kind of tires used affect maneuverability and performance.

In order to test whether *n* Power is related to automobile preferences in any systematic way, we asked a small sample of middle-class executives and various samples of Wesleyan students what kind of car they would like to have. Price limits of $5,000 for the executives and $3,000 for the students were set in order to make choices more realistic and presumably more related to actual purchases. Those who did not answer the question, or whose answers were so vague as to be useless (e.g., "any small foreign car," "Chevrolet or Ford sedan") were not included in the analysis. Various statistics and ratios were computed for the first-choice automobile of each subject, using data from

[7] I am indebted to Howard Conley for suggesting this second theme.

Figure 4.2. A Measure of Automobile Maneuverability

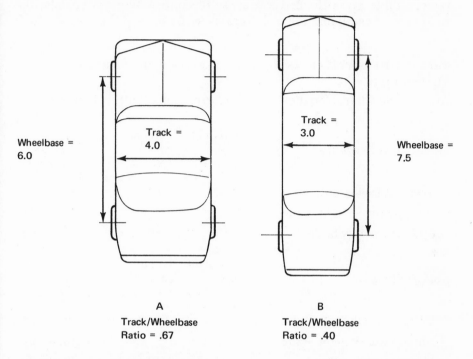

	A	B
	Track/Wheelbase	Track/Wheelbase
	Ratio = .67	Ratio = .40

On the basis of the Track/Wheelbase ratio, automobile A is more maneuverable than automobile B.

the *World Car Catalogue* (D'Angélo, 1969). Each car was assumed to be the standard version of the particular brand or model, unless the subject specified options. Table 4.10 presents the results of these computations for both groups. Within both samples, n Power is positively correlated with the maneuverability ratio and negatively correlated with the horsepower/weight ratio. However, in both samples n Power is also associated with preference for a foreign car. Foreign cars are more maneuverable than American cars, but they also may have more prestige just by being foreign. Do high n Power people like foreign cars for prestige or for their maneuverability? Inspection of the correlations of n Power times maneuverability, computed separately for American and foreign cars, suggests that they prefer foreign cars for both reasons. The correlation of maneuverability with n Power is still significant among those choosing foreign cars.

Highly-maneuverable foreign cars have prestige, but their maneuverability also suggests a deeper reason for their appeal. A car's maneuverability gives the driver a sense of control over the vehicle, the road, and presumably other drivers as well. Perhaps for people high

TABLE 4.10 n POWER AND CHARACTERISTICS OF DESIRED AUTOMOBILE

Automobile Characteristic	Correlations[a] with n Power for:		
Middle-class Executives	American cars (N = 15)	Foreign cars (N = 4)	All cars (N = 19)
Track/Wheelbase Ratio	.06	(.80)	.31, p = .10
Horsepower/Weight Ratio			−.35, p~.08
Maneuverability Scale[b]	.18	(.50)	.41, p<.05
College Students	American cars (N = 34)	Foreign cars (N = 82)	All cars (N = 116)
Track/Wheelbase Ratio	.07	.20, p<.08	.19, p<.05
Horsepower/Weight Ratio			−.15, p<.07
Maneuverability Scale[b]	−.03	.10	.22, p<.02

Group[c]	Mean n Power Score
College students choosing a foreign car (N = 82)	51.83
College students choosing an American car (N = 34)	47.91
Difference	3.92
	t = 2.06
	p<.05
	2-tailed

[a] Rank-order correlations for executives, Spearman product-moment correlations for college students.

[b] One point for each of the following: more than three gears, disc brakes at least for the front wheels, any kind of independent rear suspension, and a Track/Wheelbase ratio greater than .535 (approximate median).

[c] Among the executives, those four subjects who chose a foreign car were higher in n Power than the other 15 (p = .064, Mann-Whitney U test, 1-tailed).

in power motivation the automobile is a model for the rest of the world: that is, they characteristically view the world as a series of complex but highly maneuverable machines, which, with proper handling, will respond "instantly to your slightest whim" (in the words of a typical automobile advertisement). Canetti (1962, pp. 208–209) discusses the connection between smooth maneuverability and power. The evidence cited earlier on the kinds of friends and the use of opportunity to expand social contacts that are associated with n Power further supports this connection.

One final bit of evidence is relevant to prestige. At Wesleyan University as elsewhere, students submit term papers in a great variety of formats, bindings, and conditions of neatness. Some hand in a few ragged sheets of paper full of typing mistakes and bound precariously with a paper clip. Others submit neatly typed, carefully proofread papers which are impressively bound in colored plastic covers with plastic grips running along the left margin. To the extent that professors judge a paper by its cover—a misleading but human tendency—the paper that is neatly and impressively bound will fare a little better or at least get a favorable first reaction. In a small way, such bindings use prestige to enhance reputation—they are an "impressive show." In one introductory psychology course, those 13 students who bound their term papers in colored plastic or colored paper binders were significantly higher in Hope of Power than those 50 students who turned in ordinary papers (means = 54.92 and 49.82, t = 1.72, p~.09 2-tailed).

The evidence reviewed here all suggests that n Power is associated with prestige or putting on a good show. High n Power people try to control information about themselves; they follow fashions; they own prestige possessions; they prefer prestigious foreign cars. Prestige is valued because it is associated with power and can stand for power, since the power structures of any complex human society are largely built on such signs and symbols. Of course, in a crisis of legitimacy, the prestige of symbols collapses, and power returns to its original basis of force and domination.

STUDIES OF OTHER GROUPS

Most of the findings in this chapter were obtained with middle-class, mostly white subjects, whether college students or executives. To date there has been little research on the action correlates of n Power within other social classes, races, and cultures; such research may discover very different motive correlates. Since this is particularly likely in the case of prestige, I think it is appropriate to mention studies of other groups at this point. A social class or any other group may be viewed as a complex of varying expectancies, incentives, and learned roles, all of which interact with motives to produce quite different behaviors. In the case of the power motive, all of these behaviors may involve power; but the specific form, style, and quality of the power may be different from what has been observed with largely middle-class white groups. Thus n Power may be generally related to prestige, but what is prestige will vary widely.

Among black male college students, Greene and Winter (1971) found n Power related to holding office or being influential in black student organizations, participating in a Black Theater group, and taking Black Studies courses. However, they also found that the region in which the student spent his childhood (Northern vs. Southern United States) acted as a very important moderator variable in further relationships. Among Northern-reared students, n Power was highly associated with being rated by peers as *directly active in the black community* and *unwilling to work within the "system."* Among Southern-reared students, n Power was associated with being rated as *pragmatic*. (See Greene and Winter for detailed definitions of these rating categories.)

Winter (1968) found that most of the usual correlates of n Power were substantially attenuated among a small sample of working-class white males. Further data on working-class subjects are available from the study by Davis (1969), cited above. All of his subjects were given a TAT and a brief questionnaire about activities and sentiments before going through an experimental procedure. Among the 41 subjects who could be classified as working class (high school education or less and a blue collar job according to the Hollingshead index), n Power was associated with the number of offices held in organizations ($r = .32$, $p<.05$), a finding similar to those obtained with middle-class subjects. However, subjects were also given a list of behaviors and actions that involved impulsive and aggressive power, and were asked to indicate whether they had done each action often (scored as 4), once or twice (3), hadn't done but would like to (2), or had never considered doing (1). Among working-class subjects only, n Power was associated with the degree to which they reported doing several of these actions, and also significantly related to the total number of actions reported as having been done often. Table 4.11 presents these results.

Thus it appears that in the working class, n Power may be associated with impulsive forms of power—things that make a direct although temporary impact upon one or a few other people. These

TABLE 4.11 n POWER AND IMPULSIVE, AGGRESSIVE POWER
ACTIONS IN TWO SOCIAL CLASSES

| Item | Correlations of n Power with extent done (see text) within: | |
	Working Class[a] (N = 41)	Middle Class[b] (N = 36)
Yelled at someone in traffic	.23	.09
Threw things around the room (books, magazines etc.)	.43†	−.13
Destroyed furniture or glassware	.06	.24
Tore up books, telephone directories, etc.	.05	—
Stayed up all night for no reason	.20	.05
Got into a car and drove a long distance on the spur of the moment	−.06	−.22
Made insulting remarks to store-keepers, clerks, or the like	.24	.30
Didn't show up for a day's work because you just didn't feel like it	.33*	.01
Played out a role that you didn't really have	.18	.11
Walked off, leaving your wife or girl to fend for herself for the rest of the evening	.10	.10
Taken towels from a hotel or motel	.32*	.15
Total number of items marked as having "done often"	.36*	.01

p of difference between these
correlations = .06

* p<.05
† p<.01

Note: Subjects over age 56, and those not classifiable as either working-class or middle-class, are omitted from this analysis.

[a] Education high school or less and blue-collar job.
[b] Education beyond high school and white-collar job.

actions may not have much to do with formal social power in the middle-class sense of the term, but they may be congruent with such working-class norms and values about power as direct physical strength and aggressive confrontation (see Whyte, 1943). However, such an interpretation is hazardous and may reflect a middle-class bias. Clearly, more research needs to be done with working-class subjects.

Findings from various groups of subjects in Germany emphasize the point that while n Power may correlate with power-related activities, the particular relationships depend upon the values and traditions of the group in question. Such differing patterns could be expressed more formally as the result of different products of motive times different levels of expectancy and incentive within the different groups. For example, among a sample of 102 *Bundeswehr* (army) enlisted soldiers, Kratzsch (1971) found that n Power and Hope of Power were correlated with many of the same activities as among American college males—office-holding, playing and watching team sports, wearing a beard, and reading ordinary pictorial magazines. (See the next section of this chapter for American findings about magazine-reading.) Among a sample of 194 male secondary school students, Kruse (1971) found expected correlations with office-holding and membership in social organizations, but no correlation with sports participation. In contrast, Erdmann (1971) found among 96 engineering students that n Power and Hope of Power were related to a pattern of isolation from the world: having few girlfriends, not inviting friends to visit, thinking that others perceive one's self as remote, not listening regularly to news broadcasts, and reading regularly both technical and pictorial magazines. Are these engineers simply not interested in social power? Yet their power motive does seem to be directed into a style of behavior that emphasizes individualistic, isolated, rational striving—perhaps because of the norms and traditions of the engineering profession. McClelland, Sturr, Knapp, and Wendt (1958) described such a style as characteristic of German culture; and the pattern does fit with Albert Speer's account of his early days as an engineer (Speer, 1970). Within each of the German samples, then, the power motive appears to be related to activities that constitute meaningful, appropriate, and valued ways to have power within that sample.[8]

---

[8] The results presented here are only a selection from the wealth of findings reported by Kratzsch, Kruse, and Erdmann, and they are organized around the emphases and interpretations of the other findings reported in this chapter. Thus my account does not necessarily reflect the emphases and interpretations of the original authors.

VICARIOUS AND SUBSTITUTE POWER ACTIONS

So far, I have discussed real and potential power actions, assuming that these create an inner feeling of power and thus lead to a satisfaction of the power motive. Is n Power also correlated with other actions that are not so obviously related to social power, but which still give a person the same sort of power satisfaction?

McClelland, Davis, Kalin, and Wanner (1972) showed that there is a somewhat complicated relationship between the power motive and the consumption of liquor, on the basis of studies of individuals, arousal experiments using liquor, and the coding of cultural documents and folktales. They found that liquor consumption is predicted by high n Power and low inhibition (which combination they call "personalized power"). Data from the Wesleyan sample and from a small sample of middle-class executives confirm these results, as shown in Table 4.12. Among the students, liquor and beer consumption is positively associated with Hope of Power (which correlates with "personalized power," see Chapter 3), and negatively associated with Fear of Power. Among the executives, the same trends exist for liquor, but beer consumption is positively related to Fear of Power. McClelland *et al.* also suggest that s Power (on which the Fear of Power measure is based) is related to beer consumption among adult males generally (1972, p. 136).

Gambling is an activity that offers a chance for inner feelings of power, both through the possibility of creating a great effect on others (bluffing, making a dramatic bet or a reckless gesture) and also through the sense of doing battle against a strong opponent ("breaking the bank"). In the long run, of course, the gambler is almost certain to lose his resources and hence his power; but for the immediate moment, he may be a compelling figure who exerts a great and mysterious power of attraction over other players and the audience. Two results from the Wesleyan sample suggest that n Power is associated with the enjoyment of gambling. First, 53 students were asked to list all of the games that they had played, and then to circle those that they had ever played for money. Those 31 who reported playing at least one game for money scored higher in n Power than the 22 who said they did not gamble (means = 51.58 and 47.41, t = 1.70, p<.10 2-tailed). In a further experiment, 43 subjects played several rounds of "Auction Pitch" (a simple card game with elements of bridge) for money. Those 25 subjects who reported on a post-experiment questionnaire that they generally enjoyed

TABLE 4.12 n POWER AND ALCOHOL CONSUMPTION

Group and variable	Correlation with:	
	Hope of Power	*Fear of Power*
Wesleyan Students ($N = 117$)		
Beer consumption[a]	.19‡	−.09
Liquor consumption[a]	.16†	−.14
	t of difference between correlations = 2.19, p<.05	
Upper middle-class executives ($N = 22$)		
Beer consumption[b]	.14	.37†
Liquor consumption[b]	.34*	−.33
	t of difference between correlations = 2.06, p∼.05	

* p<.15
† p<.10
‡ p<.05

[a] Answers to the question "On an average occasion, how much (beer/liquor) do you drink?" scored on a six-point scale.

[b] Answers to the question in note *a*, times the frequency of occasions when that beverage is consumed, the latter also scored on a six-point scale.

gambling were again higher in n Power than the 18 who said that they did not (means = 52.60 and 46.28, t = 2.07, p<.05 2-tailed). There was no relationship between success at this game and n Power, although Fear of Power predicted failure, as I shall discuss in Chapter 5. While n Power inclines people toward gambling, it apparently does not lead to skill or success in gambling.

Reports of research with the Winter scoring system (Winter, 1968, 1972) showed a relationship between n Power and watching sports; also between n Power and reading "vicarious power magazines" such as *Playboy* and *Sports Illustrated*. These findings have been replicated with the present sample of Wesleyan students, as illustrated in Table 4.13. Both activities involve experiencing power at one remove or vicariously. The sports fan or the magazine reader

TABLE 4.13 *n* POWER AND VICARIOUS EXPERIENCE AMONG
WESLEYAN STUDENTS

Group	Mean Scores on:	
	Hope of Power	*Fear of Power*
Those who report that they read one or more vicarious magazine[a] (N = 159)	51.00	50.19
Those who report reading none (N = 78)	48.94	50.86
Differences	2.06	− .67
	t = 1.55	
	p<.07 1-tailed	

Variable	Correlations with (N = 117):	
	Hope of Power	*Fear of Power*
Number of college sports events watched per year[b]	.19*	−.14
Number of sports events on television watched per year[b]	.18*	−.11

* p<.05

[a] Includes: *Playboy, Sports Illustrated, Esquire,* automobile magazines, "girlie" magazines, and sports magazines.
[b] Answered and scored on a six-point scale.

can imagine himself as the actual participant, and through identification perhaps achieve what he believes to be the inner feelings of power. This behavior would be particularly likely and appropriate among the otherwise powerless—the very young, the old or physically undistinguished, and the man who has few chances for power in his occupation and his life (See Beisser, 1967).[9]

Drinking, gambling, and vicarious participation in sports and other subjective power experiences are correlated with *n* Power. Can

[9] Earlier findings (Winter, 1968) showing a relationship between *n* Power and watching vicarious television programs were not confirmed with the present Wesleyan sample data. This may be due to changing tastes, the difficulty of deciding how much and what kind of vicarious power is available in a given program series, or to great fluctuations in the viewing habits of college men.

these actions be called "power-related"? Whether they can be depends upon the definition of power that we adopt. Consider drinking: a man may feel very powerful after drinking alcoholic beverages; yet the more he drinks, the *less* powerful he actually is, until finally he is totally powerless. Is drinking therefore a power-related behavior or is it substitute, defensive behavior (see Lazarus, 1961, 1966)?

My approach has been to avoid semantic questions, and instead to map the range of action correlated with the power motive. These subjective actions do not necessarily involve social power, but they do give a vicarious, inner feeling of power satisfaction, even if the feeling is only temporary and reversible. They are important behaviors, and often have significant social and economic consequences even though they do not involve "real" power. They are a part of the whole network of relationships that constitute the construct *n* Power. Further, recall that most of the objective power-related actions discussed earlier in this chapter correlate with *n* Power only in interaction with other variables—i.e., when expectancy and incentive are high or can be assumed to be high. It is, therefore, important to know how a high *n* Power person will act when the expectancy of objective social power is low. To what other actions will he turn? Most of the vicarous and subjective correlates of *n* Power have a high expectancy of success, even approaching unity. That is, given a bottle of liquor, a person can be virtually certain of achieving the inner sense of power that goes along with being drunk, *if he wants to.* The feeling will not last, and it will be replaced with feelings of weakness and perhaps remorse. Still, this temporary feeling of power is quite certain and quite reliable. My own guess is that high *n* Power people will almost always enjoy and often carry out these vicarious and subjective actions; but the likelihood that they will do so increases as the expectancy of objective social power goes down.

An extreme case of this process is the *Götterdammerung* gesture of the power figure who faces inevitable and final defeat—for example, Ibsen's dramatic hero "John Gabriel Borkman" or the last days of Hitler in World War II (Bullock, 1962). There was absolutely no hope of recovering power; defeat was certain. The power-driven person ended his own life and destroyed as much as he could (his friends, his enemies, his possessions) in one last, grand gesture that affirmed for a final moment his power.

Whether it is because they really have power, or because vicarious activities make them feel as though they do, people high in Hope of Power, the approach aspect of the motive, do think of themselves as more powerful. Forty-six Wesleyan students in an introductory psychology course rated various concepts with a Semantic Differential set of scales (Osgood, Suci, and Tannenbaum, 1957). The Hope of Power score was correlated $+.33$ ($p<.05$) with the combined score on all "potency" scales for the concept "Myself," suggesting that Hope of Power is associated with feeling strong and powerful through whatever means.

SUMMARY

This survey of the actions and other sentiments correlated with n Power constitutes in one sense an extended validation of the scoring system. N Power is related to a great many behaviors and attitudes that involve power, and therefore the scoring system can reasonably be called a measure of the need for *power*. In another sense, the results reported in this chapter help to expand and clarify our understanding of the nature of power itself.

The power motive is related to a sequence of interpersonal styles and actions that is likely to draw attention and attract followers, so that over time high n Power people come to occupy positions of social influence and formal power. The sequence, or series of "power strategies" associated with n Power, turns out to be similar in form and content to several recent analyses of power strategies and power games, notably those by Martin and Sims (1956), Felker (1969), and Haley (1969).

N Power is further related to an intermediate class of actions which I have called "prestige" and "information control." These are intermediate in the sense that normally they serve as signs or symbols of real power and are thus part of the domain of objective social power, although they can be artificially manipulated or faked. Finally, n Power is related to a variety of vicarious actions that can serve as a substitute for objective social power.

These findings may tell us something about the nature of power itself. As shown by Kolb and Boyatsis, excessive power motivation may be maladaptive, perhaps because it leads to disaffection among followers and possibly dictatorial attempts to counter this disaffection. When under pressure, the power holder may find it easier and more comfortable to ignore real power and instead try to manipulate information and prestige so as to retain the public and private impression of power. Finally, he may even turn away from objective social power and retreat into the search for subjective (and therefore certain) feelings of potency. That is, he takes refuge in a world of inner power feelings that has little to do with the external realities of power. All of these tendencies will very likely lead to the loss of his formal social power, which may then drive him to a final destructive orgy of momentary power.

CHAPTER 5

The
Fear
of Power

In this chapter I report findings with the Fear of Power measure. The reader will recall from Chapter 3 that stories are classified as Fear of Power if the power goal is for the benefit of some other person or cause, or if the person or story writer reacts to power with doubts, conflict, irony, or feelings of deception (see Table 3.8). This classification was derived from the categories for scoring s Power used by McClelland, Davis, Kalin, and Wanner (1972). I decided to label these combined categories Fear of Power because their action correlates all seem to involve both interest in and avoidance of power. After presenting these Fear of Power findings, I shall discuss the differences between s Power and Fear of Power.

PARANOIA

The first major finding with Fear of Power was that it was associated with the specific diagnosis of paranoia among male schizophrenics. In fact, this finding led me to conceptualize the classification based on the s Power categories as Fear of Power, and thereby to diverge from the McClelland *et al.* interpretation. Therefore I think that it is important to discuss why male paranoia should be thought to involve specifically the avoidance aspect of the power motive. Unfortunately, the words "paranoia" and "paranoid" are often used in vague and confusing ways, and recently they have even become popular terms of political invective. What did they used to mean?

In his classic analysis of the case of Schreber, Freud (1911) identified two power-related themes: (1) fear of the power of someone else who forces the person to perform actions that are against his own will; and (2) belief that one possesses great, secret powers—that one has been especially chosen to save the world. Freud related these two themes to an underlying projection of unacceptable homosexual impulses that originated in the paranoid male's ambivalence toward his father.

Many later writers have stressed the power-related aspects of male paranoia, sometimes arguing that these are primary and that the homosexual ambivalence is derivative from them. Ovesey (1955) thought that the male paranoid experienced conflict with the power of parents and other siblings, so that he felt inadequate and needed to be dependent on a powerful male figure. These feelings of weakness, submission, and humiliating subjection are then symbolized by homosexual wishes and fears, because of the association of masculinity and power in our culture. Wolowitz (1965) further elaborated the power theory of male paranoia. Sensing some specific power deficit, the male paranoid tries to appropriate the power of other men, often through magical sexual and aggressive means (perhaps symbolized by sucking, biting, or being penetrated by the penis of the other). Thus the paranoid has a *desire for power*. However, he fears that the powerful male will destroy him as punishment for this wish, and so he repudiates the desire. That is, he *fears the effect of his own desire for power*, and *fears the power of other people*. Paranoid episodes are then precipitated by specific failures of power in important male-role behaviors—sex, management of subordinates, or athletics. That is, there is an additional *fear of losing power*. Thus while power is attractive, it is also aversive in several specific and rather different ways.

As evidence for this formulation, Wolowitz first had a group of pictures of men rated for "powerfulness" by a group of normal subjects. He then found that among male paranoids, there was a positive relationship between the rated "powerfulness" of a picture and aversion toward it, while for nonparanoid male schizophrenics, there was no such relationship. With pictures of women, the nonparanoids showed a relationship between rated "powerfulness" and aversion—predicted perhaps from cultural stereotypes—but the paranoids showed no such relation. Wolowitz concluded that male paranoia thus involved a specific aversion to powerful other men.

Additional support for the power interpretation of male paranoia came from the research of Wolowitz and his colleagues (Wolowitz and Shorkey, 1966, 1969; Weems and Wolowitz, 1969), who consistently found that male paranoids score relatively high in the power motive, using a modification of the Veroff scoring system. May (1970) used specially-designed TAT pictures and different scoring categories, and found some evidence for elevated power defensiveness (or anxiety about power) in male paranoid schizophrenics, as compared with nonparanoid male schizophrenics and normal males. These results, of course, do not rule out homosexual wishes and anxieties as the original cause of male paranoia, but they do at least provide evidence for linking paranoia, homosexuality, and an aversive attraction to power—in whatever causal sequence.

Therefore there are clear grounds for expecting that Fear of Power should be associated with the diagnosis of paranoia among schizophrenic males, whatever one's theoretical position on the ultimate origins of paranoia. To put the matter another way, if male paranoids score relatively higher on that classification of the power motive which was based on the s Power categories, then there are grounds for labeling that classification Fear of Power.

This is just what happened. The TATs collected by May (1970) were scored according to the revised n Power scoring system. May's subjects were 17 young male patients of two small psychiatric hospitals who had been unambiguously diagnosed as schizophrenic by a diagnostic conference team, and 20 young males matched on age, I.Q., and social class. Both samples had a median age of 22 and a median I.Q. of 114. All subjects were middle- or upper-middle class whites. The schizophrenic group had all had recent acute psychotic episodes, and had been hospitalized for a median of about twelve weeks. This was the first hospitalization for almost all schizophrenic subjects. Eight had been clearly labelled as paranoid by the diagnostic team; but this diagnosis was not known to the TAT administrator and was not of interest at the time the data were gathered, since May originally intended to study sex-role and schizophrenia generally (1969). The other nine schizophrenic males were not labelled paranoid.

May used 12 specially designed TAT cards and administered the TAT individually to all subjects. The spoken stories were tape-recorded and later transcribed. These special procedures required some adjustments in the analysis. First, only the stories told to the first six pictures were considered, following Reitman and Atkinson's note that the validity of experimentally-derived motive scores drops markedly after the first six or eight pictures (1958, pp. 666–673). Second, the clinical administration procedures introduced a substantial correlation between the length of the stories and the various motive scores. (Correlation coefficients were +.62, +.32, and +.52 with total n Power, Hope of Power, and Fear of Power, respectively; all are highly significant.) Since the relationships of score and length were approximately linear, their effect was removed by an extension of the technique described in Veroff, Atkinson, Feld, and Gurin (1960), in which the overall regression equation for score on story length is used to determine the predicted motive score for each subject, given story length, which score is then subtracted from the actual score. This correction was carried out for all subjects combined, but separately for each motive.

Table 5.1 presents the results for the paranoid schizophrenic, the nonparanoid (undifferentiated) schizophrenic, and the control groups. A one-way analysis of variance shows that the three groups differ significantly only in Fear of Power. Further comparisons among the groups show that the paranoids are significantly higher than either of the two groups, and that the nonparanoid schizophrenics and the controls do not differ significantly from each other.

Does the scoring definition for Fear of Power fit with the typical paranoid themes of persecution and megalomania? A story is classified as Fear of Power if any of the following themes are present: (1) explicit statement that the power goal is for the benefit of some other person or cause; (2) guilt, anxiety, self-doubt, or uncertainty on the part of the person concerned with power; or (3) irony and skepticism about power as shown by the story writer's style. Each of these characteristics is a kind of check or control on pure power—either by a force within the person (guilt, anxiety, doubt, irony), or by external forces that operate through social values (altruism, i.e., the use of power only to benefit others). These two kinds of forces, acting to check or restrain power, are similar to Schreber's alternating delusions of being persecuted by powerful others (guilt, anxiety, doubt, fear) and of having been especially chosen to save humanity through his own powers (altruism).

Thus it seems reasonable to label the modified s Power categories as Fear of Power, and to argue that Fear of Power is related both to diagnosis of paranoia among males, and also perhaps to ambivalent

homosexual wishes. This still does not tell us the precise nature of
the Fear of Power—what is it that is feared? Is it the fear of losing
one's own power, the fear of others' power, or the fear of one's
own power? Wolowitz's model mentioned above suggests that all
three fears are involved in male paranoia. Perhaps a study of the
action correlates of Fear of Power can help to answer the question.

First, most of the relationships reported in Chapter 4 between
n Power and office-holding, verbal hostility, and prestige possessions

TABLE 5.1 ASPECTS OF POWER MOTIVATION IN PARANOID,
NONPARANOID, AND CONTROL MALES

Group		Mean Scores on:	
	N Power	Hope of Power	Fear of Power
Paranoid Schizophrenics (N = 8)	7.97	3.91	4.05
Nonparanoid Schizophrenics (N = 9)	5.07	4.56	.52
Controls (N = 20)	6.88	5.54	1.31

Variance Table for Fear of Power Scores

Source	Sum of Squares	d.f.	Variance Estimate
Between groups	59.79	2	29.90
Within groups	289.47	34	8.51
Total	349.26	36	

$$F = 3.51, p < .05$$

Differences in Fear of Power Scores

Groups compared	Difference	t	2-tailed p
Paranoid vs. Nonparanoid Schizophrenic	3.53	2.60	.02
Paranoid vs. Controls	2.74	2.06	.05
Nonparanoid Schizophrenic vs. Controls	− .78	—	—

Note: Since each of the three subscores was corrected for the effects of story
length on motive score by a regression equation, the Hope of Power and Fear of
Power scores do not sum exactly to the total n Power score.

do not hold (or even reverse) for Fear of Power. Thus Fear of Power does not lead to most of the direct kinds of social power. It appears that just as the Fear of Power is a socialization or restraint on power in fantasy, it also involves an inhibition or restraint of obvious power-related actions. What then does Fear of Power predict?

AUTONOMY

One of the common and striking features of male paranoia is a rigid sense of autonomy (May, 1970). There is some evidence that men scoring high in Fear of Power are concerned about autonomy, or at

TABLE 5.2 FEAR OF POWER AND RESPONSES TO THE COLLEGE STUDENT QUESTIONNAIRE

Item # and Question	Cross-tabulation of Response		

			Usually a group	One friend or alone
159. Other than on dates or with your spouse, do you generally pursue leisure time and recreational activities (movies, exhibits, hobbies, etc.) with a group of friends or by yourself or with one friend?		High	37	45
	Fear of Power	Medium	28	40
		Low	43	30

$\chi^2 = 5.00$, p<.09
gamma = .18

			16 or more hours	less than 16 hours
158. As you think back over this past academic year, how much of your nonclass time per week (including the weekend) would you say you spent in casual conversation with friends or acquaintances?		High	34	79
	Fear of Power	Low	45	63

$\chi^2 = 2.74$, p<.10
gamma = .25

least about being left alone. Table 5.2 gives data from the College Student Questionnaire for Wesleyan students suggesting that Fear of Power is associated with being alone rather than in groups, but this could simply indicate less interest in affiliation. Further data from the Questionnaire clarify the point. Two hundred nineteen Wesleyan students indicated as freshmen their preferences on four different issues associated with the structure and style of academic work: the nature of knowledge, study, classes, and examinations. Relationships between these preferences and Fear of Power are given in Table 5.3. The great majority of all students chose what may be termed the "autonomous" or "independent" alternative for each question. Nevertheless, those high in Fear of Power are even more likely to prefer academic autonomy and independence. An "Academic Autonomy Scale," made up of these four items, is positively associated with Fear of Power and negatively associated with Hope of Power. Moreover, the difference between the two correlations is significant. Thus it seems clear that Fear of Power is associated with preferences for (at least academic) independence or autonomy, rather than simply disinterest in affiliation.[1]

One interpretation of these results is that the autonomy concerns of men high in Fear of Power derive from a fear of structure, especially structure that is imposed by someone else of high status or power (e.g., a professor or university administrator). Specified programs, assigned work, lectures, and "objective" examinations are all constraints on behavior that originate from "outside." Fearing the structure that someone else imposes is thus one manifestation of a fear of the potential power of other people.

Some evidence for this interpretation comes from actual academic behavior. Among approximately 175 male undergraduates in four large introductory and advanced psychology courses, 22 handed in a major term paper late (without an extension, or beyond an extension that had been given), despite clear warnings that late papers would be graded down. Eight students requested an "incomplete" grade in the course, either to finish the final paper or to postpone the final examination. Both groups of students had high Fear of Power; the combined mean for the 30 was higher than the average for the classes (mean = 56.43, t = 2.97 for difference from 50.00, $p<.01$ 2-tailed).

[1] Data from Erdmann (1971) support this point. Among 96 German engineering students, there is a nonsignificant but *positive* correlation between n Affiliation and Fear of Power ($r = .16$), while n Affiliation is negatively related to Hope of Power ($r = -.31$, $p<.01$). As noted in Table 3.13, n Affiliation and Fear of Power are uncorrelated in the Wesleyan sample.

TABLE 5.3 ASPECTS OF POWER MOTIVATION AND ACADEMIC
PREFERENCES

Item # and Question[a]	Gamma[b] statistic for association of italicized alternative with:	
	Hope of Power	Fear of Power
140. Which of the following statements comes closest to your views? —There are bodies of knowledge to be learned, and college faculty are more competent than the student to direct the student's course of study through required courses, prerequisites, etc. (19%) —*College students should be given great freedom in choosing their subjects of study and in choosing their own areas of interest within their subjects.* (81%)	−.09	.26
141. Would you prefer to have your academic work organized to allow: —A predominance of class work, class assignments, regular examinations, etc. (25%) —*A predominance of independent reading, writing, and research* (75%)	−.04	.24
142. In the average humanities or social sciences course, do you generally prefer: —Objective examinations (e.g., true-false, multiple choice) (23%) —*Essay examinations* (77%)	−.15	.14
143. If class size permitted, which type of instruction would you prefer? —All or mostly lectures (5%) —*All or mostly discussions* (95%)	−.11	.42

	(Product-moment correlations)	
Academic Autonomy Scale (1 point for each italicized alternative chosen in the above four questions)	−.11	.17*
	p of the difference between these correlations <.055	

* p<.05

In other words, students high in Fear of Power appear to have problems with course deadlines, and so they either ignore them or try to modify them.

Driving an automobile requires that one accept the constraints of a very complex structure: the traffic laws and customs, the physical structure of the road, and the constantly changing structure or "field" of other vehicles and drivers. If a driver is unable or unwilling to operate within this imposed structure, then he is likely to have an accident. The 29 Wesleyan students who had had two or more accidents tend to be higher in Fear of Power than the 170 who had not (means = 52.48 and 50.21, $t = 1.12$, $p \sim .13$ 1-tailed), although the difference does not reach usual levels of significance.

PERFORMANCE AND STRESS

Perhaps Fear of Power causes debilitating anxiety in situations involving structure; thus performance deteriorates under stress, causing mistakes, accidents, and even a loss of power or prestige. If this is true, then a high Fear of Power person would avoid such situations because he anticipates the aversive consequences of stress. Two small bits of evidence support this conclusion. First, among 46 Wesleyan undergraduates in an introductory psychology course, there is a significant correlation ($r = +.37$, $p < .01$) between Fear of Power and "General Activation" as measured by a self-report scale used by Thayer and his colleagues (Thayer, 1967). Thayer has shown that the General Activation scale is an accurate reflection of physiological measures of arousal, and proposes it as a simple measure of the activation continuum, as this concept is used by Duffy (1962), Fiske and Maddi (1961), and others. If persons high in Fear of Power generally do feel more aroused, then in important power situations their level of arousal might be so high that performance would suffer, following the familiar Yerkes-Dodson Law that performance is an inverted U-shaped function of motivation or arousal. Fear of Power may thus result from the combination of the saliency of power as an

---

Table 5.3 (*Cont.*)

Note: Overall N = 219.

a The percentage in parentheses after each alternative is the percent of the entire sample choosing that alternative.

b See Goodman and Kruskal (1954). *Gamma* is based on a 3 × 2 cross-tabulation, with motive scores divided into thirds.

area of content and a characteristic high arousal level. If the present finding holds true generally, it would explain why the avoidance component of achievement motivation (and perhaps of all motives, see footnote 12 of Chapter 3) can be successfully measured by questionnaires about general anxiety and stress.

Is the high arousal level the cause or the result of the aversive experiences which I earlier hypothesized to be the origin of the Fear of Power? If we start with possibly genetic differences in arousability, then perhaps highly-aroused persons are more likely to respond to all kinds of avoidance training and socialization (Eysenck, 1957; Schachter and Latané, 1964). Since aversive experience with power would then co-occur with many other kinds of aversive experiences, perhaps high Fear of Power persons will be generally more fearful and anxious, therefore high on other avoidance motives. Thus the *content* of early experience determines the content of later motives, but individual differences in *processes* such as arousability would determine whether these motives are primarily ones of approach or ones of avoidance.

In an attempt to study performance under conditions of some stress in a power situation, we asked forty subjects to play several rounds of "Auction Pitch" (also called "Setback"), which is a simple card game resembling bridge.[2] (See Morehead, Frey, and Mott-Smith, 1956, for the rules.) Auction Pitch was chosen because it was a game relatively unfamiliar to our subjects (37% had played it before), and because it is quickly learned and does not require much experience to be played well. All players were given $4 with which to play, with stakes of 25¢ per point per hand. If a person lost all his money, he could either withdraw or continue with his own funds. From the relationships between gambling and n Power discussed in Chapter 4, we assumed that this situation represented both an incentive and a stress in the area of power.

Several measures of performance during the game were available, and the relationship of each of these to Fear of Power is shown in Table 5.4. First, the number of times that the person won the bid, divided by the number of rounds played, is a measure of Bidding Activity (assuming that the actual quality of the cards dealt to any particular player varies randomly). Neither aspect of the power motive is correlated with Bidding Activity. Next, having won the bid, a player may fail to make that bid (i.e., be "set") for two reasons: he may have overestimated his cards in the beginning, or he may fail

[2] I am grateful to Alfred Petrocelli for designing and carrying out this study.

to play his cards in such a way as to make the score that he expected and bid. Thus, the proportion of bids that a player actually makes is a measure of the immediate skill with which he estimates and plays his cards. This measure is called "Playing Efficiency" in the table. However, a very cautious player might simply refuse to bid, and while such a strategy would avoid the chance of being set, it could scarcely lead to winning the game. Thus a longer-term measure of skill is the extent to which a player both makes bids and avoids being set during several rounds of play. This measure is called "Overall Skill" in the table. Fear of Power is negatively related to both measures of skill—especially the short-term measure, while Hope of Power is unrelated to either. In other words, while Fear of Power does not predict Bidding Activity, it does predict ineffective performance in actual play. In this one stressful situation, people high in Fear of Power do less well. This may be the reason why they seek autonomy in preference to stressful interpersonal situations, even though power is salient to them.

TABLE 5.4 ASPECTS OF POWER MOTIVATION AND PERFORMANCE AT AUCTION PITCH

| Variable | Correlations with: | |
	Hope of Power	Fear of Power
Bidding Activity[a] (N = 40)	−.14	.06
Playing Efficiency[b] (N = 28)	−.01	−.59†
Overall Skill[c] (N = 40)	−.10	−.34*

* $p<.05$
† $p<.01$

[a] Number of times won the bid/Number of rounds played.

[b] Number of times made bid/Number of times won the bid. Those 12 subjects who never won the bid are excluded. Cases where the dealer is forced to bid are excluded, so that the maximum score is 1.00.

[c] Number of times made bid—Number of times "set" (failed to make bid)/Number of rounds. Cases where the dealer is forced to bid are included here.

FAVORITE PATTERNS OF PROFANITY

In the search for a general understanding of the nature of Fear of Power and Hope of Power, some important data came from an unusual and interesting source. Fifty-nine male Wesleyan students in an introductory psychology course gave answers to the following question: "When they swear, many people find some words or phrases more expressive than others. What are your 'favorites'?"[3] Five blank lines were given for answers; the median number of phrases listed was three. Responses were searched for phrases and patterns of phrases that were associated with one or another of the three power motive scores.

None of the familiar four-letter words, either by themselves or in combinations, showed any particular pattern. However, those who used the word "motherfucker"—either as a noun or as an adjective —were significantly higher in Hope of Power, as shown in Table 5.5. Although this term has a distinctive pattern of usage among black Americans, the differences in Hope of Power held for black and white students considered separately. The only characteristic term used by high Fear of Power men was "asshole." This may suggest a connection with homosexual desires, which makes sense in terms of the relationship already cited between Fear of Power and paranoia and Freud's argument that paranoia is the result of unaccepted homosexual impulses. However, "asshole" could also indicate an anal preoccupation. To decide between these two interpretations, we then checked the Fear of Power scores of all those who listed "shit" or a synonym such as "crap," and found that they were not significantly different from the average. However, those who used any words or phrases (other than "asshole") which suggested homosexuality were significantly higher in Fear of Power, as shown at the bottom of Table 5.5. These findings were later cross-validated on another small sample of students, but they clearly need further replication. Nevertheless, they are interesting and helpful to our understanding of the approach and avoidance aspects of the power motive.

What do the results mean? I assume that people use profanity to express their desires and conflicts. If we take literally the favorite profanity of people high in Hope of Power, we would conclude that they have incestuous desires for their mothers. Likewise, those high

[3] I am indebted to Alan Hartley for his ideas in the design and preliminary analysis of data for this question.

in Fear of Power have homosexual desires or fears. Both kinds of wish seem to be linked to the strength and manner of resolution of the Oedipus complex, suggesting that a person's power motives originate or are shaped in the pattern of desires, prohibitions, identifications, and relationships that occur during the ages of 4 to 6 years. Hope of Power appears to be the result of what Freud considered to be the "usual" resolution of the Oedipus complex: the boy identifies with his father and represses the incestuous desire for the mother. (This theme is discussed in the next chapter, where the figure of Don Juan is taken as an archetype of Hope of Power.)

TABLE 5.5 ASPECTS OF POWER MOTIVATION AND FAVORITE PROFANITIES

Group	Mean scores on:	
	Hope of Power	*Fear of Power*
Those using "motherfucker" or some variation thereof (N = 8)	58.75	54.38
Those not using (N = 51)	49.98	49.04
Differences	8.77	5.34
	t = 2.58	t = 1.50
	p<.02	p<.20
Those using "asshole" or some variation thereof (N = 7)	48.57	60.14
Those not using (N = 52)	51.52	48.37
Differences	− 2.95	11.77
	t = 0.81	t = 3.25
	p = n.s.	p<.01
Those who use any homosexual expression, command, or phrase (N = 9)	48.22	55.33
Those not using[a] (N = 46)	52.26	48.24
Differences	− 4.04	7.09
	t = 1.18	t = 2.07
	p = n.s.	p<.05

Note: All tests of significance in this table are 2-tailed.

[a] Not including four subjects who used "asshole" but did not use any other expression that could be classified as homosexual.

Fear of Power seems to result from a reversal in the Oedipal stage. Here the boy identifies with his mother and becomes thereby a sexual object for the father (Freud, 1921, cap. 7). In other words, at the level of fantasy, the boy has submitted to his father, perhaps taking him as a love object. Such an impulse, either overtly or symbolically homosexual, arouses anxiety at a later age, and is therefore repressed. What we observe as Fear of Power in an adult male would thus be an anxious concern about power which is based on an earlier association of power with (possibly homosexual) submission. I put "possibly homosexual" in parentheses, because it is still not clear whether power or homosexuality is primary (Ovesey, 1955).

FAMILY BACKGROUND AND THE ORIGINS OF POWER MOTIVATION

Do these speculations about the origin of Fear of Power stand up when we look at objective data on the family backgrounds associated with Hope of Power and Fear of Power? Structural position in the family includes the number and sex of siblings, as well as the distances in age between siblings, and thus generates a large number of different categories (see Sutton-Smith and Rosenberg, 1970). I will discuss only two variables: ordinal position (eldest, middle, youngest) and number of siblings (none, one, or more than one).

What structural positions in the family should be associated with the development of a strong power motive? At this point, I want to discuss two quite different theories about the origins of power strivings. The first notion is that power strivings develop as an overcompensation for early power deprivation or feelings of weakness. Thus youngest sons, who grow up with more powerful others and thus experience greater power deprivation, should be high in the power motive. (An alternative prediction from the same theory is that youngest sons are likely to be indulged in early life, so that they will not need to have power later on; while first-born sons, as the primary targets for parental power, will feel greater powerlessness and thus overcompensate later.) This kind of explanation, in which everything is "really" its opposite, is popularly thought to derive from psychoanalysis, particularly from the work of Adler and Horney. Actually, Adler carefully distinguished normal expressions of power, which as a part of the striving for superiority were balanced with social interest in the healthy adult, from neurotic power strivings, which might result from an early inferiority complex (1927, 1928,

1930). Horney also stressed the difference between the desire for power that comes from a feeling of superior strength or commitment to a worthy cause, and the "neurotic quest for power, prestige, and possession." Only the latter come from a sense of weakness and a desire to get security. According to Horney, people with a neurotic power need avoid any situation where they are helpless or at the mercy of other people. They try to dominate others, but at the same time have strong inhibitions against domineering behavior; thus in the end they may simply try to avoid power (1937, pp. 162–187). Freud also argued that narcissism, which involves power strivings, was directly (and not inversely) related to ego strength (1914, pp. 56–57). Thus all three psychoanalytic theorists took pains to distinguish two different kinds of power: *positive power* originating in strength, and *negative power* originating in weakness. I think that this distinction, particularly as it was phrased by Horney, illuminates the differences between Hope of Power and Fear of Power, though of course more research needs to be done to establish the extent of that overlap. In any case, I think that psychoanalytic theory would predict specifically that the Fear of Power is associated with an early subordinate family position and feelings of powerlessness.

What about Hope of Power? The findings reported in Chapter 4 suggest that it is positive and involves feelings of strength. If this is close to narcissism, then psychoanalytic theory would probably predict that eldest sons are relatively high. Social learning theory suggests a simple mechanism for the learning of positive (approach) power motives: the more early power behavior which is rewarded, the stronger will be later power-seeking. Since eldest sons are likely to have more (and more successful) early experiences of exercising power over younger siblings, they should later score relatively high in the approach aspect of the power motive. Moreover, an eldest son is likely to have a stronger identification with his father because he is the first-born male. He will be encouraged to imitate his father, especially in the vicarious performance of the father's power behaviors. Thus in later life, he will have a stronger interest in power and approach toward it. Only sons will have the same strong identification and great reinforcement for modeling themselves after their fathers, although they do not have power experiences with siblings. They too should be relatively high in later power concerns.

In general, then, we would expect that Hope of Power should be high for eldest and only sons, and that Fear of Power should be high for youngest sons. Table 5.6 presents findings on the power motives and the family position of 218 students from the Wesleyan sample. Only those from intact families are considered. Data were taken from university records, and are as of the freshman year. Hope of Power tends to be high among only sons, middle sons, and eldest sons with more than one sibling. What characterizes all of these positions is the relatively great degree of maneuverability and therefore greater potential for learning power strategies and using power. Consider the possibilities of power coalitions. An only son can play off one parent against the other. A middle son is by definition in the middle of at least a triad, so that he can and must make coalitions with either his older or his younger sibling. An older son of *two* has a relatively more fixed status. His power relationship to the younger sibling is fully determined by his status; there is little possibility of gain or loss through forming coalitions. However, if the eldest son has more than one sibling, then he has to ensure that he does not lose his power to a coalition of younger siblings. If we combine all ordinal

TABLE 5.6 ASPECTS OF POWER MOTIVATION AND FAMILY STRUCTURE

Ordinal position	Mean scores on:	
	Hope of Power	Fear of Power
Only child (N = 16)	53.19	49.44
Eldest (N = 96)	49.68	50.47
Eldest, >1 sibling (N = 44)	51.23 ⎱ t = 1.47	50.41
Eldest, 1 sibling (N = 52)	48.38 ⎰ p = .16	50.50
Middle (N = 54)	51.59	49.44
Youngest (N = 52)	49.10	53.39
Youngest, >1 sibling (N = 25)	49.64	57.40 ⎱ t = 2.83
Youngest, 1 sibling (N = 27)	48.63	49.78 ⎰ p<.01
Positions of high maneuverability and power potential[a] (N = 114)	51.70 ⎱ t = 2.25	
All others (N = 104)	48.75 ⎰ p<.03	
Positions of high imposed inhibition[b] (N = 25)		57.40 ⎱ t = 3.46
All others (N = 193)		49.96 ⎰ p<.001

Note: All tests of significance in this table are 2-tailed.
[a] Eldest with more than one sibling, only, and middle children.
[b] Youngest children with more than one sibling.

positions of high maneuverability (i.e., possibility and necessity of forming power coalitions), we find that they tend to have significantly higher Hope of Power scores than all positions of low maneuverability. To be sure, this combination was made after the scores were known, so that the interpretation capitalizes on chance. Nevertheless, the grouping according to high maneuverability makes conceptual sense (see Collins and Raven, 1969). Thus early experiences in exercising power—more precisely, being able to maneuver in a situation which offers varied possibilities of coalition-formation—are the precursors of later approach or Hope of Power. This is consistent with the predictions, in that "maneuverability" in coalitions is probably associated with rewarded power behavior and thus an enhanced strength of ego, or narcissism.

The results for Fear of Power are quite different. The only group with high Fear of Power scores is youngest sons with more than one older sibling. In Table 5.6, I describe this group as having experienced high imposed inhibition, because they have the greatest number of other persons who have power over them, and because they are least likely to have power over anybody else. They also have little room for maneuver in coalition-formation, for someone else is usually in the position of initiating or confirming the final coalition. They would experience the greatest power of others, the least personal power, and hence the greatest powerlessness. For them, in short, the area of power is most likely to be associated with aversive consequences, because there are so many more people likely to punish them (and especially to punish them for trying to have power). Again, this is what we would expect on theoretical grounds.

CONCLUSION

Can all of these findings be put together into one theory about the avoidance aspect of *n* Power? Earlier I asked what it was that was feared in the Fear of Power: having power, losing power, or the power of someone else? After looking at the results, I think that all three interpretations are in part correct, in that each explains some of the findings. Fear of Power seems to combine all three fears.

Let me start with the family background and develop a speculative account of the origin and expression of Fear of Power. The more powerful siblings a person has, the greater the inhibition of his power behavior, and the higher his Fear of Power in later life. I take this to be, initially, a *fear of others' power*, since as a youngest son he had so often been the victim of that power. The most extreme later expression of this concern about being the object of another's power is the imagery of homosexual fears, whether this imagery occurs in later profanity or under stress in paranoia. At the same time, such a person also develops a *fear of own power,* because in early years the attempt to exercise or assume power often brought counterattack, defeat, and punishment from powerful others. In later years, this fear is expressed in a reluctance to participate in typical power-related actions and a tendency to be ineffective, overaroused, and thereby self-defeating when he does participate. Concomitant with this is a *fear of losing own power,* which may be a redintegration of the early family situation, where punishment by powerful others was, in effect, a loss of own power. In later life Fear of Power leads people to handle the conflict between wanting power, fearing it, and yet fearing not to have it by opting for autonomy and avoiding structure imposed by others. In other words, they try to leave the field. The data suggest that all three senses of the Fear of Power go together, and I have represented their interrelatedness in Figure 5.1. Perhaps the fear of others' power is primary.

This picture of Fear of Power thus seems to fit Horney's concept of neurotic or overcompensatory power needs, together with inhibition

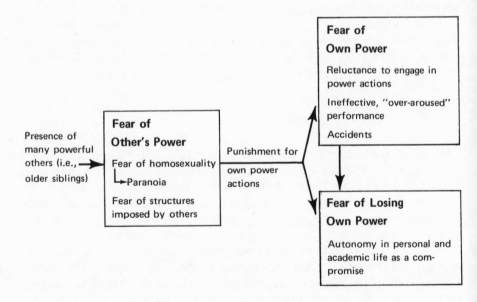

Figure 5.1. Hypothetical Structure of the Fear of Power

against them. Such a conclusion, and much of the above discussion, emphasizes the pathological aspects of the Fear of Power. To some extent this is due to the particular variables that have been studied so far. But isn't such a fear often a healthy and appropriate reaction to the excessive and often brutal power of others? I think that it is; and in Chapter 7, I shall suggest a more positive and hopeful picture of Fear of Power in its broader social aspects.

There is some evidence that Fear of Power is related to high characteristic levels of arousal and thus perhaps to a variety of other personality dispositions that involve arousal, such as introversion (Eysenck, 1957), strength and/or balance of the nervous system (Gray, 1965), anxiety or "drive" (Spence, 1964), or "customary level of activation" (Fiske and Maddi, 1961; Maddi, 1968). These dispositions, in turn, may be affected by genetic and environmental determinants quite unrelated to power as such.

The overall theory is that motive scores reflect the general interest, associative elaboration, salience, or meaningfulness of any particular content area—power, achievement, affiliation, and so forth. Whether the behavioral tendencies within a given area will be those of approach or avoidance depends on other variables. One such variable may be arousal or arousability. People with a high characteristic level of arousal may more readily develop avoidance motives in order to protect themselves against additional arousal, or (according to the Yerkes-Dodson Law) to ensure optimum performance. Arousal or arousability may also interact with parental socialization techniques, making a child relatively more sensitive to punishment, avoidance learning, and thus later avoidance behavior. Finally, socialization may have an effect in its own right. A child who is heavily punished may develop avoidance motives as a result. In each case, avoidance motives would tend to generalize across all areas of salient content. A person whose power motive is largely Fear of Power may also try to avoid failure rather than striving for success in achievement situations, and try to avoid rejection rather than strive for affiliation. Approach and avoidance may, therefore, be generalized personality dispositions.

FEAR OF POWER AND SOCIALIZED POWER (s POWER)

This chapter has reviewed the behaviors correlated with Fear of Power, and has suggested a theory about the nature and origin of this avoidance aspect of the power motive. I have called the measure "Fear of

Power" because to me such a term is the most appropriate label. The reader will recall that the Hope/Fear distinction was developed from that used to distinguish personalized and socialized power by Mc-Clelland, Davis, Kalin, and Wanner (1972, chap. 8 and appendix IV). Chapter 3 of this book reports that Fear of Power is related to Activity Inhibition in the same way as s Power, and that the two sets of distinctions intercorrelate rather highly. Both distinctions predict the consumption of liquor in the same way. Thus the reader may wonder about the conceptual and empirical connection between Fear of Power and s Power. Are they simply different names for the same thing? They certainly have different connotations; so that if they are the same thing, which name is most appropriate? Or are they related but different things?

It would be premature to try to answer these questions at the present time. We need several careful studies, of different populations, in which both distinctions are measured and correlated with the same behaviors. For example, while the two distinctions relate to drinking in the same way, McClelland *et al.* found that office-holding correlated with s Power (1972, p. 180), whereas in the present research it is consistently related to Hope of Power, along with most other kinds of power-related actions. Nevertheless, the subjects used in these two research projects are not fully comparable, and this may account for the differences in the findings. So far as empirical research is concerned, readers and researchers should remember that, although they are related, the Hope/Fear and p/s distinctions are not identical; therefore the particular measure that is used in any further research should be clearly identified.

Apart from empirical issues, it is important to note that the two distinctions rest on quite different convictions about the nature of power and of the power motive. The p/s distinction seems to be based on a sense that there are good and bad kinds of power, and that one can increase the good kind and reduce the bad kind. McClelland (1970) identifies p Power with "dominance" and s Power with "leadership," while I have suggested in Chapter 1 that such a distinction is based more on the observer's point of view and the resistance to the power action than on anything intrinsic to the action (or to the motive) itself. McClelland argues further that many of the social and moral problems of power can be resolved by increasing s Power, or "rehabilitating the positive face of power"—in short, changing p Power into s Power. Specifically, McClelland, Davis, Kalin, and Wanner have designed training procedures to do just this in the case of problem drinkers (1972, chap. 14). In terms of formal motivation theory, both p Power and s Power are thought to be approach motives, differing mainly in the nature of the particular power goal that is approached.

The Hope/Fear distinction rests on a very different notion of power. As stated in the preface to this book, I do not think that power can be so neatly divided into "good" and "bad." To me, the good and bad of power are closely woven together. The so-called good behaviors (office-holding, perhaps prestige) and the "bad" behaviors (drinking, gambling, perhaps aggression) are both related to the *same* aspect of the motive, namely, Hope of Power. If the power motive is "socialized" or controlled in *fantasy*, whether by altruism or by self-doubt, then it seems to act as an avoidance motive in *behavior*. As such, it avoids the "bad" side of power, but it may lead to paranoia, homosexual anxieties, and deterioration of performance under stress, with a resulting aversion to structure. Therefore it seems to me that both aspects of the power motive are mixed, that there are not separate "good" and "bad" power motives. Of course such a conceptualization makes the social and moral problems of power much more intractable.

While there are important theoretical and philosophical differences between these two ways of partitioning the power motive, any final choice between them, or resolution of the differences, will have to wait for further research. It seems obvious that some kind of important distinction must be made within the general domain of the power motive, but the precise nature of this distinction is not yet fully clear.

CHAPTER 6

Don Juan:
An Archetype
of the Power
Motive

The discussion of the power motive in the last two chapters is based on a survey of various empirical studies of its action correlates and related characteristics. To a great extent, I have worked from the data toward a theoretical understanding or portrait of the power motive. In this chapter, I intend a rather different approach: examining n Power as it is manifested in the legendary figure of Don Juan. This should help to bring together many of the rather atomistic empirical findings, so that we can see the various aspects of the power motive functioning in a person.

Why pick a mythic figure rather than a real person? And why Don Juan? Often we can apprehend a legend more vividly than a life, because the irrelevant features and distracting details have been stripped away. Like most legendary figures, Don Juan is not concerned with the trivia of daily life: he stands forth as a clear and forceful archetype. Moreover, careful study of a mythic figure can suggest additional hypotheses about actions and characteristics related to the power motive, and these hypotheses can be checked with the research data at hand. Finally, exploring the social context and origin of the legend can suggest broader hypotheses about the social context and origins of the power motive.

Rather early in this research, I decided that the figure of Don Juan showed many aspects of the power motive.[1] Don Juan involves sex, and the connection between sex and power has been a persistent theme in studies of either power or sex (see, for example, Hobbes, 1651; Carter, 1960; and Millett, 1970). Maeztu (1938), Pritchett (1955), and Holthusen (1960) have explicitly linked Don Juan and power. Moreover, Don Juan is one of the most persistent and durable characters in Western literature; since his first appearance in Spain around 1615, more than seventeen hundred later versions of the legend have appeared in the literature of every European country and in every era down to the present (Singer, 1965).

In this chapter, I shall first summarize the Don Juan legend in its original version. Some psychologists have written about the Don Juan figure, and I shall draw on their interpretations to construct a psychological analysis of the legend. Then, using both this interpretation and some features of the legend itself, I shall relate the Don Juan legend to the power motive, both by referring to the results reported in Chapter 4 and by testing additional hypotheses with data from the Harvard and Wesleyan samples. At the end of this chapter, I shall look at the social origins of the power motive, both by noting when and where the Don Juan legend appears with extraordinary frequency and by studying the historical situation surrounding its first appearance. Thus the legend and its interpretation, the findings, and the discussion of the social origins of the legend all together suggest a theory about the nature and origins of the power motive. The data and other evidence in this chapter will come from many sources: moving back and forth from literary imagery, the Wesleyan and Harvard samples, and historical archives. Many people think of Don Juan merely as a man obsessed with seduction; in this chapter, I hope to show that the legend means much more.

[1] I am indebted to W. Nicholas Knight for bringing the Don Juan legend to my attention, and for sustaining this attention with his inspiration and enthusiasm while we taught a joint English/Psychology course on the legend at Wesleyan University in 1969. I am further indebted to Abigail Stewart for her insights, suggestions, and criticisms in working out the interpretation of the legend that is presented in this chapter.

THE DON JUAN LEGEND[2]

The opening setting is Naples. Don Juan, the aristocratic son of an old and distinguished Spanish family, seduces the Duchess Isabel by pretending, under cover of darkness, to be her fiancé Duke Octavio. In the ensuing discovery and confusion, Don Juan escapes with the permissive assistance of his uncle, who is the Spanish ambassador to Naples. We learn that Don Juan has seduced other noble women back in Spain, and that he has been exiled by his father for that "treachery." In the course of his flight, Don Juan is shipwrecked, washed ashore at a small Spanish fishing village, and nursed back to health by Tisbea, a strong and proud woman who had heretofore been contemptuous of love. Don Juan responds by exclaiming that "I am dying for her"; with sweet words and claims of everlasting love, he then seduces her. Again he flees, this time after burning down Tisbea's hut.

Don Juan returns to his native city of Seville. His faithful servant is both frightened and fascinated; he continually urges Don Juan to reform his wicked life in order to escape death, damnation, and the torments of hell. Don Juan only laughs scornfully at such fears: "I have a long time left to worry about that!"

By chance, a note of invitation from Doña Ana to her beloved Marquis de la Mota falls into Don Juan's hands. He recognizes the chance to seduce Doña Ana through disguising himself as the Marquis (who is his friend) and sending him to another part of the city. He gains admittance to Doña Ana's rooms; she discovers his real identity, realizes that she has been tricked, and screams for help. Her father, the Comendador of the military order of Calatrava, rushes in to avenge both his daughter's dishonor and his own disgrace; but Don Juan quickly kills him and escapes again.

Don Juan now exults in his reputation as "the great deceiver of women; the Trickster of Spain." Even more than seduction, "the greatest pleasure is to trick women and leave them dishonored." Again, his servant warns him of the evil of his ways. Even his father begs him to change. But Don Juan continues to scorn their warnings: "Plenty of time for that later." His escape after the murder of the Comendador takes him to a village wedding feast; again with empty promises

[2] This précis of the legend is based on the earliest two versions, "¿Tan Largo Me Lo Fiáis?" and "El Burlador de Sevilla," both by Tirso de Molina (see Mandel, 1963, pp. 3–99 and Wade, 1969). All line citations are from the Wade edition, and are translated by the present author.

and tricks, he seduces the virgin bride only hours after the ceremony —then he flees.

Returning under cover to Seville, Don Juan and his servant enter a church. They see a stone statue over the tomb of the Comendador, whom Don Juan had so recently killed. The inscription on the base of the statue calls for vengeance; Don Juan reads it and, thinking to humiliate Doña Ana's father even more, pulls the beard of the statue and invites it to dinner at his house.

That night the statue appears at the door. Don Juan is clearly surprised and, for the first time, uneasy; but he welcomes the statue and invites it in. The statue then invites Don Juan to supper at his tomb on the next night. Don Juan accepts with a show of bravado: "Were you hell itself, I would dare to give my hand."

When Don Juan appears at the tomb, the statue of the Comendador says, "For what you have done, you must pay!" and grips Don Juan's hand to drag him down into the fiery tortures of hell. Don Juan first denies that he actually seduced Doña Ana: "She saw my deception first." Then he tries to repent by calling for a priest. "Your resolve is too late," replies the statue. With that, Don Juan dies, and the tomb sinks with him into hell.

This play, by the Spanish monk Tirso de Molina, has served as the basic model of the legend. Some later authors added details; others cut the story down to its barest outline. Regardless of these alterations, the legend consists essentially of two elements, both drawn from existing folklore (Austen, 1939; MacKay, 1943) but first combined by Tirso in about 1615: (1) Don Juan tricks and seduces a series of women; and (2) Don Juan challenges the statue of a man whom he killed in the course of his seductions, a challenge that leads ultimately to his punishment. The double title of Tirso's play stresses both elements: *The Seducer of Seville and the Stone Guest* (Weinstein, 1959). These major themes of seduction, murder, and challenge to honor, as well as the satisfaction of Don Juan with his prestigious title of "the greatest seducer of Spain," are all clear cases of Power Imagery according to the scoring system. Nor is there any evidence of altruism or self-doubt. Thus we can consider the character and legend of Don Juan as being highly saturated with Hope of Power.

PSYCHOLOGICAL INTERPRETATIONS OF
THE DON JUAN LEGEND

While there has been a great volume of literary comment, interpretation, and analysis of the Don Juan Legend (the principal sources are
cited in Weinstein, 1959, and Mandel, 1963), there has been rather
little systematic and careful use of psychological theory. To be sure,
the terms "donjuanism" and "donjuanesque" are used in clinical practice to denote a type of man who practices (or who attempts) serial
seduction. Marañón argued that this character type is "really" the
opposite of what it appears to be; that the donjuanesque male is
actually immature sexually, adolescent, weak, and effeminate in
psyche and physique. He is expressing an "indecisive masculinity"
through the pursuit of undifferentiated instinct (1940, pp. 67–83).
Reik dismissed the Don Juan type as having an "insecure ego . . .
pitiable . . . a high school boy's ideal" (1945, pp. 161, 189, 193).
Such interpretations may or may not be correct; but as they are interpretations of persons rather than of the full legend, they are not of
great concern here.[3]

Otto Rank began his analysis of the legend by referring to the
Oedipus complex: "The many women whom Don Juan has to replace
again and again represent to him the irreplaceable mother, while his
adversaries, deceived, fought, and eventually even killed, represent
the unconquerable mortal enemy, the father" (1924, p. 11; see also
Freud, 1910, on the meaning of the "endless series" of love objects
and the "injured third party" theme). The servant and the stone statue
function as increasingly powerful representatives of the ego ideal or
superego. Many features of the legend support this interpretation. The
parallel of the seduced women with the mother is very clear in the case
of the fisherwoman Tisbea. Having nearly drowned in the shipwreck
(a symbol of birth, according to Freud, 1910), Don Juan asks "Where
am I?" and Tisbea replies "In the arms of a woman." She then has him
carried to her hut, where she intends to repair his clothes and take
care of him. The Comendador is an explicit symbol of the primal
father, in that he attempts to keep Don Juan from having sex with
"his" woman, namely, his daughter Ana, and that her loss of honor
entails his own disgrace. In Thomas Shadwell's *The Libertine* (En-

---

[3] Apart from the psychological studies quoted later in this chapter, works by
Worthington (1962), Brachfeld, and Lafora (both cited by Weinstein, 1969, pp.
142–143) should be mentioned.

gland, 1676), Don Juan actually kills his own father; and as Rank notes, this more direct realization of the Oedipal wish also occurs in numerous minor versions. Usually Don Juan is hostile and even cruel in the face of his father's warnings and remonstrations.

The parallel of the final scene with Freud's account of the slaying and eating of the primal father in *Totem and Taboo* (1913) is even more obvious (Rank, 1924, pp. 38–40 and *passim*). Don Juan's initial taunt to the statue can be seen as the ultimate direct challenge to the father's potency. He pulls his beard ("the supreme insult among Arabs and . . . no doubt adopted from them by the Spaniards," Austen, 1939, p. 140), thus symbolically challenging his penis. "Tonight we shall await you at dinner . . . although it will be difficult to fight if your sword is made of stone" [lines 2259–2264]. This is the final attack, couched in the language of an invitation to (for) dinner.[4] The father then invites Don Juan to a meal at his tomb.[5] At this second dinner, which can be seen as a continuation of the same totem meal but on the father's terms, Don Juan is reluctant to eat. The food has suddenly become repulsive: scorpions, vipers, vinegar, and a stew of fingernails. After Don Juan has finished eating, the statue grips his hand. Don Juan immediately feels the flames, a symbol of remorse and guilt that follows the slaying and eating of the father. (The Spanish verb, *abrasar*, to set afire, can mean figuratively "to make ashamed.") Directly after feeling these fires, Don Juan says that "Your daughter saw my deception before I could dishonor her," and then calls for a priest to whom he can confess. These two acts—the last ones of Don Juan—seem to be striking parallels to the consequences that Freud deduced from the guilt arising after the totem

---

[4] The phrase "to have x for dinner" is ambiguous, in that x could be either the guest or the food. Thus, to await the father *for* dinner can be seen as a veiled reference, or pun, to the cannibalistic eating of the slain primal father of the *Totem and Taboo* legend. (See also Canetti, 1962, pp. 219–221.) This ambiguity exists in the Spanish preposition *a* as used by Tirso in this passage:

> Aquesta noche *a* cenar
> os aguardo en mi posada [lines 2259–2260].

[5] When Don Juan arrives, the statue says "To eat, you must raise the [stone that is covering] this tomb." Wade (1969, pp. 40, 209) notes the folk belief, especially strong in Spain, that the dead eat and drink; and he suggests, following Freud and others, that originally the dead themselves were eaten. From this belief the practice developed of offering food and drink to the dead, especially on *El dia de los Difuntos* (The Day of the Dead, or All Souls Day, November 2). Only in 1541 was this eating and drinking at the tombs in churches forbidden. To make the connection complete, I note that the Don Juan legend, in a nineteenth-century version by Zorilla, is performed throughout the Spanish-speaking world on or about November 2 each year.

feast. Denying that he had seduced the father's woman would be an attempt to undo the deed; after the fact it is an attempt to create a prohibition or taboo on the (incestuous) wish. Calling for a priest can be seen as a symbolic incoporation of the father's morality in the superego. In other words, the specific actions, sequence, and consequences of actions within the final meal scene closely follow Freud's "drama" of *Totem and Taboo*. Both legends symbolize the transformation of the Oedipal wishes into a stable social and moral order.

Nevertheless, interpreting the Don Juan legend simply as an expression of the Oedipus complex does not fully account for some striking features of the play. First, as Pratt (1960) notes, Don Juan competes with sexual rivals of his own age—"siblings" such as Octavio, the Marquis, and the village bridegroom—as well as with the "father." More striking still is his brutality toward the women whom he seduces: he burns down Tisbea's hut, he abandons women as soon as he has seduced them, and he takes greater delight in the "sport" of tricking and cheating women than he does in the act of sex itself. The contemporary Russian writer Sinyavsky has vividly described this brutal contempt for women (1972, pp. 19–20):

There is always something of the Black Mass in the sexual act. . . . The story of Don Juan is the endless search for the One Woman, as yet untouched, with whom the forbidden act will be particularly enjoyable. . . . From the strictly physiological aspect, there is little to choose between the old "object of love" and the new. But the point is just this: the new seems sweeter in anticipation because with it you will break the law for the first time and therefore act more sacrilegiously. You will turn some unknown "Donna Anna" into a slut, and her being "Donna Anna" and "unknown" is an added pleasure. "So pure, so beautiful, and this is what I'll do to you!"

Consistent with the Oedipal interpretation, one could argue that this rage directed toward the "mother" is in fact an attempt to punish her for preferring the father. Moreover, one could go on to argue that the elaborate description of Tisbea's virginity (as well as that of the other seduced women) is simply an exaggerated denial of the mother's own obvious sexual "history."

Nevertheless, it seems clear that these features strongly suggest additional pre-Oedipal elements set within the Oedipal framework. What are these elements? Pratt suggests that sibling-figures are punished and ousted because their birth disrupted the original mother-son tie, and that Don Juan cruelly abandons women because he expects that the "mother" will eventually desert him. In other words, these elements of the legend represent a disguised wish for reunion or fusion with the mother, rather than (or in addition to) sex as such.

In a related interpretation, Fenichel (1945, p. 243) argues that Don Juan is "dominated by the pre-genital aim of incorporation [i.e. re-union with or incorporation of and by the mother, Fenichel, p. 63] pervaded by narcissistic needs and tinged with sadistic impulses." If these nongenital needs are not satisfied, then sadistic reactions can develop.

If it is true that rage and aggression toward women are more important in the Don Juan figure than sexuality as such, then we may find it instructive to turn to those post-Freudian theorists who developed psychoanalytic theory toward an understanding of the roots of hate and aggression. Klein and Riviere offer a theory of the pre-Oedipal origins of aggressive and brutal contempt for women, and they apply this theory explicitly to Don Juan (1938, especially pp. 19–25 and 86). For the infant child, the mother is the original and most complete source of satisfaction of the totality of wants and pleasures. Yet this total pleasure is inevitably frustrated; Klein and Riviere argue that the child experiences this frustration as a threatened destruction— in short, the child feels hate and aggression, which can be defended against in many different ways. One such mechanism, which seems basic to psychological growth, is that of turning away from the mother, subdividing aims and pleasures, and then distributing them elsewhere. But Don Juan is unable to reject the mother in this way: while he feels frustration and rage, he continues to have an insatiable longing for the total pleasure of fusion with her. He cannot simply reject women; for he is bound to them in the classic dilemma of dependence: fusion with the mother (i.e., with all women) is at the same time both the ultimate source of pleasure *and* the source of frustration and threatened destruction. Don Juan is thus driven to approach women; but at the same time he is threatened by them, flees them, and is driven to an exaggerated male striving for sexual control, power, and prestige. As Klein and Riviere suggest, omnipotent power is a direct way "to control all potentially painful conditions, and have access to all useful, desirable things, both within one's self and without" (1937, p. 39).

Although as children all men probably experience the mother as a source of frustration and pleasure, all men do not become Don Juans.[6] Many use other mechanisms to handle aggression arising from threatened destruction, and some develop mature adult relationships.

[6] However, the popularity of the legend in Western culture since 1616 suggests that the aspects of the pattern of maternal behavior that I am going to describe may be rather general in Western culture, at least among the middle and upper classes since 1600.

Therefore the frustration and pleasure must be combined in some special way for Don Juan, in order to produce the later combination of insatiable longing *and* aggressive, deprecating rage. The basis of Don Juan's special dilemma seems to be a special kind of ambivalence, or alternating behavior, in the mother: she mixes both rejection or frustration with affection or pleasure in such a complex way that the child cannot separate them, subdivide them, and distribute them elsewhere. In short, the child cannot develop a consistent and unambivalent attitude toward the mother, nor later toward women in general. For him, women will always be alluring, loving, faithless, and treacherous. For him, therefore, women must be both approached and brutalized.

Some contradiction and ambivalence is inevitable in maternal behavior, of course; but why should a mother behave in this especially binding way? To satisfy her own needs? To control the child as an object of her own power? Since we are referring here only to male children, we might conclude that the mother ambivalently binds the male child—accepting and rejecting him—as an act of retaliation against men, specifically against the child's father and her own father. (Rank, 1924, chaps. 7–9, outlines a similar interpretation of the role of women in the Don Juan legend.) Now under what conditions would mothers be especially likely to act in such a way? Retaliation seems likely when there is a great differentiation between the sexes, such that women are suppressed and restricted by men. Thus many writers have argued that the Spanish mother is dominant, assertive, and possessive—suggesting the combination of affection and rejection—because of her restricted status vis-à-vis men (Pritchett, 1955, pp. 86–87 and 171–173; Pitt-Rivers, 1961, chap. 13; de La Souchère, 1964, pp. 13–32; and Wade, in press).[7] And at the time of Tirso's play, "the Spanish upper classes had inherited the Moorish custom of keeping their women-folk secluded" (Elliott, 1963, p. 305).

The popularity of the Don Juan legend in the West may give some clue to its social function, if this analysis is correct. Don Juan articulates compelling and yet fearful male fantasies—fantasies that probably derive from subtle changes in male/female relationships and

[7] As Rank points out, the mother's ties both to the slain father of the *Totem and Taboo* model (the oppressor) and to the heroic son (the liberator, but also the new oppressor) are ambivalent. This suggests that the explanatioin of Don Juan can be further pushed back to the relationship of his mother with her own father. Rank's full analysis deserves to be more widely known; most critics only mention the Oedipal interpretation with which Rank begins his analysis in chapters 1 to 4.

thus child-rearing that occurred in Europe (or at least in Spain) in the sixteenth century. Perhaps the legend is analogous to, or replaces, the ritual custom of defloration of virgins through the *droit du seigneur* custom (see Freud, 1918). In any case, by articulating and to some extent allaying male ambivalence, the legend makes possible some kind of stable adult relationship between men and women— though perhaps more on the terms of an unstable armed truce.[8] Thus after Don Juan is punished for his deprecation of women by the final "swallowing up" in hell, three of the seduced women are to be married (the Duchess with Octavio; Ana with the Marquis; and the village bride with the bridegroom). Presumably these will be happy marriages.

To sum up my interpretation of the legend: Don Juan seeks fusion with his mother through seducing a series of women; yet he fears this very fusion, because it is also the source of frustration and thus the threat of his own destruction. He cannot separate these two aspects of "woman," because they have been complexly bound together by his mother; and so he is driven to pursue both at once. Symbols of this complex combination of attractive and destructive femininity abound in the play: women themselves, the ocean, the statue, the tomb—all seen as incorporating or "swallowing up." Don Juan's behavior— seductions, deprecation, bragging, destruction, prestige, insolence— are thus a drive for power to defend against this incorporation, to control the chaotic and confused sources of pain and pleasure.

I suggest that this is the pre-Oedipal basis of the Don Juan legend and thereby of the power motive itself. How can such an interpretation be evaluated? Is it simply a question of the reader's predispositions toward psychoanalytic interpretation of literature—either being impressed and convinced, or else being politely amused at such a "curiosity of our indefatigable century" (Mandel, 1963, p. 624)? I intend to support this interpretation in two different ways. First, I shall refer to imagery in the original play. Then I shall show how the major features of the legend, interpreted in this way, are related to

---

[8] There are subtle as well as obvious parallels here with many other hero myths. Consider the Christian Last Supper: at a *banquet,* Jesus taught important final rituals involving food to his *male disciples.* On the cross, he was given *vinegar to drink.* He also *reconciled son and mother* ("Mother, there is your son. . . . There is your mother"; John 19:27). God the *father* allowed him to die and be *buried in a new tomb cut out of rock* with a *stone* against the entrance. After the resurrection and ascension, the *band of male disciples* waited for the animation of the Holy Spirit, which filled them with proselytizing zeal. Now *"Death is swallowed up"* (I Cor: 15:54). Jesus's principal apostle was later to preach: *"Wives, be subject to your husbands* as to the Lord; for the man is the head of the woman . . ."* (Eph. 5:22–23). (*New English Bible* translations.)

characteristics of the power motive (specifically the Hope of Power).
Psychologists have often used psychological theory and data to
"explain" literature; but rarely have they worked the analysis the
other way around. In other words, after confirming the correlations
of the power motive with the "obvious" Don Juan behaviors, can the
legend be used as a source of hypotheses about new and unanticipated
characteristics of n Power?

What is the evidence for my interpretation of the legend? First,
consider the encounter between Don Juan and Tisbea. Before she
sights the shipwreck, Tisbea exults that she is immune to the power
of love. She describes the catching of fish and the capturing of the
hearts of men in imagery that strongly suggests incorporating, en-
snaring powers:

> With a thin rod and casting net, I amuse myself by catching[9] as many
> foolish fish as lash about in the salty water down among the lodgings of
> conch-shells. . . . I live in imperious tyranny as the mistress of love, finding
> pleasure in men's pains and glory in their hellish torment. . . . I like to
> cast my rod to the winds, and give my bait to the mouth of the fish.
> [lines 395–481 *passim*]

After his rescue, Don Juan begins to flatter Tisbea with extravagant
metaphorical praise. Of course this is designed to facilitate the seduction; yet the particular images used may also suggest both the positive
and negative aspects of woman—nurturance *and* destruction:

> I left the hell of the sea for your clear sky. . . . At your feet I found a
> sheltered harbor. . . . Like the sun, you can set on fire with a glance, though
> you seem as snow. . . . You capture me in your tresses. . . . I swear, O
> beautiful eyes (which, in looking, kill me) to be your husband. . . . While
> God gives me life I will be your slave. [lines 584–588, 631–632, 937–938,
> 942–944]

To his servant, Don Juan exclaims, "I am going to die for the beautiful
fisherwoman; tonight I will enjoy possessing her" [lines 684–686],
thus directly linking sex and death-by-incorporation. Later, he uses
similar images to proclaim his love to the village bride: "Beautiful
eyes, white hands—they set me afire; I am burning" [lines 1806–
1807]. At the end of the play, of course, Don Juan is in fact "swallowed up" in the fires of hell. He has said to each woman, "Give me
your hand"; now the statue of the Commendador instructs Don Juan,
"Give me your hand." The evening of the final meeting with the statue
is the evening when Don Juan was to have been married to Isabel by
order of the king. Both marriage (often symbolized by the giving of

[9] The Spanish verb, *prendar*, can also mean "to capture" or "to copulate."

a hand) and being swallowed up by fire and the grave (after giving the hand) are thus symbols of ambivalent fusion with women (see also Canetti, 1962, pp. 203–206).

This theme of the woman who binds together both affection and rejection, pleasure and terror, is even more directly and obviously present in some later versions of the legend. In Zorilla's *Don Juan Tenorio* (Spain, 1844), which is the most popular version in Spanish-speaking countries, Don Juan breaks into a convent to seduce and carry off Doña Inez. Yet at the end of the play, she intervenes at the last moment to save him from the statue and the destructive fires of hell. After viewing Mozart's *Don Giovanni*, E. T. A. Hoffman suggested that Doña Ana had been aroused to an erotic frenzy by Don Juan, and that this raging sensuality led her to pursue revenge against him until his downfall (written in 1814; quoted in Mandel, 1963, pp. 322–326). In *Man and Superman* (England, 1901–1903), Shaw developed this interpretation into the central theme of the play: Don Juan is pursued by Doña Ana because he is to be the "instrument of Woman's purpose." Finally, in 1953 the Swiss playwright Max Frisch wrote an anti-Don Juan play in which the hero is terrified of the throngs of pursuing women. He prefers to isolate himself in order to study geometry, but he is a prisoner of his reputation. In desperation, he makes an offer to the bishop of Cordova: he will stage a faked scene of vengeance, with an actor hired to play the Comendador and a machine to produce sulphur clouds and smoke. The church will have a legend proving the justice of heaven; in return Don Juan will be given solitude in a monastery. The legend is created; Don Juan escapes to the palace of the Duchess of Ronda, who is actually a reformed prostitute and with whom he is in love against his will. At the end of the play, the futility of his attempts to break free from the pursuing women is set in more modern terms: it is again a banquet; Miranda (the "Duchess") announces that "We are going to have a child"; and the curtain falls very slowly.

Many scholars discern a fundamental departure in these later versions of the legend (Weinstein, 1959, chaps. 7 and 15; Mandel, 1963, pp. 23–26 and 547–697 *passim*). Don Juan has become "Romantic" or "Molecular"; the form of the legend is often merely a vehicle for the author's own thoughts and concerns—thoughts that may be a great or even total departure from the original legend as composed by Tirso. If my interpretation is correct—that the legend in its most basic and primitive meaning is an assertion of male power and strength against women who are both desired and feared—then there may be more unity to the different versions of the legend than scholars have suspected, for the theme of male power against female incorporation seems to run through both the early and the more recent versions of the Don Juan legend.

THE SEDUCER

Now I turn to the formal relationships between aspects of the Don Juan legend and the power motive. Surely the most salient characteristic of Don Juan, if not the most basic from a psychoanalytic view, is that he seduces women. Mozart's *Don Giovanni* gives the most thorough testimony to the sexual powers of the hero when his servant recites the "catalogue" of "beauties my master has loved": "In Italy, six hundred forty; In Germany, two hundred thirty-one; One hundred in France, ninety-one in Turkey; but in Spain there are already a thousand and three. . . . Provided she wears a skirt, you know what he does. . . ." (Act I, Scene 2).

It would be very difficult for a contemporary researcher to assemble such a catalogue of seductions and relate the total number to the power motive. However, the participants in the Harvard Student Study were asked at various times whether they had had sexual intercourse. The results are presented in Table 6.1. They show that those who had had intercourse—or who had reported that they had had intercourse— before college and during their freshman year were higher in n Power than those who had not. After freshman year, the effect of n Power diminishes. This suggests that n Power is at least related to having sexual intercourse at a relatively early age. Unfortunately, there were no accurate data available on frequency of intercourse, number of partners, or the length of relationship with any particular partner. However, Kratzsch (1971) found a significant correlation between n Power and the reported "number of sexual partners during the past two years" among a sample of 102 enlisted men in the German army ($r = +.30$, $p<.01$ 2-tailed). Thus there is at least some evidence that Hope of Power is associated with active sexual activity; and the findings reported in Table 5.5 suggest that this sexual desire or activity may be specifically directed toward the mother, although in a disguised way.

Yet Don Juan does more than seduce women. He tricks them; he abandons them; he attempts to exalt himself and debase them. Can we find an analogue of this orientation toward women that is associated with n Power? Twenty-eight Wesleyan male undergraduates were asked the following question:[10]

[10] I am indebted to Anita Miller for designing and carrying out this study.

What would you consider to be the characteristics of an ideal wife?

A. Her personality and background:
B. Her actions and feeling toward you and your family:
C. Her role as a wife and mother in the home and as an individual in society:

Most of the responses could be coded under the general headings of affiliation, independence, and dependence qualities. N Power was correlated +.16 with the number of affiliation qualities mentioned, −.36 with independence, and +.31 with dependence. While none of these coefficients reaches usual levels of statistical significance, n Power is significantly correlated with the total of dependence—inde-

TABLE 6.1 n POWER AND SEXUAL INTERCOURSE AMONG HARVARD STUDENTS

| Time period | Mean n Power Scores for: | | Difference |
	Those who had intercourse during this period	*Those who did not have intercourse*	
Precollege	5.50 (12)	3.66 (65)	1.84; t = 2.02, p<.05
During freshman year	5.60 (10)	3.70 (67)	1.90; t = 1.93, p<.08
After freshman year through sophomore year	4.53 (17)	3.78 (60)	.75
After sophomore year	4.00 (17)	4.20 (60)	− .20
During junior year	4.06 (17)	4.18 (60)	− .12
After junior year	4.33 (24)	3.98 (52)	.41
During senior year	3.93 (30)	4.20 (46)	− .27

Note: The overall number of cases in this table is 83. However, data were unavailable for various subjects during various time periods; thus the number in parentheses after each mean score is the N for that mean.

The scores are not cumulative, i.e., the means are for those having intercourse during that time period only, since the previous time period.

All tests of significance in this table are 2-tailed.

pendence qualities ($r = +.42$, $p<.05$). In other words, college men high in the power motive tend to prefer wives who are dependent and not independent. While a dependent wife may interfere with her husband's power, she probably enhances his *feelings* of power; presumably he then thinks that *he* is not dependent on *her*. Thus this combination of qualities is attractive to high *n* Power men because it gives them the same feelings of superiority over women that Don Juan enjoyed as a result of his seduction, trickery, and exploitation.

DISGUISE AND CONCEALMENT

In the original play, Don Juan carries out two of his four seductions by means of disguise, taking advantage of darkness to conceal his true identity and instead appearing as the man with whom the woman is in love: Don Octavio in the case of Isabel, and the Marquis de la Mota with Doña Ana. In later versions of the legend, especially those of Molière and Mozart, Don Juan carries dissimulation even further. He changes costume with his servant and takes on other disguises. Several interpretations of this behavior are possible. First, it is obviously a useful tactic for seduction: either the women are genuinely deceived about his identity, or else the disguise at least gives their conscience an excuse for willing participation. Following the Oedipal interpretation, one could argue that the disguise represents a fear of the father, which fear then manifests itself in a symbolic identification with the man who is being cuckolded. This is supported by the fact that Don Juan conceals his identity only when seducing women of noble or aristocratic rank (Isabel, Doña Ana), and only when the seduction occurs in a palace or a noble house. In other words, the less the displacement of the woman from the mother, the greater the anxiety and the more the resulting identification with the cuckolded father. Rank (1924) suggests such an interpretation as part of a more general discussion of the servant as conscience. Pratt (1960) connects this "substitution by disguise" to the ancient myths and rituals in which gods or priests replace the husband.

Yet Don Juan does more than disguise himself in order to seduce. When Isabel first discovers the trickery and asks "Who are you?" he replies, "I am a man without a name." The king of Naples rushes in and asks "Who's there?" Don Juan replies, "A man and a woman"— two sexes, two nameless individuals; biological forces without title or status (Wade, 1969, p. 176). At the village wedding feast, moreover, Don Juan completely reverses this tactic. He takes advantage of his rights as a nobleman to sit next to the bride, and he emphasizes his name and lineage in order to seduce her: "I am a noble caballero, of the family of the Tenorios, the ancient conquerors of Seville" [lines 2048–2051]. It is as though Don Juan has no *necessary* identity; as appropriate to the situation, he assumes whatever name, costume, and background is required. With Isabel and Doña Ana, deception is necessary; but with the village bride, the prestige of his real identity gives the greatest advantage. He does not uniformly use either his real name or a disguise; rather, his identity is adapted to the situation.

Is the power motive associated with anonymity—the concealment, or more precisely the control, of information about the self? Canetti (1962, pp. 337–384 *passim*) makes the point that power involves the control of transformations (or masks) of the self and others; thus under conditions of danger or uncertainty, such control would be manifested in a concealment of name or identity. In one Wesleyan University administration of the TAT and a questionnaire about attitudes and activities, students were told that they could use pseudonyms if they wished. The 24 students who did so were significantly higher in Hope of Power than the 35 who did not (means = 53.17 and 47.80; $t = 2.10$, $p<.05$ 2-tailed). In other words, when men high in Hope of Power fill out a questionnaire about themselves, and when the purpose of the questionnaire is somewhat vague, they tend to protect themselves by remaining anonymous. They may even distort information about themselves, as in the finding in Chapter 4 about upward distortion of the lowest reported final grade. When they are in control and it is to their advantage, they emphasize their prestige (Chapter 4). Thus when the servant proclaims that Don Juan is the "Trickster of Spain," he replies that "You have given me such an elegant name."

"I HAVE A LONG TIME LEFT . . . UNTIL DEATH!"

In the course of the play, Don Juan is reproached and warned about the consequences of his way of life. His servant says that he will have to pay eventually with death; Tisbea invokes God's punishment "if you are not bound to this choice"; his father speaks of the power of God's justice. In each case, Don Juan replies with complacent indifference: "I have a long time left until that." Until the very end of the play he seems both casual about time and unconcerned about death, that is, about the end of time. He dismisses the fear of the dead as "the most base fear"; with the village bride he even claims, "If I fail . . . let me be murdered by a man," adding smugly to himself, "by a dead man" [lines 2090–2095]. When he challenges the Comendador with the invitation to dinner, he adds the gratuitous taunt: "Your vengeance is a long time in coming" [lines 2273–2274].

What reactions to time are associated with n Power? In the sample of 70 Wesleyan undergraduates whose rooms were studied and observed (see Chapter 4), those 35 who had calendars anywhere in the room were lower in n Power than the 35 who did not (means = 52.71 and 49.00; t = 1.75, p = .08 2-tailed). A calendar can vary from a simple desk or wall calendar to an elaborate personal scheduling of events, plans, and deadlines; and its psychological significance ranges from a simple consciousness of passing time and a desire to know what the date is, to an elaborate concern about being aware of and preparing for every important future event. In any case, men high in n Power appear to have less interest in the passing of externally measured time. Perhaps they believe that "I have a long time left until that."

Are they really so casual about important future events? In the autumn of 1967, 145 Wesleyan undergraduates were asked to answer the following question:

What are your feelings about military service? Assume that you will not be 4-F or some nondraftable category. Which of the following is closest to your plans vis-à-vis the military?

_____ After college, I will probably enlist in the _____.
_____ I will take my chances of being drafted.
_____ I will seek classification as a conscientious objector.
_____ Other (Please describe).

Fifteen students chose to seek conscientious objector status, and 32 others gave miscellaneous answers including occupational, divinity, or physical grounds for exemption, "Don't know," and simple avoidance responses such as "Jail or leave the country." These 47 students were excluded from the following analysis on the grounds that by reason either of accidental factors or of strong moral convictions against conscription and the Vietnam war, they were not faced with the ordinary dilemma of the potential conscriptee[11]: Should he enlist, at some additional cost in time and commitment and with some benefits of choice and higher status? Or should he take the chance that he will not be drafted? In the autumn of 1967, this dilemma was partic-

[11] Their n Power scores were about average.

ularly acute for young American males, because of the large numbers of men who were being drafted and the very high level of conflict and casualties in the Vietnam war. Those 42 students who said that they would simply take their chances of being drafted were significantly higher in Hope of Power than the 56 who said that they planned to enlist in some branch of the military services (means = 51.40 and 47.23; t = 2.09, p<.05 2-tailed). In other words, men high in Hope of Power tend to avoid playing safe and prefer to take their chances, probably because they feel that "It can't happen to me!" or "I have a long time left to worry about that!" Thus they are prepared to gamble about military conscription, just as they also like to gamble when they play ordinary games. (See Chapter 4. It may also be true that men high in Hope of Power simply don't like being in the army if they can possibly avoid it.) Some further evidence comes from McClelland and Watson (1973), who found that when asked to gamble in a public situation, people high in n Power tend to take higher risks than those low in n Power. In Christian Grabbe's *Don Juan und Faust* (Germany, 1829), Don Juan expresses this attitude of indifference to time, risk, and death (Mandel, 1963, p. 342): "To gamble all on just one card, one little scrap of paper—your money, your life poised in mid-air, exposed to the storm of fate—that's what I call a lovely pasttime!"

ILLUSIONS

Although Don Juan denies the reality of time, he surely has few illusions about life. He tricks women, but remains aware of reality himself. When he first encounters the statue of the Comendador and begins to feel fear, he bravely asserts that it is all a product of his imagination, an illusion. Shadwell, Molière, Byron, and Shaw further developed this theme: in their versions, Don Juan himself is disillusioned and he attacks the illusions of his society. Interestingly enough, among a small sample of Wesleyan undergraduates, n Power was highly correlated with resistance to the familiar Müller-Lyer optical illusion.[12] Using the method of constant stimuli, in which the fixed stimulus was 3.5 inches long and the variable stimulus ranged from 1.83 to 3.5 inches, n Power was very significantly correlated with the Point of Subjective Equality, or length of the variable stimu-

---

[12] I am indebted to Dwight Greene for designing this study as a part of a class research project on personality factors associated with susceptibility to visual illusions, following the work of McGurk (1965).

Figure 6.1. Diagram of the Müller-Lyer Illusion as Used in This Study

A. Fixed stimulus (actually 3.5 inches long)

B. Variable stimulus (actually from 1.83 to 3.5 inches long, at 1/8-inch intervals)

Procedure: Fourteen 8 X 11-inch cards, one with each combination of fixed and variable stimuli, were shown to subjects three times in random sequence. The Point of Subjective Equality (= PSE, where B appears to be as long as A) was calculated according to procedures described by Underwood (1966, pp. 81-83).

lus which was seen as equal to the fixed stimulus (see Figure 6.1), *rho* = +.59, p<.03. In other words, *n* Power is related to accurate perception or resistance to illusion. How can this fit with the argument in Chapter 4 that *n* Power leads to distortion of information and to the creation of illusions that finally bring about the loss of power? Perhaps the two results can be reconciled by hypothesizing that the power motive is not so much related to accurate perception as such, as it is to the autonomous control of information. Men high in *n* Power are resistant to illusions fostered and cherished by others, but they are subject to the illusions that they create about themselves. Hence, while not being "taken in" by the world, they may be taken in by their own illusions and visions. Don Juan was both a cynical realist and, in the end, the victim of his own illusions.

"WHO CAN CONFINE DON JUAN?"

Don Juan seems to be in autonomous control of everyone and everything: the women he seduces, the servant who warns him, and those who would reprimand and punish him. He arranges and maneuvers every situation so that he can act upon it as he will. "Who can confine Don Juan, who is himself unconfined?" asks one servant. In the Tirso play, he twice shows real anger to his servant: once when the servant announces that Isabel is seeking to marry him [lines 2220–2223], and again when the servant anticipates his marriage (to have been held on the evening of the second meal with the statue), "with very great responsibilities" [lines 2651–2652; the Spanish word *cargas* can also suggest encumbrances or burdens]. Both sexually and socially

Don Juan strives to avoid being confined or ensnared in the demands and plans and arrangements of other people. He takes the initiative in defining and arranging his life. This theme follows directly from the interpretation of the play as representing pre-Oedipal ambivalence about reunion and fusion with the powerful mother. As I noted above, later versions of the legend have Don Juan struggling against the confinement of marriage.

Were Don Juan to be set in twentieth-century America, he would have to have a vocation or career. We can be sure that he would not be confined to an ordinary routine job or be satisfied with just another position in a hierarchy. I have already noted above that n Power is related to a preference for unassertive, dependent wives; now I will examine how it is related to career plans, looking for evidence of an analogous independence (or avoidance of confinement). One hundred thirty-six Wesleyan undergraduates were asked the following question:

If your life could go according to your plans and hopes, what would it be like in, say, twenty years? Please write out a brief description in the space below. Obviously your career plans would be an important part of this description, but try to mention other plans also.

From a comparison of the answers of ten students scoring high in n Power and ten scoring low, a scoring category of "Autonomous Control" was developed (see Appendix III for full definitions and details). In this initial comparison, men who were high in n Power tended more often either to mention some specific statement that "I will not be restrained in an ordinary job"; or to choose some self-employed career; or to list anticipated interests and activities over and above their job and family. Examples of the latter include: "I hope to be successful in some area of business at first, and then move possibly into a political or policy extension of my experience, with more social overtones." "Doing research . . . I would like to be living in a city or area in which there were a lot of exciting, stimulating activities." This category was then cross-validated by scoring blindly the remaining 116 replies. As predicted, those 50 students who mentioned one or more forms of Autonomous Control, as defined above, were higher in n Power than the 66 who did not (means = 51.80 and 49.21; t = 1.71, p<.05 1-tailed). In other words, n Power is associated with the same sort of desire for autonomy, for thinking of oneself as more than a role or roles, that Don Juan displayed with respect to marriage and society. Perhaps this is the reason why men high in n Power do not especially seek careers in bureaucracies (for example, in government), even though such careers might seem to involve power.

The reader will recall that in Chapter 5, I argued that Fear of Power was associated with autonomy concerns, while here I suggest that autonomous control is related to the power motive in general. I think that there are slight differences between the two kinds of "autonomy." Overall n Power seems to involve a concern with not being controlled by others. This is certainly characteristic of most of the specific occupations associated with n Power, as well as of the more general career and life plans discussed here. In the case of Fear of Power, the concern for autonomy seems to be more defensive and rigid. Control by others is not only unpleasant, but also a threat. Perhaps the distinction can be most clearly expressed in terms of the different reactions to things that diminish autonomy, such as externally-imposed structure. Men high in Fear of Power tend to avoid these things and to withdraw, in order to protect their autonomy. When they cannot do so, their performance (especially their power performance) suffers. Men high in Hope of Power probably would challenge such structures (see Table 4.7); but they may also play along in the hope of eventually taking over the structure, or at least attaining their own power goals. Meanwhile, when they describe their career and life plans, they are careful to define themselves as something more than just a role in a structure.

BACKGROUND

Don Juan proudly proclaimed that he is "a noble caballero"; that his father is held in reverence and esteem only lower than that of the king. Most later versions of the legend also emphasize this aristocratic background. Among 202 Wesleyan students (whites only), n Power is positively associated with father's income, although the relationship is not very strong (χ^2 for over vs. under \$14,000/year = 5.27, p = .07, $gamma$ = .23). This finding, while confirming the hypothesis from the legend, should be tempered with the caution that there were few students from poor families (income under \$6,000) in the Wesleyan sample. Among those few, there is a slight suggestion of high n Power, which would confirm the finding of Veroff, Atkinson, Feld, and Gurin (1960) that Veroff n Power had a U-shaped relationship to income. Moreover, black students were excluded from this analysis on the grounds that societal constraints on black income would obscure the relationship, if any, to n Power.

What about Don Juan's mother? For all of my psychoanalytic theorizing about the mother, she is never mentioned in Tirso's play, nor is there much discussion in later versions. The only extensive description of Don Juan's mother is to be found in Byron's poem, and even here some scholars argue that Byron's *Don Juan* is not really related to the legend (Weinstein, 1959, pp. 79–82; Mandel, 1963, p. 447). In any case, it is worthwhile to quote some of Byron's description as an hypothesis:

> His mother was a learned lady, famed
>   For every branch of every science known—
> In every Christian language ever named,
>   With virtues equall'd by her wit alone:
> She made the cleverest people quite ashamed,
>   And even the good with inward envy groan,
> Finding themselves so very much exceeded
> In their own way by all the things that she did.

* * *

> In short, she was a walking calculation,
>   Miss Edgeworth's novels stepping from their covers,
> Or Mrs. Trimmer's book on education,
>   Or "Coelebs' Wife" set out in quest of lovers,
> Morality's grim personification,
>   In which not Envy's self a flaw discovers;
> To others' share let "female errors fall,"
> For she had not even one—the worst of all.
>
> (Canto I, Stanzas 10 and 16)

How can we translate "a learned lady . . . walking calculation . . . morality's grim personification" into an hypothesis testable with college undergraduates? What is the equivalent of Byron's description in twentieth-century America? The combination of intelligence and morality is probably most like the career of teaching school (see Gorer, 1948, pp. 58ff.). Thus I would predict that men high in n Power would more often tend to have mothers who are, or were, schoolteachers. More precisely: among those men from "aristocratic" families (here taken to be father's occupation as major professional or executive), n Power should be related to having a mother who is a schoolteacher, as compared to a mother who works at another job or a mother who does not work at all. Table 6.2 gives the results of a test of this hypothesis with data from the Wesleyan sample. The analysis is restricted to white, intact, middle-class families, since among other groups the mother may often be working out of necessity rather than choice. Father's and mother's occupation were taken from records of the Admissions Office at Wesleyan, as of the year that the student applied to Wesleyan. The results give some support to the hypothesis based on Byron's description of Don Juan's mother: n Power is jointly

186   The Power Motive

associated with coming from an upper-middle class family and having a mother who is a schoolteacher.

Why should this be so? American school systems probably select for and encourage a strong sense of critical morality in teachers (as Gorer suggested), although some sort of detached moral rigor may be intrinsic to the role in any case. As Klein and Riviere note, "Teachers are . . . further removed from the child's feelings, they bring less emotion into the situation than parents do" (1937, p. 95). Thus a teacher may be (or become) disposed to mix cool affection with cool

TABLE 6.2 *n* POWER AND MOTHER'S OCCUPATION AMONG MIDDLE-CLASS WESLEYAN STUDENTS

		Mean *n* Power scores, where mother worked as:[a]		
		Not a teacher	*A teacher*[b]	*Difference*
Father's Occupational Status	Upper-middle class[c]	48.87 (N = 23)	54.20 (N = 15)	5.33; t = 1.63 p~.06 1-tailed
	Lower-middle-class[d]	52.16 (N = 31)	52.15 (N = 13)	− .01

Group[e]	Mean *n* Power Score	Difference
Mother worked as a teacher (N = 28)	53.25	
Mother worked not as a teacher (N = 54)	50.76 ⎱ 49.85	3.40; t = 1.69 p<.05 1-tailed
Mother did not work (N = 150)	49.53 ⎰	

Note: Only white, intact, middle-class families are included in this table.
[a] During the year that the son applied to college.
[b] Includes professor, but does not include librarian, guidance counselor, school psychologist, or curriculum director.
[c] Major professional or executive.
[d] Minor professional, small owner/manager, salesman, clerk, etc.
[e] From the entire middle-class sample.

rejection toward students. To the son of a woman teacher, his mother may in fact bind affection with rejection in this way, or he may perceive that she does so by generalization from his own teachers. Moreover, as Klein and Riviere note, teachers "divide their feelings among many children" (*ibid.*), and this should also act to increase the emotional distance, and perhaps sense of rejection, between a mother who is a teacher and a son. For a variety of reasons, then, men high in n Power tend to have the kind of mother that Byron described—the kind that our interpretation of the legend suggests.

Byron also notes that Don Juan's father died, leaving him "as sole heir . . . with a long minority" (Canto I, Stanza 37). These lines do not give us a very precise idea of the son's age when his father died, which is an important detail. Table 6.3 presents power motive scores for the 22 Wesleyan students whose father had died by the time that they entered college. If the father died before the son was fifteen years old, then the son tended to score significantly lower than the overall average in Hope of Power. If the father died *after* the son was fifteen, then the son's score was significantly higher than the average. At the bottom of the table, the data are arranged in a slightly different way. Among the men whose father died before they were fifteen, not only is the overall n Power score low, but also what power motivation there is tends to be Fear of Power. If the father died after the son was fifteen, the overall motive is high and it is largely an approach motive.

What then is the impact of the father's death on the power motive? Let us consider the matter in relation to the formation and passing of the Oedipus complex, which, as a source of the power motive, is important although secondary to the mother-son relationship. If the father dies while the son is relatively young (here taken roughly as before the age of fifteen, but in psychoanalytic theory probably before six), then the son may suffer great feelings of guilt because he believes that his hostile wish has somehow "caused" the father to die. This aversive guilt, attached to an early expression of a wish for power (to kill the father), then becomes the basis for a *Fear of Power* in the adult male. However, if the father's death occurs when the son is well past childhood, then he is less likely to experience guilt, and may even experience the removal of the father as a liberation and an opportunity for satisfying his own power drives. Thus Don Juan's father is driven to ask in anguish, "Is it possible that you want to kill me?" Here, as earlier in this chapter, I am certainly making a lot of interpretations of data from a sample of American college men, and so the findings need to be replicated.

TABLE 6.3 POWER MOTIVE SCORES FOR WESLEYAN STUDENTS
WITH DECEASED FATHERS

Group	n Power	Mean Score on: Hope of Power	Fear of Power
Those whose father died before they were 15 years old (N = 15)	46.60 t = 1.66 p<.07 for difference from 50	46.27 t = 1.59 p<.10 for difference from 50	50.00
Those whose father died after they were 15 years old (N = 7)	56.14 t = 1.83 p<.07 for difference from 50	58.71 t = 2.02 p<.05 for difference from 50	47.43

		Relationship of Power Motive Subscores: Hope≧Fear	Fear>Hope
Age at Father's Death	Under 15	7	8
	Over 15	5	2

p<.05
(Fisher Exact Test)

Note: The t-tests in this table are 1-tailed.

Yet they are presented because of their consistency with the theoretical interpretations of the Don Juan legend, and because they suggest something about the nature and origins of the power motive.

RED AND BLACK

How would Don Juan look? In what style and with what colors would he be dressed? The obvious answer is that he would be dressed in a manner similar to any young aristocrat in early seventeenth-century

Spain; a theatrical director would simply consult the portraits and other paintings of that time. Yet our interest may extend beyond the trivial question of period costumes, for if Don Juan is associated with the colors and styles of the time and place of his first appearance, then these associated colors and styles certainly suggest hypotheses about relationships between the power motive and aesthetic preference that may be more widely true. Such hypotheses can then be tested with modern data, just as Knapp (1958) linked n Achievement, preference for somber (green and blue) colors, and Puritan culture.

What are the dominant colors associated with powerful aristocratic men in Don Juan's day? The paintings of El Greco (c. 1541–1614) and Velásquez (1599–1660) show such men dressed in black, with a *golilla* (fancy collar) and cuffs usually of white.[13] Very often there is some red in the picture: the men are wearing the insignia of a military order (usually an embroidered red cross-like elaboration) or a red sash, or perhaps the redness of their lips and complexion is exaggerated. Thus black, white, and red are the principal colors of aristocratic men in the paintings. Is the power motive associated with a preference for these colors?

The modern evidence is necessarily indirect and therefore tenuous, since no tests of aesthetic preference as such were used in the present research. One nonreactive measure of color preference was taken from the actual TAT protocol: in what color ink (or pencil) was it written? Considering the first TAT protocols of all male Wesleyan undergraduates, those ten who wrote in red ink or pencil were significantly higher in n Power than the other 299 (means = 59.10 and 50.22; t = 2.83, p<.005 1-tailed).[14] In the study of automobile choices mentioned in Chapter 4, fifty-six Wesleyan undergraduates were asked to specify the color(s) of the car that they desired. Those ten who listed either red or black were higher in n Power than the rest, although the small numbers made this trend of only marginal significance (means = 54.10 and 50.30; t = 1.09, p<.15 1-tailed).[15]

[13] See especially, El Greco: *The Burial of Count Orgaz* (1586); *Portrait of Julián Romero el de las Hazañas* (1580–1585); and *Portrait of St. Ildefonsus de Toledo* (1607). Velásquez: *Portrait of Phillip IV* (c. 1628); *Portrait of the Duque de Olivares* (1633); and *The Surrender of Breda* (1634–1635).

[14] There was no difference between those writing in black and those writing in blue. This may be because both colors are very commonly used for writing, whereas the choice of red may reflect the power motive because it is a more unusual color.

[15] If the four persons who did not give any automobile choice at all are included as being neither red nor black, the difference is increased to 4.28; t = 1.27, p∼.10 1-tailed

The tentative finding that red and black are associated with the power motive is quite consistent with the research of Wexner (1954) and Murray and Deabler (1957) on the relationship between colors and mood-tones. Wexner showed charts with different colors to college undergraduate subjects and asked them to select the one color chart that went with each of several different clusters of words suggesting mood-tones. She found that black and red were most often associated with the mood cluster *powerful, strong, masterful,* being selected as such by over 75% of the subjects. Thus there is a thread of evidence from research in aesthetics, from the history of costume in Tirso's Spain, and from the preference of high *n* Power people that black and red are the colors associated with power.

DON JUAN IN NATIONAL LITERATURES

I have tried to establish the Don Juan figure as an archetype of the power motive, and now I will use this linkage to explore the origins of *n* Power in a broader social and historical context. First, I shall take the frequency of appearance of Don Juan versions in a nation's literature as a rough measure of levels of the power motive in that nation at that time. Then a study of the unique historical and social features of those decades when versions of the legend were very frequent will suggest hypotheses about the origins of the power motive.[16] This technique is related to McClelland's coding of motive content in cultural documents and national literatures over time (1961, chaps. 3 and 4). The difference is that here I am examining the frequency of only one literary theme; and although this theme may be closely related to the power motive, there are certainly other legends and themes which could express *n* Power. Hence the procedure may lead to an underestimation of levels of the power motive. There are other problems, too. Why assume that a version of the Don Juan legend was popular (or even known) in a particular country at a particular time, just because it was written there and then? What is to count as a version of the legend? How many features of Tirso's play must be present? Must the principal hero be called Don Juan? Nevertheless, there are good grounds for proceeding with the analysis. First, the legend *is* an elaborate and developed expression of the power motive, so that its frequency in European literatures after 1650 may well represent a good index of the saliency of power among

[16] I am indebted to Jay Wiley for suggesting this technique of analysis to me.

members of significant elite groups. Second, a reasonably thorough bibliography of Don Juan versions exists. Finally, we cannot know whether this technique will lead to useful discoveries until it is tried.

Singer's bibliography (1965) is an exhaustive compilation of all known versions of the Don Juan legend in all of the European languages, and includes a chronological list of versions with notation of the country of author or of publication. In this list, Singer rather closely defines a "Don Juan legend" as involving the themes of Tirso's play, and omits peripheral versions which are not closely related to the legend (although such versions are noted in another part of the book). Therefore I began by classifying all versions in Singer's chronological list according to country of origin and decade of appearance, for the major European countries. (Appendix V contains the coding rules used for the research reported in this section.)

Since the output of Don Juan versions is highly correlated with the output of book titles in general, it was necessary to correct the raw figures of national output per decade for the number of book titles printed in that decade. Figures for book production were taken from Iwinski (1911), corrected and added to by Schneider (1930), with more recent data taken from the *United Nations Statistical Yearbook*. For Germany, England, France, the Netherlands, Italy, and the United States, reliable data were available for a sufficiently long time-span to compute for each country a regression equation predicting the number of Don Juan versions in a decade, given the number of book titles produced in that decade. Deviations from these predicted figures were then calculated. Particular decades were selected as high in output if the actual number of Don Juan versions was two or more, *and* at least one more than the number of versions predicted on the basis of the total output of books; otherwise the decades were classified as not high. For the other countries, book production data were too fragmentary for meaningful computation. In these cases, high output decades were selected by inspection of the book production figures that were available, with the condition that all "high" decades had to have produced at least two versions. Appendix V contains the list of countries and decades of high output.

Empire. There are many grounds for predicting a relationship between the Don Juan legend and the fortunes of empire. First, the imagery of the play itself contains many references to imperial conquest. Don Juan is described as "of the family of the Tenorios, the ancient conquerors of Seville" during the Spanish Reconquest. In Molière's later version of the legend, Don Juan explicitly compares the conquest of a heart with colonial conquest: "I have the ambition of the great conquerors . . . like Alexander, I would expand my conquests to new worlds" (*Don Juan*, Act I, Scene 2). Second, Klein and Riviere argue that new territory is symbolically a "new mother"; that "both the escape from [the mother] and the original attachment to her find full expression" through the discovery and conquest of "the land flowing with milk and honey" (1937, pp. 104–106). By offering a chance to unbind the ambivalence of attraction and fear that characterizes the reaction to the mother and to some extent to all women, empire should thus be especially attractive to men of the background that we have postulated for Don Juan. Thus the Don Juan figure, or men high in the power motive, should be driven to seek empire. Moreover, the loss of empire should drive men back to their original ambivalent attitude toward women, and so increase Don Juan output (and perhaps the power motive). While the imagery of Tirso's play suggests the conquest of new territory, the play's first appearance (around 1615) occurred in a time of internal crisis and external disaster for Spain, as I shall discuss below. Thus the legend and the power motive should occur as a reaction to both gain and loss of imperial power. Finally, I note Weber's suggestion that many countries have an "internal power dynamic," which expresses itself in a concern for prestige and thus outward expansion of the nation's power (1948, pp. 159–160), as a reason for predicting a relationship.

In a general way, the Don Juan legend arose and became so very popular at about the time of Europe's great colonial expansion in the early seventeenth century. But how can the growth or contraction of an empire be more precisely measured? For example, we can speak generally about the size of the British Empire; but the precise measurement of land area under the "control" of British officials at any one time is difficult because of the elusive nature of imperial "control." How much land did the Massachusetts colonists, or the East India Company, really "control" at any particular time? One solution is simply to count the number of colonies gained or lost during a given decade and then to assume that this is a rough measure of changes in the extent of empire. Therefore I counted the number of colonies gained or lost per decade, starting in 1740 for the British Empire and in 1800 for the French Empire. These are the only two imperial countries for which we have both corrected Don Juan output data and imperial changes over a sufficiently long time period to permit an adequate test of the hypothesis. Information was taken mostly from *The Encyclopaedia Britannica* and *The Statesman's Year-Book*. The coding definitions for "colony," "gaining," and "losing," along with the data on Don Juan output and changes in the number of colonies, are given in Appendix V. For the British Empire, gains or losses in colonies are followed by increases in the output of Don Juan versions roughly two decades later, with the rank-order correlation between the two variables being +.38, p<.05. Since the lag of two decades was selected in order to maximize the correlation, it is necessary to cross-validate these results with data from the French Empire. The rank-order correlation is again positive and nearly significant (*rho* = +.35, p<.10). Thus we may conclude that there is some evidence for linking the appearance of Don Juan versions in a nation's literature to changes in the fortunes of that country's empire. More generally, the power motive may be connected with imperialism.

War. There are also grounds for predicting a relationship between the frequency of Don Juan versions and war. Aggressive war very often occurs when a country is gaining or losing an empire, and these gains and losses have already been shown to be related to the Don Juan legend. Moreover, war itself is one very direct expression of power. In the language of von Clausewitz's classic discussion, "War is thus an act of force to compel our adversary to do our will. . . . It is composed of the original violence of its essence [and] the hate and enmity which are to be regarded as blind, natural impulse" (1962, pp. 63–83 *passim*). One could hardly ask for a clearer or more vivid example of Power Imagery, or of the sentiments of Don Juan, who wanted to "expand my conquests to new worlds."

How can this hypothesized relationship between the output of Don Juan legends and the occurrence of wars be tested? It is difficult to get an accurate and complete list of wars, and of course the definition of a "war" itself is complicated. However, Richardson (1960) made a very complete list, for the entire world, of all "deadly quarrels" in which more than 316 people were killed (i.e., of magnitude 2.5 or greater) from 1820 through 1945. Wright (1965) supplements this list after 1945. The lists are quite usable for present purposes because, although they may contain inaccuracies and imprecision of detail, they are unlikely to have omitted any wars in which the countries on the present list participated. First, I counted the number of wars that each country entered per decade. (The date of entry into a war for a particular country is not always the same as the date of the beginning of the war.) Some countries enter more wars than others, for reasons such as geography which are irrelevant to the present study. Therefore, in order to identify comparable periods of "many" and "few" wars in different countries, I computed the median number of wars entered per decade for each country separately, and then noted those decades in which that country entered more or fewer wars than the median. Thus each decade in each country can be classified simultaneously in terms of its relative Don Juan output (high or low) and of its being above or below the median number of wars entered for that country. Table 6.4 presents the results of this cross-classification, relating entry into wars in one decade with Don Juan output in the following decade. (Relationships

TABLE 6.4 WAR AND THE OUTPUT OF DON JUAN VERSIONS IN FIFTEEN COUNTRIES, 1830–1959

		Output of Don Juan versions in the following decade, given the number of book titles published in that decade, for the country:	
		High[a]	Not high
Wars entered in a decade by the country:	Above median[b]	23	41
	Below median[b]	24	94

$$\chi^2 = 5.27$$
$$p < .05$$

Note: Wars were calculated for the decades 1820–1949 and corrected Don Juan versions for the decades 1830–1959. The following countries are included: Argentina, Austria, Belgium, Brazil, Denmark, France, Germany/Prussia, Great Britain, Italy, Mexico, Netherlands, Portugal, Russia, Spain, and the United States. Wars are taken from the list in Richardson (1960, pp. 32–111). In other words, each "subject" in this cross-tabulation is a country-decade.

[a] See the list of "high" output decades for each country in Appendix V.

[b] Median number of wars entered per decade calculated separately for each country.

between war-entry and Don Juan output in the same or the preceeding decade were also positive but not as significantly so.) A tentative conclusion is that there is a general association between war and the Don Juan legend, although the direction of causality is not fully clear. Table 6.5 presents a more refined analysis: the actual rank-order correlations between "overproduction" of Don Juan versions (i. e., corrected for book production) and number of wars entered in the previous decade for those six countries for which there was an accurate and complete time series of book production figures. All of the

TABLE 6.5 RELATIONSHIP BETWEEN WAR AND OUTPUT OF DON JUAN VERSIONS IN SIX COUNTRIES, 1830–1959

Country	Rank-order correlation between overproduction of Don Juan versions[a] in a decade and number of wars entered[b] in the previous decade, 1830–1959 inclusive:
France	.35 (p<.13)
Germany/Prussia	.60 (p<.02)
Great Britain	.24 (p<.21)
Italy[c]	.20 (p<.27)
Netherlands	−.07 (p<.45)
United States	−.14 (p<.33)
Combined probability estimate[d]:	z = 1.65 p<.05 1-tailed

[a] Actual number of versions appearing during the decade, minus the predicted number given the production of book titles for the decade and the correlation between versions and book production for that country.

[b] Wars of 317 or more casualties, as listed in Richardson (1960, pp. 32–111).

[c] Prior to 1860 taken to be any of the Italian states (for wars) and any version in Italian which appeared in any part of what is now Italy (for Don Juan versions).

[d] Using the Stouffer method of combining probabilities (see Mosteller and Bush, 1954, p. 329). The fact that the correlations for the Netherlands and the United States are in the reverse direction is taken into account.

correlations are positive (except for the Netherlands, in which only one Don Juan version appeared between 1820 and 1920, and for the United States, where geographic isolation and the continuous conflict with American Indians make the coding of wars in the nineteenth century difficult), and the combined probability of the results is significant. Overall, despite the obvious crudeness of the measurements—using the decade as the time unit, the data on versions, books, and wars— and despite the multitude of complex factors involved in both war and literature, there is a relationship between war and one important literary archetype of the power motive.

THE SPANISH SETTING OF TIRSO'S PLAY

By studying the social context of the Don Juan legend, imperialism and war have been isolated as two likely socio-historical determinants of the power motive. Since this is only the beginning of inquiry into the social context of n Power, I shall conclude this chapter with a further brief study of the situation in Spain at the time Tirso de Molina composed the first Don Juan play, in order to give an intensive analysis of the legend and to suggest some more hypotheses for future research. What was happening in Tirso's world around 1612–1616, when he was probably writing the play (Wade, 1969, p. 16)? How did he view these events? How and why did he come to write a play about Don Juan—a play that is "the most important play ever written if measured by its total impact directly or indirectly on world literature" (Wade, 1965, p. 254)?

These were the years when Spain was passing through acute crisis, when disillusionment and introspection flourished.[17] From the time of Ferdinand and Isabella toward the end of the fifteenth century, the kingdoms of Castile and Aragon had experienced an extraordinary growth in power, wealth, and prestige. Spain had driven out the last Moorish outpost on Spanish soil; she had discovered, conquered, and exploited a New World; her diplomacy and armies set the standard for Europe; her king ruled as Hapsburg Emperor. At home, centralized administrative control had been re-established over the towns, the church, the military orders, and the aristocracy. To be sure, there was a dark side all along: religious and ideological unity were obtained only at the cost of the expulsion

---

[17] This discussion of Spanish history is based largely on Elliott (1961; 1963, especially chap. 8), with additional sources cited in the text.

of the Jews (and later the converted Moors), while the Inquisition suppressed the slightest traces of Protestantism or other heresy. More subtly, men paid little attention to careful development of the economic infrastructure and instead pursued wealth by means of *hidalguía*—the ethic of conquest, courage, and honor. The Hapsburg involvement in Europe was soon to sap the resources and energy of Spain during the Thirty Years War. Throughout the world, Spain had been engaged in an heroic attempt to establish a unified Christian hegemony—an impossible dream which, through repeated failures, would destroy the greatness of Spain.

Toward the end of the sixteenth century, the signs of decay multiplied. The "Invincible Armada" was defeated in 1588, and the Netherlands possessions were effectively lost with the Twelve Years Truce of 1609. The wealth of the New World came suddenly into jeopardy. Because of the deaths of many of the Indians who worked in the mines, and because of the English and Dutch interference in the Caribbean, the royal supply of silver treasure from America declined by almost 50% between 1585 and 1615. One by one, the Portuguese possessions in Asia (under Spanish control during the unity of the two kingdoms) had been captured by the Dutch. In 1599–1600 a plague killed perhaps 10% of the Castilian population. The economy was in continuous crisis; as agriculture stagnated and industry declined, royal debts were repudiated in 1575, 1596, and 1607. After the death of Philip II in 1598, Spain was governed effectively by a *junta* made up of inept, corrupt, and indolent men. Events forced a retreat on foreign fronts. The junta distracted themselves at home by extravagant court fiestas. Believing that a final effort at religious unification could solve Spain's problems, they expelled the *Moriscos* (converted Moors) in 1609, an action that only exacerbated the economic crisis by removing an indispensable supply of labor. Spain was decaying and rapidly approaching disaster everywhere. The might that had been Spanish power was showing itself to be impotent. The historian Elliott concludes that "The humiliating awareness of the sharp contrast between the dying splendor of Castile and the rising of the foreigner is one of the most important clues to the psychological climate [of the times]" (1961, p. 69). This was the setting in which Tirso created Don Juan.

Who was Tirso de Molina? Much of his life remains obscure. His real name was Gabriel Téllez, and he was probably born in 1584. There is growing evidence, based not only on a disputed birth certificate, but also on an internal analysis of many of his plays, that he was the illegitimate and unrecognized son of the Duke of Osuna, Don

Juan Téllez Girón.[18] Of the rest of his immediate family, it is only
known for certain that he had a sister "resembling him in cleverness
and in unhappiness" (Wade, 1949, p. 134). Educated at the University
of Alcalá, he became a monk in the Mercedarian Order in 1600 or
1601, and began to write plays in about 1605, or roughly at the age of
twenty-one. It appears that he was fond of using plays to give advice
to people in high places (including the king), to serve as propaganda
for people and causes that he favored, and finally to attack powerful
figures—particularly his enemies—for their corruption. Whether because he antagonized powerful people or because he was thought to
be a "danger to public morals," he was forbidden to write plays after
1625. What kind of plays did he write? The theme of the woman who
tricks men was very much in the literary current of the times (Wade,
1969, p. 37). Tirso developed this theme of the *deceptive and powerful woman* in many of his own plays: wives who trick husbands,
women who compromise themselves in order to marry the man of
their choice (as the Duchess Isabel finally did with Octavio in the
Don Juan play), and men who become merely pawns in the hands
of determined women.

From 1616 to 1618 the Mercedarian Order sent him to Santo
Domingo in the New World to teach theology and to reform their
monastery. He departed for America from Seville, and it is very
likely that he spent considerable time in that city in the spring of
1616, before his departure. Here, according to the best scholarly
estimate, he created Don Juan.

What sort of place was Seville at that time?[19] It was called "the
new Babylonia" by contemporaries, and in many ways it was a
microcosm of the exaltation and decadence of Spain. The grandeur
of the *Casa de Contratación* (House of Trade) overflowing with
hundreds of cart loads of silver newly arrived from America, and the
fine clothes and magnificent coaches of the aristocracy were set
against the rest of the city, which resembled a rubbish heap—overrun
with the poor, the sick, the maimed, and abandoned children. Black
and Moorish slaves made up perhaps 7% of the population. It was
a city of wealth, vice, poverty, corruption, and fraud, in which effective policing and the maintenance of order were virtually impossible.
There were perhaps 300 gambling houses and over 3,000 houses of
prostitution—the latter often owned by the church, chaplaincies, con-
vents, or hospitals. Although prostitution was concentrated in a few

[18] Personal communication from Professor Gerald E. Wade.
[19] Most of this description is based on the work of Pike (1966, 1967).

districts, there was open soliciting throughout the city. Whores were even popularly graded along a "foodlike" scale: "trout—cod—frog" (Wade, 1964; 1969, pp. 195–196).

We can now draw together some of the things that must have been in Tirso's mind as he wrote the play: the greatness of Spain's power, now threatened and even thought of as an illusion; his own tenuous connection with the aristocracy; his mission to the New World that had been so recently conquered; Seville as the focus of this great conquest and also of the corruption and vice that lay behind it; women who were subjugated in reality, revered as the source of religious fervor and ideals (cf. Green, 1963, pp. 240–249), and feared as the demanding, tricking, powerful, and alluring harlot. Is a model needed for the character of Don Juan? Seville and Spain were full of them; but if we accept the hypothesis of his birth suggested above, Tirso could draw on his older half-brother, Pedro Téllez Girón, as one of the best. By 1600, Pedro (as the next Duke of Osuna) was already known to Seville as an irresponsible liar, adept at love intrigues, who had killed a man in a brawl.[20] From 1611 to 1616 he was the Spanish Viceroy in Sicily, thereafter in Naples until 1620. In an age of foreign policy retreat for Spain, he favored an aggressive, "messianic" nationalism to restore the greatness of Spain by returning to military conquest. While in Naples, he was supposed to have been implicated in a plot to infiltrate the Venetian Republic with foreign adventurers, and during a festival seize the city, "kill the leading men, and admit Osuna's powerful fleet into the lagoons . . ." (Trevor Davies, 1937, p. 240). Whether this particular incident with its suggestive imagery is true, he was recalled in disgrace in 1620 and died three years later.

How did Tirso use the example of Pedro, if indeed he was the model for Don Juan? Several levels of interpretation are possible; all of them may be partly true. One obvious interpretation is that Tirso wrote the play as an act of symbolic vengeance against his half-brother, who refused to recognize him as a Girón and who as the Duke of Osuna was gaining recognition and glory in Italy. At a deeper

[20] A contemporary Englishman wrote of Pedro from Madrid in 1623: "He had kept the Marquis de Campolataro's wife, sending her husband out of the way upon employment; . . . got a bastard son of a Turkish woman . . . one day at High Mass, when the Host was elevated, he drew out of his pocket a piece of gold, and held it up, intimating that that was his God . . . he had invited some of the prime courtesans of Naples to a feast, and after dinner . . . commanded them to strip themselves stark naked, and go up and down, while he shot sugar-plums at them out of a trunk . . ." *Howell's Familiar Letters*, London, 1890, pp. 208–209.

level, Tirso may be offering his own analysis and cure for the plight of Spain in 1616. If power and lust are linked together, as in Pedro, then the Don Juan play may be an attempt to revive the energy and enthusiasm of Spain's past. (The play is set in the heroic Reconquest era of the 1300s, and Don Juan is of the family that conquered Seville from the Moors.) Thus Tirso may be praising power. Men can gain and hold true power only if they are able to break free from the "encircling arms" of powerful women (Tisbea); to do this they must trick women in an attempt to establish their masculine independence. Many Spanish critics, notably Maeztu (1938) and Madariaga (quoted in Mandel, 1963, pp. 646–658) interpret the legend in this way. On the other hand, we must not forget that Tirso was rather a cynic and a moralist, as well as a theologian. The play can certainly be read as an attack on the institutions of Spain, by linking the corruption of power with the corruption of sex—both are stupid and fraudulent. This is the interpretation of Schopenhauer and of Unamuno (quoted in Wade, 1969, pp. 21–22), among others.

We do not have to choose. The play is enigmatic and ambiguous. Don Juan lives out the secret ideal of many men, and has a career of glorious conquest—until his courage and energy drive him to destruction. In an analogous way, perhaps, the legend is an imaginative treatise on the very nature of power and the power motive. Power is a form of conquest; arising from an ambivalent fear of a powerful and binding mother, and symbolized by the sexual degradation of women. Yet in the end power is a fleeting illusion, because in death it inexorably ends with the swallowing up of even the most powerful man. Power is everything; yet it is nothing, for man can never escape "the encircling arms."

CHAPTER 7

The
Power Motive,
Power, and Society

In the preceding chapters I have traced the definition and measurement of the power motive, and have reported research on the action correlates of both its approach and avoidance aspects. Through an examination of its expression in the literary archetype of Don Juan, I suggested some hypotheses about the larger historical and social context of n Power. The presentation and discussion have covered a broad range of topics and sources of evidence. Now it is time to put all of these findings together, and to try to answer some of the questions and issues that were raised in the first two chapters. How does n Power function as a motive in explaining behavior? Does it help us to understand power? How does the power motive relate to power and politics in society? The present research is obviously not going to answer all of these questions; but what has been presented above, together with some additional findings to be reported in this chapter, can certainly suggest some provocative hypotheses and point out some important directions for future research.

N POWER, MOTIVATION, AND POWER

In Chapter 2, I argued that the concept of motive refers to a goal or purpose, both as subjectively experienced by the person and as an organizing principle for understanding and predicting his observable behavior. Nevertheless, the relationship between a person's motive and his action is mediated by additional factors such as his other motives, the obstacles in the situation and his resources to overcome them, his perceptions and expectancies about the situation, and the incentive value to him of the particular goal. Thus any particular motive is associated with a great variety of different and alternative instrumental actions and even with a range of goal-satisfactions that are, to an extent, mutually substitutable. The value of the concept of motive and of the way of measuring motives proposed here is that they give an empirical basis for discovering the boundaries of a domain of related instrumental actions, and the extent of substitutability among goal satisfactions; but to predict behavior with much precision, it is necessary to consider both motive and situational variables such as expectancy and incentive.

Both points can be illustrated with the findings about the power motive. The power motive is defined empirically as those categories of the thematic apperception that increase under several different conditions of power arousal (candidacy for student offices, having the role of psychological experimenter, observing hypnosis, and seeing a film of the Kennedy inauguration). The power motive predicts many behaviors that are clearly related to social power: holding offices in organizations and having other positions of power, using interpersonal strategies that are likely to get power, controlling and even distorting information, and acquiring prestige. Most of these findings came from studies of college students and upper-middle class adult executives; for these populations it is safe to assume that the probability or expectancy of getting real social power is reasonably high. However, among other groups where the expectancies are probably lower or at least different (working-class men, Southern vs. Northern-reared black college students), n Power predicts different kinds of actions. The findings for politicians and for other occupational groups (see Chapter 4) can also be interpreted in this way. For the men of Eastport, urban renewal and self-initiated political candidacy provide greater power incentive than traditional politics. Being a psychologist, teacher, or business manager provides higher expectancy and incentive than being a lawyer.

Even among the college student and executive groups, the power motive also predicted actions such as drinking, gambling, reading vicarious magazines, watching sports, and precocious sexuality. While these actions do not involve formal social power, they do appear to be alternative goals or satisfactions of the power motive *as that motive is empirically defined.* I say that they are "alternative" goals because no one can do all of them at once, yet all are related to the power motive in thought or imagination. Thus (for American men at least) they can be thought of as alternative ways of getting the kind of satisfaction that real social power provides. Vicarious forms of power are readily available—expectancy of success is quite high, and is to a great extent under the person's own control. Thus they will be quite attractive to anyone in *n* Power, but they will be particularly attractive to those for whom the expectancy of real social power is low or sharply declining. Everyone cannot get elected to an office or be an athlete; but almost everyone can read magazines, gamble, watch sports, or drink. When a political or military empire crumbles, leaders may turn to drinking and sex. People with a strong power motive who are prevented from getting real power in a society by reasons of caste, class, or other barriers may turn to drink, sex, and perhaps more direct impact through impulsive and aggressive actions. Under certain conditions, then, aggression, sex, drinking, vicarious participation in sports and sex, gambling, and the quest for prestige are all felt subjectively as power and are thus part of the domain of power. They are mutually substitutable forms of power.

Thus the power motive leads to a great variety of actions and specific goals, either as direct and incompatible alternatives or as sequential goals. Because it unifies and relates these quite different behaviors, it can be called a motive in the sense of that concept proposed by Murray (1938, pp. 54–66), Frenkel-Brunswik ("drive," 1942), and recent theorists such as Atkinson, and Birch and Veroff ("class of incentives," 1966).

Nevertheless, the model for relating *n* Power to action has been informal and imprecise, and it depends upon making commonsense and *post facto* assumptions about expectancies and incentives within various populations—that expectancy of formal social power is low in the working class, or that routine party politics is low in power potential, for example. One urgent priority is therefore to determine expectancy and incentive in a careful and systematic way. Consider the basic Atkinson model as presented in Chapter 2:

$$\text{Action tendency } A = f \ (M_a \times E_a \times I_a)$$

How can the E and I terms be measured? Expectancy is the perceived probability of success of the particular action tendency (Atkinson, 1957); this may be close to the actual probability of success, but may also be affected by the motive itself (see McClelland, 1961, pp. 221–225; Scheibe, 1970, pp. 105–108). Expectancy might be measured by one or more of the following variables: generalized beliefs about the locus of control of resources (i.e., Rotter's I/E scale, 1966); possession of skills and resources relevant to power (the base of power in the sense of French and Raven, 1959); or favorable aspects of the situation which make being a leader easier, such as group respect, a clearly structured task, and access to sanctions (Fiedler, 1971, pp. 129–130). In any case, the probability of success of a power action depends mainly upon whether there is resistance to that action, either from the object of power or from a rival. If great resistance is perceived, then E would be low; if very little or no resistance is perceived, then E would be high.

What about incentive? In the case of the achievement motive, Atkinson did not measure I directly, but instead made the plausible assumption that I was inversely related to perceived probability of success (or $1-p$). Thus both E and I could be derived from knowing p; the more difficult the achievement task, the greater the sense of accomplishment from succeeding at it. This assumption seems reasonable for achievement tasks (although it has recently been questioned; see Heckhausen, 1968). Does it hold for power? Is it true that the greater the difficulty or the lower the expectancy of power, the greater the attractiveness or power incentive? For a person who is high in both achievement and power motives, this might be true. Some difficult power actions may also be attractive for other reasons. However, it seems to me that difficulty *per se* is not the major determinant of incentive in the case of power. What does make a particular action or outcome attractive to a person with the power motive? Surely it is the amount of power that he gains, feels, or displays in that outcome. How can this "amount of power possessed or gained" be measured? In general, two things contribute to amount of power: the *domain*, or the number of people over whom one has power; and the *range*, or the set of behaviors which one can cause in these people.[1] The overall power incentive can be represented as some function of the resulting domain and range of power. Probably the function is multiplicative, so that if either is zero, then I is also zero:

[1] These two concepts are taken from Cartwright (1959, pp. 199, 208). Dahl (1957) uses the term "scope" to indicate what is called "range" here.

$$\text{Incentive} = f \, (\text{domain} \times \text{range})$$

In other words, the more people that one can get to do the more different actions, the greater the power and thus the higher the incentive.

If incentive is defined in this way, some very interesting and important consequences follow. Incentive is not at all related to the perceived probability of success, as it may be for the achievement motive. In fact, the reverse may be true. For an absolute ruler, incentive is very high because both domain and range are high. Yet very often the absolute ruler *perceives* little resistance, so that expectancy is also high (cf. Duijker, 1961). In the case of the achievement motive, the product of E and I reaches a maximum at intermediate levels of probability of success; hence people high in the achievement motive tend to take moderate risks (Atkinson and Feather, 1966). Since the power incentive depends on other things than perceived probability of success, the product of E and I will not necessarily be maximized at intermediate probabilities; hence n Power should show no relationship to moderate risk-taking. This may explain the cyclic, "rise and fall" nature of power noted at the end of Chapter 4. If the power motive causes distortion of E (through distortion and suppression of negative information), as I suggest often happens, and if the incentives of absolute power are high, then by ignoring resistance absolute rulers will often take excessive risks and in the long run lose their power.

This analysis of expectancy and incentive in the case of power is only a preliminary hypothesis about the nature of the relationship of the power motive to action. In order to use this model in more formal theory and research, several further questions must be answered:

How can the probability of success of a power action be measured? Is it related to the amount of resistance?

Does n Power influence the perception of probability of success, and if so, in what ways?

Are domain and range the principal components of power incentive in the mind of the power-motivated person? How are they related?

The analysis of expectancy of power as some function of resistance recalls one of the major issues about the definition of power, as mentioned in Chapter 1. Dahl (1957), among others, maintains that "power" refers only to getting someone to do something that he would not otherwise do—in other words, power is power only when there is resistance. In the terminology of this chapter, Dahl is thus distinguishing low-expectancy power actions from high-expectancy power actions. Possibly he is also suggesting that incentive is inversely related to expectancy. My position is that incentive is unrelated to expectancy, and further that there is no reason to define power on the basis of expectancy (i.e., resistance). I suggest that the real problem is to find out how power-motivated people react to different levels of expectancy, and then to work out the determinants of expectancy and incentive.

Some words of caution about the concepts of "expectancy" and "incentive" are in order. They are psychological variables presumed to reflect important aspects of the social situation, and they are thought of as existing "within the person." For purposes of research and prediction, both the immediate situation and such enduring features of social structure as role, class, caste, sex, race, and culture can be defined in terms of clusters of expectancies and incentives. When this is done even in an informal way, the diverse and varying effects of motive become more intelligible. Yet defining social and cultural variables in such psychological terms carries with it the risk that we may come to think of society and culture as existing *only* in the minds of people. We can easily forget that society and culture are objective, real, and "out there" as well. If we do this, then we may come to believe that social change can be achieved simply by altering people's expectancies and incentives, forgetting that these expectancies and incentives are there in the first place because of the persistent and powerful overriding effects of society and culture. I think that this kind of thinking is one reason why "psychologizing" and even psychology itself are often charged with having a conservative, individualistic bias. To be sure, changing psychological variables sometimes can change behavior and social outcomes, but there are obvious and strong limits set by the situation and social position (see, for example, McClelland and Winter, 1969, pp. 250–254 and 311–312). Therefore I think that some precaution against "psychologizing" is appropriate. While we may wish to discuss social variables in terms of expectancy and incentive for purposes of precision in the analysis of data, we should not forget that these psychological terms really stand for the constraints and resources that exist in the objective social situation. We should not permit the social variables—class, race, culture—to "disappear" from the final description of the results.

THE POWER MOTIVE AND SOCIETY

How is the power motive related to the ways in which power is held and used in society? Let us begin by asking whether there is anything to be studied. Since political events and outcomes are obviously shaped by the inherited legacy of history and the immediate balance of institutions and social forces, how can the personalities of individuals or members of groups have any effect? Such a question recalls the dispute between the personal and situational views of power, as discussed in Chapter 1. Greenstein (1969, pp. 33–62) suggests that there is no one fixed answer to the problem of the effect of personality in politics. Under certain circumstances, individual personalities (and motives) may have an increased effect on events and outcomes: if the environment admits of restructuring; if there are no elaborate, fixed, conventional expectations; if the situation is ambiguous (new, complex, or contradictory); or if the particular person is in a "strategic" location in the system. With appropriate cautions, then, it seems reasonable to study the relationship between the power motive and society.

I think that this relationship has two different perspectives, each of which suggests different kinds of questions. First, we can consider that formal political system, and study the motives of leaders, chairmen, presidents, or other officials. How does the power motive affect their behavior, policy, and the actions of their administration as a whole? Here we think of power as the capacity or the performance of the system as a whole, and the research problem is whether the motives of leaders of the system have any relationship to the performance of that system. For example, how do leaders high in n Power behave? Do they get into wars and expand the territory of their system (their country, bureaucracy, gang, and so forth)? Are they thought of as "good" or successful leaders?

Alternatively, we can study groups within some system. Here the research questions involve the relationship between motive levels of group members and the behavior and goals of the group. For example, do groups high in n Power get more actual power? Are they more vocal, or more radical? How do they form alliances, negotiate, and react to the "authority" of the overall "system"?[2]

---

[2] These two perspectives on power and society are often called the "control" and the "influence" or "conflict" perspectives, respectively. Lipset (1959), Parsons 1960, 1963), Horton (1966), and Gamson (1968) discuss the philosophical, ideological, and academic differences between the perspectives.

The research on the social aspects of *n* Power that has been done to date involves both perspectives and sets of questions. I shall summarize these studies below, and then try to draw some preliminary conclusions about the role of the power motive in society. The studies themselves are in the nature of small-scale pilot studies, so that the data and conclusions must be only suggestive and not definitive. Nevertheless, the results are interesting, both for their own sake, and because they illustrate the kinds of social, political, and historical research that can be carried out using measures of human motives.

The power motive in two different groups. During the 1960s and 1970s, two rather different groups or movements were especially important in American society: young black participants in the new Black Identity and consciousness, and young white radicals of the New Left. Both movements attracted a wide following and an even wider interest; both were supported and opposed with great emotion; and both were the subject of much confused and conflicting analysis. Although each movement contained within it many different goals and viewpoints, both clearly emerged in response to national events and conditions; and both had a relatively clear major goal of affecting American society. Thus both clearly qualify as "interest groups" or "solidarity groups" in Gamson's (1968) sense. Some preliminary findings on motive levels within each group are interesting, because the observed differences in motives seem to fit with other differences between the two movements.

Greene and Winter (1971) studied the correlates of *n* Power in a sample of black college undergraduates, using peer ratings on dimensions that were perceived as important and relevant to black consciousness. A factor analysis of all ratings on all dimensions yielded two principal factors:

I. High ratings on being *Directly Active in the Black Community.* Perceived extramural involvement with the black community both locally and elsewhere, including participation in formal activities (Black Studies, high school courses, school breakfast programs) and informal social interaction. Low ratings on *Willingness to work within the system.* Perceived to feel that, regardless of its instrumental usefulness, the "system" is inevitably co-opting and stifling.
II. High ratings on *Pragmatism.* Perceived to subordinate immediate tasks and actions to long-term goals, rather than being "spontaneous" and believing that only the present reality counts and can be trusted.

As discussed in Chapter 4, Greene and Winter confirmed Nuttall's (1964) finding that the region of childhood-rearing acted as an important moderator variable. For Northern-reared black undergraduates, n Power was highly correlated with pooled ratings on Factor I ($r = .60$, $p<.01$), and negatively correlated with ratings on Factor II ($r = -.33$, $p<.15$). For those who were reared in the South, n Power showed the reverse pattern: a slight negative correlation with Factor I ($r = -.25$) and a strong positive correlation with Factor II ($r = .58$, $p<.01$). Among all students, n Power was related to holding office in the *Ujamaa* Familyhood (the black student organization), participating in the Black Repertory Theatre, and taking Black Studies courses. Greene and Winter conclude that n Power is associated with actions that show a militant concern and involvement in the interests and culture of the black community, but that the particular forms of power-related behavior will depend very much on the complex of learned expectancies and incentives connected with region of childhood-rearing. In other words, they argue that "we can in some sense characterize the new black presence as based on n Power."

Winter and Wiecking (1971) studied two kinds of white radicals: (1) a group of full-time, decision-making workers in New Left organizations, and (2) a group of students who occupied the office of a university president to protest campus military recruitment. As compared to appropriate control groups, both radical groups showed significantly *lower* n Power and significantly *higher* n Achievement. Winter and Wiecking suggest that this pattern reflects a "new Puritanism"—an ascetic, idealistic quest for fundamental change, which is, by turns, uninterested, ambivalent, and hostile toward power and power structures. Winter and Wiecking draw historical parallels to the radical (and sometimes violent) zeal to disrupt, innovate, and purify that was characteristic of the Puritans of earlier times—the Dutch and English Calvinists, and the American Revolutionaries of 1776.

Thus the new black presence and the white New Left appear to have almost opposite levels of the power motive. Might this difference be related to differences between these groups in action and orientation toward politics and society? For the blacks, high n Power is associated with accelerated attempts to achieve black goals and increase black power, to influence authorities, and to judge the overall power of the social system by the morality of its ends—specifically its responsibility toward the aspirations of black people. At least for this particular interest group (or solidarity group), high n Power appears to involve *increased activity* directed toward its purpose of redistributing power.

For the white radicals, low n Power and high n Achievement are associated with a very different kind of discontent and protest. They do not merely seek a change in the distribution of power, but often advocate replacing politics with "something else." In tones that sometimes seem apocalyptic, some white radicals of the New Left call for a quasi-religious enthusiasm that they believe will exorcise the spell of power and dismantle the cumbersome, inhumane bureaucracies of power. The "something else" is not fully articulated, but it seems to go beyond traditional politics and even traditional revolution. It resembles both a religious vision and a secular Utopia. Rather than trying to influence authorities, compete for power and resources, and judge the morality of the system's power, many white radicals appear to renounce both "the system" itself and any other system.[3] Perhaps it is these differences in motives and goals that distinguish the New Left from the "Old Left" (white radicals who advocate the more traditional redistribution of power). In any case, for the white radicals of the New Left, I would argue that low n Power is associated with *less activity* directed toward political competition and changing the allocation of power in the traditional political sense. But then what is the motive source for their *increased activity* directed toward more fundamental change? Winter and Wiecking suggested that it is n Achievement, and they noted both the example of the seventeenth-century Puritans and some recent empirical studies, which suggest that n Achievement is associated with religious vision and fundamental, disruptive change (see also McClelland, 1961, pp. 141–149, 367–373; Feierabend, Feierabend, and Sleet, 1967; Firestone, 1969).

These results do suggest an interesting hypothesis that can be further refined and tested: Within a particular group (whether an organized interest group or a more diffuse solidarity group), high levels of the power motive go along with competitive political activity directed toward changes in the allocation of power. Low levels of n Power may go along with activity, but activity in directions other than ordinary competitive politics and the struggle over the distribuion of power.[4]

---

[3] The differences in n Power levels and action between blacks and whites are undoubtedly due in part to differences in social class and background. White radicals, being largely upper- middle class (Keniston, 1968), have already experienced power in society as a whole, and are in effect renouncing it. Blacks are only beginning to experience power in society as a whole. Thus the motive differences have to be set in their social-developmental sequence to be fully understood (see Greenstein, 1969, pp. 36–40).

[4] Among interest or solidarity groups generally, the direction of activity should be related to whatever motives are strong: thus high n Achievement should lead

This distinction between directly political activity (the new Black Presence and the Old Left) and activity toward other goals (the New Left) seems parallel to Smelser's (1963) distinction between *norm-oriented movements*, which seek to change ways of doing things but not overall values, and *value-oriented movements*, which seek to alter basic societal values. The above hypothesis can then be restated in Smelser's terms: high n Power is associated with increased norm-oriented activity but not increased value-oriented activity; while low n Power and high other motives (especially n Achievement) may lead to increased value-oriented activity but not increased norm-oriented activity. A further refinement: within a broadly-based movement, both kinds of activity will occur and will be carried out by "specialists" with the appropriate motive constellation. The orientation and direction of the movement or group as a whole will be related to the motive levels that prevail either among the leaders or among the members generally.

This analysis certainly does not "explain away" social movements. Such interest groups and solidarity groups are not "caused" by the motives of their members, but rather by the objective social and institutional conditions that prevail (see Smelser, 1963; Milgram and Toch, 1969). This analysis is not intended to explain why such groups come into existence, but rather to suggest how motive levels affect their direction, activity, and characteristic orientations.

The conclusion that n Power is associated with movements that emphasize norms but do not attempt to change values also fits with the occupations that tend to be high in n Power: teaching, psychology, the clergy, business management, and leadership in urban renewal (see Chapter 4). Each of these groups is likely to be active in efforts to establish or strengthen norms (enlightenment, justice, happiness, mental health, adjustment, salvation, or rational efficiency, as the case may be); yet each group also tends to operate with the conviction that its basic values or conceptions of the "good" are right and should, therefore, constitute the basis of the social order. Skinner (1953, chaps. 22–26) argues that these high n Power professions are, in addition to government itself, the basic "controlling agencies" of society. Given such a conviction of the "rightness" of basic values, the power-related actions necessary to the enforcement or strengthening of norms may very likely be rationalized as "for the good of society," and *not perceived as power* by the particular group. Thus the so-called

---

to radical innovation, while high n Affiliation should lead to a concern for increasing warm, friendly human relationships (perhaps through establishing communes or "intentional communities").

helping professions, as well as business managers, may readily develop a "power shadow" or unconscious power complex (see Guggenbühl-Craig, 1971, pp. 1–19).

   The power motive in leaders: a study of American presidents. How do the motive levels of officials relate to their behavior and the performance of the system which they control or direct? Systematic research on leaders has been hampered by the lack of precise measurement techniques and, of course, by the fact that most really significant political figures are either dead or otherwise unavailable as subjects for the social scientist. Most previous researchers have therefore used one of two alternative strategies: (1) testing lower-level politicians and extrapolating upward (Browning and Jacob, 1964; Browning, 1968), and (2) making clinical interpretations of the motives of higher-level leaders (Lasswell, 1936; George and George, 1956; Freud and Bullitt, 1967). Neither strategy is fully satisfactory as an objective way to assess motive levels of major political leaders.

   Therefore Donley and Winter (1970) worked out a different strategy. They applied the scoring systems for *n* Achievement and *n* Power to the inaugural speeches of American presidents from 1905 through 1969. They argued that the inauguration presents each president with a kind of standardized situation, in which he must articulate the fundamental concerns, aspirations, fears, and projected actions of himself, "this administration," and "this country" as a whole. Thus the speeches are somewhat analogous to the individual person who reacts to an ambiguous situation as he takes a TAT. Of course many people help to write a presidential speech, so that the scores reflect the motives of the president's key advisors and speechwriters, as well as his own. Yet these associates also participate in the formation of policy and the making of decisions, so that the scores may be a good approximation of motive levels of the presidential administrations as a whole. Donley and Winter intended their study as a demonstration of a new method,[5] but I shall present their findings here in order to explore the behaviors and outcomes associated with the power motive among modern American presidents.

   There have been only twelve American presidents since 1905; such a small sample size makes drawing any conclusions difficult. Yet these twelve men are a total sample of a group who have had an enormous impact on the history of the world and the lives of millions of people

[5] See Donley and Winter (1970) for a discussion of methodological issues and problems.

over the past seventy years. Thus the significant results that emerge even in such a small sample, though tentative, can scarcely be called trivial or uninteresting.

Table 7.1 shows the *n* Power and *n* Achievement scores of the presidents, as corrected for length of the speech. N Power and *n* Achievement are highly correlated ($r = .71$, $p<.01$). Why is this so? Referring to twentieth-century chief executives, Hargrove (1966) distinguishes *Presidents of action* and *Presidents of restraint*. The former (including both Roosevelts, Wilson, Truman, Kennedy, and Johnson) have expanded the scope and powers of the presidency as an agency

TABLE 7.1 MOTIVE SCORES OF PRESIDENTIAL INAUGURAL
SPEECHES

President	Approximate number of words	Raw n Power score	n Power per 1000 words	Raw n Ach score	n Ach per 1000 words
T. Roosevelt (1905)	970	8	8.25	6	6.19
Taft (1909)	5570	11	1.97	5	.90
Wilson (1st—1913)	1670	9	5.39	5	3.00
Harding (1921)	3540	13	3.67	8	2.26
Coolidge (1925)	4200	13	3.10	7	1.67
Hoover (1929)	3960	12	3.03	16	4.04
F. D. Roosevelt (1st—1933)	1900	12	6.32	10	5.26
Truman (1949)	2460	18	7.32	10	4.07
Eisenhower (1st—1953)	2460	10	4.07	7	2.85
Kennedy (1961)	1320	11	8.33	9	6.82
Johnson (1965)	1460	10	6.85	11	7.53
Nixon (1969)	2130	11	5.16	18	8.45

Note: This table is slightly modified from Table 3 of Donley and Winter (1970). Reprinted from *Behavioral Science*, Volume 15, Number 3, 1970, by permission of James G. Miller, M.D., Ph.D., Editor.

of popular reform, through leadership of public opinion, management of legislative bodies, and control of the administrative apparatus. They are thought to be "good" or "strong" presidents. All but one were Democrats, and Table 7.1 shows that they tend to be relatively high in both motives. Presidents of restraint (including Taft, Hoover, and Eisenhower) have operated with a "Whig" theory of the office and avoided strong leadership, manipulation, emotion, and politics. They are often thought to be inactive or "weak" presidents. Presidents of this type are usually Republicans, and as expected, they are low in both motives.

For each of Hargrove's two patterns, power and achievement motives are either both high or both low. Moreover, each pattern is identified with one political party. Is there something about the American political system or American values that forces such a correlation? The ideal Republican president is restrained in both motives; the ideal Democratic president high in both. Apparently the other two possible types don't get nominated or elected to the presidency. A man high in n Power but low in n Achievement would probably seem too pragmatic, ruthless, and self-seeking; he would lack that visionary concern for excellence that Americans seem to require of their active presidents. Woodrow Wilson approaches this type—somewhat surprisingly in view of his reputation for inflexible idealism, but certainly consistent with the recent interpretation of George and George (1956, p. 320), who held that Wilson's concern for achievement was actually more of a defense mask for power needs. The man who is high in n Achievement and low in n Power may accomplish much in ordinary life; but if he ever became president, he would probably find the office unsatisfying and frustrating because he lacks political interests, sensitivity, and skill. When confronted with power issues, he may therefore be hesitant, ambivalent, and fluctuating in his behavior because he lacks the appropriate motive base. Herbert Hoover shows this motive pattern, and the above description certainly applies to his administration (see Barber, 1968). Richard Nixon tends toward the same pattern, although his n Power score is actually just below the median. Thus the very high correlation between the power and the achievement motives is probably an artifact of the peculiar constraints and values of the American political system.

Since n Power and n Achievement are so highly correlated among the presidents, it will be necessary to correct each motive for the effects of the other, in order to discover the independent effects of each motive. Therefore the results below will be presented in terms of partial correlation coefficients (partial τ, partial r, or partial point-biserial r).

The most obvious question is whether a president's n Power score is correlated with his performance in office. Does high n Power make a "good" president? In recent years, American historians have twice been polled on their evaluation of the presidents, and the correlations of motives with their ratings are shown in Table 7.2. Schlesinger (1962) simply asked 75 historians to rank all presidents on their "contribution as President," suggesting several factors that should be taken into account in making judgments. As shown in the table, neither motive is by itself significantly related to the rating.

Maranell (1970) asked 571 historians for ratings on seven different scales. According to the intercorrelations among the scales that

TABLE 7.2 PRESIDENTIAL MOTIVES AND RATINGS BY HISTORIANS

Rated Variable and Source	Relationships with:	
	n Power	n Achievement
New York Times Poll (Schlesinger, 1962), *9 Presidents*	*Kendall partial τ*	
Rank on "Overall contribution as President"[a]	−.02	.27
Maranell Poll (Maranell, 1970), *11 Presidents*	*Spearman partial r*	
A I. General prestige[b]	.49†	−.10
II. Strength of action	.44†	.08
III. Presidential activeness vs. passivity	.46†	.20
VI. Accomplishments of administration	.46†	−.05
VII. Amount of information about the President possessed by respondent	.54†	.06
B IV. Idealism vs. practicality	.19	−.19
V. Flexibility vs. inflexibility	.16	−.02

† p = .10 or lower (1-tailed)

[a] A generalized rating on characteristics such as creative approach to problems of statecraft, being the master instead of the servant of events, using the prestige of position to improve public welfare, effective use of staff, safeguarding the interests of the nation, and having an effect on the future.
[b] The Roman numerals refer to Maranell's dimensions, while the letters indicate clusters of these dimensions. See Maranell (1970) for the full definitions of the variables and the intercorrelation matrix.

Maranell presents, the seven scales constitute in effect two independent dimensions, as labelled in Table 7.2: (A) strong, prestigious,
active, accomplished much, and well-known to historians; and (B)
idealistic and inflexible vs. practical and flexible. N Power is related
to all of the scales of cluster (A) at levels that approach significance.

TABLE 7.3 PRESIDENTIAL MOTIVES AND ENTRY INTO WAR

Presidents during whose administration the United States entered a war:[a]   Presidents during whose administration the United States did not enter a war:[a]

President	n Power	n Ach	President	n Power	n Ach
Wilson	5.39	3.00	T. Roosevelt	8.25	6.19
Mexican Intervention			Taft	1.97	.90
Haiti Intervention					
World War I			Harding	3.67	2.26
Russian Intervention			Coolidge	3.10	1.67
F. D. Roosevelt	6.32	5.26	Hoover	3.03	4.04
World War II					
Truman	7.32	4.07	Eisenhower[c]	4.07	2.85
Korean War					
Kennedy	8.33	6.82			
Vietnam War[b]					
Cuban Intervention Attempt					
Johnson	6.85	7.53			
Dominican Intervention					
Mean Motive Scores	6.85	5.34		4.02	2.99
S.D.	1.10	1.87		2.19	1.90

	n Power	n Achievement
Partial point-biserial correlation with war entry	.40	.02
	p<.15	
	1-tailed	

Yet it is not related to the scales of cluster (B), which suggests that the power motive can be combined with either an inflexible ("Authoritarian"?) or flexible ("Machiavellian"?) style. As I argued in Chapters 1 and 3, the power motive and the style of using power appear to be different things. N Achievement is not related to any of the Maranell scales.

Is the power motive correlated with more specific presidential actions and outcomes? The historical events associated with the output of Don Juan versions, as discussed in the last chapter, provide some hypotheses. As we might predict, those presidents who were in office at the time that the United States entered wars tend to be higher in n Power than the others, while n Achievement is completely unrelated to war-entry.[7] Table 7.3 shows the actual motive scores of the two groups, gives the appropriate definitions and coding rules, and indicates the partial point-biserial correlation coefficients.

It is more difficult to check the relationship of presidential n Power to the growth of empire, since the United States has not usually annexed its "colonies." Nevertheless, formal gains or losses of territory (as defined in Chapter 6 and Appendix V) occurred under three presidents from 1905 to 1969:

[7] The n Power scores of the "war" and the "nonwar" presidents do not overlap, except for Theodore Roosevelt, who, in the judgment of many historians, did his best to have the United States enter a war. Hargrove records that he "preached the cult of war to the point where he turned many Americans against him. The public had always suspected that he had loved war too much . . ." (1966, p. 30). I have not included Nixon in this analysis because at the time of writing, his term as president is not complete.

Table 7.3 (*Cont.*)

[a] Definitions of "entry" and "war" are the same as those used by Richardson (1960) and Wright (1962, appendix C), which takes a war to be any quarrel involving two or more nation-states with casualties over 316 (magnitude 2.5).

[b] Assigning the entry of the United States into the Vietnam war to the Kennedy administration is a judgment based in part on the so-called Pentagon Papers documents (*New York Times*, 1971), and in part on the decision of Wright (1962, appendix C).

[c] The landing of United States troops in Lebanon in 1958 is not judged as entry into a war, because they were principally garrison troops who did not actively participate in fighting, and because they were soon removed without further involvement. Wright (1962, appendix C) does not judge that the incident was a "war." (See also R. P. Stebbins, *The United States in World Affairs 1958*, pp. 202–218. New York: Harper and Brothers, 1959.)

T. Roosevelt	Canal Zone acquired through a treaty with Panama.
Wilson	Virgin Islands purchased from Denmark.
Truman	Philippine Islands acquired independence; Okinawa and the Pacific Trust Territories acquired under United Nations mandate.

N Power is very significantly related to such gaining or losing of territory (partial $r_{pb} = .74$, p<.01 1-tailed), while n Achievement is negatively related (partial $r_{pb} = -.65$, p<.05 2-tailed).

The president is the head of a vast executive apparatus designed to implement his policies. If he has high n Power, then he may have greater difficulty in maintaining good relationships among his associates, for several reasons. He may be more critical; they may compete more for his favor; and they may disagree more with him and so become disaffected. Thus there should be a greater turnover of officials within his administration. Table 7.4 shows the number of changes of cabinet members, corrected for the number of departments and the length of presidential tenure in office. There are special difficulties in the case of the four vice-presidents who took office upon the death of a president and who, in consequence, inherited a cabinet not of their own making. The simplest way to correct for this seemed to be to consider only the cabinet changes and time in office for the term to which they were elected in their own right. All changes in the cabinet that occurred through two months after their inauguration in their own right are therefore ignored. Presumably by that point they had a cabinet of their own choosing. As predicted, the final measure of cabinet turnover is correlated with presidential n Power at a level that is modestly significant, and it is unrelated to n Achievement. Thus high n Power presidents are likely to have a group of advisors that changes more rapidly, whether for reasons of disagreement, disaffection, presidential disfavor, or simply the exhaustion of the cabinet member's energy.

Finally, presidents who are power-oriented, strong, and prestigious are likely to arouse animosity among some people. Hence n Power might predict attempts at assassination; although the causal chain between a president's motives, his behavior, reactions among potenial assassins, and appropriate circumstances for an actual attempt on his life is certainly complex and tenuous. Nevertheless, as predicted, the four presidents who had attempts made on their lives (both Roosevelts, Truman, and Kennedy) were significantly higher in n Power than the seven who had not (partial $r_{pb} = .74$, p<.01 1-tailed). There

TABLE 7.4 PRESIDENTIAL MOTIVES AND CHANGES IN THE CABINET

President	Number of changes[a] in the cabinet	Years in office[b]	Number of departments[c]	Cabinet changes per department per year
T. Roosevelt	11	4.0	9	.31
Taft	3	4.0	9	.08
Wilson	11	8.0	10	.14
Harding	3	2.4	10	.13
Coolidge	3	4.0	10	.08
Hoover	5	4.0	10	.13
F. D. Roosevelt	15	12.1	10	.12
Truman	6	4.0	9	.17
Eisenhower	11	8.0	10	.14
Kennedy	3	2.8	10	.11
Johnson	11	4.0	12	.23
Nixon	4[d]	2.5[d]	12[d]	.13[d]

	n Power	n Achievement
Partial correlations with changes per department per year	.46 $p<.08$ 1-tailed	.08

Note: Information taken from the *Biographical Directory of the American Congress 1774–1961, The World Almanac,* and newspaper reports.

[a] Changes are replacements of one cabinet member with another. The initial occupant at the beginning of an administration, and the first occupant of a new cabinet position are not counted. In the case of vice-presidents taking office upon the death of a president, only changes occurring more than two months after inauguration in their own right are counted.

[b] In the case of vice-presidents taking office upon the death of a president, only terms to which they were elected in their own right are counted.

[c] The maximum number of cabinet departments that existed during the years in office as defined above.

[d] As of July 31, 1971.

were no differences in n Achievement (partial $r_{pb} = -.38$, $p = $ n.s.). A slightly different interpretation of these results is that the potential for assassination is relatively constant, and the more active presidents who are high in n Power simply expose themselves more to the public.

The study of American presidents certainly raises problems of causal inference and method. Yet the results do give an encouraging suggestion of how a leader's power motive is likely to be reflected in his actions. Power motivation is associated with powerful actions and effects—war, territorial change, and rapid turnover of advisors. If these general qualities of strength and activity are positively valued, and if the specific outcomes are thought to be appropriate for the society, then n Power will be associated with positive judgment and evaluation, both by historians and by the leader's own constituency. However, if these qualities of the leader are thought inappropriate or are disliked, then n Power may be associated with negative evaluation and harshly critical judgment, at least in the minds of contemporary assassins and perhaps also of future historians.

Fear of Power and charisma. So far there has been no research on the social effects of Fear of Power. Nevertheless, many of the characteristics of Fear of Power resemble the features of charismatic leadership, so that the possible connection between the two deserves to be mentioned.[8] Max Weber contrasted the growth of the organized, institutional power of the nation-state or the prince with the revolutionary moral fervor of charismatic leaders, who rallied the masses to destroy institutions and other organized structures of power. According to Weber's definition, charisma is "a certain quality of an individual personality by virtue of which he is set apart from ordinary men and treated as endowed with supernatural, superhuman, or at least specifically exceptional powers or qualities" (1947, p. 358). Charisma compels recognition and obedience by followers as a "duty." For Weber, the conflict and interplay between rational bureaucratic power and charisma was the underlying dynamic of social change in human history (Eisenstadt, 1968). Now if charismatic leadership is related to the Fear of Power, then Weber's two conflicting trends of history can be identified with the two conflicting aspects of the power motive.

What are the reasons for linking charisma and the Fear of Power?

[8] I am indebted to Abigail Stewart for formulating the relationship between charismatic leadership and Fear of Power. Canetti (1962, pp. 409–462 and especially 444–448) also discusses these points.

First, power as such is very salient to the charismatic leader. He gains and maintains power and authority by proving his strength; whether through personal strength, glory in war, heroic deeds, magic, or the prophetic articulation of a revolutionary ideology, religious doctrine, or divine commandment. Yet at the same time the charismatic leader severs all ties to the established external order and rejects the routine, rational, methodical bureaucratic authority. He avoids structure and institutions. He seeks to act as an autonomous agent, unconstrained by power as it exists in organized society. Thus to him, power is both salient and aversive; in many ways the charismatic leader *fears the power of others*. He reacts by avoiding structure and leaving the situation, just as does the person high in Fear of Power. From a distance he challenges established power, and the provoked reaction of established authority combines with his own fears of power to produce a sense of persecution, which may be seen as a combination of paranoia and realistic sensitivity. This persecution acts as an important force to keep his followers together and active.

Following the conclusions of Chapter 5, the charismatic leader should also *fear his own power*. There is certainly persuasive evidence that he defends himself against such a fear. First, he holds that his power is not his own, but is a "gift of grace" or part of a divine mission that originated outside of himself. He holds that his followers obey, not out of the force of his own power, but rather out of a duty to the divine source of his power. Erikson traces the origin of this attribution in the childhood "sense of being both needed and chosen by [his father], and thus of carrying a superior destiny and duty . . . an excessive sense of unworthiness and a precocious devotion to 'ultimate concerns' " (1964, p. 203). Further, the charismatic leader rationalizes his power as being wholly for the benefit of his followers. Erikson calls this a "conviction that in the conduct of [his] individual life [he carries] the responsibility for a segment of mankind, if not for all existence" (*ibid.*). This belief seems closely related to the fusion of power and altruism in the TAT stories of people high in Fear of Power, and, in the extreme, to Freud's account (1911) of Schreber's delusion of having been chosen to save humanity. Finally, there is much evidence in the lives of charismatic leaders of a more general process of inhibition or striving to control impulses. Erikson refers to their "strong and precocious consciences." Ascetic dietary and sexual practices, and in some cases a very strong emphasis upon nonviolence, are specific forms of inhibition. Finally, as the revolutionary or prophetic movement succeeds and moves from opposition to administration, the charismatic leader often renounces power. For example, Moses was not allowed to reach the promised land, and Gandhi would not accept political office in an independent India. Sometimes he may even provoke his own assassination. Thus there seems ample evidence for arguing that charismatic leaders fear their own power.

One of the central features of charisma is that it makes no provision for its own succession. Succession occurs only upon the death or removal of the leader himself and is, therefore, always a major crisis for the followers: "What will happen to us when he dies?" This can be seen as the leader's defense against *fear of losing his own power*. If he can be replaced and followed in an orderly, agreed-upon manner, then he is only another occupant of a position of authority. If he is unique—incapable of being superseded, irreplaceable, the incarnation of an inevitable force larger than life—then his personal power is safe because it is the original and continuing bond among the followers.

Lewis's recent and provocative anthropological study of spirit possession and shamanism (1971) lends some additional support to the notion that the charismatic leader is one social manifestation of Fear of Power. First, charisma, or the "gift of grace," and possession are similar concepts: both are instruments of a "higher power," to which obedience is owed as a duty, and out of which relief from affliction and a good outcome is expected. Second, possession generally occurs among those social groups who themselves have lost power or who are oppressed by the power of others (women, depressed classes, colonized peoples). According to Lewis, ecstatic possession is a reassertion of autonomy against power, "rising to the challenge of the powers which rule [one's] life and valiently overcoming them" (1971, p. 188). It is therefore not hard to see why organized social hierarchies and established religions seek to damp down or manage such "enthusiasm" in order to preserve their power intact; and why many teachers, psychologists, clergymen, and business managers often take a dim view of uncontrolled charisma "from below."

For these reasons, I think that charismatic leadership is one social form of the Fear of Power. The argument seems to stress the pathological elements of the charismatic leader, perhaps because of the word "fear." This is not completely intended, and it is well to remember Erikson's distinction between the great innovator and the crank: "Such men and women also display an unusual energy of body, a rare concentration of mind, and a total devotion of soul, which carries them through trials and errors and near catastrophes, and, above all, helps them to bid their time, until they find their public even as their public finds and drafts them" (1964, p. 203).

THE CYCLE OF POWER AND CHANGE

Can these findings and speculations about the social aspects of the power motive be put together into some kind of general theory about the motivational dynamics of society? While it might seem premature or even absurd to attempt to construct such a theory on the basis of only a few studies, yet the effort is worthwhile both to summarize what is known and to suggest further hypotheses that might provoke research.

Let us begin with the study of Winter and Wiecking on the "puritans" of the New Left. High n Achievement—often in the form of a Protestant Ethic, a Puritan consciousness, or quasi-religious zeal—tends to bring about change, disruption, and dramatic economic progress (McClelland, 1961, chap. 4). This economic change may involve the destruction of existing beliefs, institutions, and modes of society based on stable forms of power and control. Because such a revolution threatens existing power arrangements, the innovators are likely to be scorned, ridiculed, and actively opposed by people with a stake in the existing order, who are likely to be high in n Power (Winter and Wiecking, 1971).

Over time, however, the economic changes create a new middle class or some equivalent group—people who have wealth, a stake in the new arrangements, and therefore something to lose. New institutions arise (at first they are "anti-institutions," but they are gradually transformed by the inherent dynamics of any bureaucracy). According to the outlook of this new class (which becomes the historical orientation for the nation itself), these original revolutionaries are now glorified as the "Founding Fathers" of a "Golden Age." Yet within the new middle class, several important changes are taking place. High n Achievement increases wealth and leisure. In addition to facilitating and encouraging an interest in prestige possessions, such wealth and leisure probably affect child-rearing practices so that sons grow up with lower n Achievement (see McClelland, 1961, pp. 376–378).

Will these sons also have high n Power? Their fathers will have relatively high incomes, which should lead to higher n Power. What about their mothers? Increased wealth tends to "free" women from the so-called burdens of economic work within and without the family; yet as Veblen (1899, pp. 55–60, 355–356) and others (Sampson, 1965, pp. 100–101) point out, women are thereby changed into objects of adornment and prestige, whose main power rests in the vicarious power of men and in a dominant, possessive, retaliatory attachment to children. In short, the mothers of these sons will have a kind of restricted status, and thus be likely to respond by binding together affection and rejection toward the male child—precisely the conditions that should increase the power motive of the son (see Chapter 6).

Thus there are grounds for supposing that the settled, wealthy middle class that emerges from the economic progress encouraged by n Achievement will in fact be relatively low in n Achievement and relatively high in n Power. In terms of behavior, they will be less likely to generate further economic growth through entrepreneurial effort; but they will have wealth, position, and prestige to protect and defend. In foreign affairs, concern with growth would change into a concern to protect established interests, both by means of war and by means of extending imperial control over what had been foreign industrial and commercial enterprise. At home, disruption and challenge would be perceived as the threat of "chaos . . . universal, unceasing, devastating, chilling, destructive disorder" (Berle, 1969, p. 5 and *passim*); and this threat of chaos should evoke responses of power and control.

What forces work against this trend? First of all, the power motive itself often leads to the destruction of real power, because prestige, vicarious power, and subjective feelings of potency can so easily come to replace real power (see Chapter 4). Thus over time, groups high in n Power may lose power to the challenges of other groups—new "puritans" who are, perhaps, both high in n Achievement and low in n Power.

How could such other groups arise? As a society becomes more centrally organized and thus controlled by only a few people, many men will feel a relative decline in their status and control. This loss of status may make them less dominant within the family; and thus leads to high n Achievement (and perhaps low n Power) in their sons (see Rosen and D'Andrade, 1959). Keniston (1968) argues that this pattern is characteristic of young radicals in America, and Hagen (1962) extends the same theory to account for the emergence of other radical modernizing groups. The high n Achievement sons thus become the "Puritans" of a new revolutionary movement.

In addition, the increased tendencies toward power and control should create more and more oppressed groups who have lost what power they had. Through the operation of Fear of Power, charismatic leaders would arise, around whom these new challenging groups would coalesce. Such a process is often associated with the breakup of colonial empires and the rise of new domestic classes and movements; probably these groups are most likely to be successful if the charisma of leaders is combined with high levels of n Achievement.

Thus we can sketch a repeating cycle of innovation, disruption, consolidation, and control. The achievement-motivated innovation later produces power-motivated control; while the very success of this centralizing control creates in others the motives for further innovation and change. Thus in an advanced industrial society, the central conflict is between "radical Puritans," who call for the animation of the individual as a directed agent of disruptive social change, and the "technocrats," who elaborate and extend their technologies of control through war and empire. (Recall the findings on urban renewal leaders in Chapter 4.) Such a cycle is highly speculative, for we do not know much about the conditions which produce high or low n Power. Yet it is offered as a framework for the interpretation of the power motive in history and society, and as a provocation to further analysis and research. I trust that the reader will judge whether it fits the history that he knows; and I hope that he will want to gather further evidence that would tend to prove (or disprove) the theory.

TAMING POWER

Since the time of Plato, wise men have argued that power must be tamed or controlled—by reason, morality, or altruism—lest it degenerate into despotism. Even Machiavelli argued that power had to be effective in order to serve society, and that effective power depended upon the informed art and wise action of the prince. Can power be controlled? Down to the present age, the question could be dodged by the argument that the growth and decay of societies through the *hubris* of power was part of an inevitable cycle of history; that such a cycle was essential to the evolution and change of human society and thus the development of man's potential. Empires come and go; what does it matter if the subjective seductions of power lead one leader or civilization astray, to be replaced by another which is at the moment better adapted? Does it work against the nature of man and society to try to tame the quest for power? Would that simply preserve one particular social order forever?

Yet in our own time the question must be taken more seriously, for in the present age untamed power can destroy humanity itself. I think that the problem is not power as such, which has been around for a long time; but rather the fusion of power with rapidly increasing technology in a kind of "mastery complex" (Murray, 1958; Canetti, 1962, pp. 465–470). Men who seek power through the advanced processes of technology "will not accept the fact that their unique excellence and their tragic flaw are one . . . they brush the warnings aside as early technological problems that later technologies will take care of" (Thompson, 1971, p. 52). And so we ask how power can be tamed.

The research reported in this book was directed toward identifying and measuring power as a human motive—a more precise specification of the Will to Power or the quest for power. Can it now contribute to the task of taming that power motive? Two approaches seem promising. First, what causes the power motive itself? Public policy could then be evaluated in terms of its effects on motive levels. Second, what other factors or dispositions can temper or modify the power motive? These are not easy questions; and because systematic research has scarcely begun, I can only sketch possible answers.

One of the roots of the power motive may be the restriction of the status and power of women, which through its effects on the behavior of mothers, creates a male concern with power (see Chapter 6). If this is true, then reducing the differentiation of sex-roles (particularly with respect to status and power) should reduce the power motive. Such a conclusion is quite an extension of the research evidence, but it is consistent with Gorer's (1966) observation that those cultures which do not take pleasure in domination and killing (such as the Arapesh, the Lepchas, and the Huri Pygmies) have little differentiation of sex style and no ideal of brave, aggressive masculinity. Such cultures probably would not understand the point of the Don Juan legend! This conclusion also fits with Adler's contention that the dominance of men over women can saturate the family atmosphere of a young child with power strivings (1928, pp. 168–170), especially if the mother binds the child exclusively and ambivalently to herself (1930, p. 403). It also fits with Canetti's linkage of sexual differentiation and power (1962, pp. 63–67).

Perhaps an increasing population density and the resulting crowded conditions of urban living are another origin of the power motive. Veroff, Atkinson, Feld, and Gurin (1960) found higher levels of Veroff n Power among men from large metropolitan areas, and it seems plausible that the power motive is both a product of urban living and a necessary aspect of survival in it. Studies of animal colonies suggest that many behaviors associated with the power motive increase under conditions of crowding. Yet Bailey studied the effects of population density in the Netherlands, which is the most densely populated country in the world. He concluded that crowding and urbanization there are accompanied by a turning inward, a sense of community, and low rates of violence (1970, parts I and III *passim*). In order to decide the issue, systematic studies of the effects on n Power (if any) of population density and other ecological conditions will be needed.

The range of particular institutions and aspects of social structure that might affect the power motive is great: housing, education, economic organization, the mass media, religion, and so forth. The motivational effects of these institutions can be studied either by studying institutions as such, or by studying whole societies and cultures. In the latter case, Power Imagery as scored in folktales, school readers, or other cultural documents can be correlated with aspects of social structure and institutions, or changes in the society, to test hypotheses about the social and cultural origins and effects of the power motive. (See Child, Storm, and Veroff, 1958; McClelland, 1961; and McClelland, Davis, Kalin, and Wanner, 1972, chaps. 3 and 4, as examples of this technique.) Longitudinal data of the sort collected by Kagan and Moss (1962) are a further source of evidence about the child-rearing antecedents of the power motive.

Can the power motive be tempered with something else? Affiliative concerns for other people might be one form of restraint on power, and this possibility can be explored by studying the actions associated with different configurations of motives (see Groesbeck, 1958). Many writers have followed Plato in arguing that reason should control power, although skeptics maintain that reason is the servant and not the master of human motives. In any case, the ways in which power can be inhibited by "reason" (perhaps as measured by Activity Inhibition) need to be more fully explored.

We are still a long way from being able to tame man's strivings for power; but there are at least some clear paths toward that goal, along which we can make some advance. The first task has been to identify, measure, and understand the power motive itself; and the research and theory of this book are intended as a contribution to work on this task.

Bibliography

Acton, Lord (J. E. E. Dalberg-Acton). Letter to Mandell Creighton, April 5, 1887. Reprinted in Gertrude Himmelfarb (Ed.), *Essays on freedom and power*. Glencoe, Ill.: The Free Press, 1949, pp. 358–367.

Adler, A. *Understanding human nature*. Garden City, N.Y.: Garden City Pub. Co., 1927.

———. The psychology of power. 1928. *J. individ. Psychol.*, 1966, 22, 166–172.

———. Individual psychology. In C. Murchison (Ed.), *Psychologies of 1930*. Worcester, Mass.: Clark University Press, 1930, pp. 395–405.

Adorno, T. W., Frenkel-Brunswik, E., Levinson, D.J., and Sanford, R. N. *The authoritarian personality*. New York: Harper & Brothers, 1950.

Alker, H. A. Is personality situationally specific or intrapsychically consistent? *J. pers.*, 1972, 40, 1–16.

Alpert, R. A., and Haber, R. N. Anxiety in academic achievement situations. *J. abnorm. soc. Psychol.*, 1960, 61, 207–215.

Andrews, J. D. W. The achievement motive and advancement in two types of organizations. *J. pers. soc. Psychol.*, 1967, 6, 163–168.

Arnold, M. B. *Story sequence analysis*. New York: Columbia University Press, 1962.

Atkinson, J. W. The achievement motive and the recall of interrupted tasks. *J. exp. Psychol.*, 1953, 46, 381–390.

———. Motivational determinants of risk-taking behavior. *Psychol. Rev.*, 1957, 64, 359–372.

——— (Ed.). *Motives in fantasy, action and society*. Princeton, N.J.: D. Van Nostrand Co., 1958.

————, and Birch, D. *The dynamics of action.* New York: John Wiley & Sons, Inc., 1970.

————, and Cartwright, D. Some neglected variables in contemporary conceptions of decision and performance. *Psychol. Rep.,* 1964, *14,* 575–590.

————, and Feather, N. T. *A theory of achievement motivation.* New York: John Wiley & Sons, Inc., 1966.

————, Heyns, R. W., and Veroff, J. The effect of experimental arousal of the affiliation motive on thematic apperception. *J. abnorm. soc. Psychol.,* 1954, *49,* 405–410.

————, and Raphelson, A. C. Individual differences in motivation and behavior in particular situations. *J. pers.,* 1956, *24,* 349–363.

————, and Reitman, W. R. Performance as a function of motive strength and expectancy of goal-attainment. *J. abnorm. soc. Psychol.,* 1956, *53,* 361–366.

Austen, J. *The story of Don Juan.* London: Martin Secker, 1939.

Ayllon, T., and Azrin, N. *The token economy: a motivational system for therapy and rehabilitation.* New York: Appleton-Century-Crofts, 1968.

Babbitt, I. *Democracy and leadership.* Boston: Houghton Mifflin Company, 1924.

Bachrach, P., and Baratz, M. S. Two faces of power. *Amer. poli. sci. Rev.,* 1962, *56,* 947–952.

Bailey, A. *The light in Holland.* New York: Alfred A. Knopf, 1970.

Bainton, R. H. The responsibilities of power according to Erasmus of Rotterdam. In L. Krieger and F. Stern (Eds.), *The responsibility of power: historical essays in honor of Hajo Holborn.* Garden City, N.Y.: Doubleday & Company, 1968, pp. 57–67 (Anchor Books).

Bales, R. F. *Personality and interpersonal behavior.* New York: Holt, Rinehart, and Winston, 1970.

Barber, J. D. Classifying and predicting Presidential styles: two "weak" Presidents. *J. soc. Issues,* 1968, *24,* 3, 51–80.

Barnard, C. I. *The functions of the executive.* Cambridge, Mass.: Harvard University Press, 1938.

Bass, B. M. An analysis of the leaderless group discussion. *J. abnorm. soc. Psychol.,* 1949, *33,* 527–533.

Baumrind, D. Some thoughts on ethics of research. *Amer. Psychologist,* 1964, *19,* 421–423.

Beisser, A. R. *The madness in sports.* New York: Appleton-Century-Crofts, 1967.

Bellush, J., and Hausknecht, M. Entrepreneurs and urban renewal: the new men of power. In J. Bellush and M. Hausknecht (Eds.), *Urban renewal: people, politics, and planning.* Garden City, N.Y.: Doubleday & Company, 1967, pp. 209–224 (Anchor Books).

Berg, I. A. (Ed.). *Response set in personality assessment.* Chicago: Aldine Publishing Co., 1967.

Berger, C. R. The effects of influence feedback and need influence on the relationship between incentive and magnitude of attitude change. Unpublished Ph.D. thesis, Michigan State University, 1968.

————. Need to influence and feedback regarding outcomes as determinants of the relationship between incentive magnitude and self-persuasion. *Speech Monogr.*, 1969, *36*, 435–442.

Berle, A. A. *Power*. New York: Harcourt, Brace, and World, Inc., 1969.

Berlew, D. E. A study of interpersonal sensivity. Unpublished Ph.D. thesis, Harvard University, 1959.

Berlyne, D. E. Behavior theory as personality theory. In E. F. Borgatta and W. W. Lambert (Eds.), *Handbook of personality theory and research*. Chicago: Rand McNally & Company, 1968, pp. 629–690.

Birch, D., and Veroff, J. *Motivation: a study of action*. Belmont, Calif.: Brooks/Cole Publishing Company, 1966.

Birney, R. C. Research on the achievement motive. In E. F. Borgatta and W. W. Lambert (Eds.), *Handbook of personality theory and research*. Chicago: Rand McNally and Company, 1968, pp. 857–889.

————, Burdick, H., and Teevan, R. C. *Fear of failure*. New York: Van Nostrand-Reinhold Company, 1969.

Brown, R. W. *Social Psychology*. New York: The Free Press, 1965.

Browning, R. P. Businessmen in politics: motivation and circumstance in the rise to power. Unpublished Ph.D. thesis, Yale University, 1960.

————. The interaction of personality and political system in decisions to run for office: some data and a simulation technique. *J. soc. Issues*, 1968, *24*, 3, 93–109.

————, and Jacob, H. Power motivation and the political personality. *Pub. Opin. Quart.*, 1964, *28*, 75–90.

Brunswik, E. *Perception and the representative design of psychological experiments*. Berkeley, Calif.: University of California Press, 1956.

Bullock, A. *Hitler, a study in tyranny* (Rev. Ed.). Harmondsworth, England: Penguin Books, 1962.

Byrne, D. Response to attitude similarity-dissimilarity as a function of affiliation need. *J. pers.*, 1962, *30*, 164–177.

————, McDonald, R. D., and Mikawa, J. Approach and avoidance affiliation motives. *J. pers.*, 1963, *31*, 21–37.

Canetti, E. *Crowds and power*. New York: Viking Press, 1962.

Carter, J. F. *Power and persuasion*. New York: Duell, Sloan & Pearce, 1960.

Cartwright, D. A field theoretical conception of power. In D. Cartwright (Ed.), *Studies in social power*. Ann Arbor, Mich.: Research Center for Group Dynamics, University of Michigan, 1959, pp. 183–220.

Cattell, R. B. The dynamic calculus: a system of concepts derived from objective motivation measurement. In G. Lindzey (Ed.), *Assessment of human motives*. New York: Holt, Rinehart & Winston, 1958, pp. 197–238.

Champlin, J. R. On the study of power. *Pol. and Society*, 1970, *1*, 91–111.

Child, I. L., Storm, T., and Veroff, J. Achievement themes in folk tales related to socialization practice. In J. W. Atkinson (Ed.), *Motives in fantasy, action and society.* Princeton, N.J.: D. Van Nostrand Co., 1958, pp. 479–492.

Christie, R., and Geis, F. L. *Studies in Machiavellianism.* New York and London: Academic Press, 1970.

Clark, R. A., Teevan, R. C., and Ricciuti, H. N. Hope of success and fear of failure as aspects of need for achievement. *J. abnorm. soc. Psychol.*, 1956, *53*, 182–186.

Clausewitz, K. von. *War, politics, and power.* Tr. and ed. by Col. E. M. Collins. Chicago: Henry Regnery Co., 1962 (Gateway Editions).

Coleman, J. S. *The adolescent society.* New York: The Free Press, 1961.

Collins, B. E., and Raven, B. H. Group structure: attraction, coalitions, communication, and power. In G. Lindzey and E. Aronson (Eds.), *Handbook of social psychology* (Rev. Ed.), Volume 4. Reading, Mass.: Addison-Wesley, 1969, pp. 102–204.

Combs, A. W. A comparative study of motivations as revealed in Thematic Apperception stories and autobiography. *J. clin. Psychol.*, 1947, *3*, 65–75.

Couch, A. S. The psychological determinants of interpersonal behavior. In G. S. Nielson (Ed.), *Personality research.* København: Munksgaard, 1962, pp. 111–127.

———, and Keniston, K. Yeasayers and naysayers: agreeing response set as a personality variable. *J. abnorm. soc. Psychol.*, 1960, *60*, 151–174.

Craig, G. A. Friedrich Schiller and the problems of power. In L. Krieger and F. Stern (Eds.), *The responsibility of power: historical essays in honor of Hajo Holborn.* Garden City, N.Y.: Doubleday & Company, 1968, pp. 135–156 (Anchor Books).

Cronbach, L. J., and Meehl, P. E. Construct validity in psychological tests. *Psychol. Bull.*, 1952, *52*, 281–302.

Dahl, R. A. The concept of power. *Behav. sci.*, 1957, *2*, 201–215.

———. A critique of the ruling elite model. *Amer. poli. sci. Rev.*, 1958, *52*, 463–469.

———. *Who governs?* New Haven, Conn.: Yale University Press, 1961.

———. *Modern political analysis.* Englewood Cliffs, N.J.: Prentice-Hall, 1963.

D'Angelo, S. (Ed.), *World car catalogue.* Bronxville, N.Y.: Herald Books, 1969.

Dashiell, J. F. *Fundamentals of general psychology.* Boston: Houghton Mifflin, 1949.

Davis, W. N. Drinking: a search for power or for nurturance? Unpublished Ph.D. thesis, Harvard University, 1969.

deCharms, R. C. Affiliation motivation and productivity in small groups. *J. abnorm. soc. Psychol.*, 1957, *55*, 222–226.

————. *Personal causation.* New York and London: Academic Press, 1968.
————, and Davé, P. N. Hope of success, fear of failure, and risk-taking behavior, *J. pers. soc. Psychol.*, 1965, *1*, 558–568.
————, Morrison, H. W., Reitman, W., and McClelland, D. C. Behavioral correlates of directly and indirectly measured achievement motivation. In D. C. McClelland (Ed.), *Studies in motivation.* New York: Appleton-Century-Crofts, 1955, pp. 414–423.
de La Souchère, É. *An explanation of Spain.* New York: Random House, 1964 (Vintage Books).
Domhoff, G. W. *Who rules America?* Englewood Cliffs, N.J.: Prentice-Hall, 1967 (Spectrum Books).
Donley, R. E., and Winter, D. G. Measuring the motives of public officials at a distance: an exploratory study of American presidents. *Behav. Sci.*, 1970, *15*, 227–236.
Duffy, E. *Activation and behavior.* New York: John Wiley & Sons, Inc., 1963.
Duijker, H. C. J. Het streven naar macht [The striving for power]. *Gawein— Tijdsschrift van de psychologische kring aan de Nijmeegse Universiteit*, 1961, *9*, 125–133.
Dulany, D. E. Awareness, rules, and propositional control: a confrontation with S-R theory. In D. R. Dixon and D. L. Horton (Eds.), *Verbal behavior and general behavior theory.* Englewood Cliffs, N.J.: Prentice Hall, 1968, pp. 340–387.
Educational Testing Service. *College Student Questionnaire.* Princeton, N.J., 1965.
Eisenstadt, S. N. Introduction to *Max Weber on charisma and institution building.* Chicago: Univ. of Chicago Press, 1968.
Elliott, J. H. The decline of Spain. *Past and Present*, 1961, #20, 52–75.
————. *Imperial Spain 1469–1716.* New York: St. Martin's Press, Inc., 1963.
Erdmann, R. Machtthematik und Verhalten—eine Replikation der Winterschen Arbeit und der Versuch einer Itemanalyse des Verrechnungsschlüssels. Unpublished Diplomarbeit (thesis), Phillips Universität, Marburg, 1971.
Erikson, E. H. Psychological reality and historical actuality. In *Insight and responsibility.* New York: W. W. Norton & Company, 1964, pp. 159–215.
————. *Gandhi's truth.* New York: W. W. Norton & Company, 1969.
Eysenck, H. J. *The dynamics of anxiety and hysteria.* London: Routledge and Kegan Paul, 1957.
Feather, N. T. The relation of persistence at a task to expectation of success and achievement related motives. *J. abnorm. soc. Psychol.*, 1961, *63*, 552–561.
Feierabend, R. L., Feierabend, L. K., and Sleet, D. A. Need achievement, coerciveness of government, and political unrest: a cross-national

analysis. Paper read at the American Psychological Association convention, 1967.

Feld, S. C., and Smith, C. P. An evaluation of the objectivity of the method of content analysis. In J. W. Atkinson (Ed.), *Motives in fantasy, action and society*. Princeton, N.J.: D. Van Nostrand Co., 1958, pp. 234–241.

Felker, C. (Ed.), *The power game*. New York: Simon & Schuster, 1969.

Fenichel, O. *The psychoanalytic theory of neurosis*. New York: W. W. Norton & Company, 1945.

Fiedler, F. E. Validation and extension of the contingency model of leadership effectiveness: a review of empirical findings. *Psychol. Bull.*, 1971, 76, 128–148.

Firestone, J. M. National motives and national attributes: a cross-time analysis. Buffalo, N.Y.: Cornell Aeronautical Laboratory, Inc., 1969 (Cal# VO-2653-G-3).

Fishman, D. B. Need and expectancy as determinants of affiliative behavior in small groups. *J. pers. soc. Psychol.*, 1966, 4, 155–164.

Fiske, D. W., and Maddi, S. R. (Eds.), *Functions of varied experience*. Homewood, Ill.: Dorsey Press, 1961.

Frank, J. D. *Persuasion and healing*. Baltimore: The Johns Hopkins University Press, 1961.

French, E. G. Development of a measure of complex motivation. In J. W. Atkinson (Ed.), *Motives in fantasy, action and society*. Princeton, N.J.: D. Van Nostrand Co., 1958, pp. 242–248.

————, and Lesser, G. S. Some characteristics of the achievement motive in women. *J. abnorm. soc. Psychol.*, 1964, 68, 119–128.

French, J. R. P., Jr., and Raven, B. The bases of social power. In D. Cartwright (Ed.), *Studies in social power*. Ann Arbor, Mich.: Research Center for Group Dynamics, University of Michigan, 1959, pp. 150–167.

Frenkel-Brunswik, E. Motivation and behavior. *Genet. Psychol. Monogr.*, 1942, 26, 121–265.

Freud, S. A special type of choice of object made by men. 1910. In *Collected papers*, Volume 4. London: Hogarth Press, 1924, pp. 192–202.

————. Psycho-analytic notes upon an autobiographical account of a case of paranoia (dementia paranoides). 1911. In *Collected papers*, Volume 3. London: Hogarth Press, 1924, pp. 387–470.

————. Totem and taboo. 1913. New York: W. W. Norton & Company, 1950.

————. On narcissism: an introduction. 1914. In *Collected papers*, Volume 4. London: Hogarth Press, 1924, pp. 30–60.

————. The taboo of virginity. 1918. In *Collected papers*, Volume 4. London: Hogarth Press, 1924, pp. 217–235.

————. *Group psychology and the analysis of the ego*. 1921. London: Hogarth Press, 1940.

————. *The ego and the id.* 1923. New York: W. W. Norton & Company, 1962.

————. *Civilization and its discontents.* 1930. New York: W. W. Norton & Company, 1961.

————, and Bullitt, W. C. *Thomas Woodrow Wilson: a psychological study.* Boston: Houghton Mifflin, 1967.

Galbraith, J. K. *The new industrial state.* Boston: Houghton Mifflin Company, 1967.

Gamson, W. A. *Power and discontent.* Homewood, Ill.: Dorsey Press, 1968.

George, A. and George, J. *Woodrow Wilson and Colonel House: a personality study.* New York: John Day, 1956.

Gibb, C. A. Leadership. In G. Lindzey and E. Aronson (Eds.), *Handbook of social psychology* (Rev. ed.), Volume 4. Reading, Mass.: Addison-Wesley, 1969, pp. 205–282.

Goodman, P. *The society I live in is mine.* New York: Horizon Press, 1962.

Goodman, L. A., and Kruskal, W. H. Measures of association for cross-classifications. *J. Amer. stat. Assn.,* 1954, *49,* 732–764.

Gorer, G. *The American people.* New York: W. W. Norton & Company, 1948.

————. Man has no "killer" instinct. *New York Times Magazine,* 1966, November 27, pp. 47f.

Gray, J. A. *Pavlov's typology.* New York: Macmillan, 1965.

Green, O. H. *Spain and the Western tradition,* Volume 1. Madison, Wisc.: University of Wisconsin Press, 1963.

Green, R. F., and Nowlis, V. A factor-analytic study of the domain of mood with independent validation of the factors. Paper read at the American Psychological Association convention, 1957.

Greene, D. L., and Winter, D. G. Motives, involvements, and leadership among Black college students. *J. pers.,* 1971, *39,* 319–332.

Greenstein, F. I. *Personality and politics.* Chicago: Markham Publishing Company, 1969.

Groesbeck, B. L. Toward description of personality in terms of configurations of motives. In J. W. Atkinson (Ed.), *Motives in fantasy, action and society.* Princeton, N.J.: D. Van Nostrand Co., 1958, pp. 383–399.

Guggenbühl-Craig, A. *Power in the helping professions.* Zürich: Spring Publications, 1971.

Guhl, A. M. Psychophysiological interrelations in the social behavior of chickens. *Psychol. Bull.,* 1964, *61,* 277–285.

Haber, R. N., and Alpert, R. A. The role of situation and picture cues in projective measurement of the achievement motive. In J. W. Atkinson (Ed.), *Motives in fantasy, action and society.* Princeton, N.J.: D. Van Nostrand Co., 1958, pp. 644–663.

Hagen, E. E. *On the theory of social change.* Homewood, Ill.: Dorsey Press, 1962.

.

Haley, J. *Strategies of psychotherapy.* New York: Grune & Stratton, Inc., 1963.

————. *The power tactics of Jesus Christ and other essays.* New York: Grossman, 1969.

Hardy, K. R. Determinants of conformity and attitude change. *J. abnorm. soc. Psychol.,* 1957, 54, 289–294.

Hargrove, E. C. *Presidential leadership: personality and political style.* New York: Macmillan, 1966.

Heckhausen, H. *Hoffnung und Furcht in der Leistungsmotivation.* Meisenheim am Glan: Verlag Anton Hain, 1963.

————. *The anatomy of achievement motivation.* New York and London: Academic Press, 1967.

————. Achievement motive research: current problems and some contributions towards a general theory of motivation. In W. Arnold (Ed.), *Nebraska symposium on motivation 1968.* Lincoln, Neb.: University of Nebraska Press, 1968, pp. 103–174.

————, and Weiner, B. The emergence of a cognitive psychology of motivation. In P. C. Dodwell (Ed.), *New horizons in psychology* 2. Harmondsworth, England: Penguin Books, 1972, pp. 126–147.

Heider, F. *The psychology of interpersonal relations.* New York: John Wiley & Sons, Inc., 1958.

Hobbes, T. *Leviathan,* 1651. New York: E. P. Dutton & Company, 1950.

Hobsbawm, E. J. *Primitive rebels.* New York: W. W. Norton & Company, 1965.

Hollander, E. P. *Leaders, groups, and influence.* New York: Oxford University Press, 1964.

————, and Julian, J. W. Contemporary trends in the analysis of leadership processes. *Psychol. Bull.,* 1961, 71, 387–397.

Holt, R. R. The nature of TAT stories as cognitive products: a psychoanalytic approach. In J. Kagan and G. S. Lesser (Eds.), *Contemporary issues in thematic apperceptive methods.* Springfield, Ill.: Charles C Thomas, 1961, pp. 3–43.

Holthusen, E. A concept of destiny in human literature. *Publ. Mod. Lang. Assn.,* 1960, 75, 1–10.

Horner, M. S. Sex differences in achievement motivation and performance in competitive and non-competitive situations. Unpublished Ph.D. thesis, University of Michigan, 1968.

————. Why women fail. *Psychology Today,* 1969, November, pp. 36ff.

Horney, K. *The neurotic personality of our time.* New York: W. W. Norton & Co., 1937.

Horton, J. Order and conflict theories of social problems as competing ideologies. *Amer. J. Sociol.,* 1966, 71, 701–713.

Howells, L. T., and Becker, S. W. Seating arrangements and leadership emergence. *J. abnorm. soc. Psychol.,* 1962, 64, 148–150.

Hunter, F. *Community power structure.* Chapel Hill, N.C.: University of North Carolina Press, 1953.

Inkeles, A., and Levinson, D. J. National character: the study of modal personality and sociocultural systems. In G. Lindzey and E. Aronson (Eds.), *Handbook of social psychology* (Rev. ed.), Volume 4. Reading, Mass.: Addison-Wesley, 1969, pp. 418–506.

Iwinski, M. B. La statistique internationale des imprimés. *Bull. de l'Institut Internationale de Bibliographie*, 1911, *16*, 1–139.

Jones, D. F. The need for power as a predictor of leadership and exploitation in a variety of small group settings. Unpublished Honors thesis, Wesleyan University, 1969.

Kagan, J., and Lesser G. S. (Eds.), *Contemporary issues in thematic apperceptive methods.* Springfield, Ill.: Charles C Thomas, 1961.

————, and Moss, H. A. *Birth to maturity.* New York: John Wiley & Sons, Inc., 1962.

Katz, I. The socialization of academic motivation in minority group children. In D. Levine (Ed.), *Nebraska symposium on motivation 1967.* Lincoln, Neb.: University of Nebraska Press, 1967, pp. 133–191.

Keniston, K. *Young radicals.* New York: Harcourt, Brace and World, 1968.

Klein, M., and Riviere, J. *Love, hate and reparation.* 1937. New York: W. W. Norton & Company, Inc., 1964.

Klinger, E. Fantasy need achievement as a motivational construct. *Psychol. Bull.*, 1966, *66*, 291–308.

————. Modeling effects on achievement imagery. *J. pers. soc. Psychol.* 1967, *7*, 49–62.

————. Short-term stability and concurrent validity of TAT need scores: achievement, affiliation, and hostile press. In *Proceedings of the 76th Annual Convention of the American Psychological Association 1968.* Washington: American Psychological Association, 1968, pp. 157–158.

————. *Structure and functions of fantasy.* New York: John Wiley & Sons, Inc., 1971.

————, and NcNelly, F. W., Jr. Fantasy need achievement and performance: a role analysis. *Psychol. Rev.*, 1969, *76*, 574–591.

Knapp, R. H. N Achievement and aesthetic preference. In J. W. Atkinson (Ed.), *Motives in fantasy, action and society.* Princeton, N.J.: D. Van Nostrand Co., 1958, pp. 367–372.

Kock, S. W. Management and motivation. Summary of a doctoral thesis presented at the Swedish School of Economics. Helsingfors, 1965.

Koenig, K. Social psychological correlates of self-reliance. Unpublished Ph.D. thesis, University of Michigan, 1963.

Kolb, D. A., and Boyatsis, R. On the dynamics of the helping relationship. *J. appl. behav. Sci.*, 1970, *6*, 267–289.

Kratzsch, S. Machtthematik und Verhalten. Untersuchung I: Empirische Untersuchung der Beziehung von Aspekten der Machtorientierung zu einzelen Persönlichkeitsdimensionen und Einstellungs- und Verhaltensdaten. Eine Korrelationstudie zur Machtthematik. Unpublished Diplomarbeit (thesis), Phillips Universität, Marburg, 1971.

Kropotkin, P. A. *Mutual aid, a factor of evolution.* New York: McClure, Phillips, 1902.

Kruse, A. Projektive Machtthematik, Verhalten und die Bewertung durch Gruppenmitglieder—eine Erkundungsstudie. Unpublished Diplomarbeit (thesis), Phillips Universität, Marburg, 1971.

Lasswell, H. *Psychopathology and politics.* Chicago: University of Chicago Press, 1930.

————. *Politics: who gets what, when, how.* New York: McGraw-Hill, 1936.

————, and Kaplan, A. *Power and society.* New Haven, Conn.: Yale University Press, 1950.

Lazarus, R. S. A substitute-defensive conception of apperceptive fantasy. In J. Kagan and G. S. Lesser (Eds.), *Contemporary issues in thematic apperceptive methods.* Springfield, Ill.: Charles C Thomas, 1961.

————. Story telling and the measurement of motivation: the direct vs. substitutive controversy. *J. consult. Psychol.,* 1966, 30, 483–487.

Leavitt, H. J. Some effects of certain communication patterns of group performance. *J. abnorm. soc. Psychol.,* 1951, 46, 38–50.

Lennerlöf, L. *ITAT: Studies performed with a version of TAT intended for use in industrial psychology.* Stockholm: Swedish Council for Personnel Administration, 1967 (Report #49).

Lewis, I. M. *Ecstatic religion: an anthropological study of spirit possession and shamanism.* Harmondsworth, England: Penguin Books, 1971.

Lindman, H. A. Study of motive and vocational preference in high school students. Unpublished Honors thesis, University of Michigan, 1958.

Lippitt, R., Polansky, N., Redl, F., and Rosen, S. The dynamics of power. *Hum. Rel.,* 1952, 5, 37–64.

Lipsit, S. M. Political sociology. In R. K. Merton, L. Broom, and L. S. Cottrell (Eds.), *Sociology today.* New York: Basic Books, Inc., 1959, pp. 81–114.

————, Trow, M. A., and Coleman, J. S. *Union democracy.* Glencoe, Ill.: The Free Press, 1956.

Litwin, G. H., and Stringer, R. A., Jr. *Motivation and organizational climate.* Boston: Harvard Business School, 1968.

Locke, J. *An essay concerning human understanding.* 1690. Philadelphia: Zell, n.d.

McArthur, C. The effects of need achievement on the content of TAT stories: a re-examination. *J. abnorm. soc. Psychol.,* 1953, 48, 532–536.

McClelland, D. C. *Personality.* New York: Holt, Rinehart & Winston, Inc., 1951.

————. Methods of measuring human motivation. In J. W. Atkinson (Ed.), *Motives in fantasy, action and society.* Princeton, N.J.: D. Van Nostrand Co., 1958, pp. 7–42.

————. *The achieving society.* Princeton, N.J.: D. Van Nostrand Co., 1961.

————. N Achievement and entrepreneurship: a longitudinal study. *J. pers. soc. Psychol.*, 1965, *1*, 389–392.

————. The two faces of power. *J. int. Affairs*, 1970, *24*, 29–47.

————. *Assessing human motivation.* New York: General Learning Press, 1971 (a).

————. *Motivational trends in society.* New York: General Learning Press, 1971 (b).

————, and Atkinson, J. W. The projective expression of needs: I. The effect of different intensities of the hunger drive on perception. *J. Psychol.*, 1948, 25, 205–232.

————, Atkinson, J. W., Clark, R. A., and Lowell, E. L. *The achievement motive.* New York: Appleton-Century-Crofts, 1953.

————, Davis, W. N., Kalin, R., and Wanner, E. *The drinking man.* New York: The Free Press, 1972.

————, Sturr, J. F., Knapp, R. H., and Wendt, H. W. Obligations to self and society in the United States and Germany. *J. abnorm. soc. Psychol.*, 1958, *56*, 245–255.

————, and Watson, R. I., Jr. Power motivation and risk-taking behavior. *J. pers.*, 1973, *41*, 121–139.

————, and Winter, D. G. *Motivating economic achievement.* New York: The Free Press, 1969.

McGuire, W. J. Personality and susceptibility to social influence. In E. F. Borgatta and W. W. Lambert (Eds.), *Handbook of personality theory and research.* Chicago: Rand McNally & Company, 1968, pp. 1130–1188.

McGurk, E. Susceptibility to visual illusions. *J. Psychol.*, 1965, *61*, 127–143.

MacKay, D. *The double invitation in the legend of Don Juan.* Stanford, Calif.: Stanford University Press, 1943.

McKeachie, W. J. Motivation, teaching methods, and college learning. In M. R. Jones (Ed.), *Nebraska symposium on motivation 1961.* Lincoln. Neb.: University of Nebraska Press, 1961, pp. 111–142.

Maddi, S. R. *Personality theories: a comparative analysis.* Homewood, Ill.: Dorsey Press, 1968.

Maeztu, R. de. Don Juan o el Poder. In *Don Quixote, Don Juan y la Celestina.* Madrid: Espasa-Calpe, 1938.

Mandel, O. *The theatre of Don Juan.* Lincoln, Neb.: University of Nebraska Press, 1963.

Mandler, G., and Sarason, S. B. A study of anxiety and learning. *J. abnorm. soc. Psychol.*, 1952, 47, 166–173.

Mann, R. D. A review of the relationships between personality and performance in small groups. *Psychol. Bull.*, 1959, 56, 241–270.

————, Gibbard, G. S., and Hartman, J. J. *Interpersonal styles and group development.* New York: John Wiley & Sons, Inc., 1967.

Maranell, G. M. The evaluation of presidents: an extension of the Schlesinger poll. *J. Amer. History.* 1970, 57, 104–113.

Marañón, G. *Don Juan*. Madrid: Espasa-Calpe, 1940.

Maroney, R. J., Warren, J. M., and Sinha, M. M. Stability of social dominance hierachies in monkies (Macaca mulatta). *J. soc. Psychol.*, 1959, *50*, 285–293.

Martin, N. H., and Sims, J. H. Power tactics. *Harvard Business Review*, 1956, November–December, pp. 25f. Reprinted in D. A. Kolb, I. M. Rubin, and J. M. McIntyre (Eds.), *Organizational psychology: a book of readings*. Englewood Cliffs, N.J.: Prentice-Hall, 1971, pp. 155–161.

May, R. *Psychology and the human dilemma*. Princeton, N.J.: D. Van Nostrand Co., 1967.

May, R. R. Sex differences in fantasy patterns. *J. proj. tech. persy. Assess.*, 1966, *30*, 576–586.

———. Sexual identity and sex-role conceptions in acute schizophrenia. Unpublished Ph.D. thesis, Harvard University, 1969.

———. Paranoia and power anxiety. *J. proj. tech. persy. Assess.*, 1970, *34*, 412–418.

Merei, F. Group leadership and institutionalization. *Hum. Rel.*, 1949, *2*, 23–39.

Milgram, S. Behavioral study of obedience. *J. abnorm. soc. Psychol.*, 1963, *67*, 371–378.

———. Some conditions of obedience and disobedience to authority. *Hum. Rel.*, 1965, *18*, 57–76.

———, and Toch, H. Collective behavior: crowds and social movements. In G. Lindzey and E. Aronson (Eds.), *Handbook of social psychology* (Rev. ed.), Volume 4. Reading, Mass.: Addison-Wesley, 1969, pp. 507–610.

Miller, N. E. Experimental studies of conflict. In. J. McV. Hunt (Ed.), *Personality and the behavior disorders*, Volume 1. New York: The Ronald Press Company, 1944, pp. 431–465.

Miller, R. E., Murphy, J. V., and Mirsky, I. A. Modification of social dominance in a group of monkies by inter-animal conditioning, *J. comp. physiol. Psychol.*, 1955, *48*, 392–396.

Millett, K. *Sexual politics*. Garden City, N.Y.: Doubleday & Company, 1970.

Mills, C. W. *The power elite*. New York: Oxford University Press, 1956.

Minton, H. L. Power as a personality construct. In B. A. Maher (Ed.), *Progress in experimental personality research*, Volume 4. New York and London: Academic Press, 1967, pp. 229–267.

Mischel, W. *Personality and assessment*. New York: John Wiley & Sons, Inc., 1968.

Morehead, A. H., Frey, R. L., and Mott-Smith, G. *The new complete Hoyle*. Garden City, N.Y.: Garden City Books, 1956.

Morgan, C. D., and Murray, H. A. A method for examining fantasies: the thematic apperception test. *Arch. Neurol. & Psychiat.*, 1935, *34*, 289–306.

Morgan, H. H. Measuring achievement motivation with "picture interpretation." *J. consult. Psychol.*, 1953, *17*, 289–292.

Mosteller, F., and Bush, R. R. Selected quantitative techniques. In. G. Lindzey (Ed.), *Handbook of social psychology*, Volume 1. Reading, Mass.: Addison-Wesley, 1954, pp. 289–334.

Moulton, R. W. Notes for a projective measure of fear of failure. In J. W. Atkinson (Ed.), *Motives in fantasy, action and society*. Princeton, N.J.: D. Van Nostrand Co., 1958, pp. 563–571.

Murphy, J. V., and Miller, R. E. The manipulation of dominance in monkies with conditioned fear. *J. abnorm. soc. Psychol.*, 1956, *53*, 244–248.

Murray, D. C., and Deabler, H. L. Colors and mood-tones. *J. appl. Psychol.*, 1957, *41*, 279–283.

Murray, H. A. The effects of fear upon estimates of the maliciousness of other personalities. *J. soc. Psychol.*, 1933, *4*, 310–329.

———. Techniques for a systematic investigation of fantasy. *J. Psychol.*, 1937, *3*, 115–143.

———. *Explorations in personality*. New York: Oxford University Press, 1938.

———. Drive, time, strategy, measurement, and our way of life. In G. Lindzey (Ed.), *Assessment of human motives*. New York: Holt, Rinehart & Winston, Inc., 1964, pp. 183–196.

Murstein, B. I. *Theory and research in projective techniques*. New York: John Wiley & Sons, Inc., 1963.

New York Times. *The Pentagon Papers*. New York: Bantam Books, Inc., 1971.

Nicolson, H. *The meaning of prestige*. London: Cambridge University Press, 1938.

Niebuhr, R. *Moral man and immoral society*. New York: Charles C. Scribner's, 1932.

Nuttall, R. L. Some correlates of high need for achievement among urban Northern Negroes. *J. abnorm. soc. Psychol.*, 1964, *68*, 593–600.

Olds, J. Physiological mechanisms of reward. In M. R. Jones (Ed.), *Nebraska symposium on motivation 1955*. Lincoln, Neb.: University of Nebraska Press, 1955, pp. 73–139.

Orne, M. T. On the social psychology of the psychological experiment: with particular reference to demand characteristics and their implications. *Amer. Psychologist*, 1962, *17*, 776–783.

———. Hypnosis, motivation, and the ecological validity of the psychological experiment. In W. J. Arnold and M. M. Page (Eds)., *Nebraska symposium on motivation 1970*. Lincoln, Neb.: University of Nebraska Press, 1970, pp. 187–265.

———, and Holland, C. H. On the ecological validity of laboratory deceptions. *Int. J. Psychiatry*, 1968, *6*, 282–293.

242   The Power Motive

Osgood, C. E., Suci, G. J., and Tannenbaum, P. H. *The measurement of meaning*. Urbana, Ill.: University of Illinois Press, 1957.

OSS Assessment Staff. *Assessment of men*. New York: Rinehart, 1949.

Ovesey, L. Pseudohomosexuality, the paranoid mechanism, and paranoia. *Psychiatry*, 1955, *18*, 163–173.

Parsons, T. Age and sex in the social structure of the United States. *Amer. sociol. Rev.*, 1942, 7, 604–616.

———. *The social system*. Glencoe, Ill.: The Free Press, 1951.

———. On the concept of political power. *Proc. Amer. Philos. Soc.*, 1963, *107*, 232–262.

Peters, R. S. *The concept of motivation* (2nd ed.). London: Routledge and Kegan Paul, 1960.

Pike, R. *Enterprise and adventure: the Genoese in Seville and the opening of the New World*. Ithaca, N.Y.: Cornell University Press, 1966.

———. Sevillian society in the Sixteenth Century: slaves and freemen. *Hisp. Amer. Histor. Rev.*, 1967, 47, 344–359.

Pitt-Rivers, J. A. *The people of the Sierra*. Chicago: University of Chicago Press, 1961.

Polsby, N. W. How to study community power: the pluralist alternative. *J. Pol.*, 1960, 22, 474–484.

Pratt, D. The Don Juan myth. *Amer. Imago*, 1960, *17*, 321–335.

Pritchett, V. S. *The Spanish temper*. New York: Alfred A. Knopf, 1955.

Rank, O. *Die Don Juan-Gestalt*. Leipzig and Wien: Internationaler Psychoanalytischer Verlag, 1924.

Reik, T. *Psychology of sex relations*. 1945. New York: Grove Press, 1966.

Reitman, W. R., and Atkinson, J. W. Some methodological problems in the use of thematic apperceptive measures of human motives. In J. W. Atkinson (Ed.), *Motives in fantasy, action and society*. Princeton, N.J.: D. Van Nostrand Co., 1958, pp. 664–683.

Richardson, L. F. *Statistics of deadly quarrels*. Pittsburgh and Chicago: The Boxwood Press and Quadrangle Books, 1960.

Ritter, G. *The corrupting influence of power*. Hadleigh, England: Tower Publications, 1952.

Roberts, J. M., and Sutton-Smith, B. Child-training and game involvement. *Ethnology*, 1962, *1*, 166–185.

Rosen, B. C., and D'Andrade, R. G. The psychosocial origins of achievement motivation. *Sociometry*, 1959, 22, 185–218.

Rosenthal, R. *Experimenter effects in behavioral research*. New York: Appleton-Century-Crofts, 1966.

Rotter, J. B. Generalized expectancies for internal versus external control of reinforcement. *Psychol. Monogr.*, 1966, *80*, 1 (Whole number 609).

Rubinoff, L. *The pornography of power*. New York: Ballantine Books, Inc., 1968.

Russell, B. *Power, a new social analysis*. London: Allen & Unwin, 1938.

Sampson, R. V. *The psychology of power*. London: Heineman Educational Books, Ltd., 1965.

———. Power: the enshrined heresy. *The Nation*, 1971, *212*, 1, 14–20.

Schachter, S. and Latané, B. Crime, cognition, and the central nervous system. In M. R. Jones (Ed.), *Nebraska symposium on motivation 1964*. Lincoln, Neb.: University of Nebraska Press, 1964, pp. 221–273.

Scheibe, K. E. *Beliefs and values*. New York: Holt, Rinehart & Winston, Inc., 1970.

Schlesinger, A. M., Sr. Our Presidents: a rating by seventy-five historians. *New York Times Magazines*, 1962, July 29, pp. 12–14.

Schmuck, R. *Strategies of dominance and social power. Proceedings of a symposium at the University of Michigan*. Ann Arbor, Mich.: University of Michigan Office of Research Administration, 1965.

Schneider, G. *Handbuch der Bibliographie* (4th ed.). Leipzig: Verlag Karl W. Hiersemann, 1930.

Schopler, J. Social power. In L. Berkowitz (Ed.), *Advances in experimental social psychology*, Volume 2. New York & London: Academic Press, 1965, pp. 177–218.

Schultz, D. P. The human subject in psychological research. *Psychol. Bull.*, 1969, *72*, 214–228.

Sechrest, L. Testing, measuring, and assessing people. In E. F. Borgatta and W. W. Lambert (Eds.), *Handbook of personality theory and research*. Chicago, Ill.: Rand McNally & Company, 1968, pp. 529–625.

Shils, E. Charisma, order, and status. *Amer. sociol. Rev.*, 1965, *30*, 199–213.

Shipley, T. E., Jr., and Veroff, J. A projective measure of the need for affiliation. *J. exp. Psychol.*, 1952, *43*, 349–356.

Singer, A. E. *The Don Juan theme, versions and criticism: a bibliography*. Morgantown, West Va.: West Virginia University Press, 1965.

Sinyavsky, A. *Unguarded thoughts*. London: Collins & Harvill Press, 1972.

Skinner, B. F. *Science and human behavior*. New York: Macmillan, 1953.

Skolnick, A. Motivational imagery and behavior over twenty years. *J. consult. Psychol.*, 1966, *30*, 463–478.

Slavin, J. A demotion procedure in leadership training: a pilot study. Unpublished paper, University of Michigan, 1967.

Smelser, N. *Theory of collective behavior*. New York: The Free Press, 1963.

Sommer, R. Small group ecology. *Psychol. Bull.*, 1967, *67*, 145–152.

Sorokin, P. A., and Lunden, W. A. *Power and morality*. Boston: Porter Sargent Publishers, 1959.

Southwood, K. E. Some sources of political disorder: a cross-national analysis. Unpublished Ph.D. thesis. University of Michigan, 1969.

Speer, A. *Inside the Third Reich*. New York: Macmillan, 1970.

Spence, K. W. The postulates and methods of "behaviorism." *Psychol. Rev.*, 1948, *55*, 67–78.

————. Anxiety (drive) level and performance in eyelid conditioning. *Psychol. Bull.*, 1964, *61*, 129–139.

Strodtbeck, F. L., James, R. M., and Hawkins, C. Social status in jury deliberations. In E. E. Maccoby, T. M. Newcomb, and E. L. Hartley (Eds.), *Readings in social psychology* (3rd ed.). New York: Holt, Rinehart & Winston, 1958, pp. 379–388.

————, and Mann, R. D. Sex-role differentiation in jury deliberations. *Sociometry*, 1956, *19*, 3–11.

Sutton-Smith, B. and Rosenberg, B. G. *The sibling*. New York: Holt, Rinehart & Winston, 1970.

Szasz, T. *The manufacture of madness*. New York: Harper & Row, 1970.

Talland, G. A. The assessment of group opinion by leaders and their influence on its formation. *J. abnorm. soc. Psychol.*, 1954, *49*, 431–434.

Telford, C. W. The refractory phase of voluntary and associative processes. *J. exp. Psychol.*, 1931, *13*, 1–36.

Terhune. K. W. Motives, situation, and interpersonal conflict within Prisoners' Dilemma. *J. pers. soc. Psychol. Monogr. Suppl.*, 1968, *3*, part 2 (a).

————. Studies of motives, cooperation, and conflict within laboratory microcosms. *Buffalo Studies*, 1968, *4*, 1, 29–58 (b).

Thayer, R. E. Measurement of activation through self-report. *Psychol. Rep.*, 1967, *20*, 663–678.

Thompson, W. I. *At the edge of history*. New York: Harper & Row, 1971.

Trevor Davies, R. *The golden century of Spain 1501–1621*. London: Macmillan & Co., Ltd., 1937.

Uleman, J. S. A new TAT measure of the need for power. Unpublished Ph.D. thesis, Harvard University, 1966.

————. Awareness and motivation in generalized verbal conditioning. *J. exp. res. in Persy.*, 1971, *5*, 257–267 (a).

————. Dyadic influence in an "ESP study" and TAT measures of the needs for influence and power. *J. persy. Assess.*, 1971, *35*, 248–251 (b).

————. The need for influence: development and validation of a measure, and comparison with the need for power. *Genet. Psychol. Monogr.*, 1972, *85*, 157–214.

Underwood, B. J. *Experimental psychology* (2nd ed.). New York: Appleton-Century-Crofts, 1966.

Van Doorn, J. A. A. Sociology and the problem of power. *Sociologia Neerlandica*, 1963, *1*, 3–51.

Van Duyn, R. *Message of a wise Kabouter*. 1969. London: Duckworth, 1972.

Veblen, T. *The theory of the leisure class*. New York: B. W. Huebsch, 1899.

Vernon, P. E. *Personality assessment: a critical survey*. New York: John Wiley & Sons, Inc., 1964.

Veroff, J. Development and validation of a projective measure of power motivation. *J. abnorm. soc. Psychol.*, 1957, 54, 1–8.

——, Atkinson, J. W., Feld, S. C., and Gurin, G. The use of thematic apperception to assess motivation in a nationwide interview study. *Psychol. Monogr.*, 1960, 74, 12 (Whole number 499).

——, and Feld, S. C. *Marriage and work in America.* New York: Van Nostrand-Reinhold Company, 1970.

——, and Veroff, J. P. B. Theoretical notes on power motivation. *Merrill-Palmer Quart. of Beh. & Devel.*, 1971, 17, 59–69.

——, and ——. Reconsideration of a measure of Power Motivation. *Psychol. Bull.*, 1972, 78, 279–291.

Veroff, J. P. B. An exploratory study of parental motives, parental attitudes, and social behavior of children. Unpublished Ph.D. thesis, University of Michigan, 1959.

Wade, G. E. Tirso de Molina. *Hispania*, 1949, 32, 131–140.

——. "El Burlador de Sevilla": some annotations. *Hispania*, 1964, 47, 751–761.

——. "El Burlador de Sevilla": the Tenorios and the Ulloas. *Symposium*, 1965, 19, 249–258.

—— (Ed.), *El burlador de Sevilla y convidado de piedra. An edition with introduction, notes, and glossary.* New York: Charles Scribner's Sons, 1969.

——. Review of Mercedes Saenz-Alonso's *Don Juan y el Donjuanismo. Revista de estudios Hispánicos* (in press).

Watson, R. I., Jr. Motivation and role induction. Unpublished Honors thesis, Wesleyan University, 1969.

Webb, E. J., Campbell, D. T., Schwartz, R. D., and Sechrest, L. *Unobtrusive measures: nonreactive research in the social sciences.* Chicago: Rand McNally & Company, 1966.

Weber, M. *The theory of social and economic organization.* Translated by T. Parsons and A. H. Henderson. London: Oxford University Press, 1947.

——. *From Max Weber—Essays in sociology* (Ed. H. Gerth and C. W. Mills). London: Routledge and Kegan Paul, 1948.

Weems, L. B., and Wolowitz, H. M. The relevance of power themes among male, Negro and white, paranoid and non-paranoid schizophrenics. *Int. J. soc. Psychiatry*, 1969, 15, 189–196.

Weiner, B., Frieze, I., Kukla, A., Reed, L., Rest, S., and Rosenbaum, R. M. *Perceiving the causes of success and failure.* New York: General Learning Press, 1971.

Weinstein, L. *The metamorphoses of Don Juan.* Stanford, Calif.: Stanford University Press, 1959.

Wexner, L. B. The degree to which colors (hues) are associated with mood tones. *J. appl. Psychol.*, 1954, 38, 432–435.

Whyte, W. F. *Street corner society.* Chicago: University of Chicago Press, 1943.

246 The Power Motive

Winter, D. G. Power motivation in thought and action. Unpublished Ph.D. thesis, Harvard University, 1967.

———. Need for power in thought and action. In *Proceedings of the 76th Annual Convention of the American Psychological Association 1968*. Washington: American Psychological Association, 1968, pp. 429–430.

———. The need for power in college men: action correlates and relationship to drinking. In D. C. McClelland, W. N. Davis, R. Kalin, and E. Wanner, *The drinking man*. New York: The Free Press, 1972, pp. 99–119.

———, Alpert, R. A., and McClelland, D. C. The classic personal style. *J. abnorm. soc. Psychol.*, 1963, 67, 254–265.

———, and Stewart, A. J. The power motives and Self Definition in women. Unpublished paper, Wesleyan University, 1972.

———, and Wiecking, F. A. The new Puritans: achievement and power motives of New Left radicals. *Behav. Sci.*, 1971, 16, 523–530.

Wolfe, T. The ultimate power: seeing 'em jump. In C. Felker (Ed.), *The power game*. New York: Simon & Schuster, 1969, pp. 238–244.

Wolowitz, H. M. Attraction and aversion to power: a psychoanalytic conflict theory of homosexuality in male paranoids. *J. abnorm. Psychol.*, 1965, 70, 360–370.

———, and Shorkey, C. Power themes in the TAT stories of paranoid schizophrenic males. *J. proj. tech. persy. Assess.*, 1966, 30, 591–596.

———, and ———. Power motivation in male paranoid children. *Psychiatry*, 1969, 32, 459–466.

Worthington, M. Don Juan as myth. *Lit. & Psychol.*, 1962, 12, 113–124.

Wright, Q. *A study of war* (Rev. ed.). Chicago: University of Chicago Press, 1965.

Zander, A., Cohen, A. R., and Stotland, E. Power and the relationships among professions. In D. Cartwright (Ed.), *Studies in social power*. Ann Arbor, Mich., Research Center for Group Dynamics, University of Michigan, 1959, pp. 15–34.

Revised
n Power Scoring System
and Practice Materials
for Its Use

HOW TO LEARN THE REVISED *n* POWER
SCORING SYSTEM

Appendix I contains the complete revised *n* Power scoring system, instructions for learning and using it, and practice materials. The latter include a "Self-Test" on the content of the manual, a list of the pictures used to elicit the stories, seven sets of practice stories, a sample scoring sheet, and expert scoring for these stories. These procedures are adapted from the instructions of Feld and Smith (1958; these instructions may be consulted for additional information). Careful use of the materials should enable the user to learn to score TAT stories (or other imaginative stories) for *n* Power with reliability acceptable for research purposes after about 12–15 hours of practice.

Preparation. Read the scoring manual carefully. Without consulting the manual, answer the questions on the "Self-Test"; then check your answers carefully with the manual. It is important to learn the basic scoring definitions before you actually begin to score stories.

Study the sample scoring sheet (located directly after the manual itself) and prepare similar sheets.

Scoring—Set A. After you have learned the basic scoring definitions, score the 30 stories from Set *A, one category* at a time. First, score for Power Imagery. Check your scoring with the expert scoring after each story; note the explanations and keep a record of your errors. After scoring for Imagery, score the subcategories for those stories which the expert scored for Imagery. Again, go through the stories for one category, checking after each story. Then go through the stories for the next subcategory. At all times in scoring, refer to the scoring manual, previously scored stories, and your own notes and record of errors *whenever necessary.* Do not trust your memory or impressions.

Scoring—Sets B through G. Stories from Set *B* should be scored at the next session, perhaps two days after scoring Set *A.* Score the 30 stories one story at a time. Score each story for Imagery and all subcategories, then go on to the next story. Check with the expert scoring after the first ten stories, the second ten, and the final ten. Again, notice carefully your errors.

Sets *C* through *G* should be scored at later sessions; perhaps two sets to a session. Score all 30 stories for Imagery and subcategories, one story at a time. At the end of the set, check with the expert scoring. *Refer to the manual and previous materials whenever necessary.* Before scoring Set *E,* you should check back over your errors, rereading the expert scoring explanation and the relevant sections of the manual. Note carefully those categories, or kinds of decisions, where you have consistent difficulty.

You should score all seven sets even if you attain high reliability after the first few sets. The additional sets give practice with different pictures, and help to ensure speed and accuracy.

How to check your reliability and progress. There are two ways to determine how closely your scoring agrees with the expert scoring. The most important scoring decision, of course, is whether to score Power Imagery. For each set, you can compute your percentage agreement (or Category Agreement = C.A.) with the expert scoring of Power Imagery by the following formula:

$$\frac{2 \times (\text{Number of agreements between yourself and expert on } \textit{presence} \text{ of Imagery})}{\text{Number of times you scored Imagery} + \text{Number of times expert scored Imagery}}$$

This formula is conservative, in that it does not count agreement on the absence of Imagery. By the time you have scored Set *D*, the C.A. for Imagery should be at least .85; and by the end, you should try to reach .90 or above. The C.A. formula can be used for checking reliability of scoring the subcategories, but it will give meaningful results only for those subcategories that occur relatively often.

For Sets *B* through *G*, you can compute a rank-order correlation between your total story score and the expert's total story score for the 30 stories of the set. (Consult any elementary statistics textbook for the formula and procedure.) To facilitate computations, the rank on expert's total story score is given in parentheses immediately after the total story score for each story in these sets. This rank-order correlation gives a measure of the reliability of your ordering of individuals within the set of 30. It is an essential measure of reliability. In the last four sets, your rank-order correlation should be above .85, and above .90 if possible. Should the figure drop for a particular set, carefully review your errors on that set, reread the manual where appropriate, and rescore the set before going on.[1]

In reporting research results, it is good practice to indicate the reliability that the scorer has attained on these practice materials with some statement such as the following: "The materials of the present investigation were coded by judges whose agreement with materials precoded by experts was *rho* = ._____, with Category Agreement on Power Imagery = ._____."

A REVISED SCORING SYSTEM FOR THE POWER MOTIVE (*n* POWER)*

Introduction

This revised scoring manual for the power motive is parallel to the earlier scoring systems for the achievement and affiliation motives.[2] Essentially two tasks confront the scorer. First, is there evidence that

---

* Copyright © David G. Winter, 1968 (Introduction and Definitions of Power Imagery and Subcategories).

[1] Sets *E, F,* and *G* in this appendix are not the same as the three sets that were used for measuring interscorer reliability as reported in Chapter 3. Therefore, your measures of agreement are not directly comparable to those measures.

[2] See J. W. Atkinson (Ed.), *Motives in fantasy, action, and society,* chaps. 13–15. Princeton, N.J.: Van Nostrand, 1958.

the story contains any concern about power? Thus the scorer first searches for evidence of power concern, according to the criteria listed below for scoring Power Imagery. Second, how extensive or elaborated is the power concern? If the story is concerned with power and has been scored for Power Imagery, the scorer then goes on to search for the presence of subcategories which elaborate the basic power concern. If Power Imagery has not been scored, then the scorer simply proceeds to the next story.

The subcategories are organized in a logical manner around a behavioral sequence, which is described below. The scorer may find it helpful to keep the behavioral sequence in mind as an aid to scoring the subcategories. The power behavioral sequence originates in a person who experiences a state of need or desire (N). He takes action (I) toward a goal. Blocks or obstacles (Bw) may interfere with the action. He may anticipate attainment of the goal ($Ga+$) or failure ($Ga-$). If he actually attains the goal, he is likely to experience satisfaction or positive affect ($G+$); if he fails, he may experience negative affect ($G-$). The power-related aspects of the sequence may be further enhanced if he has, or associates himself with prestige ($Pa+$) or if he lacks prestige ($Pa-$). The power theme is further enhanced if the actions create a significant or important effect (Eff). These subcategories increase the power of the act through increasing the "size" of the action and the "size" of the effect created. The power behavioral sequence is presented schematically in the figure below:

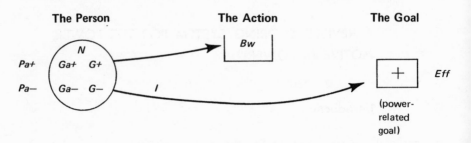

DEFINITION OF POWER IMAGERY (Pow Im)

Power Imagery is scored if some person or group of persons in the story is concerned about establishing, maintaining, or restoring his power—that is, his impact, control, or influence over another person, group of persons, or the world at large. This power concern does not have to be the only theme, or even the major theme of the story, in order to be scored; it can be a peripheral theme. There are three more specific ways in which this power concern is expressed, or can be inferred from the stories; listed below are these three criteria for scoring Power Imagery.

1. *Someone shows his power concern through actions which in themselves express his power.* This person is called the "actor." These actions can be in the past or future tense, and in the passive voice. They can be wanted, fantasied, recollected, planned, or actually carried out in the story. They do not have to be successful. There are several types of such power actions:

(*a*) Strong, forceful actions which affect others, such as assaults, attacks, chasing or catching (e.g., a criminal); verbal insults, threats, accusations, or reprimands; and sexual exploitation, where it is clear the action does not express mutuality or love. Crimes against persons or institutions (unless minor and of little effect) and gaining the upper hand or taking advantage of another's weakness in order to impose one's will on them is scored. Even such actions as begging or importuning can be scored, if they are intended to affect another's behavior or mental state. Do not score accidents. Examples of (*a*):

They plan to attack an enemy supply area.
The agents will catch the suspected people.
The company representative has bawled out the captain.
He is trying to seduce his secretary.
The guy will go out to do some panhandling.

(*b*) Giving help, assistance, advice, or support if it has not been solicited by the other person. However, solicited advice is scored where there is evidence for power concern beyond the mere answering of requests, e.g., "He asked for advice, and in reply the father tried to make the point that. . . ." Teaching is scored, unless it is only a routine description of a teacher in a classroom. Examples of (*b*):

The older man protected the younger against others.
The father is interested in teaching his son basketball.
Her husband went with her to help her, because she was stricken with grief.
She is giving the kid advice.

(*c*) Trying to control another person through regulating his behavior or the conditions of his life, or through seeking information which would affect another's life or actions: searching, investigating, checking up on, and so forth. Do not score routine requests for information, or routine ordinary requests. Thus statements such as "The sergeant tells the men where to put the tent," "John wants Jim to lift the book," or "John asks Jim to lift the book" are not scored, since they are a part of everyday action and do not indicate any special concern for power. However, "John wants to influence Jim to lift the book," "John orders Jim to lift the book," or "The sergeant threatens the men . . ." are scored, because they go beyond routine actions and indicate a special concern for control. Examples of (c):

The welfare worker arranged to transfer the kid to the country, to get him under a new influence.
The executive is visiting the branch office to determine whether the agency should handle a new account.
They are being sent to get information on the enemy troop build-up.
The newspaperman is trying to get the lowdown on the politician.
Complaints kept coming into the main office, so the businessman was sent to get a first-hand report.

(d) Trying to influence, persuade, convince, bribe, make a point, or argue with another person, so long as the concern is not to reach agreement or to avoid misunderstanding or disagreement. Mere mention of an argument or dissension would not, by itself, be scored; for example, the dissenters might come to a mutual resolution, or give up the argument in favor of affiliative activity. In other words, someone must be doing something, or wanting to do something, in order to change someone else's opinion. Examples of (d):

His father tries to interest him in ranching.
She tries to convince him to return home.
The junior executive is trying to get his point across.

(e) Trying to impress some other person or the world at large. Such actions as creative writing, making news or publicity, trying to win an election to office or identifying closely with someone else who is trying to win an election, and any action that will attract widespread attention is scorable. Trying to create a public effect or display, or gaining fame or notoriety, are scorable. The scorer should be careful to distinguish a concern for success as such from a concern for the fame or public attention that may result from success. Only the latter is scored for Power Imagery. Thus "He invents a better mousetrap" is

not scored, but ". . . and the world beats a path to his door" is scored.
Examples of (e):

The reporter is interviewing the farmer about a feature story that he
    is going to write.
An author is trying to gather thoughts for his novel.
The guy is trying to impress his date.
The man is urbane and sophisticated; he knows the right places in
    town to be seen in, and how to be seen in these spots.
She is fed up with him and is putting on a scene.
He was seen tearing hell through town in the family automobile. (A
    vigorous action, and a suggestion of public attention)

Not scored as Power Imagery: Generally actions are not
scored for Power Imagery if they are described as wholly routine, or a
wholly routine part of the role of the characters involved. Thus a
teacher teaching, or a soldier giving a routine command do not indicate a special concern for power; they are part of the routine roles of
teacher and soldier. However, a father teaching, or an ordinary person
giving a command are not routine, and are therefore scored. Actions
which are carried out *only* for the purpose of satisfying another
motive are not scored for Power Imagery. Thus mention of extra-
marital sex would not be scored if the two people were in love, or were
looking for companionship. Arguments are not scored if they are resolved as friendly discussions. Achievement-oriented actions which are
successful are not scored, even if they are important and significant
actions, unless the story also mentions that the actor will thereby become famous or achieve widespread public attention. In other words,
the scorer should carefully distinguish the achievement and the power
aspects of certain stories. Examples of things *not scored* for Power
Imagery:

They established one of the best thoroughbred farms in the world.
    (This is only about achievement, not recognition.)
A first date. Perhaps they will sleep together—they both want com-
    panionship and removal from reality. (Sex is mentioned, but the
    concern is with affiliation and not power.)
They are having a casual discussion. The man is explaining to the
    others about something they did not understand. (This is routine.)
He helped his wife carry in the groceries. (This "helping" is entirely
    routine.)

2. *Someone does something that arouses strong positive or negative emotions in others.* Here the person's power is shown by the emotional reaction of others to him: they feel pleasure, delight, awe, gratitude, respect, intense enjoyment; or fear, worry, despondency, strong jealousy, anger, or offense because of something he has done. Expressions of interest, such as "he was very interested" or "they listened intently," are not scored; but stronger expressions which indicate power or force are scored, such as "He was absolutely fascinated," or "His words compelled their attention." The action which arouses the feelings must be intentional, or under the conscious control of the actor in order to be scored; but it does not matter whether the effect or emotional arousal is intended by the actor. Thus someone's response to natural disasters, accidents, economic depressions, and the like are not scored. Examples of criterion 2:

The professional player is giving a demonstration, and the boy is thrilled.

He has taken her to a small cafe. She is enchanted by the atmosphere, and shows her delight.

He told his mother what he had been doing. She broke down and cried.

3. *Someone is described as having a concern for his reputation or position,* that is, about what someone else or the world at large will think of his power. The difference between this criterion and criterion 1 is that under criterion 1, some action at least has to be mentioned. Here, the person is concerned about his reputation or others' judgment of his power, but no powerful actions are mentioned. He may be concerned about being seen as superior, strong, or of high status; alternatively he may be concerned about avoiding a reputation for weakness, inferiority, or low status. However, the scorer should carefully distinguish concerns for reputation as involving power from concerns about success or failure in achievement strivings, which would not be scored. Thus "John finished last and was sad" would not be scored; but "John finished last and was humiliated" would be scored. The difference is that the former case involves only an inner standard, while the latter case involves a concern about public evaluation. The desire for prestige is scored. The desire for money (being rich, having a large income, etc.) is not scored as such; but if the story makes it clear that money or income is closely related to prestige, then it is scored.

In addition, Power Imagery can be scored under this criterion if a character experiences positive or negative affect in regard to a position of high or low status or prestige. Thus a character may bask in the glory of high status, or be disappointed at his inferior position. Here again, the scorer should distinguish affect about position or prestige, which is scorable, from affect about successful or unsuccessful achievement strivings, which is not scorable. Examples of criterion 3:

The girl is thinking about the attention which is focused on her.
He has taken her out because he likes her, but also because he wants to find out how his boss rated him on his last rating.
He wants some money, so that he can move out of the small room to a luxurious resort, where he would have a rug on the floor and a maid at the door to clean up after him.
The captain thinks he is not to blame, and wants to be vindicated.
The mate knows that his job depends on the executive, but doesn't want to let the crew think he let a white-collar man tell him what to do.
They are both slightly worried about the impressions they are making on each other.

Not scored under criterion 3:

He wants a job. He wants to show he can handle himself in the world. (There is no mention of public reaction or attention; the character may be trying to prove something to himself.)
The man has worked his way up through the company. He will prosper and live a happy life. (This is an achievement theme; "working up through the company" and "prospering" do not explicitly refer to public acclaim.)

If Power Imagery could be scored under more than one criterion, the scorer should select the criterion which covers the major or the most important power-related aspects of the story. If several different characters in the story display concern about power, score the character with the most highly elaborated power concern for Power Imagery and subcategories. If other characters also express power concern, score additional subcategories as appropriatae (i.e., considering them as actors), *so long as no subcategory is scored more than once per story.*

If Power Imagery is scored, then the scorer goes on to check for the presence of the subcategories, which are described below. If Power Imagery is not scored, then the scorer ignores the subcategories and proceeds to the next story.

Subcategories

Each subcategory can be scored only once per story. Any sentence can be scored for more than one subcategory. The same phrase can be scored both for Power Imagery and for any subcategory, but it cannot be scored for two subcategories. Any subcategory must be related to the power sequence or goal in the story in order to be scored. Sometimes a collectivity or group of characters are concerned about the power goal. In such cases, one or more of the subcategories can be scored on the basis of statements about one member of the group, and other subcategories can be scored on the basis of the other characters. In other words, the group may be split up for the purposes of scoring the subcategories, and the statements about each individual character may be considered to apply to the group as a whole.

PRESTIGE OF THE ACTOR (Pa+, Pa—)

Prestige is scored if the character(s) concerned about the power goal are described in ways that increase ($Pa+$) or lower ($Pa-$) their prestige. Titles[3]; adjectives of status, reputation, fame, or skill; or an alliance or association with some prestigeful person, a large number of persons, or an institution (including government agencies) are all aspects of prestige that can be scored. Mention of the legal system ("taking a case to court") is scored $Pa+$. Prestige can also be scored if the setting of the story is described as exotic or prestigeful, such as with adjectives of status, fame, or prominence. Finally, prestige can be scored if a lower-status person is trying to exert his power against a higher-status person. As an example, the prestige of David is increased when he defeats the powerful, prestigeful Goliath. The prestige can be stated at the outset of the story, or it can be acquired during the story or as a result of the power-related action. Both $Pa+$

---

[3] As a scoring convention, the words "commanding officer" or any military rank of captain or below (captain, lieutenant, sergeant, corporal, private) are not scored in stories involving the military. Ranks of major, colonel, and general (field marshal) are scored. Equivalents for naval and air force ranks, as well as for ranks of other nations, should be determined by the scorer. "Captain" is not scored when it means simply the person in charge of a ship, unless the ship is named or described with an adjective (e.g., "newest ship," "big ship," etc.).

and *Pa*− can be scored in a story, but each can be scored only once. Examples of *Pa*+ and *Pa*−:

The men are top-ranking military people. . . .
He graduated from a leading educational institution. . . .
They are sophisticated people at a very intimate, expensive, party. . . .
The man is a New York advertising agency executive. . . .
The guy is a cheap punk. (scored *Pa*−)
These men are Special Forces advisory units.

STATED NEED FOR POWER (N)

Need is scored if there is an explicit statement that some character wants to attain a power goal: to establish, maintain, or restore impact, control, or influence. Most of these statements will involve expressions such as "he wants to," "he wishes to," "he hopes to . . .," "he felt a need to . . ."; or strong evidence of desire such as "he is very interested in . . .," or "he is determined to. . . ." The goal may be broad and general, such as "he wants to persuade his son," or it may be a more specific subgoal, such as in the following: "The officer is planning an attack. The men want to get adequate information about the problems they will encounter." Here the desire for information is a specific part of the more general power goal, i.e., the attack. However, Need should be scored only when the thing that is desired is related to the power goal. Statements of one person's wanting another to do something are not scored unless they are related to the power goal. Thus the following would not be scored for Need: "The boss is trying to convince the partners. One partner wants to break for lunch." *Need is not inferred from Instrumental Activity*, no matter how vigorous or forceful the action is. Thus "he demands . . ." is not scored. It may seem obvious to the scorer that characters who take strong forceful actions toward a power goal must want to reach the goal. Need is scored, however, only when there is a definite statement of need or desire on the part of one of the characters. Examples of *N:*

He would like to impress the girl.
The inspector hopes to catch the smugglers.
He wants to have an affair with her.

INSTRUMENTAL ACTIVITY (I)

Overt or mental activity (such as planning) by a character in the story which indicates that he is actually doing something about attaining a power goal is scored as Instrumental Activity. There must be an actual statement of activity within the story, independent of both the original description of the situation and the final outcome of the story. Statements can be in the past or future tense or passive voice, so long as they are not simply descriptions of the outcome of actions. The scorer should be careful to avoid scoring statements that imply Instrumental Activity but, by the nature of the wording, merely describe situations. "There is an argument" is not scored, but "John is arguing with Jim" would be scored. Any action that is intended to lead to a power goal can be scored, even if the action is only a minor step toward the goal. However, the action must be related to the power goal and not to some other concern. Instrumental Activity is scored regardless of the outcome or success. Examples of *I:*

The man is trying emphatically to make a point.
The crew will complete the attack mission.
The captain is bitterly criticizing the other man.
He is taking her to a small cafe to impress her.

BLOCK IN THE WORLD (Bw)

Block is scored if there is an explicit obstacle or disruption to the attempt to reach a power goal. It is not scored if the person merely fails to reach the power goal. Descriptions or counteractions after the goal is reached are scored for Effect. The scorer should carefully distinguish an obstacle or disruption to an on-going activity from an obstacle that establishes the goal as power-related in the first place. Most power-related stories contain the suggestion of an initial block: there are people to be convinced, others to be impressed, or enemy troops to be attacked. Such initial obstacles merely define the power goal, and are not scored. Only disruptions and obstacles that occur along the way to the goal and hinder on-going action are scored *Bw.* Thus if one character is trying to convince another character about something, then the other character's having an explicit counter-opinion, or any characteristic of the other character or of the situation that suggests that the convincing is more difficult than is normally the case, could be scored for *Bw*. Sometimes there may be some doubt as to whether the obstacle is in the character seeking the power goal (not scored), or in the external situation. *Bw* is scored if the obstacle is at least partly in the external situation. Examples of *Bw*:

The commander is concerned about the mission, because the bridge is heavily guarded. ("Heavily guarded" goes beyond the routine resistance to attack that could be expected.)

The inspector wants to look for contraband. The captain is trying to keep him off the ship.

The girl resists his advances.

The boy has to leave town and this will cost him his reputation as a star athlete.

GOAL ANTICIPATION (Ga+, Ga−)

Goal Anticipation is scored when some character in the story is thinking about the power goal—impact, control, or influence—or is anticipating the goal, or wondering whether he will attain it. This means that a character in the story has to be thinking or anticipating; comments by the author of the story are not scored. Goal anticipations are positive (*Ga+*) if the character is having positive anticipations; they are negative (*Ga−*) if the character has negative or doubtful anticipations. The word "thinking" is Instrumental Activity if it means planning, and is a Goal Anticipation if it means "thinking about" or "wondering about." Examples of *Ga*:

The soldiers are weighing the odds of success in the coming attack. (scored *Ga−*)

He is thinking ahead to future pleasures with his mistress. (*Ga+*)

He is worried about the disgrace he will have to face. (*Ga−*)

The man is thinking that he is convincing his boss. (*Ga+*)

GOAL STATES (G+, G−)

Affective or feeling states associated with attaining or not attaining the power goals are scored *G+* or *G−*, depending on whether the affect is positive or negative. If a character is happy or pleased that he has had power (attacked, criticized, influenced another person), then $G+$ is scored. If he is angry, upset, or dissatisfied about not having power (being weak or of low status, losing an argument, failing to impress someone), then $G-$ is scored. Of course, the feelings have to be connected to the power goal; mere elation or depression in a story that is scored for Power Imagery is not automatically scored for G. These statements of affect may or may not occur at the end of the story, when the final goal is reached or not reached. However, affective states ($G+$, $G-$) should be distinguished from anticipations about the goal ($Ga+$, $Ga-$). The former occur after the goal has been attained or lost; the latter occur in the mind of the character before the goal is reached, while the outcome is in doubt. $G+$ and $G-$ can also be scored for positive or negative affect about the attainment of minor goals which occurs along the way to the central power goal of the story. Negative emotional reactions to blocks are often scorable for $G-$. Examples of G:

Seeing the girl smile serves to reassure him that he has impressed her. ($G+$)

He is amazed that he is having such a hard time in the debate. (Scored $G-$ because "amazed" is taken to connote that the man is unhappy at having a hard time)

He will lose his reputation and become bitter. ($G-$)

She is happy that attention is being focused on her. ($G+$)

EFFECT (Eff)

Effect is scored when there is some distinct response by someone to the power attempts or actions of a character in the story. There are three principal kinds of effects: (a) Strong positive or negative emotions in one person as a result of the action of another (see criterion 2 for Power Imagery); (b) an overt counterattack, counterinfluence, escape, or similar counterreaction by one person to another's attack, influence, and so forth; or (c) some indication that the power action has produced a major, striking effect, such as widespread public acclaim, suicide, or the like. Responses have to be explicit in order to be scored for effect; they cannot be inferred. They have to be described as resulting from the power-related action, and not simply occurring by chance or for another reason. Resistance to another's power is scored; but compliance that goes beyond routine acceptance of power can also be scored, if the compliance or acceptance is enthusiastic, eager, or protesting. Effect, then, is scored if there is additional evidence of someone's power through elaboration of the effects of that power. Examples of *Eff*:

While the soldiers are searching, the enemy will capture the commanding officer.
The inspector will find the contraband; however, the captain will escape and be smuggled out of the country.
Jensen will solve the boy's problem and become endeared to millions.
The boy takes his father's advice, is successful, and frequently looks to his father with respect.

Final Note

Power Imagery and each subcategory that is scored are counted +1. The total n Power score for a story is the sum of scores for Imagery and subcategories. The maximum score possible for a story is +11. If there is no Power Imagery, then the story is scored 0.

Additional Scoring for Hope of Power and Fear of Power

If a story has been scored for Power Imagery and the appropriate subcategories, then the scorer should proceed to make the following additional discrimination between *Hope* and *Fear*.

Fear of Power is scored if one or more of the following are present in the story:

1. *The power goal is for the direct or indirect benefit of another*—either a specified other person, or a cause (e.g., mankind, the Revolution, Justice, etc.). Examples:

He wants to be President so that he can lead the country out of chaos.
He's fighting the champion—chance to win a big purse. His kid is in the hospital and needs a big operation.

If more than one character is concerned with power, score Fear of Power if *any* of the characters has a power goal for the benefit of another.

Stories that involve soldiers, spies, agents of governments or companies, and reporters present a problem in the application of this criterion. In one sense, all such persons can be assumed to be carrying out a power action on behalf of their government, company, agency, newspaper, or the like. Fear of Power is scored if the country is mentioned (e.g., the country's name, "his country," "the country," etc.) in the case of soldiers and spies; Fear of Power is not scored if only "soldiers" or "the army" (navy, air force, armed forces, etc.) is mentioned. In the case of businessmen, reporters, and agents for companies or agencies, Fear of Power is scored only if the power goal is for the benefit of a person, organization, or cause above and beyond the company, newspaper, or agency. Examples:

The executive checking to see whether his agency should take the new account. (not scored)

The advertising executive is designing his agency's campaign for a new client company. (scored)

The *Daily Planet* reporter is investigating a scandal for his paper. (not scored)

The *Daily Planet* reporter is investigating a scandal; when his story is written, it will set off a campaign to restore good government to the city. (scored)

Finally, even if the power goal is for the benefit of another, but the character clearly and obviously derives extra, personal gratification from it, *Fear* is not scored. Thus a soldier fighting for his country who greatly enjoys killing would not be scored Fear of Power.

2. *The actor has doubt about his ability to influence, control, or impress others.* This does not have to be accompanied by actual failure, nor is mere failure sufficient to score Fear of Power under this criterion. Fear of Power is not scored if the actor doubts only the particular outcome; it is scored if he has basic doubts about his ability to influence, control, or impress others. Thus not all cases of *Ga−* would be scored Fear of Power. Also scored under this criterion are stories where the actor experiences confusion or emotional conflict about the power goal in the course of the story. Again, if there is more than one actor, Fear of Power is scored if any actor meets this criterion.

3. *The writer of the story suggests that power is deceptive or has a flaw,* as by the use of contrast, irony, or explicit state-

ment. Here the editorial comments or the style of the writer can be scored, rather than the power goal or the characteristics of the actor. Fear of Power can also be scored under this criterion if the relationship between outcome and affect is reversed: if a character is happy after power failure, or sad after power success. Examples:

He fights the man and demolishes him, but he feels bad, because he
  lowered himself to the other guy's level. (criterion 2 or 3 applic-
  able)
When he finally got the girl, he was chagrined to learn that she was
  his sister.
"Chet the Jet"—the world's greatest boxer—has lost to a ten-year-old.

All stories that are not scored for Fear of Power are considered as Hope of Power. The notation of *Hope* or *Fear* can be made in the margin of the scoring sheet, next to the total score for the story.

After all scoring is completed, the scorer should then add up the scores for each story in the protocol to get a Total score; and he should add the totals for those stories designated *Hope* to get a Hope of Power score, and add those totals for the stories designated *Fear* to get a Fear of Power score. The overall totals for *Hope* and *Fear* should add up to the overall *n* Power score. *Hope/Fear* is a *classification* of the score for each story; neither *Hope* nor *Fear* is given any additional point.

SELF-TEST: REVISED *n* POWER MANUAL

After reading the scoring manual, write out your answers to the following questions without consulting the manual. Then check the answers to see whether they are correct.

Imagery. What is the general basis for scoring Power Imagery? What are the three criteria for scoring Power Imagery? What kinds of statements would satisfy each of these criteria? What are the rules governing the scoring of Power Imagery in stories about solicited advice or help? Teaching or simple requests? Arguments? Success and great achievement? What is the procedure for scoring when several different characters in the story have power concerns?

Prestige. What general classes of words or phrases are scored for *Pa*+ or *Pa*−? Can *Pa* be scored on the basis of prestige which is acquired by a character during the course of the story?

Need. What is the criterion for scoring *N*? What kinds of statements of desire are not scored *N*?

Instrumental Activity. What is the criterion for scoring *I*? What are typical examples of *I*?

Blocks. What is meant by a Block? How is failure to obtain the goal scored?

Goal-anticipation States. When is *Ga* scored? How are comments by the author dealt with? What is the difference between *Ga* and planning or thinking that is scored *I*?

Goal States. What is the distinction between *Ga* and *G*? What statements of affect or feeling are not scored *G*?

Effect. What are the three principal kinds of things that can be scored *Eff*? Is any reaction to a power attempt scored *Eff*?

Hope/Fear. What is the rule for scoring cases involving an agent of a company (or government, etc.)? What is a reversed affect-outcome relationship? Do all cases of power which benefits someone else get scored for Fear of Power?

PICTURES USED TO ELICIT STORIES SCORED
FOR *n* POWER

The pictures that were used to elicit the stories for Sets A through D were as follows:

Sets A and B:

Stories 1–10:	A group of soldiers; one of whom is pointing at a map or chart (Uleman, 1972).
Stories 11–20:	Man and woman drinking beer; a guitarist in the foreground (Uleman, 1972).
Stories 21–20:	"Homeland": man and youth talking outdoors (#24 in Atkinson, 1958, pp. 832–834 catalogue).

(*Continued on page 266*)

Sample *n* Power Scoring Sheet

Story Number	Imagery 1	Imagery 2	Imagery 3	Pa+	Pa−	N	I	Bw	Ga+	Ga−	G+	G−	Eff	Total	Hope/ Fear

Sets C and D:

Stories 1–10:   Ship's captain talking with man dressed in a suit (Harvard Student Study).

Stories 11–20:   A young man lying on a bed, reading a newspaper (Harvard Student Study).

Stories 21–30:   "Mad Scientist" examining a test tube by the light of a candle (Uleman, 1972).

Sets E, F, and G:

Stories 1–10:   Conference group. Seven men variously grouped around a conference table (#83 in Atkinson catalogue).

Stories 11–20:   Two women standing by a table; one is working with test tubes (Veroff et al., 1960, p. 3).

Stories 21–30:   Father-son (#1 in Atkinson catalogue).

The stories from the practice sets were written with the following four questions, spaced out on the TAT forms, as a guide:

1. What is happening? Who are the people?
2. What has led up to this situation? That is, what has happened in the past?
3. What is being thought? What is wanted? By whom?
4. What will happen? What will be done?

The questions are not reproduced in the practice stories that follow, but their position is indicated by paragraphing. In some cases, the writer of the story ignored these guide questions and simply wrote one continuous story. Such stories are reproduced as they were written.

POWER PRACTICE STORIES: SET A

Note: Original spelling and grammar have been preserved.

A-1.   An army officer of high rank and some of his battalion leaders are going over plans for a forthcoming attack. Situation takes place in Korea during the summer of 1952.

Recently the N. Koreans have attacked and won several strategic locations in the front line. The officers are now planning a counterattack.

The officer wants these locations to be re-taken. He thinks it can be done and judging by the number of lieutenants involved, it should be a large scale attack. Each man wants to know the battle plan and what he can expect.

Fire will begin at daybreak with each battalion in an integrated drive on the enemy held positions.

A-2.   This a command briefing by the commander-in-chief of the Army's forces in the Pacific. The men he is lecturing to are his division commanders & staff.

The general is pointing out an island that is occupied by Japanese troops. That island was taken by the Japanese during the past month. It must be retaken by the U.S. forces.

The men listening to the general are duly impressed, by both the general & the task. They feel the importance of the task. The general hopes he is succeeding.

The division commanders will go back & do the same briefing for their troops. The divisions will attack the Japanese held island and take it after a very hard fight.

A-3.   The general, during the war in Europe, is pointing to an area of enemy concentration and explaining the situation to his staff officers.

The war has been going poorly with the U.S. suffering many casualties.

It has been decided that if the enemy is driven out of this position the course of the war could be changed. The strategy has been decided and the officers are being given their orders. The battle is soon to be waged and the U.S. will come out victors.

A-4.   The people are soldiers. They are looking for some people who are hiding.

The soldiers are bad. They have evil looks on their faces. They are looking for the good guys who are trying to overthrow their military rule.

The commanding officer thinks the good guys are hiding and is pointing to where he wants his men to look.

The soldiers will go looking for the good guys who are hiding—they will not find them—while they are gone the good guys will capture the commanding officer.

A-5.   These are battalion commanders being briefed by intelligence prior to some *tactical* move in combat. They are not dressed for a top level *strategic* meeting.

The enemy is dug in and a full scale assault is needed to take their position.

They are assessing the enemy's strength to determine the best plan of attack.

They will attack and the enemy will surprise them since the man in the khaki suit is a spy.

A-6.   A group of army officers has come from the pentogone to investigate a situation in the field. The officers concerned are much older than usual, and presumably therefore more senior and responsible.

They are wonder what to do about the situation, have already joined on idea of what the essentiols are of the problem. Their reaction is that it is a grave problem.

A-7.   Air Force Major & pilots.

It is a briefing situation preceding a bombing run.

Major is pointing out objectives.

They will bomb targets shortly after.

A-8.   It looks like several military leaders are discussing some point concerning current military action. The man on the left is the leader.

There is nothing in particular which has happened in the past which brings these men together. There is no sense of urgency on their faces and it appears that this is a routine strategy meeting. This situation was occasioned by the military action going on at the time.

The meeting is to discuss and formulate specific duties which each of the men is to carry out. People are trying to figure out the best way of accomplishing the task, but it looks like the man on the left is telling the others what to do.

The men, all except the man on the left, will carry out the assignments given to them.

A-9.   The leader of a reserve Army unit is pointing out to members of the Army reserve where they will carry on a certain set of maneuvers.

This is taking place during the summer bivouak that researvists must take part in each year.

These men have been called away from their jobs and businesses to take part in this mandatory exercise.

The men who are listening consider the whole thing a waste of time as does the leader who is giving the instructions.

The maneuvers will be carried out but with very little enthusiasm on the part of the leader or the soldiers.

A-10.   The captain says to his men, "We've got to hit this bridge to cut off the enemy supply route. If everybody does his job, no one will get hurt and the mission will be a success."

A higher officer has told the captain that the enemy supply trains must be stopped. The captain has chosen the bridge as the best spot. He knows that air power could do the job, but he is itching to fight.

The men are scared but they will do their jobs.

The men will blow up the bridge. Two of them will be killed. The captain will be promoted.

A-11.   The gentleman in the picture has all the moves, is urbane, sophisticated, cosmopolitan in outlook, chooses his clothes and girl friends quite discriminately and knows the right spots in town to be seen in, how to be seen in these spots—his clothes, time of arrival, types of girls his friends will like to see him, proper drinks to select—probably imported beer of a type which she isn't aware of. This guy is the boy lecher type who has made the transition from a leading educational institution to Madison Avenue or Wall Street with a great deal of finese. This guy has all the moves for the league he's pitching in.

A-12.   The guy is a cheap punk—works for a racketeer; the girl is one of the girls that hangs around with the gang; he has taken her to a local joint—is planning a big night.

The girl is new w/the mob—she just came in; she trusts the guy but she has been around; the guy has played around w/many girls in the past.

The girl is happy—she thinks she has found an exciting life—away from her poor bkground. The guy is just thinking of her in bed—she will be an easy one.

They will go to his pad—spend the night there; they will have an affair—when she gets pregnant he throws her out.

A-13.   The people are in New York City. They are not married, but have gone out together a lot. They are in a small bar, having a few drinks, before going out to dinner.

They have been out together many times before. But tonight the man will ask the woman to become engaged, while the woman is really not prepared for this event.

After diner, the couple will go to his apartment. The woman will refuse the man's ring.

A-14.   The handsome man has taken his newest girl friend to his favorite lounge knowing that she likes classic guitar music and booze. Since her interests fit perfectly with the offerings of the bar, he feels this will be a great opportunity to impress her. Seeing her smile as the guitarists plays for them, serves to reassure him that his efforts have paid off—("She's snowed"). His thoughts are naturally then planning ahead to future pleasures that may be shared. However, after the 2 become better acquainted he soon looses interest and turns to other potential mistresses to repeat the episodes.

A-15.   This is a San Francisco bar where the people go who are really IN, so it is not crowded. The man is a NY ad agency executive visiting the San Francisco branch office in order to determine whether the SF agency should handle a new international account for a company with its main office in Tokyo.

He is with an old girlfriend who is a SF model who lives in Carmel and is separated from her husband who is a famous commercial artist.

A-16.   The man has just met the woman this afternoon on a business trip. Now, after work, he is taking her to a small, romantic little cafe he knows.

The woman is enchanted by the atmosphere and shows her delight. The man sits back satisfied & somewhat bemused. He is making a very good impression, just as he had hoped.

He will try to take advantage of it.

A-17.   A gentleman is wining and dining a woman not his wife. The gentlemen is rather pressed for funds since they are drinking beer in what appear to be a fairly expensive club. The lady has just requested that the guitarist play her favorite song. She is apparently enraptured by the whole affair. The gentlemen is rather smuggly congratulating himself on a successful snow-job and is eagerly awaiting the more amorous adventure which the evening portends.

A-18.   It is early in the evening at a quiet little restaurant in some fair sized city. The two people in the front are being sarinaded at the request of the gentleman. It is some special ocation, not as formal as an birthday since they are drinking "Bud" but maybe a nice event has just taken place. Even after a ball game.

The song is the favorite of the girl.

A-19.   A man & his wife have gone abroad on a business trip, and during the evening they are enjoying supper at a small café.

The man has been asked to leave on business with short warning & has elected to take his wife. Because the "deal" will probably be successful, & because he has worked hard for this deal, they probably plan to end the trip in a holiday. The man probably is confident of success, the wife is only enjoying the opportunity of being in Europe—it is *not* her first trip for she appears confident.

The "deal" will probably be successful and the holiday will be started as planned. About half way through the holiday the man will be called back to America on business.

A-20.   A man is out on a date on his vacation. He is a top-executive who has met a very nice lady in a hotel—

This man always goes out with other girls, and impresses them with good restaurants and night clubs.

The girl really likes the music and the man thinks of the nice night he is going to spend with her—

She meets another friend in the restaurant and ignores the man. He is frustrated because that never happened before in his life—

A-21.   Dave Jensen, alias "The Fugitive" is currently (for this episode only) stuck on a farm in the Kentucky Blue grass country.

Jensen got into this particular situation when he fell out of a plane which had just landed at the airport by not waiting for the unloading ramp.

It seems the young man doesn't know what to do since he loves horses, but suffers from hay fever and can not stay in the country.

Using his medical knowledge Jensen will recommend that

use of pills that will solve the boys problem & endear Jensen to many more devoted listeners.

A-22.   The boy is an orphan, and the city slicker is trying to make the scene with the kid's sister who has raised him since he was 6 and his Mom & Dad died. The slicker thinks the only way to score with Sister to get on the kids side.

But the kid sees through the fancy airs, and sees the slicker for what he really is, a nogoodnik.

Sis will finally see the light too, and tell guy where to go.

A-23.   The two men are rural citizens in the farming country of Indiana. The man sitting is a farmer whose first child recently died at birth. The other is the doctor who delivered the child.

The doctor has come to see the man regarding the farmers wife who has been severly depressed since the child's death 6 months ago. She can have no other children.

The farmer is bitter, the recent tragedy and his increasing debt have caused him to consider leaving the farm inherited from his father. The doctor is worried about the couples health.

The couple will stay on the farm and adopt 2 children.

A-24.   Father who is a gentleman farmer type out on his country place for the weekend is trying to reach his son through a father to son heart to heart talk. Dad bought this place to hopefully educate or provide a different type environment for his son to be aware of. Conversations such as these probably occur infrequently because of Dad's time pressures during the week and out in the country unrestrained by people Dad hopes to get to know his son better as he wishes to provide the best in life for his son by opportunities he is able to afford.

A-25.   Looks like Dad, a relative or the local preacher stopped by to give junior a little advice. Junior did something a little bad— perhaps he was seen tearing hell through town in the family roadster. Then he went back home and continued choring on the farm, until Dad or Uncle Louis or whoever it is came out and called him on his actions.

Junior doesn't seem angry—kind of resigned to the fact that he's been caught and almost tactly admitting it was a pretty foolish thing to do.

All live through it! And probably happily thereafter.

A-26. A father and son are talking over the son's future. He wants to be a rancher and has taken a job for the summer in Arizona. His father has come to visit him and they are talking of the great like the son has found for ranch work. The father is a business man perhaps a salesman and wants his son to do what he would like best but is still concerned with insuring the son will be happy.

A-27. The man in the shirt is young perhaps the suited man's younger brother. The suited man is giving him advise.

The young man has by some action expressed his indecision at a critical point in life. He has possibly just graduated from high school and is undecided about farming, as a career.

The younger man wants counseling from the older, who has travelled or had army service. The older man wants to help the younger.

The younger man will listen to the older but will make own decision. He will leave farm.

A-28. Son is having heart-to-heart talk with Dad concerning future colege plans. The Dad is a successful businessman-rancher and son is undecided about interests.

Dad really doesn't want to push kid into any area of study and is reassuring him of full support in what ever he chooses. He just wants son to sincerely try at what ever area he enters before deciding upon chances.

The son consequently seriously contemplates future, decides upon a field of concentration, and is successful frequently looking to father with respect.

A-29. The boy has been having problems and has been sent to a work farm to help him readjust. There he is talking with the counselor. He is trying to explain the troubles he has been having and the counselor is listening sympathetically. The boy is grateful as it is the first time someone has seemed to take a genuine interest in him.

Soon he will respond to this therapy and recover.

A-30. This is a discussion between a N.Y. Times reporter and one of the managers of a politician's ranch. The newpaperman is trying to get the lowdown on the real politician.

The reporter is in Texas since he has been invited to a barbecue the next day.

The worker is an old pro at ignoring these questions and will not divulge any of their boss's idiosyncracies. This man has some political savvy and will lead the reporter on enough to find out what the reporter thinks of his boss. He will probably relate to his boss what questions the reporter asked. The reporter will not be asked to any more barbecues since he is too nosy.

POWER PRACTICE STORIES: SET B

B-1.   A U.S. officer is showing a group of subordinates some plan to be followed on a map. They are at a base under semi-adverse conditions

The men have been leading their men in war games. All has been successful the present briefing is further routine

The fellows in back are bored

B-2.   A army general is briefing his staff— The men are commanders of divisions. There has been a surprise invasion of a South American country— The president & his cabinet has made the decision to retaliate with an invasion force. Planning of this attack has been completed and the officers are being given their respective roles. They can not question the task—they show concern over the correctness of the political decision and are concerned about the outcome of the invasion. They are now in battle dress at the push off point in Central America— the attack is coming within the hour. They are confident superior U.S. military will win but are uncertain of repercussions that come later.

B-3.   These are GI's on a mission. The Commanding Officer is explaining the details of the job to be done, pointing to a chart or detail of the area in which the job to be done is located. The men are confident that they can do the job. No one is tense or nervous.

Concentration is directed at the map. The commanding officer is likewise fairly confident in the ability of his men. He directs his attention at them and the job at the same time.

The area is informally run, reflecting the cooperation which can be expected from the men. There is no "command"

required. The men feel responsible, they know what they have
to do.

B-4.   A U.S. soldier is showing a map to a Chinese communist soldier and asking for information.
        The communist soldier has been captured in a battle. He
has been treated well.
        The U.S. soldier wants information about the location of
troops & ammunition. The communist is worried the U.S. will
"beat it out of him"
        The communist will supply the information & the U.S. will
attack those positions.

B-5.   A general is giving his field commanders his views on how to
conduct the campaign.
        The general plan has been laid out, and only the details are
now being discussed. Each man knows his objectives & is now
reviewing the details of how he is to carry out that objective
        The general is asking for critical details. Some of the com-
manders disagree with him and some of the others, but for
expediencies sake they will quickly come to agreement.
        Having developed detailed plans, the commanders will
hasten to complete the mission. —This will only be one of
many such missions.

B-6.   The Army major is briefing his division officers on a plan of
action to be taken in the present war games. The division people will relay the big picture to each of their units. The briefing
appears to be taking place in an aircraft but is posible in a
quansut hut.
        The war game have started and this is an up dateing of
information. The men are each thinking of their positions in
the big picture

B-7.   The people are Army officers being briefed by an Air Force
intelligence officer. They are planning some sort of strategic
raid against an enemy and are thinking about their needs.
        The officers are in a quonset hut overseas—probably in a
cold region. They have engaged in an overall war and are
planning a tactical strike against the enemy. Their concerned
look shows that they have been losing.
        They wants to wipe out the enemy—the enemy has been

hurting them and they are thinking of ways to retaliate. The Air Force officer doesn't care, but the army are thinking of the cold and the coming battle.

The army officer will try to use the A.F. intelligence and will find it faulty. They will blame him for his incompetence.

B-8. This is a group of army officers in a multi-national force receiving a briefing on their next operation. The officer pointing to the map was the commanding officer of the group that was to launch an attack at dawn. The attack was designed to break the back of the invasion of a small association which had been launched against that nation by a giant neighboring country.

The men are thinking about their respective jobs in the coming attack and are particularly interested in receiving adequate information from the C.O. about their duties and the specific problems they might encounter.

The attack will probably be only partially successful and will result in only part of the objective being accomplished.

B-9. Comander pointing out attack area—others are line officers —a serios situation—they give impression of being prepared but not tense—cross section of army types differnt forms of battle dress—America has integrated. It could be subhous, underground or in special Bunker of some type—

This is an assault group—We have been attacked (or have some reason—if any can be given) for attacking. A crucial scientific area of other side—hit them where they will feel it the most.

Pain, sadness, responsibility—"Why did I get into this"— and desire to do a good job no matter what—

They will succeed—some will be shot up some not—

B-10. These are Army personnel planning an offensive operation. They seem to be in a foreign country, judging by other people who are also in the crowd.

This offensive is part of a campaign to assist a friendly government.

The individual pointing to the map is showing where the operation is to take place. The others will be responsible for executing it.

It appears that this will be a small raid or perhaps a patrol.

B-11.   These people are obviously posing for a beer ad. They have been placed in this setting and practiced the "act" several times. They are almost frozen or glued into their positions. Finally, the photographer signols for the actual "take" and everyone puts on their best phoney smile. In a moment, they will all break up after the photo is taken and talk about the next job they will model for.

B-12.   The couple in the foreground are on their first date. They met at the office where they both work. She is his bosses secretary. He has taken her out because he likes her and thinks she is pretty, but also because he wants to find out how his boss has rated him on his last rating, since he did not get the raise he was expecting and is not satisfied with the bosses explanation —the girl has no conception of the man's ultimate design, but is merely enjoying herself and his company and the surroundings of the cocktail lounge. She has been trying to attract his attention for several months, and so was quite happy to be asked out.

B-13.   This is an add for beer and they are filming the add. The people are actors.
        They have been hired for the add because they are good looking & have done this type of thing in the past.
        The people are trying to look happy, as the director wants.
        The scene will be accepted & shown on T.V.

B-14.   The fellow has taken this woman out to lunch. He's dated her a couple of times before. She's flighty & used to having people court her. He's been around, has plenty of money and has given himself the afternoon off to carry on his conversation with her.
        They are both probably on vacation in a Spanish country. He invited her to the place because he liked it and wanted to impress her. They ordered beers but neither were thirsty and she doesn't like beer.—
        He's getting put out that she isn't showing any more interest in him but hopes that she is enjoying herself and will soon pay him with some attention.

B-15.   Zeke has taken Carol to his favorite bar and is smiling while Zeke's friend is singing that Carol is a lucky girl to be dating Zeke because he is such a famous hustler of fine women that he will certainly improve her reputation among the cool set. Carol is thinking that this sure is a great evening. Zeke is thinking that she will try hustle him into the sack before the evening is over. She'll try, but all she will get is a goodnight kiss because Zeke is so cool!

B-16.   This is a TV Ad showing two models drinking Budweiser in Club Henri IV—they're eating potato chips—they're singing some corny "lively people" slogan—But Beer!!??

The people were hired for their good looks and "liveliness" —the guitar was included for kind of a "folksy modern" effect —(same reason for check table cloth)—

The actors are thinking "this ad is lousy because its unbelievable"—I wish they'd let me have a drink of the beer under these hot lights.

The people will get paid $100—plus $50 for the reruns. The guitarist will feel happy because he got his hands on T.V.—the man looks like a sleazy "slim tie" type from Queens.

B-17.   The young couple are enjoying an evening out. They may be engaged or newly married.

The couple has been to a show or other entertainment and have stopped for a late snack.

The girl thinks the guitar player is a wonderful musician and very charming. The man thinks he is foolish and is amused by the incident.

Girl will listen to guitar player, man will drink his beer and order many more. He will be carried home by date.

B-18.   She is first date—they are at a fine bar drinking—She has lost herself in the music—has removed her thinking from the problems of the world. He is thinking about her—She is beautiful, fun, but what is she really like—He sees her now mostly as a good time—perhaps they will even sleep together—if not tonight—perhaps another time. They both want companionship—and removal from reality. It looks like their finding just that in each other—they will have good times for a period of time—but then it will end.

B-19.   Well Yes! Rod Brick is taking out a young lady he met at a cocktail party. They are in a cafe on Alvaro St. It in Los Angeles California it is 4:00

She is only visiting L.A. and will only be there another week. She is a receptionist in San Francisco. He offered to show here L.A. on Friday—today is friday.

B-20.   Harry is impressing his mistress with a trip to Puerto Rico. Harry's "too great" for his wife and her country squire. His mistress's name is Mary. She's "not a nice girl."

Harry's good looks drew Mary out of the secretary pool in N.Y.C. and they soon set up shop in an mid-town apt. Harry's supposed to be on a business trip to Flatbush for a couple of days, but he's not . . .

Harry's thinking what a cool bastard he is, Mary's thinking that the guitar player looks like her brother.

Harry and Mary won't be together too long, because Harry's wife's too nosey & smart.

B-21.   The boy is the son of the father. The Man just returned from the ctiy and is thinking of leaving the country and moving the whole family into the city.

The father hasn't been able to make money on his farm. He's always been machanically minded & now wants to take a responsible position with an urban engineering firm.

The boy's angry because he's the local baseball star and leaving town will cost him his reputation. He also loves the smell of horses . . .

The father will move (w/his family) but they won't sell the farm until after the baseball season's over. During this time he'll read-up on specific engineering studies

B-22.   This is a drawing of a photograph. The picture was of two schoolmates who had great plans for this Kentucky farm that they bought. They had come from another part of the country, but desired the chance to raise horses and race them. They subsequently established on this land one of the best through-breed farms in the world here.

At that point they were considering the financing involved (the banker took the picture). The fence-sitters daughter has copied the picture for art class.

B-23.   The man is a college professor who is driving across the country to begin a new teaching job. His family are going to follow him after he finds a house. He has stopped to stretch his legs and has struck up a conversation with the farm boy who was working in the field. The two are talking about the importance of education to young people, especially college education. The boy is interested in chemistry and in science in general, but fears that his father and mother, neither of whom went past the 8th grade, and who are third generation farmers, will not pay for any schooling beyond high school or ever let him go to college.

B-24.   Pop tries to talk to junior about college: "Son, you could get a fine scholarship to state u. with your baseball talent." But junior still has another year of High School left before he must make the post H.S. decision of what to do.

Pop has been away a month working his head off in the big city & junior knows that Pop is a goof for working so hard. He isn't happy and he doesn't make in money either. Jr. wants to go out with Judy and that is all he can think about. Pop isn't really sincere anyway 'cause he doesn't care.

B-25.   A boy and his father are talking together, sitting on a fence outside their farm home.

The father has just come home from his job in the city and found his son, quietly contemplating while sitting on the fence.

The father wants very much to help his son and give him advice and good suggestions about life. But the son realizes that he is different than his father and that he must go his own way.

The son will soon leave home, perhaps to go to college. The father will continue to give advice & help to his son.

B-26.   The man in the suit is the father of the boy on the fence. The father is a businessman who also owns a small cattle farm. The boy is working on his father's farm for the summer.

It is Sunday, and the boys parents came out to the farm for the weekend, the mother is in the main ranchhouse fixing lunch—they are expecting another couple and their boy to join them.

The father is talking to the boy about the future—the boy's future. He is saying that he is proud of the boy and the hard work he is showing he can do.

B-27.   The Dept of Agriculture employee is trying to get the young
        boy to accept the idea of Benson's "land bank" soil program.
        The boy has just been left 200 acres by his father to farm.
            Prior to this time, the boys father was violently against
        the Dept of Ag's program & would threaten to shoot anyone
        who came on his land. Now the boy can do anything he wants.
            The boy thinks the program sounds good and would give
        him more $ than he could get raising corn. The D of A
        employee thinks that he will get promoted if he can swing the
        deal.
            The boy's father will come out of the house with a shotgun
        and blast the D of A employee. The father will get the chair.
        The son will sell his farm and go to Business School, thinking
        this to be his best bet.

B-28.   I think the boy is an inmate of an orphanage or some other
        form of institution (perhaps correctional) and the adult is a
        teacher and administrator. Perhaps the boy has asked for help
        or otherwise indicated a need for counsel. The boy wants at-
        tention or help with his problem and appears to be getting it.

B-29.   The boy is a high school athlete and the man is a coach from
        a well known Eastern University who has come to the boy's
        home (farm) to discuss the possibilities of a scholarship or
        loan to come to that well known University. The coach is flat-
        tering the boy by asking him a lot of questions about himself
        which the boy enjoys talking about. The coach is trying to be
        debonair and to impress the young man with his wordly ways.
        The young fellow is truly flattered and proud to have the coach
        come to see him. He will probably take the offer more because
        he feels wanted and appreciated than because of his innate
        desire to go to the school.

B-30.   The reporter (in the suit) is interviewing the farmer on the
        fence in regard to a feature story that he is about to write. The
        story is on changes that have taken place on the farm over the
        last two decades.
            The reporter is asking the young farmer why he is a
        farmer—given the low income and other negative factors
        which the farmer has indicated. The farmer tells him that
        there is nothing else he can do and, in general, tells a "sob

story." The reporter feels that there is much human interest in the whole farm situation and hopes to do a good job.

POWER PRACTICE STORIES: SET C

C-1.   The man in uniform is a captain of a freighter—the other man is an inspecter from the customs dept. The inspecter is checking over the ship as it has just come into port.

The captain is a smuggler—bringing opium into the country. The inspecter has been tipped off and is checking up on the ship. The customs Dept. has been suspicious of the captain in the past.

The inspecter feels he finally will catch the captain—a feeling of triumph—or of revenge because he can put the captain who makes a lot of money behind bars. The captain doesn't feel much fear—he has been through this before; he is telling the inspecter to "go to hell"—the captain is too smart for him—it's a bluff.

The inspecter will search and find the dope; however the captain will escape and be smuggled out of the country.

C-2.   The captain is speaking with the member of the home office of the company which owns the liner. The home office representative has just bawled out the captain about arrangements during departure. The captain is angry at this reprimand, and is telling the representative to stick to the dockside part of business, and let him run the business area.

The ship will make a record run under the impetus of the captain venting his pent up emotions on making the ship more efficient.

C-3.   The man in uniform is a merchant marine captain welcoming aboard a member of management of the company, U.S. Lines. It seems the company man has come aboard to make a routine inspection just prior to sailing. The captain will conduct him through the ship, pointing out recent improvements, problems on board, and making general conversation. The two are personally well acquainted and will exchange personal frivalities during the tour.

C-4.   An American manufacturer or businessman is speaking with a captain of an American merchant ship. They are in a foreign port, and the businessman desires that the captain accept his cargo for shipment.

This cargo must be shipped as soon as possible, but the captain explains that his ship is almost finished loading. The businessman askes him to rearrange the stoage of the ships cargo so that his own cargo will can be put on. Finally, the bus man offer to pay a preimum price, and the captain agrees to take the cargo with some modifications.

C-5.   The president of a steamship line is coming aboard one of the steamship of the line to talk to a skipper and see what's going on.

In a board meeting recently, the company's affairs decided that they should get out and see the operation firsthand.

The captain is explaining to the president some of the problems he is encountering in the field and the president is trying to grasp these problems in company terms.

He will go back and report along with the other and company policy will be formulated to alleviate some of these problems.

C-6.   One person is the commander of the ship, a naval admiral the other one is a congressman who has come to the ship in order to inspect some naval facilities.

The congressman is a recently elected junior senator who is trying to gain publicity for himself by somehow exposing waste in government.

Thus, the congressman is trying in any way he can to find some example of waste. The admiral is on his guard for anything.

They will make an inspection of the facilities together, and the congressman will make a public statement.

C-7.   A reporter is interviewing a captain of a passenger ship which has just collided with a tanker in the harbour with the loss of 30 lives.

The captain has had a perfect record for his 35 years on the sea and is the ablest in the fleet. The collision was entirely the fault of the tanker. The captain is married has no children.

The captain is tired, being awake for 2 days; he is bitterly explaining the error of the other ship. He fears his job.

He will lose his captaincy of this, the fleets top liner and will be bitter about the fates of captains of liners which collide.

C-8.   The busy executive man in the suit is paying his fare to ride the Hudson River Day Line excursion boat up to Bear Mountain.

He just wants to get away from the hustle of the city, which has been depressing him lately.

He'll get mixed up with a crowd of drunks who will throw chairs overboard and he'll be arrested and disgraced and will lose his job.

Then he'll find something more pleasant and worthwhile to do with his time rather than working 9–5.

C-9.   Government agent has just indicated his desire to search the ship for contriband. Captain is trying to persuade agent of the discomfort such a course would cause his passengers and the criticism of the line as a result of such a search. Captain insists that there is no substance to the report that smuggling is, in fact, going on aboard his ship.

C-10.   The man in civilian clothes is the owner of a very large steamship line. He is discussing the refinishing of the great liner in the background with the commander of the ship. The vessel is not getting the required revenue to support its operations. A better selling effort is required. The owner will refinish the vessel in an attempt to attract more travelers to his line. The captain will recommend some.

C-11.   Peter searches the want ads for summer employment. He's just finished his first year at college and needs money for the next year. He hasn't picked a field yet, but wants to get a job that will be (1) Profitable (2) Interesting (3) Good Experience.

In college Peter experienced a good deal of disappointment in the loose sense of structure and direction in the courses he had taken.

C-12.   This is a young G.I trying to kill time waiting for his unit to transfer to the front. He is nervous, and a little afraid for the future.

His brother is there already, and he is wondering if their units will hook up once there.

The two brothers will not meet up, and in reality, the boys unit is not even going to the front, but to a training base in Germany.

C-13.   This is a guy in a dormitory room; he is just relaxing after going through some rough exams.

De The boy has just had finals—they were rough—he did well; there is a feeling of peaceful exhaustion. He has been priming himself for weeks—the moment has just passed.

He is glad it is all over; he would like to unwind now; he would also like to get the results—to prove that he did well—to justify the effort he put in.

He will go to the movies—get drunk tonight; in a few days, he will get the test results—he will have done mediocre—passed the exams but not highly; he will be disappointed and bitter—as a reaction, next year he will study hard.

C-14.   Jobless worker is reading want-ads for potential jobs in his area.

He has lost several jobs because of young age and lack of higher education and has consequently become quite dissatisfied. However he is intelligent and is determined to wait until a particularly interesting job with a possible future appears. In the mean time he will be satisfied living on unemployment and waiting. Since he is not married or has no real obligations, this std. of living can be tolerated for a while.

His efforts don't pay off however because no jobs of that nature appear.

C-15.   The boy is scanning the want ads for a job in the late afternoon in his bare apartment. He has no family and has recently left the service.

The boy quit high school and enlisted in the Army at 17. Two years later is now looking for a job in NYC. He has few friends and has had little luck in job hunting for the past month.

He wants love. He wants money and will find neither.

He will leave for California in 2 weeks.

C-16.   Whew! I'm tired of looking for a job. But, I'm going to have to get some money somewhere so that I can get these clothes washed and some breakfast. But before I do, I think I alright to see what Dick Tracy did yesterday.

It is really a shame that I cannot find a job. No one seems to want to hire me. I don't understand why. Maybe if I could get some money I could get out of this hole and move to a luxurious resort where I would have a rug on the floor and a maid at the door to clean up after me whenever I wanted.

C-17.   A high school senior is laying on his bed in his room reading the paper his father has just brought home.

His parents
The high school boy has been playing baseball after school as he does everyday. He had been constantly contemplating quiting school and playing professional baseball. His parents are set against this and plan to send him to college. He reads the sports section everyday and keeps up with every aspect of baseball.

He will, however, never quit highschool. He will go on to college, study a profession and be a success.

C-18.   Joe College has just come in from working in the fraternity house. He wondering whether to finish reading the paper or go on to sleep before supper.

The fraternity house must be fixed up for rush week. Joe doesn't particularly like work but he knows a clean house is essential for a good impression on the rushees.

Joe is tired—He's interested in the sports page but he won't read much longer—he's worried about his dirty clothes but not too worried.

Joe will go on to bed.

C-19.   Harry is checking over want ads in the paper and musing over possible effects of his plan somehow to display Sgt Murphy's incompetence. Things are in apparent disarray in his bunkroom reflecting the fact that Harry is not really a model soldier himself. Nevertheless he would like to excel in making Murphy look silly.

Harry will probably organize all corps members to collect data and call an inspection team from Washington. But he will have insufficient evidence and be court martialled.

C-20.   Young man who is having trouble with college work and fears he will flunk out.

Girl trouble. Heartbroken because his girl-friend jilted him.

He has two problems. (1) Explaining grades to parents (2) In an effort to demonstrate his independence he is looking for a job in the city of his college.

Grade won't be that bad, so he will remain in school. Another girl will come along.

C-21.   A moral conflict. To lead the unions against the company or not.

Union boss knows that strike will mean hardship on members. Disagreement about working conditions and safety factors. Workers do not demand higher wages—only safer conditions.

Are the improved conditions worth the long strike? Would it be better to press the issue next year?

He will strike. He will feel responsibility for the decision. Later, any guilt-feelings will be overridden by rationalization.

C-22.   A diabolical plot to rob the largest bank in New York is being planned by this man, an ex-convict. This mans desire for wealth no matter how attained has warped his mind so that this is all right and this is the reason for his previous imprisonment. He is thinking of all the small details, trying to make sure of no slip ups. He knows these caused his capture before and he does not want this to happen. He will rob the bank successfully. However he will be captured at his hideout, maybe not immediately but just a little way in the future and he will be sentenced to mental observation while in jail.

C-23.   Man is meditating whether or not he should replace his kerosene lamp with an electric one.

Smoke gets in his eyes.

How expensive the electricity is vs. how bad the kerosene lamp is.

Only the shadow knows.

C-24.   A novelist and critic is puzzling over a problem in the book he is writing. "Is this passage true to life? Why? Why Not?"

The man has written an number of novels and critical essays of definite value.

The author is attempting to create the passage in order to reflect real life accurately and at the same time illuminate some aspect of real life.

He will succeed in his attempt, but only partially.

C-25.   A man deep in thought is doing creative writing at a desk, and is carefully getting down his thoughts and looking critically at what he is writing.

The man is a writer who has had an inspiration, an idea,

for a work and has been developing it mentally before putting it onto paper.

The man is thinking of how his words sound, whether they say what he wants them to. He wants to get his feeling into words.

The man will revise his work, finally set it aside until he can return to continue preparation of the final copy.

C-26. This is a man in a mining camp. This man is the foreman, and he is thinking.

He, the foreman, has had some trouble with the job concerning some of his men and their work.

He, the foreman is thinking of a way to solve his problem with the men. He is looking for a solution to his problem.

He seems fairly competent and will seemingly succeed in his action that he will take the next day, for this evening he is burning the midnight oil.

C-27. This man by the lamp is watching the flames and dreaming. He sees odd and strange patterns in the flickering light.

Something unfortunate happened in his life today and he is reflecting upon it.

The man would like to know why this had to happen to him.

He will try to correct the situation but will not be able to do it.

C-28. The guy is sitting in a restaurant having a cigarette and a drink. He is an unhappy married man and has just become depressed.

His wife just walked out on him, even though he had a business success. She thinks he's spending his salary on liquor which is probably correct.

He is thinking it would be nice if his wife came back, but he can see that he shouldn't have drunk so much.

He will show up at this bar a lot, his wife will never come back, he will lose his job, and become an alcoholic.

C-29. The drunkard is sitting at this table with a sad face and a tremor in his whole body. He is alone.

The drunkard's wife has suddenly died and the poor man

realizes for the first time that he was wrong. She died because of him and he feels guilty.

He thinks that life could've been different if he only had the strength to live a responsible life. He desperately wants his wife back to show her that he can change.

He'll go out right away and start drinking like mad— He'll come back to the same room and break everything on his way.

C-30.   It looks like a mad scientist pondering over the question of who will be his next victim.

He was angry at his wife and his anger generalized to mankind.

He is thinking about how happy he is.

His next victim will be you!

POWER PRACTICE STORIES: SET D

D-1.   Captain of luxereous pleasure ship is dealing with potential insurance agent concerning proper coverages, risks, and costs.

The captain has been approached by the interested agent and convinced to let the agent appraise the situation in an effort to save the Captain (owner) insurance expenses.

The agent has asked some rather personal questions which offended the captain somewhat. Consequently, he is telling the agent what he feels to be the relevant facts which he is either to take as given or forget the appraisel. The captain is currently quite satisfied with his current insurance company anyway and consequently rejects the proposal.

D-2.   The captain of the cargo frieghter is talking with an scheduling executive of the shipping company.

The ship has lain idle at the pier for several days waiting to be loaded. The longshoremen are on strike.

The two men are discussing the immediate future of the negotiations to settle the strike. Neither is directly involved in the negotiations. They both are anxious to get the ship to sea.

The men will soon finish their discussion and generally take it easy until the strike is settled probably in a few days.

D-3.   The captain of an ocean liner is explaining the administration of a ship to a midwestern businessman who is on tour with a group of similar men.

The businessman has asked a general question of administration, mostly to make conversation, and the captain has responded earnestly, as he has great interest in his work.

The businessman thinks the talk is somewhat boring—the captain is oblivious of the narrowness of his conversation and feels that he is pleasing his guest.

The captain will terminate, the businessman will excuse himself and leave.

D-4.   The ships commander is explaining to the senator the layout of his new ship.

The ship is the first of a new fleet authorized by congress, and opposed by this senator.

The commander wants to convince the senator that the ship was worth the price. The senator has his back up—growls around and shows his displeasure.

The senator will make a press statement that the new ship is worthwhile.

D-5.   Welcome aboard the ship. I'm your captain, and I hope you enjoy your cruise. We have here a wonderful crew who will do there best to make you comfortable.

No, it does look as though we may have trouble with the weather. However we take good care of the vessel, she is in top notch condition. We should have no trouble.

Yes, we will do everything to see that you are in time to make the meeting in Cairo. We have never been late, except where the safety of the passengers and crew dictated that we change course. We will try our best to get you there.

If you have any questions, the first mate should be able to help you.

D-6.   The civilian is getting information from the cargo ships captain about the operations of his ship. The civilian is a Port Authority representative and there has been some question about the ships operation. The captain is explaining very carefully exactly what he thinks the civilian wants to hear. He cannot be disrespectful since he must keep good relations in order to return to this port. He will succeed

D-7.   An American naval ex officer is leaving to go abroad, probably on a training mission. His staff secretary has come down (in formally) to see him off and get any last minute information about how to handle a specific situation that has come up.

       The mission has been planned for a long time and finally all preparations and plans for the mission are complete. Just before sailing time, something urgent has come up and the officer has called his secy to come down to be briefed.

       The officer wants some specific action taken.

       The secretary use his own initiative to solve the problem and will wire the ex officer and advise him of success

D-8.   One man is a merchant ship captain, the other a representative of the Shipping firm. The Captain is explaining an unfavorable event.

       There has been a strike of workers on the ship and the ship failed to reach port on time.

       The Captain thinks he is not to blame for the incident and wants to be vindicated. The man in the suit wants information

       The man in the suit will report to mgm't. The Captain will be disciplined.

D-9.   The ship has just arrived in port and the captain is taling to a customs agent before passengers debark.

       There has been much smuggling and the captain feels he knows who the cusserals are. He is giving his tips to the customs agents.

       When the passengers come off the boat the agents will apprehend the people suspected by the captain.

D-10. These two men are having a calm discussion. The man on the left is an insurance man and he is talking to the captain of a passenger ship.

       This steamship line has had trouble in the past with van-delism and various unfortunate experiences. The insurance company is considering raising the charges.

       The captain is answering some questions posed to him by the insurance man. The insurance man does not know whether to believe the captain, but he does want him to describe the operating procedures while at sea.

       The insurance company will raise the rates and the steam-ship company will do something about the vandelism.

D-11.   A high school dropout is lying on a bed in a disorderly room reading a paper. The window is dirty the furniture shabby. He is reading the sports page to kill time.

Having unsuccessfully tried to gain employment with his background, he has become disgruntled and frustrated.

He is without ambition and feels society has given up on him. He wants to gain a secure position but the paths open to him are limited.

He will continue to be frustrated until he resumes his education. This he will accomplish and he will ultimately have a happy creative life.

D-12.   This guy is resting after spending all day of K.P. He is in the Army, and is expecting to be discharged in a few months.

The first sergeant has designated that he take KP on this weekend, and it is the second weekend in a row for him. He is pretty sick of it.

He is thinking of what movies are in the paper for him to go to. He wants to have some fun, but is pretty lonely, and can't think how to get it.

He will get dressed soon and go out and raise some hell. But when it is over, he only feels worse.

D-13.   The boy in the picture is a "high school dropout" who is checking the papers for some indication that a job might be available.

He left school to take what he thought was a good job, but was laid off, and for the past few weeks has been searching for other opportunities.

The boy would like to work but the motivation to get out and work at getting the job is lacking. He is content to lie back and hope that something will turn up.

In order to eat he will have to go get a job no matter of what kind.

D-14.   This is Joe college relaxing on a weekend in his room. Joe doesn't have to study too hard because he is taking a lot of easy courses this term. There is only one bed in the room because Joe is a lone wolf. He likes to take it easy and keep to himself. His dirty clothes are the result of washing his Corvette for a big date tonight with one of the campus queens. Right now all he wants to do is be by himself and relax for the night to come.

Studying doesn't mean much to Joe because he has always been given everything he needs.

D-15.   This fellow is either cutting work or else it is his day off. The sun at the window is too bright—as if it were midday—to be evening or later afternoon in which case the man could be resting after a hard day's work.

The man went out and got a paper—the room is too bare and suggests he is living their only temporily for the paper to have been delivered. He's relaxing and reading the paper, quite completely too—by the fact that his shoes are off and his feet are up.

D-16.   After the completion of the patrol, which was successful, Juan was able to read of his exploits in the papers.

The U.S. papers played up the demolition of the rebel camp as a major victory for the loyalist forces. These forces had been on the defensive and were badly in need of a victory to raise moral and rally the people. It was Juan's opinion that the patrol had accomplished this goal and he was quite satisfied with his role as patrol leader.

D-17.   This is a college student relaxing in his room, reading the paper.

There is much that is happening in the world and he is keeping himself informed.

As he reads about events in far off places he thinks about how lucky he is to have such a soft existence here.

After he finished reading the paper he will forget all about what he has read.

D-18.   This boy is reading the newspaper, not because he wants to know what is in the news, but because he is relaxing and needs something with which to relax. The boy looks like a student at some university.

The night before the boy got drunk and does not feel like doing very much early in the morning.

The boy is concentrating somewhat on the words he is reading, but his mind is generally daydreaming about nothing in particular. The boy is thinking in the back of his mind that he must soon get busy with his chores for the day.

In about an hour, the boy will get up, clean up the room a little and they get to work.

D-19.   This is me on a sunny afternoon in May at college. The very last thing I want to do is study. I have just returned from driving golf balls and am reading the sports section of the *New York Post*. The Yankees lost again and I am pretty upset. I'm glad I did well at the driving range: if I hit golf balls poorly *and* the Yankees lost I would have been too depressed to work tonight.

D-20.   This is a Sunday morning scene. The guy on the bed, with no cases to do for about six hours is enjoying his hangover and Sunday paper.

Saturday night and no homework usually leads to this type of situation. It is obvious he has a headache from the uncomfortable position of his arm and the "vertilated feet" position, obviously hot, itchy feet from Saturday night.

Generally he is thinking—how much of what am I reading true, what can be done about; my head hurts, I must go work.

He will get up and go to breakfast and begin to work.

D-21.   This man is a farmer who is looking over his bills. It is winter time and he is wondering how much of the money he got for his crops will be needed to pay them. As he thinks he smokes continually. In the past, his profits have decreased every year. He still makes a good profit, but he wonders how long he can continue to do so. Costs have risen and the prices he is getting for his crops have not. He is thinking that maybe his farm is not all that it seems to be at other times when bills are not due. His profits will be smaller than the preceding year's profits. But not so small as to discourage him from keeping his farm, and remaining in the work he likes so well.

D-22.   He often wrote at night. His latest book must be finished for the trip to New York. He was nominated as a Pulitzer Prize winner. His ideas seem to flow at night by candlelight—this he feels a necessity. His book has been in the making for a great many years and his creative insight has finally taken hold. He writes. His mind picks bits of information and puts the ideas in print. The book will be published. The story will be a million seller and a movie made about the novel. The title: *Candle*.

D-23.   In a quite secluded working area a man is carefully working with a substance and heat is being applied. The man has made

previous attempts and is trying to arrive at a suitable conclusion. The man is thinking of possible results. The man after
a few more tries will arrive at what he feels is a suitable conclusion.

D-24. A man is lighting a lamp for night seeing. It has become dark
outside and the need for light has become necessary. So he
decides to light the lamps. The man hopes the lamp will light
and that he will not burn himself before the lamp is lit. The
lamp will light and he will be able to read or do whatever he
pleases once.

D-25. A scientist working in his home laboratory on an invention
which he feels will benefit mankind. He has felt a need all his
life to do something different and really worthwhile. He is
noticing that his plans are near complete. Upon completion of
his plans he will begin intricate construction of his worthwhile
invention. He will be a complete success and it will lead other
men on to utilize the invention.

D-26. This man is a doctor in the late eighteen hundreds. He is preparing medicine for a patient. He was called at midnight on
this emergency call. The patient is very sick and near death.
The doctor feels that this is a disease which he has been re-
searching, and decided to use his toxin, successfully tried on
animals, on this dying patient. The toxin works, and the
patient recovers. The doctor has wiped out a disease that had
deadly potential and reduced it to the status of a cold.

D-27. In the cellar of the mad scientist's house, an elaborate laboratory has been developed for the experimentation of X plague.
When he was a little boy, the town mocked him for studying
chemistry and physics. They ridiculed him and did not allow
their children to associate with him. They made him the lone-
liest person in the world. He is attempting to develop a plague
which will destroy all those who mocked and ridiculed him
during his childhood. After spending five more years of research, the mad scientist will approach the town and release
his discovery on them.

D-28. We are at a secret laboratory. The man is a Russian scientist
who has been assigned to invent a secret weapon to be used
against his country's enemies. He is experimenting in order to

find a device to be used for a secret program of which he cannot be disclosed. He is entirely devoted to his country and to the cause he is working for. He will continue experimenting into long hours of the night in order to perfect the device he is working on. His undying devotion will ultimately be rewarded because he will invent the device he wished to use and it will be perfect for its purpose.

D-29.   Doctor Yes is just adding some HCl to his formula for fast drying paint. He feels that the Armor Paint Research Laboratory will profit greatly from his discovery. The Armor Research Laboratory got a call about ten o'clock A.M. that their new fast drying paint they just marketed was causing deterioration of metal. Doctor Yes was assigned to fix the problem. I wonder if I add HCl what will happen to the other acids in the mixture. This could be very harmful or counter act the others thought Doctor Yes. The paint was found very defective and although Doctor Yes spent many hours trying to fix it, it was to no avail and the project had to be scrapped.

D-30.   This is Tom Edison and he is meditating about the possibility of making an electric light. He has read a little about electricity and it fascinates him, especially since very little is known about it. He has just gotten a job and now has a few tools to work with. He is wondering where to begin his experiments. As yet there is little space and very little money to work with. He also wants to marry. He marries. But only after making a different invention to get the money. He will work many man hours on the bulb. But due to his brilliance he will be kept from creating the electric light for a long time. Late in life he finally fulfills his heart's desires.

POWER PRACTICE STORIES: SET E

E-1.   This is some sort of business meeting. The executives are sitting around trying to figure out a problem—as they are members of an insurance company they are discussing no-fault insurance. Their biggest worry is to see how they can lobby in order to get the bill passed. They realize that the big trial lawyers won't want it to go through since it would cut out plenty of their expensive cases. Also, many lawyers being in government will have much control in the passage. What is being discussed here is how the best way is to handle it—make it appealing to the voter so they will put pressure on the legislature or just lobby or a combination. One man has gotten up he is going to get a drink of water since this has been

E-2.   Archibald was always the one who came up with the strange ideas. There doesn't seem to be any real story here, but it is interesting to watch the reactions which his various associates have to the points dramatized by his stabbing finger. He never quite takes his sayings seriously, but most other people seem to. As Archie elaborates on his latest thoughts on Utopian society, their reactions are alternately serious, amused, skeptical, mildly excited, or mixed.

E-3.   The people are business executives who are finishing up their lunch break at the office. They are in a happy mood because the business firm is going to have a vacation starting at the end of the day

    The men were eating out, but these men have come back to the office early (as they usually do) to sit around reading the paper or to talk with each other

    The men are excited about the vacation coming up, and they are talking about their vacations and what they're going to do.

    Soon the lunch break will be over and they'll go to their offices to work.

E-4.   This is an executive meeting of the bosses of 2 large firms which have decided to merge.

    Due to economic hardships & overlap of outgoing monetary expenses two firms have joined together to try to cut expenses & become a profit making company.

    The man who has left the table is disgusted & hostile because he hasn't been chosen as the new head of the joint corporation. The man sitting at the head of the table is the new president & is overly optimistic, enthusiastic, and impressed with his new power. The others are equally optimistic, yet not quite as sure of the security of their optimism.

E-5.   This is a meeting of junior executives of a small company.

    This is just a routine meeting. Nothing exciting or important happened.

Everybody wants to get a better job in the company; they appear friendly to each other but would prefer to see the other guys "screw up" badly.

Nothing will happen for a year.

E-6.   A business meeting. John: "I got a plan to make a million but I need you guys to invest in my ideas."

Bob: "But what about last time, I know your harebrained schemes. They never work."

John: "Aw, don't listen to him, this one is really surefire."

Bob: "But he said that last time & the time before."

Pete: "But this one doesn't sound too bad."

John: "That's right, trust me, I know it'll work."

Bob: "I wouldn't if I were you."

Pete: "Well you're not me & I resent your trying always to tell me how to run things. Maybe its not such a bad idea anyway."

Bob: "OK throw your money away, just remember that I warned you."

E-7.   "Our company is showing a rise in both its ingenuity and in its production," the chairman responds.

"Yes but will this new extricate us from our deficit?" the 1st board member asks.

"Sales will go up if the product is better," the chairman replies.

"I'm sure," said the 2nd man. "Just like our sales of pink shoelaces. We had the best laces on the market."

"Should we go ahead and build a new plant?" asked the building advisor.

"If we stay in the old one we're in now, we'll die of negligence," commented one board member.

"I think that we should attempt an all round improvement in both procedure & facility."

"Let's ask the president."

E-8.   This is a board meeting in which the members are hopeful of adopting a new policy. The policy ignores moralism for the sake of material gain.

All but one of the men are enthusiastic. They see great gains ahead. The lone fellow is saddened and frustrated. He sees his fellow men poluted by selfishness

The board will meet with great quarrels from within. All will find themselves extremely self. The lone man will be viewed with disdain For he alone makes the others see themselves.

E-9. The men are discussing the merging of their company with another. Their company will soon go bankrupt and they want to join another. However there is one member that is a little too optimistic and want to keep on working, that is the man who is standing by the window. He doesn't agree with anything that is being said he has been working for the company for 10 years and thinks that it will go on. The other member know that is was a result of his bad handling of the company that it is in financial difficulties now. Finally they decide to merge with the other company and the man at the window resigns because he himself know that he was not doing a very good job.

E-10. The introduction of a new idea at a corporate officials meeting has been received with mixed feelings. Like most new ideas this one has been hatched by one person who has either accidentally or purposefully examined a problem in a different way.

The need for some change was apparent when the men sat down for a discussion. When the idea was injected into the conversation it forced some to modify the idea in their own mind, others rejected the idea as foriegn and unrealistic.

E-11. A quiet, dedicated student scientist proceeds with her work with the utmost care as her bitchy professor looks on. The girl comes from a peaceful family that immigrated from Germany. There was a strong (though not expressed) feeling of love among the family, but with it was a stern discipline & an emphasis on learning. She has a cool balance within her. She knows where she's going. She has family security & internal peace & she plugs toward her goal with resilience & courage. The prof. lacks this balance. She never had this peace. She looks upon with a mixture of jealousy, regret, & admiration.

E-12. The woman in the foreground is working on a research project attempting to develop an effective but safe pesticide to protect trees from gypsy moth invasions. Her assistant, in the background, is displeased with the way the research has been going, for many of her suggestions have been ignored and her attempts to conduct her own research have been thwarted.

E-13.   The lady with the test tube is a newcomer to the staff at the research center. She came from a college a month ago and has worked long hours towards a discovery. She has made great strides. Confident. Assured. Single-minded. Other woman is head. She is jealous of the discovery. The girl thinks little of the rewards or material benefits she can reap from her find. The woman could kick herself because she won't be getting that attention. The old head might try to buy the discovery— or try to manipulate it towards her ends.

E-14.   The lady chemist is very impressed with her work for she is on the brink of a new discovery and she must be sure that she gets the proper mixture of chemicals. Her co-worker, Joan, doesn't seemed to be impressed either way and is standing by idly. Partly in not understanding the experiment and partly in not caring. The chemist, Andrea, is about to discover the cure of a disease that she has wanted to cure for a long time. Since the death of her father from the rare disease her life has been dedicate to finding the appropriate cure. The time is almost here. As she mixes the chemicals all she can think of is how this could have helped her father and even so it will help others. The cure is found and Andrea leaves her research aside and goes out in the world.

E-15.   This woman is devoted to biological research and although a little lonely, enjoys her work and is very much absorbed in it, and has little else in her life. Her mother has come to visit her, and as usual has invited her to dinner with her and some friends.

Both love and respect each other very much, and the daughter will accept the invitation, politely, mostly to make her mother happy. Eventually the mother will understand she wants to

E-16.   The woman with the pipette is not of the same type of personality as the woman with the glasses, however she values her professional opinion and has asked her for advice in interpreting the results of the procedure she is about to perform in the picture.

The woman performing the procedure has, she thinks, discovered something new and wishes to obtain the opinion of the second woman.

The woman performing the procedure hopes the second will approve of her interpretations. The second woman is interested only somewhat in the procedure, however she will give her honest opinion.

The results will be conclusive and the second woman will encourage the first to continue along in the same area.

E-17. Late, on the evening of Sept 5 Marie and Jeanette Le Duc finally discovered the cure for cancer. The two scientists had been doing cancer research for 30 years.

E-18. The younger woman is a student performing an experiment. The older one looking on is her professor.

The younger one has been coming to classes and the labs and the older one is simply checking on her to see how she's doing.

The younger one is concentrating on her work and the older one is trying to see if she is making any mistakes. The younger one is hoping that she is doing okay.

The younger one will finish okay and the older one will go "pick on" someone else.

E-19. A mother has come to find out the results of tests done on her child, who is 7 yrs. old & has been strong and healthy until a few months ago.

Quite suddenly he's been losing weight and been generally fatigued. They are a middle-class family; he is an only child; had a younger brother who died in childbirth.

The mother senses a certain tension & knows the news is not good. The doctor has told her that her son is going to die of leukemia.

Being a calm, controlled woman she sits still, collapses in a chair & says nothing. What is there to say? Nothing can be done & nothing will be done.

E-20. The two lab technicians were in the criminology department of a large city Police Department. They are almost never told what their tests have to do with specific cases; they merely work and fill out lab reports, which the lab manager then coordinates with the cases they are assisting.

This case was different. Even the interdepartmental secrecy of the bureau couldn't keep this case secret. The lab technicians were especially careful today; the case was in the public eye and the results of this very test determined the guilt or innocense of a very prominent person. His lawyer was the lab technician's husband.

E-21. This is Mr. Adams the senior partner in his law firm and Mr. Johnson his junior partner. As they are discussing a special case that has come up Mr. Adams glances at Mr. J. As he does Mr. A. thinks of him—how he was when he came in—a fresh law graduate—how he has changed—how he thinks a little differently now—much more practical and not as much text book oriented—how he will change even more in years to come. Still he will have those forthright eyes, that proud chin and hopefully that sincere and intelligent way about him. Mr. J. is all that Mr. A. hoped he himself had been.

E-22. The two are a young man and his father. The young man is being "pensive", and the father is trying to help his son out, but realises he can't.

The young man has graduated from college, and is now home after graduation.

The young man realises he has to find a job now, although he feels he doesn't want to work for the rest of his life. He also realizes he must move out of the house and live on his own as soon as he can.

The young man will stay home with his parents the rest of the day, then go out looking for a job. He finds one with an insurance company, gets married, finds a beautiful little cottage in the country, and lives happily ever after!

E-23. "Gosh, Dad, I sure am glad you're here," said young Freddy nervously. "It sure is nice to know that you felt the same way before *your* first time in front of those people!" The old man chuckled quietly to himself. "They're awful hard on you at first, but you've just got to stand up and show 'em you can take it. After awhile, they let up on you."

"Well, thanks for coming by, Pa. I guess I'd better get on in there. But I sure do dread having to go in there and try to convince all those students in my lecture."

E-24. This is a psychiatrist talking to a patient who is a manic depressive.

No one incident has led up to the unbearable melancholic state which this man is in, but his whole life seems to be a trail of ambitions which were shattered and a loss of all idealism and hope.

The man after just going through a divorce & separation from his 3 children has seen the last remnants of his dignity and concrete examples of his masculinity and existence being taken from him, is contemplating suicide. The Dr. is scrutinizing the patient to see how extensive these feelings really are.

E-25. Two notorious underworld figures are discussing how they're going to get the big load of heroin through customs.

Both of these dudes are concerned that they may get caught.

The young brash one will escape with his own neck and the older one will make it behind bars. The younger one wouldn't help out in the crunch.

E-26. "Why do you reject what I offer you in life. You could have a very nice steady life, if you'd just accept things."

"But don't you see that I just can't. I don't want to just be thought of as a rich man's son I want to make something of myself. Can't you understand. I think it's better that I leave. Maybe I should go to California far away from the East Coast high society. This just isn't for me."

"But what have I worked for all these years I always only wanted the best for you. Don't you understand."

"I do understand but I have to make a go out of my own life not just be an extension of yours. I'm leaving."

E-27. The thoughts raced wildly in the mind of the father as he stared solemnly at his son. His son seemed troubled, yet could not confide his inner feelings to his own father. "He has come from me and he is all I have—yet I don't even have him. He is now like a foreigner to me. How I remember how close we used to be. But then, that girl came between us and I had to go through 2 yrs. of silence & not understanding. And even now that it is over, there's still no communication between us. He has not emptied his mind to anyone else—of this I am sure.

But why, even in their troubled separation, does he have to reject me and think only of what has passed."

E-28.   The old man is scolding his son for placing badly in his college's rowing crew.

   The night before the big race, the son went on an all-night spree of drinking in his fraternity.

   The son is ashamed, but he nurtures a secret death wish for his old man. The father is deeply disappointed & wants his son to achieve the best

   The son will not disappoint his father. He will go on to win races. Eventually, he will receive a large inheritance upon the death of his proud father.

E-29.   An older man, who is quite wealthy and has many business interests, runs his operations from a center in South America somewhere. The younger man is a hired employee, not a native, and is a servant and body guard. Occasionally, this estate being the economic center of the area, there are parties, or celebrations in the large home for "friends". The older man is making an indirectly complimentary remark about one of the people present, unknown to him, a man not well liked by his employee.

E-30.   "Experience is the best teacher." This saying holds true if the experience is one's own. In the picture the older man is relating his experiences of the past; confident that they can teach others what he has learned. The younger man is sceptical of the advice he hears. He believes that experiences from the past can not be as educational as those to come.

   The older man feels that his experiences have taught him much and he only seeks to impart his knowledge on someone who can gain from them. The young man feels more directly responsible for his education and prefers not to learn vicariously.

POWER PRACTICE STORIES: SET F

F-1.   Brian Gardner, a brilliant up & coming executive, has just been hired by a company because of his advertising ideas in relation to the company's brand new product, a remarkable brand new chemical to use in house. An executive meeting has been called in order for Brian to promote his campaign ideas to the other executives. Brian's ideas are discussed enthusiastically and he is excepted by the other men, not only for his knowledge of the field but also for his humble personality.

Now the executives will take different phases of the new advertising plan back to their individual departments to have plans drawn up and to get the ball rolling in their factories across the country.

F-2.   Left-handed liberation. These men have taken off from work in order that they might be able to plan a rally for their movement. Basically they are all middle-class people who have a common ambition to liberate themselves from the ugly American view of left-handedness.

Years of frustration and persecution. The men believe the time has come to resolve their guilt because there is no longer a reason.

Their thinking how they will be able to bring left-handed people from all over the country together in the hope of establishing the respect and understanding of their fellow American.

They will succeed.

F-3.   Some sort of business meeting is in progress.

A plan is being offered by one or more of the men, and the action seems to be in convincing the others of the quality of the plan.

The man at the window seems unconvinced the man being swayed at the table seems favorable to the plan offered, but again unsure. The presenters of the plan seem confident.

The man at the table will agree with the plan; the man at the window will remain unconvinced but will abstain, thus the plan will be adopted.

F-4.   John Jumper, Bill Stat's friend (?), is proposing a new product for their company. John, the president, recently came out against diversifying; he and Bill talking it through beforehand. Bill had argued with John that the plan, although alluring to the board, would be bad for the company. Now however John is presenting the idea to the board hoping to win their confidence. Bill is very much taken aback at first & is now staring out the window deciding what he should do.

F-5. Debate-conversation. One speaks enthusiastically; another does not see the meaning of blank talk and watches scenes thru the window. Others sit in various ways and either listen or let their minds wander. Anyway they will end up in the same place. Nowhere.

What is a discussion? Especially one involving business types. Carrying on a system which is nearing doom; returning it to the beginning.

F-6. The Hammelburger family now had seven males between the ages of 20–40 who were now preparing to take over the family. The boys had gone through high school together and had always been close friends. Now they were involved in financing the political overthrow of a South American gov't. hostile to them and their economic interests. In order for their revolution to be successful it had to be led by guerillas in the name of the people. They had been carefully training a group of 5000 citizens in guerillla warfare on an island they owned in the S. Pacific and finally after 2 yrs. of painstaking preparation they were planning to launch their revolution the following week.

F-7. It appears to be a break after a business discussion. The men act towards each other with varying degrees of familiarity. The man looking out the window appears to need a break from these people as well as a meeting break. The rest seem excited and happy about a new venture they hope to carry out with each other and appear optimistic yet relatively inexperienced.

F-8. A group of men get together after being a long way apart— they are having some kind of a reunion.

The men, years previous, had been close buddies. When they "reconvened", some of the men find that their minds have drifted far apart from that of the others. A couple of the men are not even listening to one recount what has occurred to him. Others find that they still do fit in with the group of their old friends.

The "loners" only want the meeting to end, and to stop "living in the past." Some of the others want to forget the present

The meeting will end, and they will be forced to return to their present lives.

F-9.   This is a gathering of the Board of Ministry of the Church of
        Christ. The standing man is giving testimonial to how Christ
        has come into his life & fulfilled it.

        The man who is being embraced has recently been shaken
        in his faith. He is not sure now that Christ is the way. But the
        others are sure that they will bring him back into the fold.

        The standing man is a long standing member of the church
        and has always been accepted by the others as being one of the
        saved and yet he has inner doubts that have always been with
        him as to whether he is right.

F-10.   It's a business meeting for some medium sized company. All
        are celebrating their 10th year in the business and the meeting
        deals with the large profits the company has made in the past
        year and a vastely improved market.

        One man, the one by the window, seriously doubts the sig-
        nificance of the company's success and the personal impor-
        tance the company has for him. He is going through a period
        of self-examination. Perhaps considering a move or a change.
        Perhaps he is not satisfied completely with the ethics of the
        company. He probably will stay on for lack of anything else.

F-11.   Student and teacher engaged in lab work. Hilda undertakes
        elementary tasks under the critical observation of Dr. Over-
        lock. Intelligent, articulate, Hilda is potentially a peer of Over-
        lock's but she must master techniques; at this she works
        arduously with quiet self-confidence. In her dour way, the
        doctor approves of his disciple. It will be difficult, but Hilda
        has the potential

F-12.   Two women professors in the chemistry department of State
        University are conducting an experiment. One of them is pre-
        paring a solution they will use in an experiment.

        The experiment came about as a result of a discussion
        they had with their male associates. The women disagreed
        with the men and they are now trying to prove their point.

        The woman who is watching is thinking about the discus-
        sion and is having second thoughts about the experiment. She
        thinks she and the other woman may have been wrong.

        The other woman is just about finished with making the
        solution. They will find out in a few minutes who is right.

F-13.   As they both stared at the thermometer in the test tube, different thoughts passed through each's mind.

The lab assistant thought darkly to herself, "She seems so calm and collected. I wonder if I could ever be so smooth & unruffled about such an important scientific endeavor. Maybe she really doesn't care about it. I think my concern with finding a cure for the disease is far greater than her's. Why?"

The scientist calmly surveyed the thermometer & thought to herself about her growth as a scientist & how she had once been as excited as the perspiring lab assistant. Yet now she considered herself a more careful & knowledgable scientist. Her calmness was a reflection of her inner conviction that science must be a technically precise study. Yet she did realize that the calmness was only superficial & that she too was sweating profusely

F-14.   In the chemistry lab at a hospital, a technician is doing a glucose tolerance test on several patients' serum.

Observe the woman with the glasses looking on. She is a technician also but with a subjective interest especially in one serum—her child's who would show if the sugar is high-diabetes. The chemistry is a scientific test—which will give a definite result—despite either technician's feeling. But somehow this mother watches very closely with a feeling of approaching doom as a certain reagent is added. If the test turns purple or a dark pink—the diagnosis will be diabetes.

The child will, I hope, not be a victim of diabetes and the mother will find her mind whirling around in joyous relief.

F-15.   They are two research scientists. One is taking a sample of the fluid. They are mature, capable women who know what they are doing. The other woman is waiting for the results. The sample of fluid is only one of many they have taken in their effort to find a cure for cancer. The results will not give them any answers, but they will keep on trying.

F-16.   Apparently, an experiment is taking place and two biochemists have decided to get together and research a hypothesis that they have formulated.

One of the biochemists discovered something different about eating a certain kind of fruit and that is if you eat this fruit, something in it will alleviate pains from certain diseases.

The government has refused them a grant on the basis that there is no evidence to support this hypothesis. The biochemists feel, naturally, that the government is wrong and are attempting to work with as much of the funds as they can.

At this point, they are not sure of the results but are quite confident and optimistic about their results. They hope to use these results to help people.

F-17. The two women are scientists. The one in the background is an assistant, watching her superior test the blood of a patient in a lab. The assistant is new and is being shown how certain tests are administered and how the results are discovered.

The blood being tested at the moment was taken from a patient having a routine check-up. The assistant is amazed at the other's skill and is slightly afraid of her own ability. However, she will prove to be just as skilled and will be able to help the superior one in many experiments.

F-18. This is a nurse and a lab assistant in a small clinic in central Ohio. They have just finished taking various samples from a middle-aged lady who has come in and who they fear may have encephylitis. There was a recent outbreak of it in the town in a number of pigeons, and the doctors fear that this lady's constant associations with the park and the pigeons may have led to her contracting the disease. The ladies are now on the brink of deciding whether or not she really has the disease or if it is simply an allergy to potted asparagus.

F-19. The woman is testing a blood sample for leukemia. The blood belongs to the daughter of the woman watching her.

The daughter, Linda, has been ill for a long time, & has been having lots of tests taken. This is one of them.

The women, who are good friends, are worried & tense that the result may be positive. Both want it to be negative. Dorothy, the one doing the test, wants to make absolutely sure, even more than usual, that her analysis is correct, for she is very emotionally involved.

The test completed, it was found to be negative. Instead, Linda has a rare blood disease that can be treated.

F-20. The woman with the pipette is a research assistant at a medical laboratory. The woman watching her is telling her something—an anecdote, story of her home.

The woman had many idealistic feelings while she was in college, about helping mankind, discovering cures, etc. The woman watching had no such thoughts, but merely works to help support her family, as her husband is unemployed. She spends a lot of time talking of her hardships.

The research assistant imagines and fantasizes about the substance in the test tube, imagining it to be some great discovery, a cure for cancer, or the like. It is actually simply a hormone extract used to make aspirin, and a very routine job at that.

She finally will break down and tell the complaining woman to stop turning to her for an ear. She will walk home alone.

F-21.   Tom Jones is on trial for 1st degree murder. He unfortunately was at first innocently implicated the crime but circumstantial evidence was against him and he finds his prospects growing dim despite the expert legal counselling of a very good defense attorney, Jerry Boyd.

The trial is into its second week and the state prosecutor has just brought a surprise witness onto the stand. Jerry Boyd was unprepared to the surprising and damaging testimony of the eyewitness who claims she saw the accused slay his wife.

Jerry Boyd confers with Tom to see if Tom has any knowledge of this witness or to her motive for adding false evidence.

Tom offers no information but is unable to take his eyes off the witness. Jerry will eventually solve the relationship between Tom & the woman & thus Tom will be declared innocent.

F-22.   A man and his father are sitting silently next to each other. They were just told on T.V. that the son had been defeated in his election for the House of Representatives.

Three months of strenuous campaigning; consisting of Friday nite talks at the local gym and speechs every Sunday in the park.

The son regards the defeat as meaning that his life long ambition to be a politician is no longer possible. The father is trying to console him, though he also realizes that his son is not.

Life will go on.

F-23.   An old man is reflecting upon his own life through his son. The old man is a musician and has trained his son.

   The old man was a virtuoso pianist & his son is about to give his first performance.

   The old man is both anxious & proud. His talent has faded, & he wants to continue through his son. The son is determined.

   The look on the face of the son assures his success. The old man feels a deep sense of accomplishment.

F-24.   John Sr., and John Jr., one the chip off the old block of the other. Too much so though. John Sr. is a socialite through & through and will not permit his son to continue as the playboy he now is. They are both at a party and Jojo (Jr's latest conquest) is walking towards them. Mr. Miller has just told his son that he will either end this affair quickly as a promise for the future, or he will be disinherited. Jr. is contemplating what to do he doesn't want either. He has always hated his father and is contemplating murder.

F-25.   The younger man, perhaps the son of the older, appears to be faced with a very difficult choice or problem to deal with. His father or perhaps just a devious character does not offer kind advice but has let the other know how he feels. The younger, wanting to do what is right in his own mind appears to disagree with the "suggestion" of the other. He however is not sure as to what action to take.

F-26.   A father and son are having a discussion. The son is involved in some internal conflict, causing him to be in misery. The father is putting pressure on the son to make a certain decision, one that the son is not prepared to make.

   The son has avoided making this important decision for a long time, and he is now going to be forced into making a decision by circumstance.

   The father eagerly wants the son to follow in his footsteps, and do some of the things that *he* was not able to do when he was younger. The son is ripped by his duty to his father and other considerations.

   The son, unable to decide for himself, will allow the decision to be made for him.

F-27.   Father & son. Father over middle age enough to have a son in his middle or late 20's. The two are talking things out which is rather extraordinary, because usually they remain silent and keep a respected distance away from each other.

The son feels lost—he has finished school and he must decide what he's going to do with himself. He has begun a job he doesn't like because it has given him a view of the "real" world. He hates the world and the people in it—it is cold and dishonest.

The father has seen the disturbed look on his son's face and he's sat down to talk with him to give him a little confidence and show him the good side of the world. The father, too, has recalled the time in his own life when he felt this way and now begins to think about how old he is and how little time he has.

The son wants freedom and pleasure—happiness.

Greater understanding between father & son will occur

F-28.   The young man is there with his father. John is following his father's wishes to serve in the army as his father did during WW II. His father is very proud of him. John is joining without resistance to his father for he has always loved and respected him. John fears however what will become of himself in the army, does not want to join, and there is a great conflict in his mind.

John will suffer from his experience in the army. Not physically, but mentally. He will not be a full person because of his father's wishes.

F-29.   Here is a faculty adviser facing the student with the question of a major. The student whose interests are very broad does not want nor will he allow himself to be forced into limiting his choice of careers. He is in the process of sorting out his alternatives. He decides for now to follow a pre-med program but including courses in other fields to balance him out. This is only a temporary solution, however, and the student is thinking that the only alternative may be to find some study outside of the college to help keep him open, on his own.

F-30.   The elderly man is consoling his son on the divorce of the son's good friend. The son, young and newly married, was idealistic and naive about love. The death of his friend's love for his wife shocks him deeply, creating fears about the durability of his own love over the years. The father is upset but resigned in the manner of too many men who've experienced hardships. Such tragedies no longer touch him deeply. He can close his eyes.

POWER PRACTICE STORIES: SET G

G-1.   This is an ethics discussion. These young men decided to continue the day's discussion later in the afternoon and as they're in a prep school they find the teacher easily available. One boy has just finished a testimonial on a past experience concerning his home town centering around his feeling of moving away from his old community. This feeling is shared by most but the teacher doesn't seem to think that alienation is necessary. They discuss the ethics of the situation.

G-2.   This group of young men are eagerly discussing some new business proposition that promises wealth. Their reactions and participation in the meetings are determined by their personalities. The man in the center, gesturing and smiling confidently, seems the most likely to be a leader, to be successful. He is able to forget personal fears and concentrate on the problem to be solved. The man with his arm around another is less ambitious. He is more excited by the jolly, hearty comraderie of the situation than the actual proposal. There are several fringe members, such as the man with glasses and the man by the window, who are bored or unhappy with the meeting.

G-3.   The presence of only males seems to suggest some type of business meeting or convention, but since I am here in college I prefer to imagine that these men are a group of ex-college students at a reunion. The talk isn't political, it's just light reminiscing. The man in the front with his arm around his friend has just been carried away by the feeling of camraderie which he hasn't felt since his school days.

The man who is talking in the center is enjoying his role as leader of the group—he has failed in his business life & hasn't "led" since school.

The man on the left standing up has realized that his memories of his school days & his "group" were false—he never could fit in, & he can't now.

G-4.   It appears to be a meeting of salesmen, who have just listened to a presentation by the sales manager (the man standing). After his presentation someone perhaps asked a question, and the man at the end of the table who is pointing w/ his finger and is the hot-shot dynamo of all the salesmen has taken it on himself to answer, thus usurping the sales manager.

The sales manager is smiling to hide his uneasiness at being usurpted. The other salesmen are thinking about the hot-shot, "What a b-s artist." Secretly, the hot-shot agrees with them, but he wants the sales manager's job.

Depending on the rigidity of the hierarchy of the company, the hot-shot will leave the company, or get promoted.

G-5.   It's a small reunion of a few high-school buddies.

A very close cliche in school. They were all on a track team together and had graduated together. A year later, they get together and one or two find that for some reason, they have grown in different directions from their school-mates.

The person on the far left is affected by a much stronger degree than the 2nd from the right, but he is thinking of how he wished he had never come. That way he could remember his friends, and they him—the way they were and he was.

The ties are broken. They will probably not try to stay in touch.

G-6.   This is a picture of a business meeting. Present are businessmen.

The meeting was convened for discussion of a decision that must be made between colleagues—whether to accept a merger proposal with another related firm. They are all thinking over, silently and aloud, the pros & cons of the merger.

It is a tough decision for all because the merger could mean years of relative hardship before the benefits are felt. Some men are undecided whether it is worth the risk, some are sure it is, & the rest don't want to take chances. They are all either trying to make up their minds or persuade the others to their point of view.

G-7.   The people are at a committee-meeting for a medium-size industrial corporation. It had been going on for an hour or so, but now was time for a small break, and friendly conversation ensued. The men enjoy their work usually, and always find their fellow workers friendly and hard-working. They had worked hard to reach their posts; a couple of them had hoped for better, but they were happy, just the same.

In a few minutes friendly conversation will become businesslike discussion, discussion over internal problems, and reasons why things aren't as good as they could be.

G-8.   Some type of organizational mtg of men with common interests—perhaps common professions or fields. Engaged in semiserious discussion. The men are all involved in some sport—training, coaching, reporting of some man's sport.

The group are brought together perhaps at a conference. One recounts a past exper. to support his view of the topic of disc. They have perhaps taken a break from serious conference activities.

All are relaxed. Interested in what is being talked about. Their minds are concentrated on the sport.

The disc. will end casually to bgin work or go to a dinner.

G-9.   A jury is discussing in an unfeeling manner a trial.

A man in a situation similar to Hugo's *Les Miserables* is being tried.

The majority of the men on the jury will try to convict the man on trial, but the one man looking out the window cannot find it within himself to vote "guilty". He feels detached from the group, but in no way would want to ever be a part of the unfeeling mob.

Dut to the one man's vote of "not guilty" the case will result in a hung jury with the one man moving slowly & sadly through life.

G-10.   "No, no. I definately think we've got to double our expenditures."

"Something a little larger might suit the public's fancy."
"Maybe if we made it out of wood."
"Or with a picture inside."
"I say we make it round."
"Out of Plastic."
"The public doesn't care as long as we stamp 'reduced from $7.50' on it."
"That's right—dupe the public."
"Then," said J.B. clearing his throat and rising, "I think

the little ashtray we have here is perfect, it was good enough
for my father, the late J.B.J.B. Marshall, wasn't it?"
"Check, J.B."
"Check, J.B."
"Check, J.B."
. . . .

G-11. The lab research technicians in the state bacteriology lab at
the University are running their tests on the urine specimens
of "Native Dancer." Up to this point, no trace of drugs had
shown up. However, this indicator being applied now is turning from the characteristic blue to pink. Something is present.
Whether or not they will have to turn in an affirmative report
to the Racing Commission won't be known until more extensive testing.

G-12. These two women work in a laboratory at a hospital. They are
testing a patient's blood sample to see if he still has traces of
a disease he once had. The women are looking grave because
it seems, by the tests they have made on the blood sample, that
the disease is recurring. The young man had just gotten well,
had just been released from the hospital and was about to go
back to school. He had been lucky in recovering so quickly
from the disease, but now he would have to return to the hospital again.
    The two women are thinking what a shame it is that the
young man will have to be so sick again.
    The young man will have to re-enter the hospital.

G-13. Jean Molina's life was her research. She spent hours upon
hours in her lab. She had no time for anything else. Her social
circle was limited to few highly intelligent and dedicated
fellow scientists. The only person she thought of as a friend
was her assistant and constant companion, Nancy.

G-14. A female doctor is making LSD for clinical use in hospitals
while her lab. assistant, a student at a nearby college, looks on.
    The lab assistant, Judy Junkee, is watching carefully the
process for making the "acid".
    She plans on stealing the chemical and formula in order
to get herself high and make a big sale on campus.
    Judy ends up taking an overdose of LSD and is delivered

to the same hospital where she stole the chemical. She is treated by the doctor who taught her the formula.

G-15.   The woman on the left, the one conducting the experiment is highly trained in medical research, specializing in cancer research. She is within a few short months of completing one of her most important experiments. However, she herself— by some twist of fate—is slowly being consumed by the disease and growing weaker every day. All that matters to her is to complete her experiment and help alleviate some human suffering.

Her assistant, not as educated, watches the woman in awe. The assistant, seeing herself as less valuable than the other, wishes only that she could be taken, leaving the woman to complete her vital work.

G-16.   There are two women—the one off to the side, in glasses, is a teacher—Miss James. Miss James is watching Maria, a student, attempt an experiment on her own. Miss James does not like Maria, and secretly hopes she'll make an awful mistake.

Maria is the prize pupil of the institution—many say she is much more able than most of her instructors. Rumor has it that she will be offered a teaching position next year. It has also been true that many have complained of Miss James's uselessness as a teacher—no good.

Miss James fears for her job. She focusses her antagonism at Maria, attempting to make her look bad at every turn, without herself appearing the cause.

G-17.   The women pictured are two doctors in the lab.

They are presently testing a certain solution which will indicate whether or not a certain patient is going to die of an incurable disease. The patient happens to be a teenager with no father and a younger brother. Her mother has already been heart-broken by her husband's death, and an older son's death, by the same disease. The doctors want the test to be negative, as do everyone else involved.

Unfortunately, the tests confirm the presence of the disease, and the doctors plan a comfortable death for the teenager, and the mother is again heart-broken, thinking how much more of her family will be snatched away by this horrible disease.

G-18. Helen, a first year graduate student, held the test tube tensely, as a lab assistant looked on. One drop too many and hours of research would be destroyed. Always fascinated by biology, Helen had found her particular interest in the recreation of the human embryo in a test tube. Naturally there had been criticism. After all she was only 22 and a female in a male dominated field. Yet she had determination and insisted on carrying out her experiments.

Then the war had struck and all biological experimentation turned to that effort. Forced underground she continued her research and appeared on the brink of a major discovery.

G-19. Two women scientists are experimenting with the raising of recently cultured test tube babies.

From sperm and egg banks specific desired genetic requirements were commanded for 6 different types of children to emerge. Scientists have been interested in determining or creating mass personality types so to elliminate all undesireable ones and only produce personalities suited for each level of society.

The women are quite concerned over the maturation & condition of the fetuses & are totally taken in by the philosophy of mass produced personalities. They themselves are almost brainwashed.

G-20. Dr Karen Jones after yrs of research has discovered a perfect contraceptive which injected once in either a male or female will stop production of sperm or eggs respectively for a period of 10–20 yrs. This drug would allow whoever controlled to control all population & foster effective breeding. Allowing only those people deemed most fit or acceptable to the forces in power to reproduce. Now that she has made the discovery and could certainly become famous, Dr. Jones is having second thoughts as she firmly believes in the rights of individuals to control their own lives & bodies and therefore she is now thinking of not revealing her discovery to anyone at all.

G-21. Now sitting in front of the television screen he was anxiously watching the results pour in from all over the country. John was with him. He had been his father's best friend and now John was his most trusted advisor.

The campaign had gone well. All of the major cities were

voting his way but still there was a chance, maybe he could not swing enough votes. John left & got him a cold glass of water. He took it and smiled grateful at John only a second, then returned his attention to the voters on the screen.

The chances began to look better. There were only two others in the room besides himself. They were all just as tense waiting and waiting.

All the work was now to be seen if effective.

The announcer came on and.

G-22. The older man is revealing to the younger one a very signifi-cant event of his early years which has great implications for the younger individual.

The two men have developed a close relationship, culmi-nating at this moment in the telling of this great secret. Both trust each other, but this trust has taken many years to mold. The young man has little knowledge of his early years; the old man is now filling in important gaps.

The young man's thoughts are ones of amazement and gratitude at finally knowing answers to matters that have puzzled him greatly.

G-23. The young man is faced with an important decision in his career. It is not his first, nor shall it be his last, but for him now, his life revolves about making the right decision. As with the older children, the father lets his son grow into his re-sponsibility; in not many years the son will not have his father to turn to—perhaps a wife or friend. But for now his father acts with restrained love, knowing that his son will make the right decision, if allowed to do so on his own, and that is the most important thing in his life.

G-24. The young man must make a difficult decision pert. to his future. The older man, father, tries to help in some way.

The younger fluctuates from one side of the decision to another. He is not willingly accepting the advise of the older man—who feels sympathy but cannot reach his son. He wishes to help—the older one.

The two will reach some pt. from which they can, together attempt to resolve the problem. The older one will understand more clearly what is going on within the younger.

G-25.   The younger man is a sensitive and very pained individual. He feels put off by a society he cannot understand.

The man with the moustache cannot understand the other man, as it is simple to him (the moustached man) that one must take in life what one can get and that the chief rule is survival.

The younger man has been extremely upset by something he has seen happen to another. The older man is impatiently trying to explain to the other that since it does not directly affect him to forget about it.

The older man—lack of comprehension.

The young man—pain.

Neither can change.

G-26.   The two men are really criminals. However also well to do businessmen. The elder is telling the younger man he wants a job set up against a certain competitor.

The older man had gone to his competitor to ask for a favor. The competitor refused. The older man decides that his competitor needs some roughing up & calls the younger man to set the job up.

The older man wants to teach his competitor a lesson. He wants the younger man to get in contact with his criminal friends & do something about his competitor.

The competitor's business will be ruined. His store may be mysteriously burned or robbed & wrecked.

G-27.   These two businessmen consult over financial matters. The work together as president and V.P. of a firm.

The younger man is making his way up in the company and has learned from the older.

On this day they work out the terms for the purchase a smaller corporation which they intend to finalize shortly.

Eventually the older man will retire and his prodigee will replace him and continue to work at building this corporation.

G-28.   Father and son. The land that the family bought in Colorado has just been taken away from them by a crafty real-estate broker.

The son wants revenge. He is young and hot-blooded. The father on the other hand, realizes that revenge will serve no purpose unless it will help to get the land back, which it will not.

The son's immediate anger will soon die down. He will come to an understanding with his father and together they will move logically to recover their stolen land.

G-29. This picture is of a father and his grown son. The son, finished with his education, is unable to find a job. He is married and so needs the money desperately, and has gone to his father partly to be comforted and partly in hopes that his father will offer him money, though he hates to take it. The father looks upon his son with sadness, realizing his situation and how hopeless it must seem to the young man. He is proud of his son and of the way he raised him and yet is inwardly ashamed that his son should be unable to work. Of course, he will offer the money. In spite of the fact that he strongly disapproved of the girl his son married, he doesn't wish the son any hard luck and so, will provide money for the family to survive upon. Hopefully, he thinks, the unemployment will be temporary, and his son will soon regain his financial standing and ego.

G-30. This young man is now faced with a decision which will affect his entire life; whether or not to take over his father's business. Ever since he was a youth he has dreamed of becoming an airplane pilot and now that he has come of age he must decide upon which way he will go. The boy's father has recently died and the older man talking to him is his father's close friend and legal advisor. The advisor is attempting to subtly sway the young man into taking over a promising and prospering business rather than pursuing his dream in the sky. The young man is going through a tortuous mental battle in which all his values are being tested. He is faced with a double attraction choice which has placed tremendous pressure upon him. He will finally decide to fly the planes and he sells the business.

EXPERT SCORING FOR *n* POWER PRACTICE STORIES

Expert scoring for each set of practice stories is given below.

SET A—EXPERT SCORING

The expert's scoring decisions for the thirty stories of Set A are briefly explained below, one category at a time. In general, only instances where a subcategory is scored are discussed; although if the decision not to score a subcategory is a difficult one, it is also discussed.

Imagery

A-1.   *Pow Im.* Criterion 1. "The officers are now planning a counter-attack" indicates strong forceful action which can affect others; therefore a concern with power. Other statements in the story, such as "wants these locations to be re-taken" (implies by military action) or "it should be a large scale attack" would be sufficient grounds for scoring *Pow Im.*

A-2.   *Pow Im.* Criterion 1. The island "must be retaken," which involves actions that indicate power. Moreover, the general "hopes that he is succeeding" in impressing the officers with the importance of the task and with himself: these statements would also be grounds for scoring *Pow Im.*

A-3.   *Pow Im.* Criterion 1. Again, mention is made of a battle, of "driving out" an enemy—both of which actions indicate power concern. Note that *Pow Im* is scored even though it is unclear from the story whether the battle has in fact taken place. The manual states that actions can be wanted, fantasied, recollected, *or* carried out; but they do not have to be carried out in order to be scored for *Pow Im.*

A-4.   *Pow Im.* Criterion 1. There are two separate instances of *Pow Im* in this story: the "good guys" are "trying to overthrow," and the "soldiers will go looking for the good guys. . . ." Either is sufficient for scoring; the scorer should choose the most highly elaborated theme, which seems to be search by the soldiers.

A-5.   *Pow Im.* Criterion 1. "Attack" and "assault" are clear evidences of power concern.

A-6.   *No Imagery.* While the officers are concerned about a "grave problem," there is no indication that any action which expresses power is planned, contemplated, or carried out. For example, the "problem" could be that food rations are spoiling, or that sunspots are interfering with radio communication. In other words, this story involves problem-solving, but not necessarily power. If the "problem" were explicitly stated to be an enemy threat, and some sort of attack were mentioned, then Imagery could be scored; but without such explicit statements, Imagery cannot be scored.

A-7.   *Pow Im.* Criterion 1. Bombing is a form of attack, and hence a power-related action.

A-8.   *No Imagery.* "Military action" does not explicitly refer to an attack or assault; it could be some routine field exercise. Indeed, the story is further elaborated in a way that suggests routine problem-solving, and not a conflict or battle. "Telling the others what to do" is part of the routine role of "the man on the left."

A-9.   *No Imagery.* Again, this is routine army life, with no special concern for power. The leader of the unit is "pointing out" and "giving instructions," but these are entirely routine for his role, and there is no suggestion that the leader has any concern for power, as, for example, through statements such as "The leader is trying to convince the men to feel enthusiasm," or "The leader is demanding that they follow orders." While the men have been "called away" for a "mandatory exercise," no actor responsible for this is mentioned. Hence Imagery is not scored.

A-10.   *Pow Im.* Criterion 1. This story is filled with Power Imagery: "hit this bridge," "itching to fight," "will blow up the bridge."

A-11.   *Pow Im.* Criterion 1 or 3. "Chooses discriminately" and "knows the right spots in town to be seen in, how to be seen in these spots" indicates a concern with impressing the world, or a concern about one's status and reputation. The decision to score criterion 1 rather than 3 is based on the assumption that "chooses" and "being seen" are minimal kinds of action; if the story had said only "wants to be known as urbane and sophisticated," then Power Imagery would probably be scored under criterion 3.

A-12.   *Pow Im.* Criterion 1. The story clearly involves sexual exploitation, which is a kind of action that indicates power concern. It might be thought that the girl's happiness and thinking that "she has found an exciting life" is a positive emotion aroused by the man, and hence criterion 2 could be the basis for scoring Power Imagery. However, it is not altogether clear that her happiness comes from the one man's actions, rather than from hanging around with the gang. Therefore, criterion 1 is the clearest basis for scoring Imagery.

A-13.   *No Imagery.* There is no evidence of any actions which indicate a concern for power; rather, the man seems to be concerned about love.

A-14.   *Pow Im.* Criterion 1. The man is concerned about impressing the girl; moreover, there is the suggestion of sexual exploitation.

A-15.   *Pow Im.* The executive is visiting the city "in order to determine whether the agency should handle a new international account." In other words, he is in the position of actively regulating the behavior or conditions of life of another person, i.e., the S.F. agency. This evidence of his control is therefore scored as Imagery under criterion 1(*c*).

A-16.   *Pow Im.* Criterion 2. The woman is experiencing strong positive emotions ("is enchanted by the atmosphere") which are the result of the man's action. Moreover, he is "making a good impression," which would be scorable under criterion 1.

A-17.   *Pow Im.* Criterion 2. The lady is "enraptured" by being taken to the club; that is, the man's action arouses strong positive emotion in another person. Again, the man's action is further described as a "snow-job," and so would also qualify under criterion 1.

A-18.   *No Imagery.* No one is taking an action which arouses strong emotions in others.

A-19.   *No Imagery.* While the woman is enjoying herself, her emotion is not described in strong terms; moreover, it is not clear that the husband's action had anything to do with her enjoyment. As for the man, his actions and concerns are exclusively oriented around his business, which is an achievement goal rather than a power goal.

A-20.   *Pow Im.* Criterion 2. "Impresses them" is a power-related action.

A-21.   *Pow Im.* Jensen gives unsolicited help, which is scorable under criterion 1(*b*). In addition, his action has a great public effect, which would be scorable under criterion 1(*e*) or 2.

A-22.   Pow *Im.* The city slicker is concerned either about sexual exploitation or making a good impression, both of which are scorable under criterion 1. The reaction of the sister would also be scorable, but the city slicker's action seems to be the principal theme.

A-23.   *Pow Im.* The doctor presumably is trying to give unsolicited help.

A-24.   *Pow Im.* Criterion 1(*c*). The father is trying to change his son's behavior through rearranging the environment or conditions of the son's life.

A-25.   *Pow Im.* The older man is giving unsolicited advice (criterion 1(*b*)). Also, junior's "tearing hell through town" is a scorable under criterion 1(*e*), since he was "seen"—i.e., connotation of public attention.

A-26.   *No Imagery.* The conversation has nothing to do with power. Although the father "wants his son to do what he would like best," this is not expressed in desiring to influence or actually influencing the son in any way. Hence the statement of "wants" does not indicate any special concern for power. If the story had said "The father wants to influence the son to make up his own mind," then Power Imagery would be scored.

A-27.   *No Imagery.* Probably the advice has been solicited by the younger brother, even though the solicitation is not fully explicit. Thus Imagery is not scored, even though the solicitation is mentioned later in the story.

A-28.   *Pow Im.* The father is reassuring the son of his support, which is scorable under criterion 1(*b*), since the son has not explicitly solicited this support. The story could also be scored under criterion 2, since the father has aroused respect in the son.

A-29.   *Pow Im.* Criterion 2. The boy's gratitude is a strong positive emotion, in response to the action of the counselor. "Listening sympathetically," while passive in form, is an action under the conscious control of the counselor.

A-30.   *Pow Im.* Criterion 1. There are two power themes: the reporter trying to find out important information, and the manager trying to mislead the reporter. Either is scorable under criterion 1; probably the reporter's action is the primary theme, since the manager's counteraction occurs as a response to it.

Prestige of the Actor

A-1.   *Pa+.* "An army officer of high rank" indicates prestige, as does his association with "some of his battalion leaders."

A-2.   *Pa+.* "Commander-in-chief of the Army's forces in the Pacific."

A-3.   *Pa+.* "The general," which is a title higher than major.

A-4.   *Pa+.* "Good guys."
        Pa−. "The soldiers are bad. They have evil looks on their faces." Even though these phrases have a stereotyped quality,

they nevertheless indicate an elaboration of the reputation or status of the soldiers. Note that *both* subcategories can be scored for actor's prestige, since there are two power themes.

A-5.   *Pa+*. Battalion commanders are normally of the rank of major; moreover, they are "being briefed by intelligence"; i.e., there is an association with a prestigeful person, unit, or institution.

A-7.   *Pa+*. "Air Force Major."

A-10.   *Pa+*. First, the captain has been given orders to stop the enemy by "a higher officer." Second, the captain is promoted at the end, and the next rank above captain is major. *Pa+* can be scored for prestige that is acquired in the course of the story.

A-11.   *Pa+*. Almost every phrase describing the person could be scored for *Pa+*.
        Pa−. "Boy lecher type" indicates low prestige.

A-12.   *Pa−*. "Cheap punk" indicates low, or at least doubtful, status and reputation.

A-14.   *Pa+*. The man is described as "handsome," which is an attribute that suggests ability or experience in this context.

A-15.   *Pa+*. The man is identified as a "NY ad agency executive," which is scorable. Also, the bar is described as "where the people go who are really IN," which suggests prestige.

A-16.   *Pa+*. While the man is described in ordinary terms, the setting ("small, romantic little cafe") suggests prestige.

A-17.   *Pa+*. "Fairly expensive club."

A-20.   *Pa+*. "He is a top-executive."

A-21.   *Pa+*. The principal character is described in terms that suggest he is a radio or television celebrity.

A-22.   *Pa−*. "City slicker" suggests at least doubtful reputation, and so is scored as *Pa−*.

A-23.   *No Pa*. Without any adjective of prestige, "doctor" (like "lawyer" or "professor") is not scored for *Pa+*.

A-24.   *Pa+*. The father is described as "the gentleman farmer type," which suggests a man of money, leisure, and hence status.

A-25.   *Pa−*. Junior "did something a little bad" is scored, even though this is a secondary power theme.

A-28.   *Pa+*. The father is a "successful businessman-rancher," which suggests status.

A-29.   *No Pa*.

A-30.   *Pa+*. The fact that the reporter is associated with the "N.Y. Times," a prestigeful institution, is one basis for scoring *Pa+*. Also the fact that he is intruding upon a (prestigeful) politician would be another basis for scoring *Pa+*.

Need

A-1.   *N*. "The officer wants these locations to be retaken."
A-2.   *No*. *N*. "The general hopes he is succeeding" could be scored as *N*, but it seems more appropriate to consider it as *Ga+*.
A-3.   *No N*.
A-4.   *N*. ". . . pointing to where he wants his men to look" is an explicit statement of wanting or desiring something relevant to power, in this case information.
A-5.   *No N*. While the story says that "a full-scale assault is needed," this need is not attributed to any character in the story, and is not scored *N*.
A-7.   *No N*.
A-10.   *N*. "Itching to fight" is here taken to mean "wants to fight," although it could be considered *Ga+* instead.
A-11.   *No N*.   A-12.   *No N*.
A-14.   *No N*.   A-15.   *No N*.
A-16.   *N*. "The man is making a very good impression, just as he had hoped." Hoping is scored *N*.
A-17.   *No N*.   A-20.   *No N*.
A-21.   *No N*.   A-22.   *No N*.
A-23.   *No N*.
A-24.   *N*. ". . . Dad . . . wishes to provide the best in life for his son . . ." indicates desire for impact via giving support. "He hopes to get to know his son" is not *N*, because it refers to an affiliation concern.
A-25.   *No N*.   A-28.   *No N*.
A-29.   *No N*.   A-30.   *No N*.

Instrumental Activity

A-1.   *I*. "Fire will begin at daybreak with each battalion in an integrated drive. . . ." Although this action appears in the final sentence of the story, it clearly goes beyond a mere summary, and is scored *I*.
A-2.   *I*. "Lecturing," ". . . will attack" are clear statements of instrumental activity oriented toward power goals.
A-3.   *I*. ". . . the officers are being given their orders," although in the passive voice, is an activity that is related to the power goal

of driving out the enemy. Note that the mere giving of orders, in a military situation, would not be evidence of a power goal; here, however, it is a step toward the attack, which is a power goal.

A-4.   *I.* "They are looking for the good guys. . . ."

A-5.   *I.* "They are assessing the enemy's strength to determine the best plan of attack" is planning, which is scored *I.* The final sentence of the story would probably not be scored for *I* by itself, since it indicates only the outcome of the story.

A-7.   *I.* "Pointing out objective" in a briefing session is a form of planning or preparation, and hence is scored *I.* "They will bomb targets" is simply the conclusion of the story.

A-10.   *I.* "The captain has chosen the bridge as the best spot" is a rather weak statement of planning activity, but it is scored *I.* "The men will blow up the bridge" could also be scored *I.*

A-11.   *No I.* There is no explicit statement of activity within the story.

A-12.   *I.* ". . . he has taken her to a local joint—is planning a big night." While this sentence also suggests anticipations, it does indicate instrumental activity towards having an effect on the girl.

A-14.   *I.* "His thoughts are naturally planning ahead . . ." does suggest anticipation as well as planning as an instrumental activity, but this seems to be a minimal case of instrumental planning.

A-15.   *I.* The visit is instrumental to the power goal.

A-16.   *I.* The action of the man ("taking her to a small, romantic cafe") creates the effect on the woman.

A-17.   *No I.* While it can be inferred that the woman's feelings have been aroused by the man's action, this action is not stated explicitly enough in the story to be scored *I.*

A-20.   *No I.* "This man always goes out with other girls, and impresses them" seems to be a statement of the man's habits or traits, rather than a statement of past instrumental activities.

A-21.   *I.* Jensen's recommendation is an overt activity designed to create impact.

A-22.   *I.* "He thinks the only way to score with Sister" suggests instrumental planning.

A-23.   *No I.*

A-24.   *I.* The purchase of the country place is an activity related to the goal of having impact on the son.

A-25.   *I.* "Tearing hell through town," which creates public notice, is an overt activity. The older man "called him on his actions" is also scorable for *I.*

A-28. *I.* The father's giving reassurance is instrumental activity.

A-29. *I.* "Listening" is, in this context, an activity of the counselor, and since it contributes to his impact ("the boy is grateful"), it is scored *I.*

A-30. *I.* There are numerous statements of instrumental activity on the part of both of the major characters in this story.

Blocks in the World

A-1. *No Bw.* In this story, the fact that the enemy has won locations is not an obstacle to on-going power activity, but in fact defines the power goal itself, i.e., "re-taking" the locations.

A-2. *No Bw.* See remarks for story A-1 above.

A-3. *No Bw.*

A-4. *No Bw.* The retaliation of the "good guys," who capture the commanding officer, is scored for *Eff* and not *Bw,* since it is really a turnabout and not an obstacle.

A-5. *No Bw.* See remarks for story A-4 above.

A-7. *No Bw.*   A-10. *No Bw.*

A-11. *No Bw.*   A-12. *No Bw.*

A-14. *No Bw.*   A-15. *No Bw.*

A-16. *No Bw.*   A-17. *No Bw.*

A-20. *Bw.* The girl "ignores the man," which is surely an obstacle to his goal of impressing her.

A-21. *No Bw.*

A-22. *Bw.* The boy, because he "sees through the fancy airs," is an obstacle to the "city slicker."

A-23. *No Bw.*   A-24. *No Bw.*

A-25. *No Bw.*   A-28. *No Bw.*

A-29. *No Bw.*

A-30. *Bw.* The farm manager's actions are certainly an obstacle to the reporter's power goal, which is to find out information about the politician.

Goal Anticipations

A-1. *Ga+.* The officer "thinks it can be done," which is a positive anticipation or expectation.

A-2. *Ga+.* "The general hopes he is succeeding," if not scored *N,* would be scored *Ga+.*

A-3.   *No Ga.*   A-4.   *No Ga.*
A-5.   *No Ga.*   A-7.   *No Ga.*
A-10. *Ga—.* "The men are scared" is a negative anticipation.
A-11. *No Ga.*
A-12. *Ga+.* "The guy is thinking of her in bed—she will be an easy one" is a clear positive anticipation.
A-14. *Ga+.* "He feels this will be a great opportunity to impress her."
A-15. *No Ga.*   A-16. *No Ga.*
A-17. *Ga+.* "The gentleman . . . is eagerly awaiting the more amorous adventure. . . ."
A-20. *Ga+.* "The man thinks of the nice night he is going to spend. . . ."
A-21. *No Ga.*
A-22. *No Ga.* The city slicker's thoughts are really planning rather than anticipations.
A-23. *No Ga.* The doctor is worried about the wife, but not about the outcome of his help, considered as a power action.
A-24. *No Ga.*   A-25. *No Ga.*
A-28. *No Ga.*   A-29. *No Ga.*
A-30. *No Ga.*

Goal States

A-1.   *No G.*   A-2.   *No G.*
A-3.   *No G.*   A-4.   *No G.*
A-5.   *No G.*   A-7.   *No G.*
A-10. *No G.*   A-11. *No G.*
A-12. *No G.*   A-14. *No G.*
A-15. *No G.*
A-16. *G+.* "The man sits back satisfied and somewhat bemused." "He is making a very good impression, just as he had hoped." These sentences indicate positive affect accompanying the attainment of a power goal, i.e., making an impression on someone else, and are therefore scored *G+.*
A-17. *G+.* "The gentleman is rather smugly congratulating himself on a successful snow-job . . ." indicates positive affect accompanying the attainment of the power goal.
A-20. *G—.* "She . . . ignores the man. He is frustrated because that never happened before in his life. . . ." Here there is failure to attain the power goal of impressing the girl, and the man con-

sequently feels frustration, which indicates negative affect. Therefore *G*— is scored.

A-21.	*No G.*	A-22.	*No G.*
A-23.	*No G.*	A-24.	*No G.*
A-25.	*No G.*	A-28.	*No G.*
A-29.	*No G.*	A-30.	*No G.*

Effect

A-1. *No Eff.*

A-2. *No Eff.* The men "are duly impressed" suggests, in this context, routine acceptance of power rather than the arousal of emotion.

A-3. *No Eff.* Changing the course of the war is a hypothetical major striking effect, but it is not actually produced in the story.

A-4. *Eff.* The "good guys" counterattack, and so *Eff* is scored.

A-5. *Eff.* The fact that "the man in the khaki suit is a spy" and that his actions in some way lead to the enemy's surprising the forces suggests the theme of counterattack or counterreaction, and thus *Eff* is scored.

A-7. *No Eff.*   A-10. *No Eff.*

A-11. *No Eff.*

A-12. *Eff.* "The girl is happy—she thinks she has found an exciting life" seems to be strong positive emotion, and this emotion is probably aroused to some extent by the fact that the man has taken her out for the night. However, it could be argued that the emotion is really because the girl is "new with the mob," and thus *Eff* would not be scored, since the mob has not taken any specific action which aroused the emotion. The case is borderline.

A-14. *Eff.* "She's snowed" suggests strong positive emotion as a result of the action of another.

A-15. *No Eff.*

A-16. *Eff.* "The woman is enchanted by the atmosphere. . . ."

A-17. *Eff.* "She is apparently enraptured by the whole affair."

A-20. *No Eff.*

A-21. *Eff.* ". . . and endear Jensen to many more devoted listeners" suggests both strong positive emotions aroused in others, and also a major striking effect such as widespread public acclaim. Both are possible criteria for scoring *Eff*.

A-22.   *Eff.* The sister will "tell guy where to go," a strong counterreaction.

A-23.   *No Eff.*   A-24.   *No Eff.*

A-25.   *Eff.* Junior's being "called" on his actions is *Eff*, though it could not be scored if it had been scored as the only basis for *I*.

A-28.   *Eff.* "Son . . . frequently looking to father with respect." Respect suggests a strong positive emotional reaction aroused in part by the father's acts.

A-29.   *Eff.* "The boy is grateful as it is the first time someone has seemed to take a genuine interest in him."

A-30.   *Eff.* The manager makes a clear counterreaction to the probing questions of the reporter.

Hope/Fear Distinction

A-1.   *Hope.* There is no mention of the country on whose behalf the army is attacking. Therefore *Fear* cannot be scored.

A-2.   *Fear.* "U.S. forces" makes clear that the attack is for the benefit of a country, namely, the United States.

A-3.   *Fear.* Mention of the "U.S."

A-4.   *Hope.* There is no mention of any country or beneficiary other than the actors themselves.

A-5.   *Hope.* No mention of the country.

A-7.   *Hope.* No mention of the country for which the Air Force is acting.

A-10.   *Hope.* No mention of the country; moreover, the captain himself is "itching to fight," so that there is a clear personal concern for power.

A-11.   *Hope.*   A-12.   *Hope.*

A-14.   *Hope.*

A-15.   *Hope.* While the executive is acting for his agency, no further beneficiary is mentioned. The rule is that agents acting solely for their agency are scored *Hope,* so long as there is no mention of the beneficiary of the agency's action as carried out by the agent.

A-16.   *Hope.* While the woman is "enchanted," the man's actions are clearly for his own benefit.

A-17.   *Hope.*

A-20.   *Hope.* His frustration is appropriate after failure, and there was no anticipation of failure or doubt about ability.

A-21.   *Fear.* Jensen's action for the benefit of the boy is sufficient to score *Fear,* even though there is also benefit to Jensen himself.

A-22. *Hope.*

A-23. *Fear.* The doctor's action is for the benefit of the wife (or also the man).

A-24. *Fear.* The father's actions are for the benefit of the son.

A-25. *Fear.* Although "tearing hell" and "calling" someone on his actions would usually be scored *Hope,* giving advice is *Fear* because it is presumed to be for Junior's benefit. When both *Hope* and *Fear* could be scored, then score *Fear.* Finally, there is some suggestion of the writer's disapproval of power through his phrasing and editorial comments.

A-29. *Fear.* The action of the counselor seems to be for the benefit of the boy.

A-30. *Fear.* While the reporter is working on behalf of himself and his newspaper only, the "old pro" is clearly working on behalf of his boss, who is a separate person. When there are two power themes, *Fear* is scored if either of the two themes could be scored *Fear.*

SET B—EXPERT SCORING

The expert scoring below may be read as follows: first, the expert's scoring decisions are briefly explained; second, the total score is given; and third, in parentheses, is the rank of that story on total *N* Power (with the highest score of the set given a rank of 1 and the lowest score a rank of 30). The latter is useful for computing rank order agreement with the expert scoring (see Atkinson, 1958, pp. 238, 688). In general, only instances where a subcategory is scored are discussed, although difficult decisions not to score subcategories are also discussed.

B-1. *No Imagery.* There is no evidence of any concern for power; this is a routine military situation. 0 (25)

B-2. *Pow Im.* Many statements could be scored for Power Imagery: the first invasion, the decision to retaliate, or the plans.
Pa+. The man is identified as an "army general"; moreover, "The president and his cabinet" are also involved.
I. Planning and giving roles in the attack.
No Bw. The first invasion is not an obstacle, but merely defines the power goal.

Ga+. "They are confident superior U.S. military will win. . . ."
Ga−. ". . . but are uncertain of repercussions that come later." "They . . . show concern about the outcome of the invasion." 5 (4.5)

Fear. The country is mentioned; moreover, there is concern "about the correctness of the political decision" and uncertainty "about the political repercussions," which suggests doubt about the consequences of achieving the power goal (reversed outcome-affect relationship).

B-3.　*No Imagery.* There is great concern and involvement about a mission or "the job," but there is no suggestion that this job in any way involves power. 0 (25)

B-4.　*Pow Im.* "The U.S. soldier wants information about the location of troops." This is clearly information of an important sort (criterion 1). Note that the fear of the other soldier that "the U.S. will 'beat it out of him' " is also scorable under criterion 2.
N. The soldier "wants information."
Eff. The other soldier is "worried the U.S. will 'beat it out of him,' " which indicates a negative emotion aroused by the action of the first soldier. 3 (12)
Fear. The country is mentioned.

B-5.　*Pow Im.* The "mission" is too vague to be scored, and the men who disagree are really concerned to come to an agreement. However, the use of "campaign," in conjunction with "field commanders," suggests a battle. Hence Imagery is scored.
Pa+.
I. There is a good deal of instrumental action. 3 (12)
Hope. No country is mentioned.

B-6.　*No Imagery.* This is a routine briefing. 0 (25)

B-7.　*Pow Im.* "They are planning some sort of strategic raid against an enemy . . ." as well as several other statements.
Pa+. "Army officers being briefed by an Air Force intelligence officer" indicates association with a prestigeful person, i.e., the intelligence officer.
N. "They want to wipe out the enemy."
I. Many statements of planning related to the power goal.
Bw. ". . . the enemy has been hurting them" seems to go beyond a simple definition of the original power goal; moreover, "they will try to use the A.F. intelligence and will find it faulty" clearly indicates an obstacle.
Ga−. "Their concerned look shows that they have been losing." This might be taken as negative (or doubtful) affect at failure

to reach a previous power goal, but it seems rather to be a doubtful anticipation of the future in this context. 6 (2)

Hope. No mention of a country.

B-8.　*Pow Im.* Many statements involving an attack.

Pa+. "Multinational force" indicates a prestigeful alliance, whereas a mere "group of officers" does not.

No N. "The men . . . are particularly interested in receiving adequate information" is not a specific statement of Need.

I. "The attack was designed to break . . ." is doubtful, but the men's thinking suggests planning.

No Bw. The invasion merely defines the power goal of an attack; it is not a disruption to ongoing power activites.

No Ga. "The men are thinking about their respective jobs . . . the specific problems they might encounter" seems to be instrumental, rather than an affective anticipation. 3 (12)

Fear. The "nation" seems a clear beneficiary, although it is not named.

B-9.　*Pow Im.* There is mention of an attack, an assault group, and the goal to "hit them where they will feel it the most."

Pa+. The phrases "special bunker" and "assault group" go beyond the description of a routine military unit, and are scored *Pa+.*

No N. The phrase "desire to do a good job no matter what" reflects a stated need for achievement (a good job) rather than power (e.g., "desire to attack no matter what").

Ga−. "Pain, sadness, responsibility . . ." are presumably felt by the soldiers, and so qualify as doubtful anticipations. 3 (12)

Fear. Doubts about the use of power ("Why did I get into this?").

B-10.　*Pow Im.* "Planning an offensive operation," "part of a campaign to assist a friendly government," and "a small raid" are all indications of Power Imagery.

I. "Showing where the operation is to take place" is an activity oriented toward the power goal (offensive operation, raid, or assistance). 2 (17.5)

Fear. Benefit of another ("friendly government").

B-11.　*No Imagery.* A routine task, and a routine request by the photographer. 0 (25)

B-12.　*Pow Im.* ". . . he wants to find out how the boss rated him" indicates a concern for his reputation and for controlling or finding out important evaluative information. Also, the girl had been "trying to attract his attention."

N. ". . . he wants to find out."

I. Taking out the girl is an activity related to his power goal.

G+. While the man "was not satisfied with the bosses explanation," this does not suggest strong affect at failure to attain a power goal, in the context. However, the girl's happiness is scored *G+* (subcategory used for the secondary power theme), although it could instead have been scored as *Eff* following upon his action. 4 (7)

Hope. Both power themes are for the benefit of the actor only.

B-13. *No Imagery.* The director "wants" the people to look happy, but this is a routine request in this situation. 0 (25)

B-14. *Pow Im.* The man is trying to impress the woman.

Pa+. "He's been around, has plenty of money. . . ."

N. "He . . . wanted to impress her."

I. "He invited her to the place. . . ."

Ga+. "He . . . hopes that she is enjoying herself and will soon pay him with some attention." This is a clear statement of an anticipated goal state.

G−. "He's getting put out that she isn't showing any more interest in him . . ." is a clear statement of negative affect at failure to arouse the girl's interest. 6 (2)   *Hope.*

B-15. *Pow Im.* This is actually a complicated story. Carol's response to Zeke's action is not really strongly emotional, nor is there any evidence that Carol herself is concerned "to improve her reputation among the cool set." However, Carol does try—presumably—"to hustle him into the sack," which suggests an attempt to affect his behavior.

Pa−. Zeke's (doubtful) prestige would then reflect on Carol.

Eff. Zeke probably counterreacts to Carol's attempt, although this is not completely clear. 3 (12)

Fear. The ironic tone of the story suggests that power is illusory or deceptive.

B-16. *Pow Im.* Although the story involves an advertising theme, there is evidence that the task is not simply routine, and that several characters are interested in the impact of advertising. The guitarist "will feel happy because he got his hands on T.V.," i.e., that he is getting public exposure in the medium; the actors are concerned about the believability of the advertisement, which suggests a concern with the reaction of the world at large.

Pa+. The location, "Club Henri IV," suggests prestige. The symbols and images connected with the actors suggest further

prestige: "good looks," "liveliness," and "folksy modern effect."
Pa—. "The man looks like a sleezy 'slim tie' type from Queens."
Ga—. "The actors are thinking 'this ad is lousy because it's unbelievable' " indicates negative anticipations about their final
impact on the public.
G+. "The guitarist will feel happy because he got his hands
on T.V." is positive affect at attaining a power goal, i.e., being
on T.V. 5 (4.5)
Fear. The ironic, deprecating tone of the story.

B-17.   *No Imagery*. The girl's reaction to the guitarist does not involve
strong emotions to an extent sufficient to justify scoring *Pow
Im* under criterion 2. 0 (25)

B-18.   *No Imagery*. This story is about affiliation, romance, and
"removal from reality," but not about power. 0 (25)

B-19.   *No Imagery*. Although the man has offered to show the city to
the lady, this seems too routine, in the context, to be scored as
giving help, assistance, or advice. 0 (25)

B-20.   *Pow Im*. Harry is impressing the woman, and his "good looks
drew Mary out of the secretarial pool," which indicates that
he has created an effect.
Pa+. A "trip to Puerto Rico" is prestigeful.
No Bw. The reaction of Harry's wife is not clearly an obstacle
to his power goal as stated in the story, i.e., "impressing his
mistress."
G+. "Harry's thinking what a cool bastard he is," a thought
that presumably involves positive affect on attainment of a
power goal.
No Eff. Mary's reaction is not described in terms that suggest
strong emotion, nor is the wife's reaction spelled out; therefore
Eff is not scored. 3 (12)
Fear. The writer's comments suggest that Harry's power goals
are deceptive or illusory.

B-21.   *Pow Im*. "The boy's angry because he's the local baseball star
and leaving town will cost him his reputation." (criterion 3)
Pa+. "Local baseball star."
Bw. The move to the city is an obstacle to the power goal,
which is the maintenance of the boy's reputation. Note that
maintaining a reputation is a continuous, on-going activity, so
that the move is an obstacle; it does not merely define the
power goal.
Ga—. The boy is angry at the thought that he will lose his
reputation. This is scored as a negative anticipation because

he does not in fact lose his reputation. If the story had said "The boy has lost his reputation and is angry," then $G-$ would be scored. 4 (7)

Hope. The boy's power goal is for his own benefit only.

B-22.   *No Imagery.* The establishment of "one of the best thorough-breed farms in the world" is an achievement goal. It would take some mention of widespread public attention or acclaim to make this a power goal. 0 (25)

B-23.   *No Imagery.* There is no direct evidence that the parents are controlling the conditions of the boy's life, nor does he attempt to influence them. 0 (25)

B-24.   *Pow Im.* Perhaps a marginal case. The father seems to be try-ing to convince the son to go to college, rather than talking about college. However, the father's actual concern about con-vincing is questioned in the last sentence.

Pa−. "Pop is a goof. . . ."

Bw. "Jr wants to go out with Judy & that is all he can think about" indicates an obstacle to the father's argument that is beyond the obvious initial fact that the son has to be con-vinced. 3 (12)

Fear. Writer's tone suggests that power is corrupt or evil.

B-25.   *Pow Im.* The father is concerned about giving advice that had not been solicited by the son.

N. "The father wants very much to help his son and give him advice and good suggestions about life."

No Bw. Although the son does not take the advice, this ap-parently doesn't hamper the father from giving it. 2 (17.5)

Fear.

B-26.   *No Imagery.* Here the father is simply talking about the future, and not trying to talk the son into doing anything (compare story B-24). 0 (25)

B-27.   *Pow Im.* The Department of Agriculture employee is trying to convince the boy to do something.

Pa+. "Department of Agriculture" is a prestigeful government institution, and this prestige reflects on the employee.

I. The father's threats are an action related to a secondary power goal.

Ga+. "The D of A employee thinks that he will get promoted if he can swing the deal." This is anticipation of achievement (promotion), but is also anticipation of power (swinging the deal).

Bw. The previous opposition of the father is an obstacle that goes beyond that mere fact that the boy has to be convinced.

Eff. The father's shooting of the employee goes beyond a mere block; in fact it is a counterreaction or turnabout, and is scored *Eff.* 6 (2)

Hope. All characters are concerned only for their own benefit. (Even the Dept. of Agriculture employee is concerned only about his own position.)

B-28.   *Pow Im.* The boy "wants attention."
N. 2 (17.5)
Hope.

B-29.   *Pow Im.* The coach is attempting to convince and recruit the boy.
Pa+. The coach is from a "well known Eastern University."
I. Many instrumental activities are mentioned: "trying to be debonair," "flattering the boy," "asking him questions."
Eff. "The young fellow is truly flattered and proud . . . feels wanted and appreciated. . . .," all of which suggest strong positive emotion resulting from the coach's actions. 4 (7)
Hope. There is no evidence that the boy is or was intended to be helped by the coach.

B-30.   *Pow Im.* The reporter is writing a "feature story," which can be assumed to create impact on the world as large (criterion 1(e)). The story is later described as having great "human interest." The Imagery is marginal, however.
No N. Although the reporter "hopes to do a good job," this stated need refers to an achievement goal—doing something well or better—and not to the power goal as such. N would be scored if the story had said, "The reporter hopes to arouse great human interest among the readers."
I. "The reporter is asking the young farmer . . .," which is activity relevant to the power goal of creating impact through a feature story.
No Eff. Although the story may arouse a great public reaction, this effect is not explicitly produced within the story, and so *Eff* is not scored. 2 (17.5)
Hope.

SET C—EXPERT SCORING

C-1.   *Pow Im, Pa+, I, Ga+, Eff. Hope.* 5 (3.5)
C-2.   *Pow Im, Pa+* ("home office"), *I, G−, Eff. Hope.* 5 (3.5)
C-3.   *No Imagery.* 0 (23)

C-4. *Pow Im* (scored because the businessman's offer of a premium price makes his request more than routine), *Pa+* (foreign port), *I*. No *N* (very marginal) or *Bw* (since the captain's refusal merely defines the power situation). *Hope*. 3 (10)

C-5. *No Imagery*. The information sought is routine. 0 (23)

C-6. *Pow Im, Pa+, I. Hope*. 3 (10)

C-7. *No Imagery*. The story is concerned with achievement. The captain is not explicitly concerned about his reputation, rather he is concerned about his "job." 0 (23)

C-8. *Pow Im, Pa+, Pa−, I. Fear* (The writer suggests that power is futile). 4 (6.5)

C-9. *Pow Im, Pa+, I* (the captain's activity), *Eff. Fear* (the passengers are the beneficiaries). 4 (6.5)

C-10. *Pow Im* ("Attracting more passengers" is a concern about impact), *Pa+, I. Hope*. 3 (10)

C-11. *No Imagery*. 0 (23)

C-12. *No Imagery*. 0 (23)

C-13. *No Imagery*. Achievement is the only concern. 0 (23)

C-14. *No Imagery*. There is no clear concern with status. 0 (23)

C-15. *No Imagery*. 0 (23)

C-16. *Pow Im* (a weak example of anticipated power over someone, i.e., the maid), *Ga+. Hope*. 2 (13)

C-17. *No Imagery*. No actual arguing, controlling, or reaction thereto takes place within the story. 0 (23)

C-18. *Pow Im. Hope*. 1 (15)

C-19. *Pow Im, Pa+* (alliance with the "team from Washington"), *Pa−* (court-martialled), *I, Ga−, Eff*. No *N* (it is related to achievement). *Fear* (The writer suggests that Harry's power is flawed). 6 (1.5)

C-20. *Pow Im* (criterion 2; her actions affected him), *Eff* (he is heartbroken). *Hope*. 2 (13)

C-21. *Pow Im, Pa+, I, Ga−. Fear* (The man has doubts about the use of power). 4 (6.5)

C-22. *Pow Im, Pa+* (he is taking on "the largest bank in New York"), *Pa−, N* (he "does not want" capture—i.e., he wants to avoid any obstacle to his goal), *I, Eff. Hope*. 6 (1.5)

C-23. *No Imagery*. 0 (23)

C-24. *No Imagery*. While creative writing often indicates a concern for public impact, in this story the man's concerns seem to be purely technical. 0 (23)

C-25. *No Imagery*. See comments on the previous story. 0 (23)

C-26. *No Imagery*. 0 (23)

C-27. *No Imagery*. 0 (23)

C-28. *Pow Im* (criterion 2), *Eff*. *Hope*. 2 (13)

C-29. *No Imagery*. Whatever caused the negative emotion in the man, it was not a conscious, intended action of another person. The actual role of the drunk in his wife's death is not spelled out clearly enough to be power; for example, it could have been an accident. 0 (23)

C-30. *Pow Im, Pa−, Ga+, G+. Hope*. 4 (6.5)

SET D—EXPERT SCORING

D-1. *Pow Im, Pa+, I, Eff. Fear* (The agent is allegedly acting for the captain's benefit). 4 (2.5)

D-2. *No Imagery*. 0 (21.5)

D-3. *No Imagery*. "Pleasing" the guest is routine here; there is no special concern for power. 0 (21.5)

D-4. *Pow Im, Pa+, N, Bw. Hope*. 4 (2.5)

D-5. *No Imagery*. While there are suggestions of status and having effects on others, the entire story is in fact a routine speech. 0 (21.5)

D-6. *Pow Im* (the Port Authority representative is seeking important information), *Pa+, Eff* (the captain's compliance goes beyond the routine). *Hope*. 3 (7.5)

D-7. *No Imagery*. 0 (21.5)

D-8. *Pow Im, N, I. Hope*. 3 (7.5)

D-9. *Pow Im, Pa+, I. Hope*. 3 (7.5)

D-10. *Pow Im* (the raising of rates by the insurance company probably has caused the steamship company to do something), *I. Hope*. 2 (11)

D-11. *No Imagery*. 0 (21.5)

D-12. *Pow Im* ("He will . . . raise some hell."). *Fear* (reversed outcome-affect relationship). 1 (12)

D-13. *No Imagery*. 0 (21.5)

D-14. *No Imagery*. 0 (21.5)

D-15. *No Imagery*. 0 (21.5)

D-16. *Pow Im, Pa+, G+, Eff* (a major public effect). *Fear* (the goal of the demolition was to rally the people). 4 (2.5)

D-17. *No Imagery*. 0 (21.5)

D-18. *No Imagery*. 0 (21.5)

D-19. *No Imagery*. The loss of the Yankees was presumably not intended, and therefore its effect is not scorable under criterion 2. 0 (21.5)

D-20. *No Imagery.* 0 (21.5)

D-21. *No Imagery.* 0 (21.5)

D-22. *Pow Im, Pa+, I, Eff. Hope.* 4 (2.5)

D-23. *No Imagery.* 0 (21.5)

D-24. *No Imagery.* 0 (21.5)

D-25. *Pow Im* (The success of the invention itself is achievement concern; but the fact that it "will lead other men on to utilize the invention" is power concern), *Pa+, I. Fear.* 3 (7.5)

D-26. *No Imagery.* Here, although great public benefits may be inferred, there is no explicit mention of public reaction. See the discussion under criterion 1 in the manual. 0 (21.5)

D-27. *Pow Im, Pa−, I, Eff* (the town's ridicule, a secondary power theme, causes a great effect). *Hope.* 3 (7.5)

D-28. *Pow Im, Pa+, I. Fear.* This story also contains a strong achievement theme. 3 (7.5)

D-29. *No Imagery.* 0 (21.5)

D-30. *No Imagery.* 0 (21.5)

SET E—EXPERT SCORING

E-1. *Pow Im, Pa+, I, Bw. Hope.* 4 (4.5)

E-2. *Pow Im, I, Eff. Hope.* 3 (9.5)

E-3. *No Imagery.* 0 (25)

E-4. *Pow Im, Pa+, G+, G−. Hope.* 4 (4.5)

E-5. *No Imagery.* The concern of the men suggests achievement rather than power. 0 (25)

E-6. *Pow Im* (the conversation itself is an attempt to persuade), *Pa−* ("hare-brained schemes"), *I* (John's statements are instrumental acts), *Bw* (Bob's opposition), *Eff* (Pete resents Bob's attempted influence). *No N* (the "need" is for money, not for persuasion itself), *No Ga* (anticipations refer to the plan, rather than to the influence process). *Hope.* 5 (1.5)

E-7. *No Imagery.* Here the conversation seems exclusively concerned with problem-solving and achievement. 0 (25)

E-8. *No Imagery.* 0 (25)

E-9. *No Imagery.* While the man standing by the window does not agree, there is no evidence of arguing, disagreeing, or trying to convince. 0 (25)

E-10.   *Pow Im.* The diffuse quality of the actor makes scoring of sub-categories impossible. *Hope.* 1 (19)

E-11.   *Pow Im* (the effects of the family's treatment), *Eff* (both on the girl and in a secondary way on the professor). *Fear.* 2 (15.5)

E-12.   *Pow Im, Eff. No Bw* (the thwarting is power imagery itself, not a block). *Hope.* 2 (15.5)

E-13.   *Pow Im, Pa+, G−. Hope.* 3 (9.5)

E-14.   *Pow Im, I, Ga+. Fear* (the cure benefits others, and there is the suggestion of a reversed outcome-affect relationship). 3 (9.5)

E-15.   *No Imagery.* 0 (25)

E-16.   *Pow Im, Pa+. Fear.* 2 (15.5)

E-17.   *No Imagery.* 0 (25)

E-18.   *Pow Im, I, Eff. Hope.* 3 (9.5)

E-19.   *No Imagery.* 0 (25)

E-20.   *Pow Im, Pa+, I. Hope.* 3 (9.5)

E-21.   *No Imagery.* 0 (25)

E-22.   *Pow Im, I. Fear.* 2 (15.5)

E-23.   *Pow Im, Ga−. Fear.* 2 (15.5)

E-24.   *Pow Im* (criterion 3), *G−. Fear.* 2 (15.5)

E-25.   *Pow Im, Pa−, I, Ga−. Hope.* 4 (4.5)

E-26.   *Pow Im, Pa+, N, I, Eff. Fear.* 5 (1.5)

E-27.   *No Imagery.* 0 (25)

E-28.   *Pow Im, Pa+, Eff* (death wish). *Hope.* 3 (9.5)

E-29.   *No Imagery.* 0 (25)

E-30.   *Pow Im, I, Bw, Ga+. Fear.* 4 (4.5)

SET F—EXPERT SCORING

F-1.   *Pow Im, Pa+, I, Eff. Hope.* 4 (5.5)

F-2.   *Pow Im* (scored on the basis of concern to establish respect in the public at large, *not* on the basis of the concern to liberate themselves), *Pa−, I, Ga+. Hope.* 4 (5.5)

F-3.   *Pow Im, I, Ga+. Hope.* 3 (12)

F-4.   *Pow Im, Pa+, I, Ga+, Eff. Hope.* 5 (2)

F-5.   *No Imagery.* 0 (24.5)

F-6.   *Pow Im, Pa+, I. Hope.* 3 (12)

F-7.   *No Imagery.* 0 (24.5)

F-8.   *No Imagery.* 0 (24.5)

F-9.   *Pow Im, Pa+, Ga+. Fear* (Bringing the man back "into the fold" is presumably for his own benefit). 3 (12)

F-10.   *No Imagery.* 0 (24.5)

F-11.   *Pow Im, Pa+, I. Hope.* 3 (12)

F-12.   *Pow Im, Pa+, I, Ga−. Fear* (doubts about ability). 4 (5.5)

F-13.   *No Imagery.* 0 (24.5)

F-14.   *No Imagery.* 0 (24.5)

F-15.   *No Imagery.* 0 (24.5)

F-16.   *Pow Im, Pa+, N, I, Bw, Ga−. Fear.* 6 (1)

F-17.   *Pow Im* (criterion 2; not criterion 1, since her "help" is routine), *Pa+, Eff. Hope.* 3 (12)

F-18.   *No Imagery.* 0 (24.5)

F-19.   *No Imagery.* 0 (24.5)

F-20.   *Pow Im* (helping themes), *I* (request to stop). *Fear.* 2 (16)

F-21.   *Pow Im* (the trial, especially the prosecutor's witness), *Pa+, I. No Eff* (the counterreaction of the defense is not explicit enough to be scored). *Hope.* 3 (12)

F-22.   *Pow Im, Pa+, I, G−. Fear* (some suggestion of the son's doubt, and the father's consolation as for the son's benefit). 4 (5.5)

F-23.   *No Imagery.* The father's "want" is not clearly an attempt to control the son's life, and it is clearly an achievement goal. 0 (24.5)

F-24.   *Pow Im, Pa+, I, Eff. Hope.* 4 (5.5)

F-25.   *No Imagery.* No disagreement is actually occurring, nor is the older man clearly offering advice or help. 0 (24.5)

F-26.   *Pow Im, N, I, Eff. Hope.* 4 (5.5)

F-27.   *Pow Im. No I* (Borderline case: the father's "action" seems to be a part of the setting of the story, even though it is mentioned in the middle of the story. *I* might be scored.). *Fear.* 1 (17.5)

F-28.   *Pow Im, N, G+. Hope* (The writer's comments are probably not strong enough to classify this as *Fear*). 3 (12)

F-29.   *No Imagery.* 0 (24.5)

F-30.   *Pow Im. Fear.* 1 (17.5)

SET G—EXPERT SCORING

G-1.   *No Imagery.* 0 (25)

G-2.   *No Imagery.* 0 (25)

G-3.   *Pow Im, G+. Hope.* 2 (16)

G-4.   *Pow Im, Pa+, Pa−, I. Fear* (editorial comments and inner skepticism about power). 4 (5.5)

G-5.   *No Imagery.* 0 (25)

G-6.   *Pow Im. No I* (the act only occurs in the last phrase). *Hope.* 1 (19)

G-7.   *No Imagery.* 0 (25)

G-8.   *No Imagery.* 0 (25)

G-9.   *Pow Im, Pa+* (jury in a courtroom), *I* (vote on the man's fate). *Fear* (the "one man" is reluctant to use power). 3 (10.5)

G-10. *Pow Im, Pa+, I, Eff* (exaggerated compliance). *Fear* (style of the writer). 4 (5.5)

G-11. *Pow Im, Pa+, I. Fear* (on behalf of the Racing Commission). 3 (10.5)

G-12. *No Imagery.* 0 (25)

G-13. *No Imagery.* 0 (25)

G-14. *Pow Im, I. Fear* (irony). 2 (16)

G-15. *Pow Im, I, Eff. Fear.* 3 (10.5)

G-16. *Pow Im, Pa+, Pa−, I, Ga+. Hope.* 5 (2.5)

G-17. *Pow Im* (not the testing, but the "planning a comfortable death"), *I. Fear.* 2 (16)

G-18. *Pow Im* (the creation of a human embryo would be, in a sense, ultimate power over the other person), *Pa+, I. Hope.* 3 (10.5)

G-19. *Pow Im, I, Ga−. Fear* (editorial comments). 3 (10.5)

G-20. *No Imagery.* Dr. Smith is interested in science, not in the power applications of science. 0 (25)

G-21. *Pow Im, Pa+* ("major cities"), *Ga+, Ga−. Fear.* 4 (5.5)

G-22. *Pow Im* (criterion 2), *Eff. Hope.* 2 (16)

G-23. *No Imagery.* 0 (25)

G-24. *Pow Im, N, I, Bw. Fear.* 4 (5.5)

G-25. *Pow Im, I. Hope.* 2 (16)

G-26. *Pow Im, Pa+, Pa−, N, I, Eff. Hope.* 6 (1)

G-27. *No Imagery.* 0 (25)

G-28. *Pow Im, Pa−, N* (the son's revenge, in the secondary power theme), *I, Eff. Hope.* 5 (2.5)

G-29. *No Imagery.* 0 (25)

G-30. *Pow Im, I, Eff. Hope.* 3 (10.5)

APPENDIX II

Activities Questionnaire Used with College Students

The following questions are a composite of all those used with the various populations of Wesleyan undergraduates described in Chapters 4 to 6. The questions used with any one group varied somewhat.

Name:

1. Are you: married _____ engaged _____ going steady _____ totally single _____

2. Where are you living this year? dormitory _____ fraternity _____ off campus _____ other _____

3. Have you ever taken a leave of absence, or left college for any other reason since you first entered?

4. Age: _____ Year in college: _____

5. What organizations do you now belong to, or have you belonged to, during your years in college? (Include fraternities but not sports.) Have you ever been an officer in any of these organizations? If so, what office and when?

6. Do you now participate, or have you ever participated, in any organized sports at college or elsewhere? Which sports, what kind of team, and for how many years?

7. Do you participate, or have you participated, in outdoor activities such as camping, hiking, mountain-climbing, sailing or yachting, ski-ing, and so forth? Which? For how many years?

8. Following is a list of games and other informal activities. Please check the column "Never," "Occasionally," or "Often" for each game or activity, as appropriate:

ping pong	Monopoly	chess	parchesi
billiards or pool	pinball machines	checkers	rummy
Frisbee	bridge	Go	set-back (pitch)
bowling	poker	cribbage	war (the card game)
karate	hearts	scrabble	other games:

Do you play any of the above games for money? Please circle those which (at least sometimes) you play or have played for money, even for small stakes.

9. On the average, over a college year, how many varsity sports events do you attend in person?[1]

10. On the average, how often do you watch sports on television?[2]

11. Assume a typical party or other occasion where you might be drinking beer. How many cans of beer would you generally drink?[3]

How often during the past year have you been at such a party or similar occasion where you were drinking beer (on the average)?[4]

[1] Alternatives given were: more than 30 _____ between 10–30 _____ between 5–10 _____ fewer than 5 _____ none _____

[2] Alternatives given were: once or more a week _____ one to three times a month _____ five to eleven times a year _____ one to four times a year _____ never _____

[3] Alternatives given were: 9 or more cans (drinks) _____ 6–8 cans (drinks) _____ 3–5 cans (drinks) _____ 1–2 cans (drinks) _____ less than 1 can (drink) _____ don't drink _____

[4] Alternatives given were: 4 or more times a week _____ 2–3 times a week _____ 2–4 times a month _____ 6–12 times a year _____ 1–5 times a year _____ never _____

The Power Motive

12. Now assume a typical party or similar occasion where you might be drinking hard liquor. How many drinks would you generally have?[5]
How often during the past year you been at such a party or similar occasion where you were drinking hard liquor (on the average)?[6]

13. If you were going to buy any car costing $5,000 or less [$3,000 or less], what kind of car would you buy? Assume a new car only. What color?

14. What is the fastest speed that you have ever driven a car?

15. How many credit cards do you have in your wallet or elsewhere?

16. What magazines do you read or look at fairly regularly?

17. What television shows do you like to watch?

18. What books, other than required course reading, have you read, in whole or in large part, in the past two weeks?

19. Have you ever been in an automobile accident, as a driver? If so, how many times?

20. Have you ever received a ticket for a moving traffic violation? If so, how many times?

21. Within the past three years, have you been in a physical fight?

22. How many loud, vehement arguments have you had within the past month? Circle the appropriate number.
0   1   2   3   4   5   6   7   8   9   10 or more

23. Have you ever broken a bone or sprained a joint?

24. On the average, how many times would you estimate that you swear during a normal day (regardless of the reason)? Circle the appropriate number.
0   1   2   3   4   5   6   7   8   9   10 or more

25. When they do swear, many people find some words or phrases more expressive than others. What are your "favorites"?

26. If you could say one sentence—any sentence—to anyone, any-

[5] Alternatives given were: 9 or more cans (drinks) _____ 6–8 cans (drinks) _____ 3–5 cans (drinks) _____ 1–2 cans (drinks) _____ less than 1 can (drink) _____ don't drink _____

[6] Alternatives given were: 4 or more times a week _____ 2–3 times a week _____ 2–4 times a month _____ 6–12 times a year _____ 1–5 times a year _____ never _____

where in the world, in person and without fear of reprisal, what would you say, and to whom?

I would say "_____" to _____.

27. Do you own any of the following?

automobile ____

motorcycle or
  motorscooter ____

television set ____

stereo components (not a 1-piece
  package set) ____

special furniture[7] ____

original works of art or quality
  reproductions ____

your own carpeting or rug[8] ____

electric office typewriter ____

cooking equipment (hot plate or
  electric frying pan[9]) ____

rifle or pistol ____

fully-equipped bar ____

tape recorder ____

cloth wall-hanging ____

28. Below is a list of different activities. Please indicate how many hours you spend at each activity during an average week in the college year.

bull sessions _____

watching television, sports,
  etc. _____

studying _____

extra-curricular activities _____

reading (not for
  courses) _____

dating _____

29. While your career plans are no doubt uncertain, please list three careers that you would want to have, or would strongly consider (be as specific as you can):

30. Have you ever signed a petition or a group letter?

31. Have you ever written a letter of protest?

32. Have you ever participated in a demonstration, picketing, march, etc.?

33. Have you ever attended an "open meeting" (a meeting called to discuss some specific issue, not a regular meeting of an organization)?

[7,8,9] These items were analyzed only for students living in dormitories.

APPENDIX III

Codes Used for Scoring Occupation and Career Plans

CODES USED FOR CLASSIFYING OCCUPATIONS

Teaching. Any mention of teaching, "teaching and/or research," or "an academic career" at any level—elementary, secondary school, or college. Educational administration is also included. Being a graduate student in fields where teaching is the obvious final career (e.g., History of Ideas, English, languages, etc.) is counted as teaching even though teaching as such is not mentioned. Being a graduate student in fields where teaching is not necessarily the final career (e.g., science, music) are not counted unless teaching is specifically mentioned.

Business management. Any mention of managing, including sales, marketing, advertising, etc. Business school graduate students included unless specifically excluded by what follows. The following are not counted: auditor, analyst, finance, investments, personnel and various technical positions (computer programmer, systems engineer, engineering, research, operations research, etc.).

Psychology. Any mention of the field of psychology, including academic teaching and research (in any field of psychology), clinical psychology, psychoanalyst, social work, etc. Psychiatry is counted, including being a resident in psychiatry (but not being a medical student with a "preference" for psychiatry).

Clergy. Being a clergyman of any religion. Administrative positions with a religious organization (national organization, religiously-affiliated charity, etc.) are counted if the person has had specialized training in religion.

Journalism. Any job that involves writing or broadcasting news or opinion, or supervising, editing, or managing those who write or broadcast. Purely entertainment or business functions (e.g., disc jockey, advertising manager) are not counted.

SCORING OF CAREER PLANS FOR AUTONOMOUS CONTROL

This code was designed to score responses to the following question:

If your life could go according to your plans and hopes, what would it be like in, say, twenty years? Please write out a brief description in the space below. Obviously your career plans would be an important part of this description, but try to mention other plans also.

Autonomous Control can be scored if any of the following occur:

1. A general statement such as "I will do what I want" or "I will not be restricted to an ordinary job." Examples:

I would never occupy myself too long with one occupation, for I find a "job" not an end but a catalyst to life.

I would not like to feel restricted, but rather do what I felt like doing at the present time.

Like to have ability to do whatever I want . . . without having to restrict myself to routine.

My career plans are not yet concrete. . . . I don't want to be type-cast or stultified by my job.

2. Specific statements that the person will be self-employed, will or hopes to start his own business or in some way establish his own career. Mention of any occupation or profession which usually involves self-employment is also counted. Examples:

I'll be self-employed.

I will be a partner in a firm which I had started on graduation from law school.

By that time I'll be a doctor.

3. Mention of an interest, with implied activity, beyond job or family. In other words, some desire to have an effect on the environment or in some way to act beyond routine role expectations of a career. Some action or strong positive interest is necessary; it is not sufficient merely to reject (or to endorse) conventional patterns of living. Examples:

Further education through reading and the arts, live Thoreau-style and *en rapport* with nature, refuting complacency to remain obnoxious to the status quo. . . .

I would hope to become a professor . . . also hope to do some writing (poetry, plays).

I hope to be successful in some area of business at first, and then move possibly into a political or policy extension of my experience, with more social overtones.

Doing research—I would like to be living in a city or area in which there were a lot of exciting, stimulating activities.

A doctor . . . active in civic affairs and sports, such as ski-ing and country clubs.

APPENDIX IV

Materials
Used in the
Small-Group Study*

QUESTION FOR GROUP DISCUSSION

D. is currently a junior at Wesleyan, who has during the past year become more and more dissatisfied with the academic atmosphere, and confused about his plans for the future. He would like to take a leave of absence for a year to think about his future plans and discover something in which he might develop a strong interest. However, he is also aware that if he leaves school, he will become eligible for the draft and face the possibility of serving in the Army and fighting in Vietnam in a war and for a cause about which he has definite doubts. Both elements of this situation are things that D. feels strongly about, and he is apprehensive both about the thought of staying at Wesleyan, and about spending time in the armed services.

Imagine that you are advising D. Listed below are several probabilities or odds of being able to take a leave of absence without getting drafted.

Please check the *lowest* probability that you would consider acceptable for D. to take a leave of absence in this situation.

Chances (out of 10)   1   2   3   4   5   6   7   8   9   10

* From Jones, 1969.

SOCIOMETRIC QUESTIONNAIRE

GROUP MEMBERSHIP QUESTIONNAIRE

Name:

1. Whom do you think most influenced the other participants? (You may include yourself when answering these questions.)
2. Who most clearly defined the problems?
3. Who offered the best solutions to the problems?
4. Whom do you think worked the hardest to get the job done and come to a good conclusion?
5. Who encouraged the others to participate?
6. Whom do you like best? (Do not include yourself on this one.)
7. Whom do you think tried to keep the group running smoothly, and encouraged cooperation?
8. Overall, who was the "leader" in this group?

POST-SESSION QUESTIONNAIRE[1]

1. How involved did you feel in the discussion, *not* necessarily the topic itself, but the discussion? (This does not mean how much you talked, but how interested and alert or involved you felt.)

Very uninvolved; I took part mainly for the money	Moderately involved	Very involved; the discussion was interesting and enjoyable

2. How many hours a week do you spend in bull sessions or informal talks?
3. Do you think that the people in your group would be able to carry

---

[1] Filled out several days later.

on an interesting and stimulating conversation about a topic you
are interested in?

I doubt very much that	so-so	They seemed like
the group would be		they would be able
interesting no matter		to have an interesting
what the topic.		talk on any topic.

Material from the Study of the Don Juan Legend in National Literatures

PROCEDURES USED TO ESTIMATE THE OUTPUT OF DON JUAN VERSIONS

First, the number of Don Juan versions per country per decade was tabulated from the chronological list given by Singer (1965, pp. 352–370), counting only those versions where the place of publication was given, or where the language of the version made the determination of the national literature clear. "Germany" includes all places of publication which fall within the 1919–1938 boundaries of Germany, if the work was written in German. "Austria" means any German-language version published within the pre-1919 boundaries of Austria-Hungary. "Italy" includes all versions in the Italian language, if they were published within the boundaries of peninsular Italy. In the case of operas, the place of publication rather than the language is definitive: thus Mozart's *Don Giovanni* is counted as Austrian even though it was written in Italian.

COUNTRIES AND DECADES OF RELATIVELY HIGH OUTPUT OF DON
JUAN VERSIONS

Austria	1780	1800	1900	1920	1940			
Argentina	1920							
Belgium	1940							
Brazil	1920							
Denmark	1840	1860	1870					
England	1670	1720	1810	1820	1870	1930	1950	
France	1660	1710	1830	1900	1920	1930	1950	
Germany	1760	1800	1820	1850	1880	1910	1920	
Italy	1650	1670	1780	1790	1830	1880	1900	1910	1920
Mexico	1900	1930						
Netherlands	1720	1920	1930	1940				
Portugal	1860	1870	1890	1920				
Russia	1830	1880						
Spain	1840	1900	1910	1920				
United States	1840	1850	1910	1940	1950			

PROCEDURES USED TO ESTIMATE THE GROWTH AND DECLINE OF AN EMPIRE

The growth or decline of an empire during a decade is estimated by the number of colonies gained or lost in that decade. The following rules were adopted in order to define "colony," "gained," and "lost."

1. No territory of less than 100 square miles in area is counted. Shifts of territory during wars, if restored within 20 years, are not counted—as in the case of the French and Dutch colonies during the Napoleonic Wars.

2. A "colony" is territory over which a country exercises sovereignty, including territory which is contiguous. Whether a colony is counted as one or as several depends upon the previous status, the relatedness of the acquiring (or losing) actions, the internal contiguity of the territory, and the unity of subsequent administration. Thus: the independence of the United States of America is the loss of

one colony (though originally the gain of several). The Malay States are the gain of one colony. Bengal, Oudh, and the Punjab/Northwest Frontier Provinces are counted as separate gains; but India is considered a single loss. Northern and Southern Rhodesia are counted as two colonies. Each of the German colonies acquired by Britain and France in World War I is counted as one colony.

3. The date of gaining a colony is the date when the first major *de facto* sovereignty is exercised over a significant portion of the territory. This can be the date of annexation or proclamation of a protectorate, but it is earlier if there is a significant event (capture, successful attack, major concerted settlement, etc.) that led only later to annexation or protectorate status. Thus shifts of territory after wars are counted from the date of *original* capture. *De jure* sovereignty which occurs long before the actual exercise of any significant *de facto* sovereignty is not counted, until the later *de facto* exercise of sovereignty, as in the case of the Falkland Islands or French Somaliland.

4. Losses via independence are counted as of the date of the treaty; other losses are counted as of the date of capture by another country.

5. The following events are not counted: division of previously acquired territory over which sovereignty had been exercised, as with the various additional administrative divisions of Australia or French African territory; gradual penetration of influence or control from an established colonial outpost; and mandates or protectorates over states that are essentially independent. For the latter point, Palestine between the wars is counted, but Trans-Jordan and Iraq are not.

6. Continuous processes of conquest, extending over a long period of time, can be counted for each significant event that involved an expansion of sovereignty over territory. Thus the gradual British expansion of sovereignty over the Indian Subcontinent can be broken down into several distinct events, as listed in the following tables. Similarly, the French and British expansion into Africa can be broken down into several specific gains.

COLONIES GAINED AND LOST IN THE BRITISH AND
FRENCH EMPIRES, 1740–1939

British Empire

Decade	Colonies Gained or *Lost*
1740	———
1750	Plassey and Arcot[a]
1760	French Canada
1770	———
1780	*U.S. America;* New South Wales; Sierra Leone; British Honduras
1790	Malta; Guiana; Trinidad; Ceylon; Straits Settlements; Cape of Good Hope; Seychelles; Muscat and Oman
1800	Maratha territory in India; Madras territory in India; Tasmania; St. Lucia
1810	The Gambia; Mauritius; Tobago
1820	Burma/Assam; West Australia; Gold Coast
1830	Aden; South Australia; Falkland Islands; Natal; New Zealand
1840	Punjab/Northwest Frontier Provinces; Pegu; Hong Kong
1850	Oudh; Nagpur Provinces
1860	Lagos
1870	Fiji; Cyprus; Malay States; Transvaal; Baluchistan; Egypt
1880	Somaliland; British North Borneo; Sarawak; Brunei; Nigeria; Papua; Basutoland; Bechuanaland; Bahrein; Qatar; New Hebrides (condominium with France)
1890	Northern Rhodesia; Southern Rhodesia; Kenya; Uganda; Zanzibar; Nyasaland; Ashanti; Sudan; Tonga; Kuwait; Trucial Coast; Wei-hai-wei; Gilbert and Ellice Islands; Solomon Islands
1900	Orange Free State; Swaziland; Protected Malay States
1910	German New Guinea; German Samoa; Tanganyika; South West Africa; Kamerun; Togoland; Palestine
1920	*Ireland; Egypt*
1930	*Canada; New Zealand; Australia; Union of South Africa; Newfoundland*[b]*; Wei-hai-wei*

Colonies Gained and Lost in the British and French Empires (1740–1939) (*cont.*)

French Empire

Decade	Colonies Gained or *Lost*
1800	*St. Lucia; Haiti*
1810	*Mauritius; Tobago*
1820	———
1830	Algeria
1840	Guinea; Ivory Coast; Mayotte; Tahiti and islands; Gabon
1850	New Caledonia; Senegal
1860	Cambodia; Cochin-China
1870	*Alsace-Lorraine*
1880	Madagascar; Annam; Tonking; Tunis; Equatorial Africa; French Somaliland; New Hebrides (condominium with Britain)
1890	Laos; Sudan/Volta; Dahomey
1900	Morocco[c]; Mauretania; Karem/Wadai/Northern Sahara
1910	Alsace-Lorraine; Niger; Kamerun; Togo
1920	Syria/Lebanon
1930	———

Note: For definitions, exclusions, and coding rules, see above. All colonies are referred to by their names as used in imperial histories.

[a] Military victories that represented substantial British control over Bengal and Madras, respectively.

[b] The Statute of Westminster (1931) is considered to have conferred self-governing status on these so-called White Dominions.

[c] *De facto* control was assured during this decade by treaties with Great Britain, Germany, and Italy.

DON JUAN OUTPUT AND CHANGES IN
COLONIES TWO DECADES EARLIER

British Empire

Don Juan Output (deviation from prediction)		Changes in number of colonies	
1760	−2.46	1740	0
1770	−2.46	1750	1
1780	−1.46	1760	1
1790	−2.46	1770	0
1800	− .56	1780	4
1810	5.34	1790	8
1820	9.10	1800	4
1830	0.00	1810	3
1840	−2.59	1820	3
1850	−1.17	1830	5
1860	.27	1840	3
1870	4.63	1850	2
1880	− .66	1860	1
1890	−3.06	1870	6
1900	−1.60	1880	11
1910	− .33	1890	14
1920	−4.02	1900	3
1930	2.40	1910	7
1940	−2.41	1920	2
1950	3.68	1930	6

French Empire

1820	−3.04	1800	2
1830	3.75	1810	2
1840	−5.97	1820	0
1850	−3.62	1830	1

Don Juan Output and Changes in Colonies Two Decades Earlier (*cont.*)
French Empire (*cont.*)

1860	−5.30	1840	5
1870	−4.15	1850	2
1880	−5.39	1860	2
1890	−5.68	1870	1
1900	7.07	1880	7
1910	−3.25	1890	3
1920	13.60	1900	3
1930	14.09	1910	4
1940	−1.53	1920	1
1950	3.10	1930	0

Index

INDEX

Achievement motive (*n* Achievement),
  10*n*., 39*n*., 40-41, 45, 48, 109,
  224
  in American presidents, 212-20
  in radicals, 209-11, 223
  relation to *n* Power, 93-95
Activation, and Fear of Power, 151
Activity Inhibition, 80, 227
  relation to Fear of Power, 82*t*., 84
Acton, Lord, 2
Adler, A., 2, 3, 156-57
Adorno, T. W., 17, 19
Affiliation motive (*n* Affiliation), 48,
  79, 115, 211*n*.
  relation to Fear of Power, 94*t*.,
  149*n*.
  relation to Hope of Power, 94*t*.,
  149*n*.
  relation to *n* Power, 94*t*.
Alker, H. A., 28
Alpert, R. A., 2, 64, 87
Andrews, J. D. W., 53
Approach motive, 29*n*., 42-44, 76-79;
  see also Hope of Power
  sums to total with avoidance motive,
  79, 85
Arnold, M. B., 10*n*.
Atkinson, J. W., 20, 28, 36, 37*n*., 40-
  41, 44-45, 48, 52, 65, 76, 77,
  78, 85, 87, 91, 99, 103, 104,
  123, 146, 184, 203-204, 205,
  226
Atkinson model, 40-45, 54, 77, 99,
  121, 203-204
  criticisms of, 45, 204
Attribution theory, 17*n*.
Austen, J., 167, 169
Authoritarianism, 13, 17-19, 217
Authority, 8
Avoidance motive, 29*n*., 42-44; *see
  also* Fear of Power
  measuring, 76-79

sums to total with approach motive,
  79, 85
Ayllon, T., 111
Azrin, N., 111

Babbitt, I., 2
Bachrach, P., 11*n*.
Bailey, A., 226
Bainton, R. H., 2
Bales, R. F., 119, 123
Baratz, M. S., 11*n*.
Barber, J. D., 214
Barnard, C. I., 109
Bass, B. M., 120
Baumrind, D., 111
Becker, S. W., 13, 120
Beisser, A. R., 100, 139
Bellush, J., 104
Berger, C. R., 60
Berle, A. A., 224
Berlew, D. E., 52, 54
Berlyne, D. E., 27
Berzon, B., 119
Birch, D., 40, 44, 203
Birney, R. C., 37, 39*n*., 45, 77-78, 85,
  86, 89
Black male college students and *n*
  Power, 134, 208-209
Book production, used to correct Don
  Juan output, 191
Boyatsis, R., 124, 141
Brachfeld, F. O., 168*n*.
Brown, R. W., 64, 100, 120, 125
Browning, R. P., 40, 53, 103-104, 212
Brunswik, E., 39
Bullitt, W. C., 212
Bullock, A., 140
Burdick, H., 77-78, 85, 86
Bush, R. R., 74*n*., 75*t*., 195*t*.
Business executives, high in *n* Power,
  106-110, 211
Byrne, D., 77

Maeztu, R. de, 165, 200
Mandel, O., 166*n*., 168, 173, 175,
    185, 200
Mandler, G., 78
Mann, R. D., 12, 119, 123
Maranell, G. M., 215-17
Marañón, G., 168
Maroney, R. J., 125
Martin, N. H., 112, 126, 141
May, R., 111
May, R. R., 65, 145, 148
McArthur, C., 10*n*.
McClelland, D. C., 2, 10*n*., 30, 36, 39,
    45, 48, 49, 55, 64, 77, 78*n*., 80-
    84, 86, 87, 89, 90*t*., 91, 95, 107,
    108-109, 115, 136, 137-38, 143-
    44, 162, 181, 190, 204, 206, 223
McClelland-Atkinson research strategy,
    10, 37-40
  cross-validation in, 64
  illustration of process of empirical
    derivation of scoring systems, 64-
    69
McDonald, R. D., 79
McGuire, W. J., 28
McGurk, E., 181
McKeachie, W. J., 51
McNelly, F. W., Jr., 107
Merei, F., 14
Mikawa, J., 79
Milgram, S., 111, 211
Milgram experiments, 111
Miller, N. E., 42, 76, 85
Miller, R. E., 125
Millett, K., 165
Mills, C. W., 11*n*.
Minton, H. L., 17, 18*n*.
Mirsky, I. A., 125
Mischel, W., 26-28, 31
Moderator variables, 123, 134, 209;
    see also Interaction (statistical)
Molière, J., 178, 181, 192
Morehead, A. H., 152
Morgan, C. D., 34-35, 49
Morgan, H. H., 88
Moss, H., 227
Mosteller, F., 74*n*., 75*t*., 195*t*.
Motive; *see also* Approach motive,
    Avoidance motive, Power motive
  and action, 25, 29-30, 203; *see also*
    Atkinson model
  concept of, in explanation of

behavior, 21-24, 202, 203
  and conflict, 25
  criterion groups to measure, 39-40
  experimental arousal of, to measure,
    37-39
  and homeostasis, 24
  and neural mechanisms, 24
Mott-Smith, G., 152
Moulton, R. W., 77
Movements, social, and motives, 209-
    212
  norm-oriented vs. value-oriented,
    211
Mozart, W. A., 176, 178
Murphy, J. V., 125
Murray, D. C., 190
Murray, H. A., 7, 30, 31, 33-36, 49,
    87, 93, 203, 225
Murstein, B. I., 36, 88, 89

Narcissism, and power motive, 118
National Sample study, 52-53, 184
Netherlands, 226-27
Nicolson, H., 126
Niebuhr, R., 2
Nietzsche, F., 2
Nixon, R. M., 213*t*., 214, 217*n*., 219*t*.
Nonreactive measures, 28, 97
Nowlis, V., 63
Nuttall, R. L., 209

Oedipus complex
  and Don Juan legend, 168-70, 178
  and Fear of Power, 156, 188
  and Hope of Power, 155, 188
Olds, J., 24
Orne, M. T., 33, 88, 111
Osgood, C. E., 9, 141
OSS assessment staff, 31
Ovesey, L., 144, 156

Paranoia; *see also* Veroff scoring sys-
    tem, correlates of
  power defensiveness in, 145
  nature of, 143-45
  relation to Fear of Power, 83, 145-
    47
Parsons, T., 103, 109, 207
Persistence, 30, 31-32
Personality, concept and theory of,
    27*n*.
Personalized power (p Power), 80-83,